Front cover: based on one of the Guildown Saxon burials (after Lowther 1931, pl 1 upper).

Frontispiece.   I D Margary at Fishbourne. (*Photograph by courtesy of Fishbourne Roman Palace*)

This book is dedicated to the memory of
Ivan D Margary

THE ARCHAEOLOGY of SURREY

to 1540

EDITED BY
Joanna Bird and DG Bird

SURREY ARCHAEOLOGICAL SOCIETY
Castle Arch, Guildford

© Surrey Archaeological Society and the individual authors 1987

ISBN 0-9501345-6-2

Printed by Adlard & Son Ltd, The Garden City Press, Dorking, Surrey

Contents

Geological map, on foldout 1

Map of major places mentioned in the text, on foldout 2

List of contributors

D G Bird, BA, PhD, Conservation & Archaeology Section, Planning Department, Surrey County Council, County Hall, Kingston upon Thames, Surrey, KT1 2DT

Joanna Bird, BA, FSA, 14, Kings Road, Guildford, Surrey, GU1 4JW

Jonathan F Cotton, MA, 5, Auckland Drive, Kingston upon Thames, Surrey, KT1 3BG

Roger L Ellaby, 47, Priory Drive, Reigate, Surrey, RH2 8AF

David J Field, 95, Mount Road, Chessington, Surrey, KT9 1JH

Rosamond Hanworth, FSA, Quoin Cottage, Shamley Green, Guildford, Surrey, GU5 0UJ

F A Hastings, BEM, 19, Dulverton Court, Adelaide Road, Surbiton, Surrey, KT6 4TB

Richard Macphail, BSc, MSc, PhD, Institute of Archaeology, University College London, 31–34, Gordon Square, London, WC1H 0PY

Stuart Needham, BA, PhD, FSA, Department of Prehistoric & Romano-British Antiquities, British Museum, London, WC1B 3DG

Rob Poulton, BA, MA, Conservation & Archaeology Section, Planning Department, Surrey County Council, County Hall, Kingston upon Thames, Surrey, KT1 2DT

Rob Scaife, BSc, PhD, FRGS, Historic Buildings & Monuments Commission for England, Fortress House, 23, Savile Row, London, W1X 2HE

D J Turner, BSc, FSA, FSA Scot, 21, Evesham Road, Reigate, Surrey, RH2 9DL

David W Williams, 39, Nutley Lane, Reigate, Surrey, RH2 9HP

E S Wood, BA, FSA, The Granary, Honey Lane, Selborne, Alton, Hants, GU34 3BY

J J Wymer, MA, FSA, The Vines, The Street, Great Cressingham, Thetford, Norfolk, IP25 6NL

Ivan Donald Margary

'...he doth bestride the narrow world
Like a Colossus...'

This book is dedicated to Donald Margary, and to illuminate this dedication a brief note on his life may be appropriate.

Margary was a larger than life person – physically an imposing figure, exceptional in intellect and ability, and of conspicuous dignity, goodness and integrity. He was patient, humble and courteous. He was generous, not only of his time, but of his wealth; he saw needs, and met them, unobtrusively. He became, over the years, an outstanding benefactor of the Surrey Archaeological Society, and the main Library Room at Castle Arch is named in his honour.

He joined the Society in 1927, and became a Vice-President in 1947. He was a valuable and assiduous member of Council until his death, and took a deep interest in the Society's affairs and welfare. The war years had depleted the Society's membership and resources, and it became clear that it was not going to be easy to finance the expansion of activities and facilities necessary to bring the Society up to date. At this juncture Margary donated the then not inconsiderable sum of £6000 – with no strings, but with the hope that more money would thus be available to assist the *Collections*, and for other publications which up to then could not be afforded: a category which includes the present book. This altered the Society's situation overnight. As Honorary Secretary at the time, it fell to me to handle this cheque, and I vividly remember the general excitement with which it was received: certainly to handle a cheque for this kind of money was a new experience for me! Margary followed this up by gifts of books and money for the Library over the years.

When he died he left the Society a share of his residuary estate, which turned out to be a sum large enough to raise the Society to an unexpected prosperity and safety. Successive Treasurers have husbanded this money very ably, as the annual accounts show. Similarly substantial sums were also left to the Sussex Archaeological Society (always high in Margary's affections – he was its President from 1964 to 1967, and they also have a Margary Room); the Kent Archaeological Society; the Society of Antiquaries; the Royal Archaeological Institute, and other bodies.

At Council meetings Margary would listen quietly, and spoke sparingly and diffidently; but when he did he spoke to great effect, clarifying issues and pointing the way to satisfactory solutions.

Ivan Donald Margary was born in 1896, and died on 18 February 1976. He was a graduate in chemistry of Exeter College, Oxford, after war service. He combined his life as a substantial farmer at Chartham Park, near East Grinstead, with his interests in meteorology, geography and archaeology, of which the latter gradually became central. The discovery of a stretch of Roman road on his estate led him to study the south-eastern network in detail, and resulted in his classic *Roman ways in the Weald* in 1948. This was followed by an authoritative survey of the whole country, leading to the two-volume *Roman roads in Britain* (1955, with revised editions in 1967 and 1973 – he was always willing to amend his conclusions in the light of later knowledge). He published over 60 papers, mostly on Surrey, Sussex and Kent, and was elected Fellow of the Society of Antiquaries in 1932.

Margary followed up his archaeological interests, not only in this way, which included field-walking and meticulous inspection, but by direct material furtherance of worthwhile objects. Thus, he contributed to the acquisition of Avebury for the National Trust (1943); to the building of a new (Margary) quadrangle at Exeter College; to rooms at the British School in Rome; and to the restoration of Kelmscott. He is perhaps best known for his purchase of the site of the Roman Palace at Fishbourne in 1962, which enabled its excavation to take place, and for the building of its protective structure. For these benefactions the nation itself is in his debt. From 1946 to 1962 he leased his 40-room Chartham Park to the Westminster Hospital rent-free as a convalescent home, and from then on lived in Yew Lodge on the estate.

All honours, although so richly deserved, were declined, on the grounds that he was privileged to share his wealth and his knowledge. We are all the poorer for his passing.

ERIC S WOOD

Introduction

In recent years several books have been published on the archaeology of a series of different counties, and it has seemed appropriate to the Surrey Archaeological Society that there should also be such a book for Surrey. As has become the pattern, many of the ideas published here were first put forward at a conference, held in October 1983. It has taken longer than we had hoped to prepare the material as a book; some papers were delayed, others needed more attention, and the editors found difficulties in pursuing the project with the necessary vigour at times. Paradoxically, therefore, the most efficient authors are now the most out of date. The person most affected is John Wymer, his paper being now over three years old. Nevertheless, in most cases the delays have led to a better book.

This volume aims to fill a major gap: there has been no general survey of Surrey's archaeology for over 50 years, since the publication of D C Whimster's book, *The archaeology of Surrey*, in 1931. In the modern fashion the present book has a number of different authors, as it is becoming difficult for any one person to keep up with the many advances now being made in archaeology. The geographical and environmental chapter may be thought by some to be rather technical, but it is a very important aspect of modern studies and emphasises how little we know, especially in Surrey. Its position as the second chapter may look odd, but has seemed to us to be logical as it does specifically relate to the situation after the last Ice Age. Other papers should prove less technical and we hope that they will be of use to everyone who wishes to know about the early story of our county, even if they have no previous knowledge of archaeology. The book also has the major aim of summing up current knowledge so as to act as a basis for future work.

It has been difficult to decide which area to cover: archaeology does not stop conveniently at county limits, and matters have been made worse by the vagaries of politicians, forever tinkering with long established boundaries. The book aims to cover the whole of the historic county – that is including the south-west London boroughs right up to the Thames – plus the area of the modern Borough of Spelthorne, north of the Thames and formerly in Middlesex. These boundaries are of course artificial, and contributors were allowed to stray outside them whenever it seemed appropriate. The authors also received guidelines as to what topics should be included, but obviously there are differences in how these instructions have been interpreted – inevitably the different archaeological periods lead to differences of approach and emphasis. We hope, however, that the book's overall aim of presenting a comprehensive picture of Surrey's past has been achieved.

The organisation of archaeology in Surrey may be briefly mentioned. The Surrey Archaeological Society, founded in 1854, has always taken the historic county as its area of interest. On the other hand the County Archaeologist, who is based in the Conservation & Archaeology Section of the County Council's Planning Department, is responsible for administrative Surrey, including Spelthorne where the London & Middlesex Archaeological Society retains an interest. Professional cover of the former historic county in the London area is now provided by the Museum of London through the teams of its Department of Greater London Archaeology. There are several other museums throughout the area, both public and private, with widely varying resources. Unfortunately, there is no county museum service, but the Surrey Archaeological Society has been able, over the years, to establish a representative county archaeological collection, based at Guildford Museum.

Modern field archaeology is skilful, painstaking, time-consuming and labour intensive. When excavation has been completed, many hours of cataloguing, drawing and finds research are needed before the final report can be written. Few would now argue with the statement that without the intention to prepare and publish a report, archaeological excavation should not be undertaken. For this reason most recent work in Surrey has concentrated on 'rescue' archaeology – where sites have been threatened with destruction, for example by development. Inevitably major schemes, especially where time is limited by redevelopment proposals, need full-time work, usually paid for by HBMC (the Historic Buildings & Monuments Commission for England), or, increasingly, by the developer involved. Surrey's development companies have a good record in this respect. Even so, there are difficulties in arranging a proper response to each situation, with everything on an *ad hoc* basis. Although there are now professional teams, the day of the amateur is far from over, and Surrey has many active amateur archaeologists: one measure of this is that several of our authors are amateurs; another is the range of material published regularly in the county journal, the *Surrey Archaeological Collections*. There are several local societies, more or less one per District or Borough, although not necessarily specifically organised in that way. They vary in degree and type of activity from society to society and time to time, being obviously very dependent on personnel. Amateurs may undertake smaller scale or longer term excavations than the professionals, and have a particularly vital role to play in local fieldwork, especially in conjunction with others more interested in local history and buildings.

Professional and amateur effort in Surrey is coordinated through the Surrey Archaeological Society's Excavations Committee. Successful cooperation between amateur and professional is obviously very important and happily is usually achieved, despite the organisational problems experienced by the professionals because of their employment difficulties and restrictions. Many examples could be quoted; for instance, Surrey Archaeological Society itself originally set up the post of administrative county archaeological officer, and the professional team for south-west

Fig 1. Late Bronze Age socketed axe with wooden head and handle (the wood survives in five pieces, one in the head of the axe), from Shepperton. Now in Chertsey Museum. Length of handle: 27.5 cm. (*Photograph by Rob Poulton, Surrey County Planning Department*)

London now absorbed into the Museum of London's organisation. At Reigate Old Vicarage the upper, medieval, levels were dug by the local amateur team and the lower Saxo-Norman levels were then taken over by professionals because time was thought to be pressing. Such major sites as Runnymede Bridge and the Goblin Works Saxon cemetery near Leatherhead owe their discovery to amateurs. Most recently the excavation of the Roman temple site at Wanborough has demonstrated the very close cooperation possible between Surrey Archaeological Society and Surrey County Council. Always, of course, amateurs turn out to dig and walk fields in all weathers, and put in long hours processing the finds.

Mention of Wanborough must bring to mind the problem of metal detectors. As so often, it is the irresponsible few who cause the trouble, the treasure hunters who care nothing for our archaeological heritage or the rights of ownership. At Wanborough hundreds and perhaps thousands of Iron Age and Roman gold and silver coins were taken without permission by people using metal detectors and working mostly at night. They dug through standing crops and part of a hedgerow, and destroyed over 300 m² of archaeological deposit. They came from all over the country, and their finds have largely disappeared on to the black market, without record. Thus archaeologists, already hard pressed to deal with sites under threat of development, find supposedly safe sites, even those protected by law, being destroyed by treasure hunters. Our heritage is irreplaceable: each site is a different collection of evidence in the soil which tells of its past use – traces of rubbish pits, ditches, fences, tracks, buildings and so on. To the archaeologist finds matter for what they tell us – they provide a date (is it Neolithic? Iron Age? Medieval?) and evidence for such varied aspects as trade, skills, food and religion: in fact a whole way of life, for which archaeology is usually the *only* evidence. The relationship between a find and its 'context' (its precise position in the soil) is vital, and once destroyed can never been restored.

It should be noted that the contributors to this book have had to generalise; our knowledge is often so limited that a few new sites – even one – could fundamentally alter any one of the chapters. Even as this book was being prepared there were major discoveries. Two unique finds were made in gravel digging: a Late Bronze Age axe and wooden handle was found near Shepperton (fig 1) and an Iron Age bronze shield was discovered near Chertsey (fig 2). Both were found with other objects of interest. Two previously unknown surviving earthworks were located, one possibly Bronze Age at Nore Hill, Chelsham, the other apparently late Iron Age at Felday near Holmbury (fig 6.17G). Probably Britain's greatest ever single find of Iron Age coins (figs 6.13, 6.14) and a new Romano-Celtic temple (fig 7.15C) were discovered at Wanborough. There have been major new finds in Southwark, especially on the Winchester Palace site. Two previously unknown Saxon cemeteries have been found, at the Goblin Works near Leatherhead and near Tadworth; and there has been much new and important work at Merton Priory and around Kingston's medieval bridge. These and other new discoveries could only be partly assimilated in the book. They help to emphasise the continuing importance of Surrey's archaeology even at national level.

ACKNOWLEDGEMENTS

The individual authors acknowledge assistance for their own sections, but obviously the editors also owe a great debt to many people. They cannot all be singled out but some must be mentioned by name. Roger Ellaby proposed the original idea at an Excavations Committee meeting, and he and the members of the Committee provided useful support and ideas thereafter; the Society's Council and especially Dr John Gower and Rosamond Hanworth were always helpful; the University of Surrey's Department of Educational Studies kindly arranged the facilities for the Conference; Rob Poulton introduced several ideas; and Surrey County Council generously provided assistance, especially with typing. The line drawings, based for the most part on material supplied by the authors, are, except where otherwise noted, the work of David Williams, who also provided the cover and made a number of valuable suggestions; some of the drawings were based on material originally prepared by Martin O'Connell. Thanks should also go to Eric Wood for the dedication, to Fred Hastings for the index and to Dr Nigel Barker, Stan Clapham, Dr John Kent,

Fig 2. Front (left) and back of Iron Age bronze shield from near Chertsey, now in the British Museum. Length of shield: 83.5 cm.
(*Photograph by kind permission of the Trustees of the British Museum*)

Harry Margary, Dr Stuart Needham, David Rudkin and Karen Webster for their help in arranging a number of photographs at short notice. Last, but by no means least, in this list come the authors (especially those who prepared their texts to time!). To everyone who helped we offer our grateful thanks, and hope that they will find the book worthy of their efforts.

Note on radiocarbon dates

This book follows the convention by which dates based on radiocarbon (C14) measurements are expressed in years bc. By contrast years BC indicate calendar dates, worked out using information provided by the study of tree rings (dendrochronology), historical data or the recalibration of radiocarbon dates. (For discussion of radiocarbon dating see Gillespie 1984.) A new convention was established late in 1986 but it was not possible to introduce it into the text at this late stage.

The Palaeolithic period in Surrey

J J WYMER

For something like half a million years, small groups of Palaeolithic people have, intermittently, roamed across that part of the north-west European peninsula we now refer to as Surrey.[1] They hunted, foraged, raised young, died and somehow maintained a lowly but effective culture, transmitted from one generation to another, which, to judge presumptuously from the only tangible relics of their presence, was static for the greater part of this enormous span of time. Yet their ancestors can be traced back to the more southerly latitudes of the Old World for another one and a half million years, so even the earliest occupants of this part of Europe were long separated from the first expressions of human behaviour. The apparently static nature of their culture may mark a phase of consolidation. It emphasises the success of their balance with the environment, although it was probably their ingenuity in coping with the rigours of the northern climates that eventually precipitated the ever-increasing changes culminating in the sophisticated hunting communities of the Upper Palaeolithic. Most of the Palaeolithic flint tools and chips found in Europe belong to this long, slow process of change. Those from Surrey are no exception, but they represent only fragments of a general pattern of cultural evolution: the lithic litter of sporadic groups, divided from each other by enormous periods of time by historical standards. There is no question of any continuum of occupation. For much of the time all of Britain would have been a cold, cheerless, inclement place like northern Scandinavia today, although not, of course, with winters of perpetual darkness. At other times, ice sheets were as close to Surrey as the Midlands or East Anglia; at one time only a few miles away in north London. These glacial phases lasted many thousands of years at different times and, although occupation was perhaps not impossible during summer months, it is unlikely that hunters would have braved the area, or had any need to.

The climatic oscillations of the Middle and Late Pleistocene had a drastic effect upon the Surrey landscape. Some of the geological processes were slow, others rapid and occasionally catastrophic. In the beginning of the period under consideration the map of Surrey would have looked somewhat different. There would have been some general similarities, with chalk hills to the south, and something like the Weald beyond, but the River Thames was much further to the north, and the drainage pattern formed by the familiar Surrey rivers of today – the Wey, Mole and Wandle – did not exist. Precursors of these streams flowed across the soft Tertiary rocks north of the Chalk at higher levels, gradually forming mature valleys, only to be diverted from them as one river or tributary captured another. The capture of the Blackwater by the Guildford Wey in the Late Pleistocene, so clearly summarised by Oakley (1939) for the Surrey Archaeological Society's special volume on the prehistory of the Farnham area, is one of the best examples of such an event to be seen in southern England. Many similar changes have taken place, with the Blackwater either joining the Thames in the Reading–Shiplake area (as it does now) or being confluent in its earlier stages with an easterly flowing major river from the west, responsible for the high spreads of gravel south and east of Reading, on Hartfordbridge Flats and Chobham Common. At one time, it seems that the Mole and Wey met near Weybridge. These geological matters have received considerable attention during the last decade (Gibbard 1979; 1982; Clarke & Dixon 1981; Peake 1982; Fisher *et al* 1983),[2] and it is not the purpose of this paper to do more than relate some of the more certain conclusions to the Palaeolithic evidence and to cite them as evidence for the great geographical changes that have taken place. The sites have to be considered in the context of their Quaternary environment, not their present one.

The Palaeolithic sites of Surrey are not as numerous as in some of the adjacent counties. In his CBA gazetteer, Roe (1968a) lists 124 sites, and by sites he means any place where one or more (possibly hundreds) of Palaeolithic flints have been found. In comparison, Kent has 492 sites, Hampshire has 471. To quote more statistics, he lists 1117 hand-axes from Surrey, 7673 from Kent and 5583 from Hampshire. The sites of Surrey occur in three groups (fig 1.1):

Hand Axes

▴ SINGLE FIND

▲ 2 to 19

▲ 20 or more

Levallois Flakes

☐ SINGLE FIND

■ 2 or more

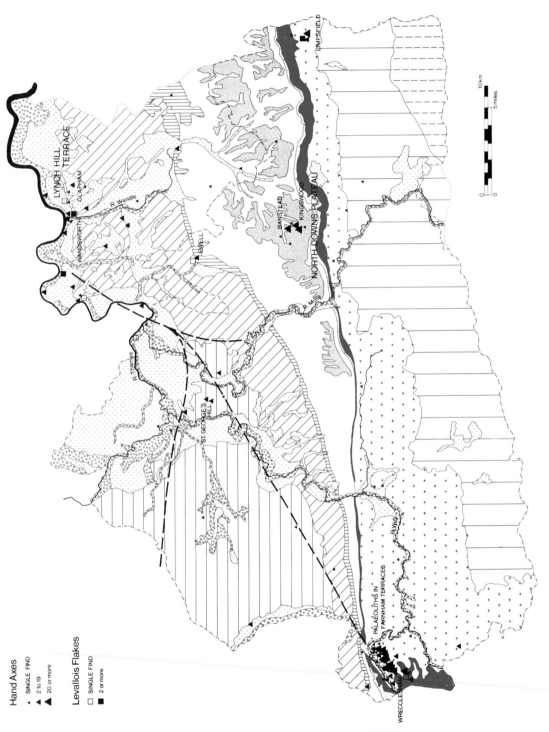

Fig 1.1.   Distribution of Lower Palaeolithic sites in Surrey. Dashes represent possible courses of Middle Pleistocene rivers prior to the main effects of the Anglian Stage glaciation. (For key to geological background see foldout 1)

1 the Farnham Terrace sequence;
2 the North Downs plateau around Walton on the Hill and Banstead and the High Level gravels and brickearth at Limpsfield;
3 isolated sites, mainly in the river gravels within the Tertiary basin, particularly in the Thames gravels between Wandsworth and Clapham; also a few flints dredged from the Thames.

As already mentioned, it is only possible to understand these sites in relation to the development of the landscape since the first humans explored the area. It is not really possible to be sure when this was, but those palaeoliths in the earliest geological contexts at least give us a positive starting point. The earliest dated occurrences are those flakes and hand-axes which are found in the high gravel spread at Farnham, referred to as Terrace A, and at St George's Hill, Weybridge. Recent geological work, discussed in more detail below, tentatively puts the deposition of these gravels during the latter part, possibly at the end of, the great glaciation which pushed the Thames from its course through the Vale of St Albans, southwards into its present valley. This great ice sheet has, apart from its obliteration or diversion of previously existing drainage patterns, left in its wake a mantle of rock waste as boulder clay or outwash gravels. Surrey, just beyond the southern limits of this ice sheet, received none of this, but its rivers had to adjust to changes. This happened during the geological stage in the British Quaternary sequence named the Anglian which, on some present chronometric dating assessments, is thought to have ended about 400,000 years ago. Others would prefer a younger date, but the writer favours the 'long chronology'.

If this is accepted, it follows that the hand-axes in Terrace A at Farnham were incorporated into those gravels somewhat before this date. They could belong to a milder climatic oscillation during the latter part of the Anglian, or even be derived from the destroyed land surface of a previous interglacial. Alternatively, they could have been discarded by bands of people making hunting forays on the veritable edge of the ice sheets, conceivable in summer months. We do not know; although there is some evidence for the presence of people in southern Britain during the preceding interglacial (the Cromerian Stage), it does not come from Surrey.

At the close of the Anglian Stage, the climate ameliorated and the ensuing interglacial is referred to as the Hoxnian Stage. By this time, the landscape and drainage pattern would have been familiar in some respects: the North Downs and their escarpment were more or less where they are today, with the Weald to the south, the Thames flowed north of Heathrow Airport and across central London, and the Surrey rivers existed, although not flowing exactly along their present courses. The Wey, at Farnham, flowed through what is now the Hale Gap, following the line of the present Blackwater. The Wandle would have been further to the east and the confluence of the Mole and what is now the Wey would have been around Weybridge. Unfortunately, there are no geological sediments in Surrey, or rarely elsewhere in south-east England, that can be related to this Hoxnian Stage. Alluvium, hillwash, peats and marsh clays must have accumulated, and flints and bones remaining from Palaeolithic camp sites must occasionally have become incorporated within them, but they have not been found. Some may exist, but it seems certain that the majority were destroyed during the long, succeeding geological stage known as the Wolstonian. This covered a vast length of time, from about 350,000 years to 120,000 years ago on the 'longer chronology'. For most of the time it was cold. Glacial ice may have reached the Midlands and part of East Anglia for part of the time. Milder periods certainly existed within the Wolstonian: interstadials or even interglacials. The rivers eroded, changed their courses, diverted others and slowly wore down their valleys, especially where they flowed through the soft rocks of the London Basin. Gravel terraces remain as partial evidence for these changes, and within them are more flint tools and flakes, either washed off earlier (?Hoxnian) land surfaces or contemporary with their deposition during the Wolstonian. Out of the river valleys, sub-aerial erosion, solifluction and chemical dissolution gradually wore away at the landscape; the Chalk escarpment receded and slope deposits formed. These changes were not necessarily very drastic, but it does mean that the actual land surfaces on which Palaeolithic man trod have gone, or been disturbed beyond recognition.

The following interglacial of the Ipswichian Stage, which can safely be described as the last interglacial before the one in which we now live, dates from somewhere between 120,000 years to 75,000 years ago; the date at the recent end being more reliable than the other. This was a pleasantly warm period for much of the time, somewhat warmer than the present climate. Elephant and hippopotamus abounded in the Thames Valley, as is known from the site at Trafalgar Square, but evidence for the presence of man is very scanty in the whole of Britain, probably because of the relatively high sea level and the existence of an English Channel. There are no deposits in Surrey that can be attributed to this stage, with the possible exception of some of the lower terraces at Farnham.

Cooler conditions set in at the close of the Ipswichian Stage, but it was not until about 20,000 BC that glacial ice once again covered much of Britain. It came no further south than north Norfolk, and Surrey only suffered some periglacial disturbances and adjustments of its rivers to low sea levels. A few hand-axes in Surrey are of a type usually associated with the earlier part of this stage, ie before the maximum advance of glacial ice.

Into this very generalised summary of the development of the Surrey landscape in the last half a million years the Palaeolithic sites can be fitted with varying degrees of accuracy, some sort of sequence suggested and, where possible, an assessment made of the environment with which the people were coping. The three geographical groupings listed above are now considered in order.

1 The Farnham Terrace sequence

The archaeology and geology of this classic flight of river terraces has recently been reviewed by Roe (1981) and his diagrammatic section across them is reproduced here (fig 1.2) with his kind permission. He summarises the work of Lasham (1893a), Bury (1913; 1916; 1917; 1935), Wade (1927), Wade & Smith (1934), Oakley (1939) and Rankine (1935; 1946–7a; 1953–4), and emphasises that, in spite of the large numbers of palaeoliths that have been found and recorded from these Farnham terraces, relatively few have been preserved with full details of their provenances. However, there is sufficient to establish that hand-axes and other artefacts occur in the gravels underlying Terrace A, and also in those of the lower terraces, B, C, and D. The interpretation of terrace deposits is fraught with difficulties, apart from knowing whether the palaeoliths are contemporary with the deposit in which they are found, or have been derived from earlier land surfaces or terrace gravels. It will be generally true that the sediments on a flight of

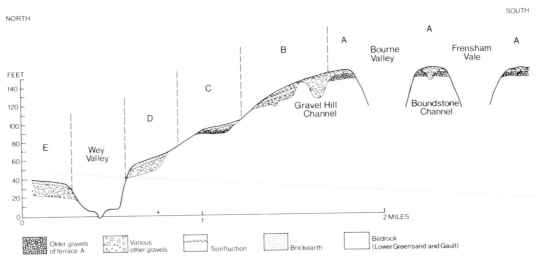

Fig 1.2. Diagrammatic section across the Wey Valley at Farnham to show the sequence of Terraces A–E (after Roe 1981; original drawing by M H R Cook).

terraces, such as at Farnham, will be progressively older as their height increases above the present river. Thus, the palaeoliths which have been found in the gravel of Terrace A qualify for being regarded as the earliest in the sequence, for none has been found in any higher gravel in the area, ie in the Old Park Terrace and the Dippenhall Gravels.

In order to establish the earliest evidence for Palaeolithic man in Surrey, the date of Farnham Terrace A is critical. At present this can only be inferred by tentative correlations with the terrace deposits of the Thames, and the dating of these is by no means conclusive. It is also apparent that Terrace A is a complex, composite feature, with channels cut through the main body of the gravel, filled with more gravels also containing hand-axes. Thus, it is the few hand-axes which can with certainty be related to the pre-channel gravel that may be regarded as the earliest. They are of 'archaic' character, ie crude and stone-struck, classified by Roe (1968b) as his Group V, which also includes the hand-axes at Fordwich, Kent, which are in a similar, early geological position. However, there is no reason to suppose that this crudity is related to their antiquity, for finely made hand-axes are known elsewhere in the world some hundreds of thousands of years earlier than these could possibly be. Yet it is obvious that they are still of great antiquity, for the great valley which one can observe from the top of the Tilford road, south of the town of Farnham, has been eroded since these hand-axes were washed into the Terrace A gravels. The hand-axes from the channels cut in this same terrace are probably not far removed in time from them (fig 1.3:1–2).

It has already been mentioned above that these gravels have been tentatively dated to the latter part of the Anglian Stage, but this date is not accepted by all workers. Clarke & Dixon (1981) base their dating on the correlation of Terrace A with the Boyn Hill Terrace of the Thames, although they emphasise that it is conjectural. They equate the Boyn Hill with the later part of the Anglian Stage. Gibbard (1979 and pers comm), although also correlating Terrace A with the Boyn Hill, equates the latter with the early Wolstonian Stage (Gibbard 1985). No more can be done here than state these contradictory conclusions (see also Fisher *et al* 1983) and the subjective opinion of the writer is that the earlier date is more likely to be the correct one, an opinion which is perhaps substantiated by considering a site beyond the Farnham district near Weybridge, St George's Hill (Longley 1976). Here, a few hand-axes have apparently come from this high level gravel (74m OD) which Gibbard (1979; 1982), on firmer ground, correlates with the Black Park Stage of the Thames, ie the time when the Thames and the Mole/Wey were diverted by the end moraine of the Anglian glaciation in the Finchley Depression of north London, and the landscape and drainage pattern was beginning to assume its present form.

The palaeoliths from the gravels of the lower terraces at Farnham have been well described. Terrace B has produced numerous hand-axes of various forms, crude or elegant, unabraded or worn (fig 1.3:3–4); also well-made side-scrapers previously described as Clactonian (Oakley 1939, 35–7) but now known to be a feature of some Acheulian hand-axe industries, such as in the Upper Hoxne Industry (Wymer 1974). Neither here nor anywhere else in Surrey is there anything justifying the claim of the presence of a Clactonian Industry. Terrace C has produced several hand-axes, some very thin and elegant, or of plano-convex section, and some Levalloisian flakes (fig 1.3:5–6). Both Terraces B and C almost certainly belong to the Wolstonian Stage, and have been tentatively dated as such by Clarke & Dixon (1981). The appearance of Levalloisian flakes in the latter part of the Wolstonian Stage can be paralleled by sequences in the Thames Valley and East Anglia (Wymer 1968; 1985).

Terrace D, at 76m OD, represents the last course of the Wey/Blackwater before its capture by the Tilford/Godalming river. Clarke and Dixon would date this as late Wolstonian, but an early to mid-Devensian date seems more likely to the writer, especially as it contains the typical hand-axes and Levalloisian flakes of a distinctive British Mousterian of Acheulian Tradition Industry (Roe 1981, 265) (fig 1.3:7). However, this industry could be earlier. Recent work by Bryant *et al* (1983) on the sediments of Terrace D includes the application of radiocarbon and thermo-luminescent dating methods. Unfortunately the results are contradictory, with a radiocarbon date of $36,000 \pm ^{2400}_{1800}$ bp (Q 2354) and a TL date of 106,000.

Future work will eventually produce a reliable, dated sequence for this classic flight of terraces. The probable sequence is summarised in Table 1.

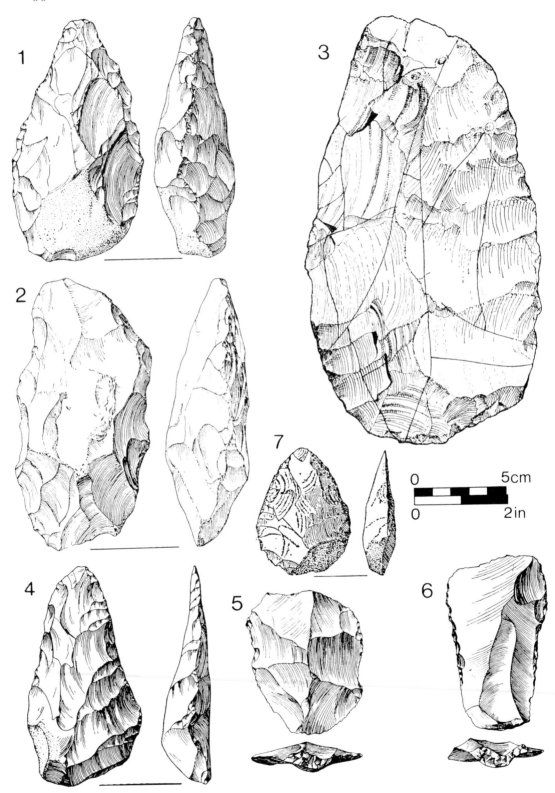

GEOLOGICAL STAGE	ESTIMATED DATE BP (after Kukla 1977)	WEY/BLACKWATER	PALAEOLITHIC INDUSTRY
	———13,000———		
Devensian Mainly cold with major ice advance as far south as north Norfolk coast *c* 15–20,000 bp		Diversion into present Wey valley Terrace D	Mousterian of Acheulian Tradition
	———70,000———		
Ipswichian Interglacial*			
	———120,000———		
Wolstonian Mainly cold but probably several interstadial or interglacial episodes contained within this stage. Distribution and extent of ice sheet not fully understood, but unlikely to have been further south than the Midlands and possibly NW Norfolk/ Suffolk		Terrace C Terrace B	Acheulian with Levalloisian Acheulian
	———367,000———		
Hoxnian Interglacial*			
	———400,000———		
Anglian Most extensive ice sheet for which there is evidence in Britain. Ice reached Chilterns and Thames Valley		St George's Hill Gravel of Mole/Wey Terrace A and incised channels	Acheulian
	———472,000———		

* The absence of known industries during the interglacial stages of the Hoxnian and Ipswichian may be a reflection of the obliteration of land surfaces and almost total erosion of interglacial sediments by later periglacial conditions.

TABLE 1.   The Palaeolithic sequence at Farnham

Fig 1.3. Palaeoliths from the Farnham terraces: 1, 2, stone-struck Acheulian hand-axes from gravels of Terrace A (after Oakley 1939; original drawing by M Leakey); 3, large Acheulian ovate hand-axe with tranchet cutting edge from Terrace B (after Rankine 1953–4; original drawing by W F Rankine); 4, pointed hand-axe with plano-convex section from Terrace B (after Oakley 1939; original drawing by M Leakey); 5, 6, Levalloisian flakes from Terrace C (after Oakley 1939; original drawing by M Leakey); 7, small, cordate hand-axe from Terrace D (after Bury 1913). All 1:2

2 The North Downs plateau at Walton on the Hill and the high level gravels and brickearths at Limpsfield

The second group of Surrey Palaeolithic sites includes material which is found in very different circumstances from the Farnham terrace gravels. The richest and most studied sites are those on the high plateau of Walton and Banstead Heaths, where the Chalk is mantled by Clay-with-flints. In the upper levels of the Clay-with-flints, within reach of the plough, numerous hand-axes and flakes have been recovered (Carpenter 1955; 1956; 1960; 1963; Walls & Cotton 1980). They are generally patinated white and often frost-cracked. Sometimes the chemical dissolution (patination) is so advanced that the struck flint surfaces have virtually reverted to cortex. A trial excavation at Rookery Farm by F Pemberton in 1969–70 produced a few flakes *in situ* at the same level as some patinated and frost-shattered flints (Pemberton 1971). There can be no doubt that these artefacts represent activity on the spot. Unfortunately it cannot be concluded that they lie precisely on an ancient, undisturbed land surface, for normal weathering processes and periglacial effects have altered the top metre or so of the Clay-with-flints, although nothing has moved far. There is no method of dating this spread of hand-axes, other than recognising that they are products of an Acheulian Industry; no Levallois is present nor any hand-axes particularly distinctive of very late Acheulian Industries (fig 1.4:1–7). On these tenuous grounds it seems unlikely that they represent Palaeolithic activity later than the Wolstonian Stage. They could well be the equivalent of those found within Terrace B at Farnham. The great interest of these discoveries is that they demonstrate the presence of Palaeolithic people on high ground, on heavy soils, well out of the river valleys. Whether this was during a cold or warm phase, or both, cannot be assessed. The former would seem more likely as the vegetational cover would have been thin. However, warm conditions need not imply dense, impenetrable scrub and woodland, for we probably underestimate the effect of grazing herds of large mammals. Elephants, rhinoceros, deer, bovids and horses would have been present. Most likely, it was these herds which attracted hunters and the hand-axes remain to mark their butchering sites.

Whereas the palaeoliths from Walton on the Hill, Kingswood and nearby can almost be regarded as being in primary context, the same seems unlikely for those found in the brickearth at Limpsfield. They were collected mainly at the end of the last century, apparently from numerous small pits on the Lower Greensand escarpment at heights up to 180m OD. There are many published references to these discoveries, and also to those in the gravel on Limpsfield Common (eg Prestwich 1891; Evans 1897; Clinch 1902a; Martin & Treacher 1910; Smith 1917; 1926; Whimster 1931) but no detailed report, which is unfortunate in view of the unusual nature of the site. The brickearth has produced small hand-axes and Levalloisian flakes so a Mousterian of Acheulian Tradition Industry may be represented (fig 1.4:8). The artefacts are nearly all patinated a creamy white, like those from Walton on the Hill, but the brickearth is not Clay-with-flints but probably a solifluction deposit formed down the slope of the Greensand. It is described as very stony.

Even less is known of the gravel on Limpsfield Common, which has also produced palaeoliths. Ochreous, ovate hand-axes have come from the surface of this gravel and probably relate more to the material from the brickearth than to the gravel itself. Martin & Treacher (1910) emphasise the unstratified nature of the gravel and its similarity to the brickearth, but conclude it cannot be the same as it does not contain Lower Greensand material. It was clearly deposited at the foot of the Chalk escarpment and Fagg (1923) estimates that the escarpment has since receded by nearly half a kilometre, so it must be a feature of considerable age, but whether it was formed by solifluction or fluviatile activity is uncertain. Whatever its age, the hand-axes which have been found in the gravel may be intrusive. Information is so scanty that it is useless to speculate further, but the importance of these sites at Limpsfield is that, again, they demonstrate the exploitation of high ground, well away from any major river valley.

Fig 1.4. Palaeoliths from the North Downs: 1–7, from the subsoil of the Clay-with-flints at Walton on the Hill and Lower Kingswood (1, 5, 7 after Carpenter 1956; 2–4, 6 after Walls & Cotton 1980); 8, ovate hand-axe from Limpsfield, probably from brickearth (after Smith 1931). All 1:2

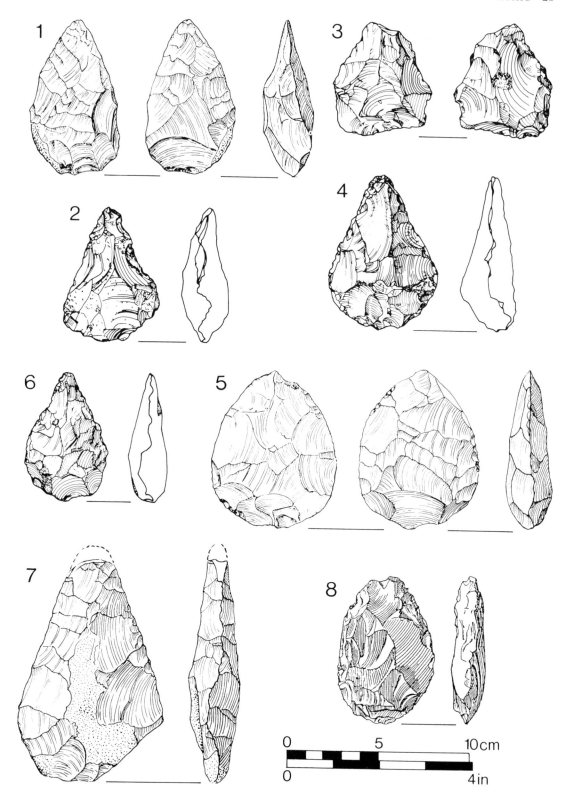

3 Isolated sites

Reference to the distribution map of sites (fig 1.1) shows a small scatter of Palaeolithic find spots between the North Downs and the Thames. There are no prolific sites or areas, with the possible exception of the spread of Thames Terrace gravel between Wandsworth and Battersea. Here, at a height of about 21–30m OD is a remnant of the ancient Thames, making a conspicuous flat feature, seen well on Clapham Common. On the basis of altitude and its Palaeolithic contents, this terrace is almost certainly the equivalent of the Lynch Hill Terrace of the middle Thames, which is now generally agreed to be of Wolstonian age. The Wandle and the Falcon Brook cut through it at right angles in order to join the main river, making the steep hills of Wandsworth Hill, Lavender Hill, East and West Hill, St Anne's Hill, St John's Hill and Battersea Rise, all rising from the valley floor to the terrace flat above. These transverse valleys contain more recent deposits which are of particular interest, as will be seen below, but when the Surrey tributaries met the Thames at this level, they must have flowed across broad flood plains themselves, frequently swollen with melt-waters during the colder parts of the Wolstonian. The flat, gravelly flood plains produced at river confluences were, not surprisingly, attractive places for large mammals and their Palaeolithic hunters. This confluence of the former, larger Wandle and the Thames was no exception, and the hand-axes discarded by these people became incorporated into the river beds at flood times. They have been discovered at Wandsworth Common, at the top of East and West Hill, on St John's Hill and various places around Clapham Common, never in any quantity and generally somewhat rolled, battered or broken through being dispersed by surging water and the movement of gravel on the ancient flood plain. Some details of these discoveries can be found in the Victoria County History (Clinch 1902a), Whimster's short chapter and gazetteer in his *Archaeology of Surrey* (Whimster 1931), Roe's (1968a) gazetteer for the CBA, and my own book on the Thames valley (Wymer 1968). The same sources refer to several of the isolated sites now to be discussed, but it is thought that a brief review of them would be useful here, in terms of the current understanding of the period.

Several of the sites support the conclusion that Levalloisian technique was not used, perhaps with rare exceptions, before the latter part of the Wolstonian Stage, ie after the time of the terrace gravel at Wandsworth and Clapham as mentioned above. This is certainly the case with the few Levallois flakes that have been found in the low-lying deposits within the valleys which cut through the actual Wandsworth–Clapham spread of terrace gravel. There is a double-ridged Levallois blade in a rolled condition from Clapham Junction in the British Museum Sturge Collection, and a few other Levallois flakes from Wandsworth in sharp condition. G F Lawrence (1890) claimed to have found a 'floor' on St Anne's Hill with 3000 flakes and implements. This cannot be substantiated, and I am indebted to L Adkins for information on the Palaeolithic discoveries in this area contained in her thesis (Adkins 1982). She lists numerous find spots around Wandsworth of hand-axes and flakes, but nothing consistent with a large quantity of material in primary context. L W Carpenter found a Levallois flake in a rolled condition at Ruxley Farm, Malden, in 1957 (pers comm), apparently from gravels which are more likely to be Late Pleistocene rather than Middle. The same probably applies to another Levallois flake found by Tom Walls in 1960 (pers comm) at Castle Avenue, Ewell, in gravel capping Thanet Sand, together with two small hand-axes and three other flakes. Levallois flakes have been dredged from the bed of the present River Thames, from gravel of the Flood Plain Terrace or Buried Channel, such as at Mortlake and Richmond, but in very rolled condition.

There is only one site in Surrey known to the writer where there is a good association between Palaeolithic flints and mammalian remains: Gosden Farm Pit near Bramley, well reported by North (1931). A small hand-axe in sharp condition was found in a gravelly sand together with several teeth of mammoth and some bones of Giant Deer.

Hand-axes have been recorded from Wimbledon Common and Richmond Park, from gravels equivalent to the Black Park Terrace of the Thames (Gibbard 1979). It is difficult to substantiate the exact provenances of the few hand-axes found but Adkins (1979a) gives Wimbledon Recreation Ground and Kingston Road. Nicolaysen (1983) has located three hand-axes in the John Evelyn Museum at Wimbledon but none come from the high terrace.

One hand-axe comes from the surface of the gravel in Richmond Park near White Lodge (Wymer 1968, 275), and one fragment of a rolled flake from nearby, in the spoil of a trench dug into the gravel (E N William, pers comm). These scanty remains can be equated with the earliest Palaeolithic material from Surrey mentioned in section 1, from St George's Hill, Weybridge, and possibly Terrace A at Farnham.

Apart from the Levallois flakes mentioned above, several hand-axes have also been found in the modern bed of the Thames, at East Molesey, Runnymede, Kingston, Richmond, Kew, Putney, Battersea and Wandsworth. Some are so rolled, virtually reduced to pebbles, that they must have been worked and re-worked from one gravel bed to another, possibly starting their life in one of the higher terraces. Some may be from Mousterian of Acheulian Tradition industries of the early Devensian Stage. This would certainly seem to be true of the occasional discoveries of flat-butted cordate hand-axes which are distinctive of this industry. They have come from the Thames at Putney (Cambridge Museum of Archaeology and Ethnology), Wandsworth (Museum of London) and Richmond (Roe 1981). They are also all in a rolled or very rolled condition. Roe (1981, 265–6) gives a very useful summary of the Surrey hand-axes of this type, which he terms *bout coupé*, referring to discoveries of them at Balham, Terrace D at Farnham and at least two from the brickearth at Limpsfield.

Hand-axes and flakes have been reported from several other sites, as shown on the map (fig 1.1), usually in patches of gravel 15m or more above the rivers of the present drainage system and rarely able to be related to any datable succession of terraces, or even to the actual rivers which deposited them. The Middle Pleistocene evolution of the Blackwater, Mole, Wey, Wandle and other streams is still imperfectly understood, but there have been many changes, particularly in response to the River Thames cutting off the lower parts of the northward flowing streams when it was diverted by the Anglian ice into its present valley. Unlike the Thames, which, since Anglian times, has maintained the general course of its valley, merely tending to shift southwards each time changing sea levels forced it to cut lower flood plains, the Surrey rivers have a long history of capturing each other with consequent change of direction and erosion of their old beds. There are no clear flights of terraces such as are so well preserved on the north bank of the Middle Thames. Other hand-axes have been found on the surface, or their condition is such that they could never have been transported in gravel. Sometimes it is difficult to know whether some of the old finds are from river deposits, brickearth or the surface. Some of these sites are listed below:

Abinger Hammer (Collins 1936): hand-axe from ?Tillingbourne Terrace Gravel

Abinger (Guildford Museum): rolled cleaver

Albury, Farley Heath (Lasham 1892): fragment of ovate axe from surface

Chaldon, Heath (Farley 1973): two hand-axes

Chertsey, south bank of Bourne (Kingston Museum records): cordate hand-axe in sharp condition

Chobham (Roe 1968a, 282): ?Blackwater gravels

Cobham, beside Old Portsmouth Road (Weybridge Museum, P Nicolaysen, pers comm): pointed hand-axe in sharp condition, another slightly rolled; from Mole Gravels

Croydon area: surface finds at Addington, Shirley (Thornhill 1971), from Wandle Gravels (Adkins 1979b)

Frensham, between the two ponds (R Clarke, pers comm): broken ovate hand-axe in fresh condition

Hurley, Salfords (Ellaby 1978): rolled and broken ovate hand-axe associated with traces of superficial gravel on Weald Clay on a terrace of the upper Mole at 70m OD

Mitcham (Roe 1968a, 292; Adkins 1979a, 10): a few flakes and animal bones recorded but not necessarily associated

Mitcham, Common (Adkins 1979a, 10): hand-axe reported from 1.30m deep in Wandle Gravel

Reigate, Woodhatch (Roe 1968a, 292; Hooper 1937a, b): deeply ochreous and rolled hand-axe in sewer trench just above the 61m contour

Shalford, Peasmarsh (Evans 1897, 594): hand-axe in gravel on Weald Clay or Lower Greensand, found *c* 1842; earliest discovery of palaeolith in Surrey; remains of mammoth and traces of old land surface claimed

Walton-on-Thames, Rydens Road (Weybridge Museum, P Nicolaysen, pers comm): three hand-axes in sharp condition

Walton-on-Thames, Sevenhills Road (Weybridge Museum, P Nicolaysen, pers comm): two pointed hand-axes

Wandsworth L B, Earlsfield (Smith 1931, 62): cordate hand-axe found 2m deep in brickearth on lower terrace of Wandle

Weybridge, Melrose Road (Weybridge Museum, P Nicolaysen pers comm): small hand-axe, and (Longley 1976) two hand-axes nearby

Wonersh (Roe 1968a, 295): Levallois flake, but found on churchyard path and possibly imported with gravel

Worplesdon (Whimster 1931): hand-axes found by labourers in 1887 and traced to gravel coming from Farnham, leading to Palaeolithic discoveries there

The sum of the evidence from Surrey for the Palaeolithic period is considerable, although it would be difficult to interpret unless placed within the context of what is known of this remote period as a whole. The first evidence for human activity in Britain is, rather surprisingly, on the fringe of the highland zone in the West Country, at Westbury-sub-Mendip and Kent's Cavern near Torquay. The former is restricted to a few flakes and at least one core tool associated with a Cromerian fauna; the latter to some crude, stone-struck flint hand-axes that may have been associated with a Cromerian fauna. High Lodge, in Suffolk, may also be of this age. There is nothing in Surrey, or the rest of south-east England, as old as this, as far as can be judged, but there is mounting evidence for the presence of hunting groups within the Anglian Stage of the Middle Pleistocene. This was a time when glacial ice came further south than any other known ice sheet before or afterwards. It reached the Thames valley and Surrey must have suffered periglacial conditions. Human occupation was presumably restricted to warmer phases within this stage, but the geological evidence has not survived; only the flint tools and flaking debris remain in the gravel accumulations of succeeding colder phases. The Black Park Terrace of the Thames dates to the end of this Anglian Stage and, in the Caversham Channel, there are prolific Clactonian and Acheulian industries. The few hand-axes from St George's Hill at Weybridge, Richmond Park and Wimbledon Common can be correlated with the Black Park Terrace, and probably Terrace A at Farnham. Archaeological typology does not support this, as there is no Clactonian Industry known at these Surrey sites, and the hand-axes are of different forms. However, such is the variety of tool forms and industrial traditions within the Lower Palaeolithic that this need not contradict the geological evidence. If the dating is correct, people were present in Surrey some time before the end of the Anglian, estimated at 400,000 years ago. The only human fossil fragment for this time in north-west Europe is the Mauer jaw from West Germany (Cook *et al* 1982), considered by some as belonging to *Homo erectus*, so possibly it was one of these people who made the Farnham Terrace A hand-axes, and was perhaps present at the other sites. However, our knowledge of human physical evolution at this time is very thin, and a primitive form of *Homo sapiens*, akin to the remains from Swanscombe and Steinheim, may have been around.

Surrey is not alone in being unable to produce any Palaeolithic evidence for the succeeding Hoxnian Interglacial period for, at present, the only site which has produced unequivocal proof of human occupation of Britain in this period is Clacton on Sea, where the Clactonian Industry continues into the Early-temperate zone of the interglacial. The Acheulian industries at Hoxne itself belong to the cool period immediately following the Hoxnian and there must be some doubt as to the provenance of the few pieces which have been found in interglacial lake muds there. However, it would be very strange if southern England had been unoccupied by people making hand-axes during the Hoxnian, and the explanation is probably the usual one that interglacial deposits tend to be destroyed in succeeding glacial or periglacial episodes and that chance has not yet revealed those which have survived. It also seems very likely that many of the hand-axes found in gravels which can be dated to the earlier part of the Wolstonian Stage have been derived from Hoxnian land surfaces. This would include some but presumably not all of the hand-axes in Terrace B at Farnham and the gravel spreads of Wandsworth and Clapham, as well as many of those from the undated isolated sites. However, there is a strong possibility that Palaeolithic occupation may have been restricted to periods when the landscape was a more open one, at times of cooler climate. Unsatisfactory as the evidence is, there is sufficient to show that several different environments were being exploited prior to the last interglacial, the Ipswichian Stage. The Walton on the Hill–Kingswood–Banstead sites, with hand-axes virtually in primary context in the upper part of the Clay-with-flints, are unique in this respect, for they demonstrate the exploitation of the high Chalk plateaux, well away from contemporary river valleys. Hand-axes have been found high on the Hampshire and Wiltshire Downs, and on the North Downs of Kent, but only in small numbers over wide areas, and usually they are very worn and patinated, unlike those from the Surrey Clay-with-flints sites where they are generally patinated but otherwise well-preserved. It is impossible to date them, other than to observe that there is no Levalloisian element so an Early Wolstonian date is more probable than a later one.

The palaeoliths in the river gravels thought to date to this time must, for the most part, reflect human activity along the rivers, both main and tributary streams. Straight-tusked elephant, horse, giant ox, rhinoceros and several forms of deer provided protein, but what proportion was hunted or scavenged is unknown. The Swanscombe skull fragments, associated with pointed Acheulian hand-axes, belong to this time: modern man, but with distinct Neanderthal traits.

A few Levallois flakes appear in Terrace C at Farnham, and in the deposits that post-date the Wandsworth gravels, but Surrey cannot boast of any rich Levalloisian site such as Baker's Hole, Northfleet, Kent, where flint was being exploited on the grand scale. The Mousterian of Acheulian Tradition Industry is poorly represented, but enough has been found to show that Surrey was not unoccupied in this latest phase of the Palaeolithic, prior to the appearance in Europe of the sophisticated Upper Palaeolithic industries based on blade production. The Limpsfield brickearth artefacts indicate that these hunters came up from the valleys on to the Greensand escarpment. They would have been contemporary with the inhabitants of the Oldbury rock shelter sites in Kent. Whether they were of Neanderthal stock is unknown, but likely.

This brief survey has only been made possible by the work and observations of many dedicated people during the last century, whose names frequently appear in the published *Collections* of the Surrey Archaeological Society. It is hoped that this tradition will continue, with the collaboration of geologists, palynologists, physicists and other scientists when suitable sites are found. Apart from new sites to be discovered, which must exist, there is still much that should be done on the old material: the palaeoliths that are described and drawn in Bury's notebooks, thankfully preserved at Farnham Museum, need to be related to the actual specimens so that there is a better sample of the contents of the Farnham Terraces. This will mean that someone will have to visit several museums. It would also be good to know more of the Limpsfield artefacts and of the site itself.[3]

NOTES

1 (This paper was completed in January 1984: Eds). I wish to express my thanks to all those people in the past who have so kindly informed me of new discoveries or the result of their studies. My files bulge with letters from the late W F Rankine, L W Carpenter, Tom Walls and (more recently) Lesley Smith, F Pemberton, L Adkins and R Scott, and I am sure there are others. Jonathan Cotton kindly allowed me to consult his exhaustive bibliography, and thanks are due to the curators at Kingston, Guildford and Farnham Museums for giving me the opportunity to make some brief checks on the Palaeolithic material they conserve. Also, my thanks are due to Pat Nicolaysen for her enthusiasm and practical assistance. In addition to the full references for those authors cited in the text, other relevant publications to the study of this period in Surrey have been included in the bibliography.

2 Editor's note: Richard Macphail and Rob Scaife asked Dr P Fisher for comment on the period earlier than that covered by them in the following chapter. It has seemed appropriate to add it here as a note, with John Wymer's agreement. Peter Fisher writes: 'The Quaternary history of Surrey is on the point of undergoing major revision. Probably the earliest Quaternary deposits in Surrey, although they may actually be of Late Tertiary age, are the Headley Formations of the North Downs (John 1980). These were thought to contain the Red Crag fossils at Netley Heath, but recent work has suggested that these fossils are in fact surficial to the deposits, and so cannot be used to date the Headley Formation,

which may be pre- or post Red Crag (John & Fisher 1984). The Caesar's Camp Gravels of the Upper Hale Plateau near Farnham, which were also widely believed to have originated during the Red Crag Transgression, have recently been shown to be a very early Quaternary fluvial deposit (Clarke & Fisher 1983).

'After a lack of research on the fluvial gravels in Surrey for more than 50 years, conclusions from very recent work (Clarke & Dixon 1981; Fisher 1982; Gibbard 1979; 1982) are making the evolution and routes of early Quaternary rivers in Surrey another matter for contention (Dixon *et al* 1983). There are two alternative hypotheses. Gibbard suggests that proto-Blackwater, -Mole and -Wey rivers formed a confluence in the vicinity of present Weybridge, and the resulting river flowed north through the Finchley Depression to join the Thames near Ware. By contrast Clarke & Dixon, who studied only the Blackwater, and Fisher, who again has examined the gravels of all three rivers, argue that the rivers followed northerly courses throughout the Quaternary. All are agreed that following the Anglian diversion of the Thames the rivers gradually adopted their present routes.'

3 Work on the Limpsfield material has now been started by members of the Lithic Tools Research Group (Surrey) (Cotton *et al* 1984).

The geographical and environmental background

R I MACPHAIL and R G SCAIFE

Introduction

This chapter seeks to provide a broad appreciation of the character of Surrey during the period spanning the Upper Palaeolithic of the last glacial stage (Devensian) to around AD 1500.[1] Changes which have occurred include natural climatic, vegetational and geomorphological alterations and equally importantly those effects on the landscape resulting from man's activities. This period has undoubtedly been one of profound changes in the environment resulting from the overall move-ment from a periglacial regime – as ice sheets did not cover Surrey – to the mid-Flandrian interglacial climatic optimum and subsequent climatic deterioration. Associated with these changes are the developmental sequences of both soil and vegetation. During the Late Devensian, the landscape was subjected to harsh periglacial conditions interspersed by the relatively milder Allerød/Windermere interstadial (11,800–11,000 bp). This pedologically unstable and vegetatively diverse period forms the basis for development of soils influenced firstly by the additions of cover loam or loess (Catt 1977; 1978), and secondly by an open heliophilous, largely herbaceous, vegetation into which the principal deciduous and coniferous woodland elements migrated from their glacial refugia. Although Allerød temperatures may have sustained *Betula* woodland and allowed the formation of some stable soils, as for example found at Brook, Kent (Kerney *et al* 1964) and Sevenoaks (Skempton & Weeks 1976), the majority of such major successional changes started *c* 10,000 bp, at the close of the Late Devensian. Subsequently climate did not remain constant and the broad and generally accepted Flandrian chronozones apply. Within this broad framework, lesser fluctuations have been evidenced, such as the 'mini warm phase' of late Saxon times and the 'little Ice Age' of the Tudor period.

Anthropogenic activity has further complicated and modified such natural vegetational and pedological successional events evident in previous interglacial cycles. Changes occurring at their most extreme include the formation of an agricultural or managed landscape. Less obvious but profound changes occurred during different phases of prehistoric activity. Forest clearances led to the creation of secondary and tertiary woodland types or the establishment and maintenance of plagioclimax communities, that is, those plant communities maintained by man such as the chalk downland pastures and heathlands. Periglacial soliflual conditions had resulted in spreads of colluvial material along the lower slopes of the Downs (Atkins & Sallnow 1975). Conversely, man has been responsible for later colluviation/hillwash resulting from valley side agrarianism.

The sources of evidence for these events as a whole are varied, coming from a range of natural science disciplines. At the outset, it has to be stated that Surrey itself is somewhat impoverished in such analyses. Where there are detailed studies available these are referred to, but as with other areas of southern England some recourse to environmental evidence for the region as a whole is necessary.

The present day geographical environment

Surrey can be divided into a number of areas differentiated by their geological, geomorphological and drainage characteristics. Temporally these have produced varying environments with par-ticular soil (fig 2.1), vegetation and consequently land-use types. A clearer understanding of these can be reached by study of Lousley's *Flora of Surrey* (1976) and examination of the 1:250,000 map of the Soil Survey of England and Wales (Jarvis *et al* 1983) on which are presented Soil Associations, which relate to where similar soils of a number of soil series form an extensive and often dominant cover. Identifiable regions are:

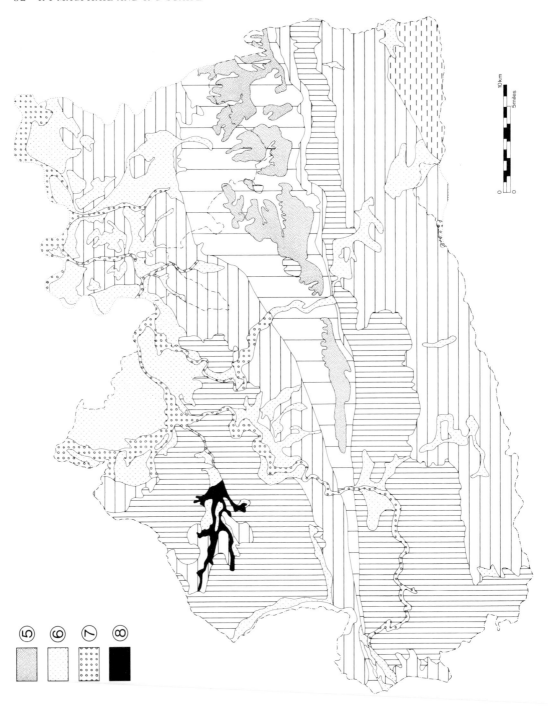

1 *The Central Weald.* An outcrop of the Upper Hastings Beds (Tunbridge Wells Sand) produced high ground in the extreme south-east of the county. Elevations of over 168m OD are reached at the Dry Hill hillfort (TQ 432417). Here, the soils are a dominant cover of stagnogleyic argillic brown earths (Avery 1980) of the Curtisden Association (Jarvis *et al* 1983). Locally, the area is well drained and well wooded.

2 *The Low Weald.* Further north and dominating the south and south-east of Surrey is the Wealden Clay tract (Lower Cretaceous), a belt which averages only 61m OD in height. This area features poor natural drainage due to its relatively low elevation and its flatness, and because of the impermeable character of its soils and the lithology. These are typical stagnogleys of the Wickham Association developed on the Weald Clay. Covers of alluvium and valley gravels give rise to typical argillic gley soils of the Shabbington Association, as for example along the Rivers Mole and Wey. The Low Weald becomes more wooded to the west compared with the east.

3 *The High Weald.* This elevated area is composed of the relatively more resistant Lower Greensand belts to the north and west of the Weald. These attain maximum elevations at such notable landmarks as Holmbury Hill (261m OD; TQ 083426) and Leith Hill (294m OD; TQ 138432). Much of this predominantly sandy outcrop is wooded but supported large expanses of open heathland until this century. The existing, generally acid, cover varies from humo-ferric podzols (Shirrell Heath 2 Association: Jarvis *et al* 1983) as at Blackheath (TQ 040460) (Macphail 1979) and Hindhead (SU 890360) to argillic brown sand (Frilford Association) at Albury (TQ 048478). Typical argillic brown earths (Fyfield 2 Association) occur where there is a fine brickearth cover (eg Farley Heath TQ 053054) or where there is a 'fine' component in the Lower Greensand (eg Fullers Earth at Redhill). In addition, there is low ground (approximately 61m OD) between Reigate and Dorking where the River Mole cuts the Lower Greensand. Here, areas of typical argillic gley soils exist on alluvium and river gravels.

4 *The North Downs.* These extend across the county, being 11km wide in the east but thinning to half a kilometre in the west at the Hog's Back. Scarp edges range between 183 and 233m OD in the east, as at Colley Hill, near Reigate (TQ 250519; 233m) and Hackhurst Downs (TQ 100490; 233m), but are lower in the west, being less than 152m along the Hog's Back. Dipslope elevations decline north-westwards. The base-rich chalk lithology also, however, carries extensive areas of acid superficial deposits. West of Reigate, the Gault and Upper Greensand outcrops are very narrow and are largely obscured by solifluction head derived from the North Downs. To the east, more extensive outcrops of these strata have produced areas of pelo-stagnogley soils (the Denchworth Association), as for example around Limpsfield (Jarvis *et al* 1983).

The area between the Lower Greensand and the Chalk is covered by valley gravels and head deposits on which are developed typical argillic gley soils (on coarse drift) and typical brown calcareous earths (Coombe Association on the Head). As soils become thinner up the scarp slope, grey rendzinas (Upton Association) become dominant. The most common chalkland soil cover of the dipslope is, however, a slightly deeper brown rendzina of the Andover Association. These are

Fig 2.1. Map of the main areas of different soils in Surrey, after the *Soil Survey of England and Wales sheet 6, 1:250,000* (Jarvis *et al* 1983); the soil cover in urban areas unmapped by the Soil Survey has been interpolated.
1: slowly permeable silty soils (stagnogleyic argillic brown earths).
2: poorly drained heavy soils (typical and pelo-stagnogley soils).
3: generally acid, mainly freely drained light soils (humo-ferric and stagnogley podzols, argillic brown sands, typical argillic brown earths).
4: base-rich shallow to deep light to loamy soils (rendzinas, brown calcareous earths, colluvial brown calcareous earths).
5: acid, poorly drained, heavy, stony soils (typical and stagnogleyic palaeo-argillic brown earths).
6: generally permeable light to loamy soils, often affected by ground water (typical argillic gley soils, argillic brown earths, some podzols).
7: loamy to heavy soils, often affected by ground water (typical and pelo-alluvial gley soils).
8: fen peat.

found, for example, around Leatherhead. The scarp area supports the floristically rich short turf communities of plagioclimax nature and arable agriculture in areas with less severe gradients.

Superficial or drift deposits on the Downs (John 1980) have resulted in a number of soil types. On the freely draining Netley Heath deposits, including the Headley Sand at Headley Heath (TQ 190533), sands and gravels give rise to a cover of humo-ferric podzols (Macphail 1979; 1983) or more commonly to argillic brown soils similar to those of the Lower Greensand. In contrast, the Clay-with-flints (Plateau Drift) carries either typical or stagnogleyic palaeo-argillic brown earths (Marlow or Batcombe Association). These soils were affected by clay movement during an earlier interglacial cycle – hence the term palaeo-argillic. They are silty to clayey, flinty soils which often suffer poor drainage. Few areas on this soil type support arable activities, with most kept under deciduous or coniferous plantations, for example Ranmore Common (TQ 140510). The River Mole gap itself carries typical argillic brown earths of the Hucklesbrook Association overlying calcareous gravel.

5   *The Eocene Basin.* This area occupies all of Surrey north and north-west of the dip slope of the North Downs. Generally, it is relatively low-lying ground usually less than 61m OD descending to less than 15m OD near the River Thames. Exceptions are the areas of Bagshot Beds, as for example at Chobham Common (SU 970650) at 74m OD. These Eocene lithologies comprise the mainly sands, loams and clays of the Woolwich and Reading Beds and London Clay. Like the Chalk, these become less extensive towards the west. In addition, these early Tertiary sequences are extensively covered by fluvial (Terrace) gravels especially towards the north and the Thames. The Woolwich and Reading Beds commonly carry typical or gleyic argillic brown earths (Bursledon or Hucklesbrook Association: Jarvis *et al* 1983). The London

Fig 2.2. Surrey landscape: the southern end of the Mole gap near Dorking. Greensand hills are visible in the background. (*Photograph by Richard Evans, Surrey County Planning Department*)

Clay is less well drained and a cover of typical stagnogley soils (Wickham Association) is frequent where there is some drift. Pelo-stagnogley soils (Windsor Association) have developed on the London Clay itself. Pelo-alluvial gley soils are present on Thames alluvium, whereas on the extensive Thames Terrace gravels typical palaeo-argillic brown earths occur (the Bockmer or Sonning Association). The valley of the River Wey is typified by pelo-alluvial gley soils of the Fladbury Association. As described later, these areas have probably had a history of poor drainage, exacerbated in low-lying alluvial areas by seasonal floods.

The more sandy and loamy acid parent materials of the Bagshot, Bracklesham and Barton Beds, north-west of the London Clay, carry humo-ferric podzols where well drained (Macphail 1979; 1983), but often produce stagnogley podzols (Holiday Hill Association) as the result of underlying less permeable loams and clays, which occur as lenses within these beds. This soil association may also be present on local valley and Eocene gravels as, for example, at Chobham Common. In some areas where terrace gravels cover the Eocene sands, palaeo-argillic podzols (Southampton Association) occur.

In summary, Surrey today contains the following areas of soil types.

(a) Poorly drained, heavy clay soils which are difficult to cultivate. These are present on Weald Clay, Clay-with-flints and London Clay.
(b) Shallow and deep base-rich soils on Chalk.
(c) Three distinct areas of freely drained light acid soils – podzols on the Lower Greensand, the sandy superficial deposits on the Downs and the Eocene sand.
(d) A variety of soil types on river alluvium which relate to local parent materials.

Fig 2.3. Surrey landscape: heathland. Chobham Common. (*Photograph by Richard Evans, Surrey County Planning Department*)

PERIOD	SOILS AND GEOMORPHOLOGY	VEGETATION AND LANDUSE	ARCHAEOLOGY
FLANDRIAN (Pollen Zone) Modern (VIII)	Arable expansion on to heavy clay soils. Use of ridge and furrow to offset poor drainage and possibly poor heathland soils	Clearance of woodlands on wet clay soils (eg Wealden Clay)	Medieval Saxon
–c AD 450 Sub-Atlantic (VIII)	Accelerated soil erosion and development of colluvial soils. Increased alluvial sedimentation, causing flooding down river	Intensification of arable agriculture. Woodland clearance of Clay-with-flints and Plateau Gravels, and possibly Hythe Beds	Romano-British Iron Age
–c 2500 bp Sub-Boreal (VIIb)	Major development of podzols on heathlands. Continued development of rendzinas on Chalk plateaux and colluvial brown soils in dry valleys. Continued erosion through clearance and agriculture. Continued alluviation	Major forest clearance on 'heathlands' with ensuing *Corylus* scrub followed by *Calluna*. Continued deforestation on chalk and development of pastures	Bronze Age
	Flandrian Chronozone III Mature soil profiles increasingly affected by Neolithic land use, eg clearance and cultivation, causing soil erosion and deposition of dry valley and alluvial sediments; loss of decalcified argillic soils from chalk plateau areas; replaced by shallow base-rich rendzinas	Much forest clearance. On lighter soils common secondary woodland; small areas of shifting cultivation; development of pastures extant to the present	Neolithic
–c 5000 bp Atlantic (VIIa)	Flandrian Chronozone II Development of mature argillic and other brown soils; few podzols on anthropically affected acid parent materials. Increasing drainage impedance on lowland clay areas	Maximum development of mixed deciduous forest even on the chalk; localised heath associated with occupation	Late Mesolithic
–c 7500 bp Boreal (VI) Boreal (V)	Flandrian Chronozone I Developing soil profiles, decalcification, acidification. Early shallow podzols; initial clay translocation. Some valleyside instability and alluvial sedimentation	Rise of deciduous forests after pioneer Juniper, Birch, Pine and *Corylus* as climate rapidly warmed up	Mesolithic
–c 9600 bp Pre-Boreal (IV)	Melt-water muds weakly formed fragipan horizons, weathering substrates, eg decalcification		

PERIOD	SOILS AND GEOMORPHOLOGY	VEGETATION AND LANDUSE	ARCHAEOLOGY
LATE DEVENSIAN (LATE GLACIAL) (Zones I–III)			
–c 10,000 bp Zone III ('Younger Dryas')	Major periglacial reworking of earlier structures and sediments by cryoturbation	Treeless tundra-heath	
–c 11,000 bp Zone II ('Allerød/Windermere insterstadial')	Short-lived soil formation humose rendzinas; meltwater muds. Strongly formed fragipan horizons. Decalcification of sediments	Presence of Birch and Pine	Upper Palaeolithic
–c 11,800 bp Zone I ('Older Dryas')	Periglacial structures; convolutions, stone stripes, ice wedge polygons, pingoes; solifluction Head. Deposition of cover sands and loess	Treeless tundra	
–c 15,000 bp			
DEVENSIAN			

TABLE 1. Suggested environmental changes in southern England (Surrey) through the late Devensian and Flandrian

The environment from 15,000 bp

Information relating to the character and changes in Pleistocene and Holocene environments can be provided from a number of sources. It is this information which can be used as a background to the environments of prehistoric and later man. The discipline of environmental archaeology places special emphasis on archaeological sites and their immediate surrounds in order to elucidate reasons for their establishment, their contemporary environments and possible anthropogenic effects. Importantly, information can be gained on the character of human life and subsistence. The sources of such information have come from the application of disciplines within the natural sciences with palaeoecology, archaeobotany, zooarchaeology and geomorphological/pedological studies being of special importance. As noted above, Surrey is somewhat unfortunate, having few data available which relate to many of the questions which are frequently asked regarding man and his changing environments. The present character of Surrey includes, however, many of the types of environment suited to such investigations and therefore has great potential. It is hoped that the nature of materials which can be utilised and the sorts of information which can be derived from the respective studies will become evident in the subsequent discussion on the environmental changes pertaining to the principal prehistoric and historic periods.

THE LATE DEVENSIAN (GLACIAL) PERIOD

The last (Devensian) glacial stage spanned the period 90,000–10,000 years bp and it is the latter part of this period (the Late Devensian Zones I, II and III, from 12,000–10,000 bp: Pennington 1975) which may be used as a basis for discussion of the environments of the Upper Palaeolithic and ensuing Holocene/Flandrian archaeological activities. The Late Devensian, which earlier texts refer to as the late glacial, embraces the Zones I–III of Blytt (1876) and Sernander (1908) and pollen Zones I–III of Godwin (1940).

During the Pleistocene, Surrey was never covered by extensive ice sheets. It must nevertheless have been strongly affected by periglaciation, for evidence of geomorphological structures resulting from permafrost occurs within Surrey. Carpenter & Woodcock (1981) have suggested that Elstead Bog (SU 910420) is the most southerly pingo remnant in England. This geomorphological phenomenon occurs when an intrusion of groundwater between permafrost and frozen soil produces a hummock of frozen water (ice). On melting and collapse, a crater is formed which at Elstead has produced conditions suited to organogenic deposition during the ensuing Late Devensian and Early Flandrian (post-glacial) periods. Analyses of plant macroscopic fossils and pollen (Seagrief 1956; Seagrief & Godwin 1960; Brooks unpublished; Carpenter & Woodcock 1981) have produced one of the most valuable vegetation records for Surrey and southern England. Other geomorphological phenomena have also been described (Atkins & Sallnow 1975; John 1974). These include fragipans (fig 2.4), soil convolutions, stone stripes, ice wedge polygons and soliflucted/head deposit. Zones of deflation in front of the ice sheet lying to the north also resulted in cover sands and loess (cover loam) being deposited in south-east England (Catt 1977; 1978). Much of this material from earlier glacials was either cryoturbated into such deposits as Clay-with-flints (Plateau Drift) or, during the Devensian, soliflucted into valley deposits (Catt 1979). In some locations, eg Headley Heath on the North Downs (John 1974) and Farley Heath on the Lower Greensand plateau (Dines & Edmunds 1929; Macphail 1979), cover loams can still be identified. At Oxted a sequence of steeply dipping (28°) Late Devensian deposits have been researched by Kerney (1963). A number of meltwater muds were separated by a fossil rendzina of possible Allerød interstadial date (fig 2.4) which contained land mollusca relating to this climatic fluctuation. Similar calcareous Allerød soils have been identified at Brook, Kent (Kerney *et al* 1964) and Pitstone, Buckinghamshire (Evans & Valentine 1974). At Sevenoaks, Kent (Skempton & Weeks 1976), an Allerød palaeosol has been radiocarbon dated at 12,250±280 bp.

The status of Zone II vegetation (11,800–11,000 bp) in southern England is still problematical because of a marked paucity of polliniferous sites of this age. The two palaeosols in Kent have both been radiocarbon dated and yielded poorly preserved pollen and plant macroscopic fossils. At both sites pollen of herbs was abundant, but with *Pinus* (Pine) and *Betula* (Birch) present in the Zone II at Brook, Kent. Lambert (in Kerney *et al* 1964, 193) did, however, suggest that this might have

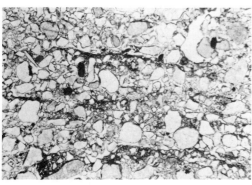

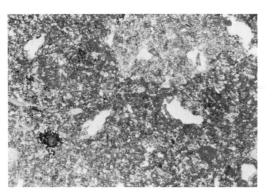
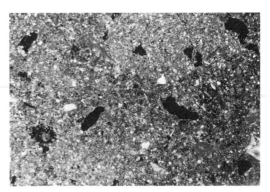

Fig 2.4. Photomicrographs of 'Late Glacial' soils.

Top left: strongly formed link cappings of silt and clay in a fragipan horizon probably developed in Zone II as surface soils (previously frozen) melted in spring, and silt and clay were washed by meltwater into the dry zone above subsoil permafrost. Plane polarised light (PPL); length of frame is 5.225mm (Hengistbury Head, Dorset).

Bottom left: heterogeneous, calcareous meltwater colluvium containing rendzina fragments from Allerød soil formation on chalk. PPL: length of frame is 5.225mm (Holborough, Kent).

Bottom right: as previous, crossed polarised light (XPL). Note high birefringence (brightness) caused by presence of calcium carbonate.

been of long-distance origin or resulting from differential preservation and over-representation in these poor pollen preserving conditions. The presence of *Betula* (as charcoal) was taken as evidence for local growth of this taxon (Levey in Kerney *et al* 1964, 197). It seems likely, therefore, that Zone II had *Betula* woodland and possibly *Pinus* colonisation during this Late Devensian interstadial, but a waterlogged stratigraphical sequence is required in order to draw firm conclusions as to the vegetational status of this interlude.

Sediments of Zone III (Younger Dryas) date containing pollen are rare in southern England. This has resulted in much weight being placed upon the evidence from a small number of sites analysed some 20–30 years ago. Analysis of Elstead (Seagrief 1956; Seagrief & Godwin 1960) led to the conclusion, on the basis of pollen and plant macrofossil evidence, that the Younger Dryas consisted of a landscape comprising *Pinus* and *Betula* woodland with a rich herbaceous flora. Scaife (1980; 1982) has drawn attention to the fact that these early pollen data were calculated as a percentage of arboreal pollen. In consequence, only the relative inputs of *Betula* and *Pinus* were being compared and not their actual relationship to the remaining pollen spectra of largely herbaceous character. Importantly, therefore, there has been an overestimation of the significance of trees for this period. The presence of extensive scatters of *Betula* and especially *Pinus* is contradictory to evidence obtained by more recent investigation of Elstead (Carpenter & Woodcock 1981), which suggests harsh and possibly continental conditions. Other such analyses from southern England indicating cold tundra-like conditions have been reviewed in the Isle of Wight (Scaife 1980; 1982) and Kent (Kerney *et al* 1964). At the former, pollen analyses of two sites show that *Betula* may have been very locally present but that the majority of *Betula* and *Pinus* pollen was probably of long distance origin. From this corpus it is suggested that the Younger Dryas had a much more open herbaceous vegetation than inferred in the past. One of the most interesting features of the vegetation is its marked floristic diversity and the varied phytogeographical elements. These reflect the variety of microclimatic, edaphic and geological conditions present. This diversity can also be shown from pollen and plant macrofossil analyses of the Lea Valley arctic plant bed (Allison *et al* 1952; Reid 1949) and at West Drayton, Middlesex (Gibbard & Hall 1982) and Colnbrook, Buckinghamshire (Gibbard *et al* 1982).

This view of harsher conditions than earlier postulated on the evidence of palaeobotanical data is commensurate with the evidence from Coleoptera fossil assemblages. It has been suggested that regionally changing climate and sharply declining temperatures occurred in Zone III (Osborne 1971; 1972; 1974). This change may have annihilated earlier Zone II (Allerød/Windermere interstadial) vegetation. Osborne (1971) has shown such rigorous conditions from assemblages of Coleoptera recovered from an organic lens in the gravels of the River Wandle, at Croydon, radiocarbon dated to the Younger Dryas at 10,130 bp.

FLANDRIAN CHRONOZONE I: pre-Boreal and Boreal Mesolithic forest

Rapidly-rising temperatures at *c* 10,000 bp initiated the successional rise to dominance of the Flandrian forest. Coleopteran evidence illustrates that temperatures rose rapidly to high mean annual values (Osborne 1974) over a short period of time. This rapid change coupled with the openness of vegetation in Zone III initiated a period of expansion of pioneer arboreal vegetation types into the landscape. The nature of this seral development and the time of arrival of different tree taxa were dependent upon the competition and dispersal characteristics of the species and on the distances of their journey from their Devensian refugia. These changes in vegetation were rapid, reflecting a complex reaction of communities to variations in controlling factors as understood in terms of dynamic phytosociology.

Surrey is fortunate in having one of the few sites providing a pollen profile and therefore sequences of vegetational change spanning the early Flandrian. Elstead, investigated by Seagrief and Godwin (Seagrief 1956; Seagrief & Godwin 1960), has been reconsidered by Brooks (unpublished) and Carpenter & Woodcock (1981). The sequence of events displays a broadly similar pattern to those of southern England (Scaife 1982). A summary of changes shown by Carpenter & Woodcock is as follows (oldest first).

(a) A mosaic of herb and heath communities at the close of Zone III (harsh climate).

(b) Pioneer communities (*Juniperus* and *Betula*).

(c) *Betula* forest.

(d) *Pinus* dominated forest community.

(e) *Pinus* and *Corylus* (Hazel) domination with the arrival of *Quercus* (Oak) and *Ulmus* (Elm) (mild winters).

(f) Mixed forest community (winters mild).

(g) Arrival of *Tilia* (Lime) and local *Alnus* (Alder) dominating with *Pinus* virtually disappearing.

Clearly seen here is the successional rise to dominance of deciduous woodland during the Late Devensian/Flandrian transition (*Juniperus*), pre-Boreal (*Betula*), Early Boreal (*Pinus–Corylus*) and Later Boreal establishment of broad-leaved forest. The uppermost levels are typical of the Boreal/Atlantic transition (Godwin's pollen Zone VI/VIIa). With succession the competitive removal of pioneer elements occurred. Those heliophilous herbaceous elements present during the Late Devensian were replaced by shade-tolerant woodland taxa. It is interesting, however, that at Elstead certain pioneer elements were noted as surviving for longer periods. It is in this period of rapidly changing vegetation that earlier Mesolithic man lived. The nature of his subsistence was

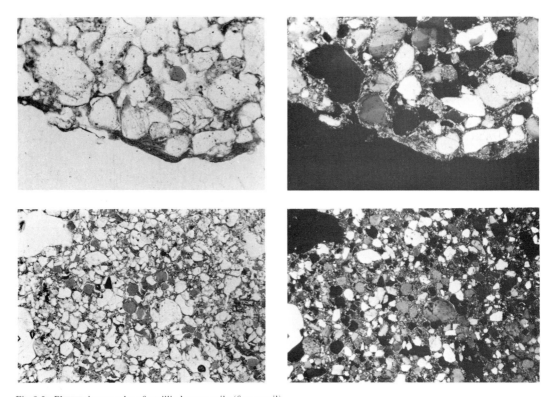

Fig 2.5. Photomicrographs of argillic brown soils (forest soil).
Top left: on this soil channel two phases of clay translocation can be seen: (i) a primary limpid clay phase, and (ii) a secondary dusty clay phase. These are interpreted as (i) primary 'pure' clay illuviation (argillic or Bt horizon formation) under undisturbed deciduous forest, and (ii) dusty clay illuviation as the forest canopy was opened, causing minor soil disturbance, possibly as early as Mesolithic times. PPL, length of frame is 1.348mm (Selmeston, Sussex).
Top right: as previous, XPL. Note clay coatings are birefringent (bright).
Bottom left: argillic Bt horizon featuring accumulated translocated clay in voids in a mainly sandy matrix. PPL, length of frame 5.225mm (Selmeston, Sussex).
Bottom right: as previous, XPL. Note birefringent clay infills.

such that he possibly had little effect upon the vegetation which might be discernible in the pollen record. Certainly, little is immediately apparent in the record from Elstead or from other pollen sequences from lowland southern sites. It has been argued that man might have had a more extensive influence on certain vegetation elements. The status of *Corylus* has long been discussed (Smith 1970; Jacobi 1978a) and man's use of fire in game herding may have influenced clay translocation in early argillic brown soils (fig 2.5 upper) (Scaife & Macphail 1983) and geomorphic processes such as valley side run-off and flood-plain alluviation (Scaife & Burrin 1983; Burrin & Scaife 1984).

FLANDRIAN CHRONOZONE II: Atlantic Later Mesolithic

The Atlantic Mesocratic period of Flandrian chronozone II (Godwin's pollen Zone VIIa) corresponds with the Late Mesolithic period, that is between *c* 7500 and 5000 bp. This period was apparently one of vegetational stability with dominant forest showing maximum extension and development of thermophilous deciduous woodland. Traditionally for southern England this period was viewed as being one of mixed deciduous woodland/forest (*Quercetum-Mixtum*) with strong representation of *Tilia*, *Ilex* (Holly), *Alnus*, *Fraxinus* (Ash) and *Corylus* in woodland of *Quercus* and *Ulmus*. In contrast to the monoclimax view of *Quercetum-Mixtum* blanketing the landscape, a polyclimax view is now more realistically held. Locally variable edaphic, drainage, topographical and geological factors resulted in differing locally dominant taxa (fig 2.6).

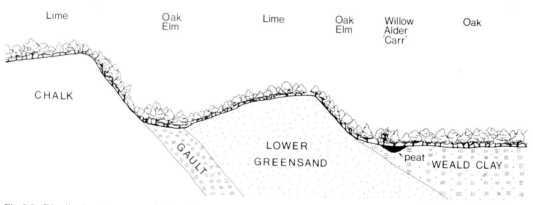

Fig 2.6. Distribution of tree types in the mixed deciduous forest of the Atlantic-Flandrian II period: lime on well-drained plateau, oak and elm on less well-drained lower slopes, oak on poorly drained soils and willow and alder 'carr' along river valleys where high water tables occur.

By this period, in areas of plateau drift, as for example, the loess and Clay-with-flints, mature argillic brown earths (ie soils affected by major clay illuviation) had developed (fig 2.5 lower). It is likely that brown earths, including argillic brown earths and stagnogleys, were present on the claylands of Surrey, the latter because of drainage impedance in heavy textured soils.

On the Chalk it is also probable that rendzinas were deeper on the scarps than at present and that in the valley bottoms, calcareous brown earths were shallower (fig 2.7). Vegetatively, the status of the chalklands has long been debated. Early views held the post-glacial status of chalkland vegetation to have been of open grass-sward character throughout (Wooldridge & Linton 1933). Recent palynological investigations of peat mires occurring adjacent to chalklands in southern England (Thorley 1981; Scaife 1980; Waton 1982) have shown that in fact the downland plant communities are of plagioclimax status, the result of anthropogenic activity.

No pollen data are available for Surrey, but studies from Sussex (Thorley 1971b; 1981), Hampshire (Waton 1982) and the Isle of Wight (Scaife 1980) would indicate dominance of *Quercus* and *Corylus* (Sussex) and possibly pure stands of *Tilia* (Isle of Wight). Calcareous rendzina soils are

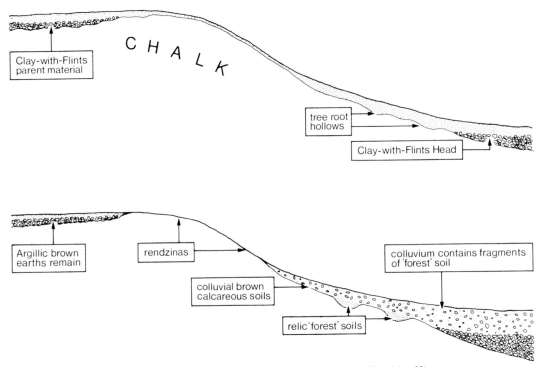

Fig 2.7. Above: decalcified argillic brown earths formed under deciduous forest (Flandrian II).
Below: Neolithic and later forest clearance and agriculture erode decalcified soil cover exposing the Chalk to produce shallow rendzinas and deeper alluvial soils.

not generally conducive to pollen preservation; they are, however, suited to the preservation of molluscs. Woodland fauna present in tree hollows on chalk soils testify to the existence of a woodland/forest vegetation at this time (Evans 1972).

The greater soil acidity of the Lower Greensand soils and associated drainage has allowed the availability of a greater number of palaeovegetational data relating to this lithology. Both peat mire and soil palynological data are present for southern England spanning this and later periods. Data from the Isle of Wight (Scaife 1980) have shown the domination of *Tilia* woodland on these well-drained soils, and by analogy with soil pollen sequences this may well have been the typical dominant woodland for the Greensand scarp in general. Mesolithic forest clearance and burning had produced localised areas of heath and scrub. Such sites as Iping Common, Sussex (Keef *et al* 1965) and West Heath, Sussex (Scaife 1983; Scaife & Macphail 1983; Scaife 1985), clearly illustrate this.

It is generally believed that clearance and replacement of woodland by heath (especially during the Bronze Age) allowed sandy brown soils to deteriorate into podzols (Mackney 1961; Dimbleby 1962; Duchaufour 1977) and in fact relic microfabrics of brown soils occur in humo-ferric podzols on Surrey heaths (Macphail 1979). There is growing evidence, however, to suggest that heath flora of the Late Devensian growing on raw soils had persisted as isolated pockets of heathland or in open scrub (Scaife & Macphail 1983) throughout the Flandrian. These areas had been subject to expansion and contraction throughout the Flandrian in response to differing levels of anthropogenic pressure. The initiation of strong podzolisation, ie the eluviation of iron and aluminium with organic matter from the upper soil Ea horizon (fig 2.8 upper) to an illuvial Bh horizon at West Heath, Sussex, has been tentatively dated to the Mesolithic. Here, a mean residence radiocarbon date of 3770 ± 80 bp (HAR-4840) of the Bh horizon (fig 2.8 lower) beneath a Bronze Age barrow has been obtained (Scaife & Macphail 1983). These studies fall outside the

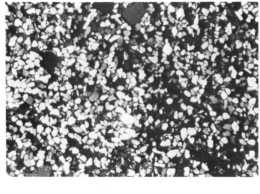

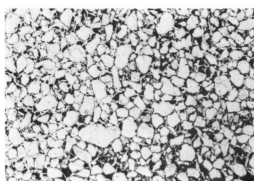

Fig 2.8. Photomicrographs of 'podzolisation'.

Top left: a leached Ea horizon from a podzol. Only clean quartz sand remains after the loss of iron and clay (acid leaching) from this horizon. It has also lost organic matter. Note only quartz sand is visible. XPL, length of frame is 5.225mm (Hengistbury Head, Dorset).

Bottom left: a Bh horizon in a podzol comprising quartz sand and translocated organic matter only (translocated iron is found deeper in this soil). PPL, length of frame 5.225mm (West Heath, Sussex).

Bottom right: as previous, XPL. Note lack of birefringence, except for quartz sand.

Surrey county boundary but are probably applicable to the large expanses of Surrey heath. Research is, however, needed to elucidate further the character of these areas.

FLANDRIAN III: later prehistoric

The Neolithic

It is from the Late Mesolithic onwards that knowledge of vegetation history and man's anthropogenic impact on southern England becomes especially scant. There is still, despite recent investigations, an absence of botanical evidence showing the nature, extent and impact of the Neolithic on the vegetation. This is important in terms of evidence of initial clearance of forest for arable and pastoral subsistence economies introduced at this time, and its secondary effects on the soils and vegetation. A number of phenomena are apparent. The 'primary *Ulmus* (Elm) decline' has been extensively dated throughout Britain (Smith & Pilcher 1973) and falls between 5335 bp and 4570 bp. This phenomenon (earlier used to delineate the Atlantic/Sub-Boreal transition) has been shown in many areas to mark the arrival, at least in the vegetational record, of Neolithic economy. A small number of closely spaced sampled pollen analyses have been carried out on this horizon, providing greater temporal resolutions and understanding. Pollen of cereals and associated weeds often also first appears at this time of declining *Ulmus* pollen which in some areas of southern England (eg the Isle of Wight) was followed by phases of shifting clearance and crop cultivation in a predominantly wooded environment closely adjacent to habitation sites (Tomalin & Scaife 1979; Scaife 1980). The causal factors of the marked decline in *Ulmus* pollen at this time have been much debated and range across climatic change; the use of *Ulmus* leaves as fodder; *Ulmus* forest clearance; differential pollen dispersion factors and disease (see Smith 1970 and Smith *et al* 1981 for appraisals). It is, however, clear that this decline is an extremely complex phenomenon, and one with which Early (pioneer?) Neolithic economy is temporally associated. Close correspondence between the pollen of cereals and weeds and the *Ulmus* decline might favour the possibility of introduced disease such as encountered during the 1970s, when the *Cerotocystis ulmi* fungus was transported by *Scolytus* beetles) (Girling & Greig 1977; Scaife forthcoming).

Pre-*Ulmus* decline activities of Neolithic man are not clear, nor is there any evidence of his transitional interaction with the existing Mesolithic populations. Edwards & Hirons (1984) have brought together evidence for pre-*Ulmus* decline cereal pollen records which have largely come from the west of Britain and Ireland. One such record, however, comes from Rimsmoor, Dorset (Waton 1982), and it is both reasonable and necessary that attention should be paid to sediments of this date from southern England, including Surrey. Subsequent to the *Ulmus* decline, there is no doubt that Neolithic forest clearance occurred at varying scales from the localised shifting clearances noted above to more widespread effects. Burrin (1981; 1983) has shown that a number of valleys in the southern Weald area have extensive thicknesses of valley sediments of aeolian character and reworked loessal origin. Results from geomorphological, lithostratigraphical and biostratigraphical investigations of southern Wealden rivers show that valley alluviation has been largely in response to anthropogenic valley side forest clearance from the Mesolithic period onwards (Scaife & Burrin 1983; Burrin & Scaife 1984). It is suggested that prehistoric man was capable, albeit inadvertently, of making a significant impact on floodplain geomorphological development. Allied to this are the possible effects on dry valley colluviation. At Brook, Kent (Burleigh & Kerney 1982), and at Pitstone, Bucks (Evans & Valentine 1974; Valentine & Dalrymple 1976), Neolithic clearance and agriculture caused significant soil erosion and colluvial deposition (fig 2.7). Such activity probably contributed towards shallow rendzina development on the steep slopes.

Neolithic man obviously did not clear all forested areas and many of those areas which were deforested apparently saw regeneration to secondary forest, especially during the late Neolithic (Whittle 1978; Tomalin & Scaife 1979; Scaife 1980; Scaife, in Wilkinson forthcoming). He may have ignored the less desirable soils (Wooldridge & Linton 1933) of the heavy textured plateau drift and clays. For the Chalk, specific evidence obtained from molluscs on archaeological sites and in dry valley colluvial sequences has contributed to our understanding. Again there is no direct evidence from Surrey and it is therefore difficult to suggest what was happening specifically. Our most comprehensive evidence comes from Wessex (Evans 1972) and Sussex (Thomas 1982) and portrays differing environments across southern England. According to the data from beneath Neolithic monuments in Wessex, these structures were generally constructed in open areas some time after forest clearance. They were placed either on grassland or on areas of arable land utilised until the time of burial (Evans 1972; Evans & Dimbleby 1976; Ashbee *et al* 1979). Work on prehistoric monuments in Sussex (Thomas 1982) indicates, however, that here clearance around the field monuments was localised and short-lived. Evidence of forest clearance and sometimes cultivation is recorded in the soil microfabrics (fig 2.9 upper) of a number of Neolithic buried soils on chalk from Wiltshire, Hampshire and the Yorkshire Wolds (Macphail forthcoming: analyses of IW Cornwall's earlier soil thin sections), and from the Jurassic limestone of Gloucestershire. The forest clearance of the chalklands and their subsequent use as pasture was responsible for the very marked diverse flora of the chalk grassland. This ecosystem is a plagioclimax and as with heathland has been maintained through continued anthropogenic pressure and grazing. Lousley (1976) has provided a most detailed flora of Surrey dealing with the floristic records for these areas.

Unlike the preceding Mesolithic period, during the Neolithic there was an apparent lack of interest in the sandy areas. Little archaeological evidence for the Neolithic period has been found on southern English heathlands. The presence of worm-sorted Neolithic struck flakes at Rackham, Sussex (Dimbleby & Bradley 1975), in a now podzolised soil and the associated palynological data clearly show that the soil was unpodzolised at this time. There is also evidence from sandy soils at Broome Heath, Norfolk (Dimbleby & Evans 1972), and West Heslerton, Yorkshire (Fisher & Macphail 1985), that many areas of present day heathland could still have had a brown earth cover soil during the Neolithic and Early Bronze Age (see below). This may well have been the case for Surrey.

The Bronze Age

As with the Neolithic, our knowledge of the overall effect of Bronze Age man on the environment remains somewhat enigmatic, with our primary source of palaeoenvironmental data coming from soil palynology, molluscan evidence and soil studies. Subsequent to possibly localised Late Neolithic forest regeneration, more extensive clearances occurred on the heathlands and those areas of remaining deciduous woodland on the Chalk. It is likely that the soils of heavy texture remained largely wooded. On the Chalk, evidence from mollusca from beneath round barrows (Evans 1972) and a single pollen diagram from such a context at Gallibury Down, Isle of Wight (Scaife 1982; Scaife, in Tomalin forthcoming), attest to the predominantly pastoral grassland character on shallow rendzina soils (fig 2.9 centre). It has become clear from such recent work that these upland areas were of substantial importance to the Bronze Age peoples as a result of extensive forest clearance which has led to the establishment of the downlands as they exist today. Regional variation in the date of clearance occurs. In Kent there is evidence for clearance at 1000 bc (Kerney *et al* 1964); in Sussex in the Middle Bronze Age (Thorley 1981); and in the Isle of Wight at an Early Bronze Age date (Scaife 1980; 1982). Later Bronze Age dates have been shown in the Hampshire region (Waton 1982). At Wen barrow on the Hog's Back, Surrey (Allen 1984), it is suggested from molluscan data that the environment within which it was constructed was one of scrub cover which continued to exist upon the Chalk. Bell (1981b; 1983) has dated colluvial deposits from three dry valleys in Sussex and Hampshire and has shown that arable agriculture possibly continued, producing stony colluvium, alternating with pastoral grassland phases which allowed stone-free zones to form within the deposit. In addition, the former may arise from high energy rill wash on arable land (Allen pers comm). Similar downslope movement of soil materials and continuance of floodplain alluviation occurred in Sussex (Burrin & Scaife 1984). Such river valley areas were probably regarded as marginal (eg Needham, in this volume) because of regular flooding.

It was during the Bronze Age that the major human impact on the sandy soils of southern England took place. This produced, through repeated clearance, burning and in some cases agriculture, the major extension and development of heathlands and their podzolic soils (Dimbleby 1962; Duchaufour 1977). The heathland itself is, along with the downlands, a plagioclimax ecosystem maintained by grazing and burning (Gimmingham 1972), which in Surrey occurred until this century (Macphail 1979). The removal of tree cover also had an effect on soil drainage and promoted the formation of wet and dry heath as at Thursley Common (Rose 1953). Pollen evidence from Ockley Bog, Thursley Common (Moore & Willmot 1976), shows probable Bronze Age woodland clearance. This also produced significant soil erosion at this time and was possibly allied to the beginning of this large Surrey mire. Here, there were two phases of clearance and probable agriculture followed by abandonment and regeneration of *Betula*, *Corylus* and ericaceous heathland. Pollen recovered from deep soil profiles at Headley Heath and Ockham Common may also provide evidence for *Corylus* scrub prior to full heathland (Macphail 1979), a pattern widely recognised in soil pollen profiles from beneath Bronze Age barrows in southern England (Dimbleby 1962).

Astonishingly, there are no pollen or buried soil data from any Bronze Age sites occurring on Surrey heathlands other than podzols being recorded beneath undated but possibly Bronze Age earth circles at St Martha's Hill (Wood 1953–4). Many English Bronze Age barrows bury soils which show various degrees of podzolisation. These range from incipient podzolisation as at Wallis Down, Dorset (Cornwall 1952; 1953), and Burley, Hampshire (Dimbleby 1962), to fully developed (Dimbleby 1962) humo-ferric podzols as found, for example, beneath the multi-barrow nucleated cemetery at West Heath, Sussex (Drewett 1976; Macphail 1981a; Scaife 1983; Scaife & Macphail 1983). Indeed, a barrow excavated at Deerleap Wood, Wotton, Surrey, on the Folkestone Beds, also apparently buries a podzol (authors' interpretation of Corcoran 1963). Soil development on the Hythe Beds of Wotton Common is discussed below in the case study.

Surrey is very rich in heathlands developed on a number of acid but variable ferruginous Eocene sands, for example at Ockham Common. These may have podzolised more rapidly than the more ferruginous, fine sandy Hythe Beds of the Lower Greensand. Despite this degradation there

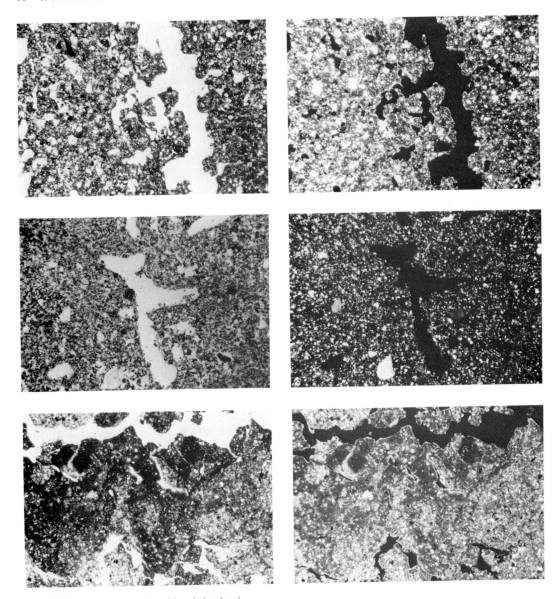

Fig 2.9. Photomicrographs of 'prehistoric landuse'.

Top left: very dusty clay coatings in soil pores of a cultivated Neolithic brown soil. In this surface horizon arding breaks up the soil and makes it vulnerable to slaking, and matrix material is washed into pores when it rains. PPL, length of frame is 5.225mm (Hazelton, Gloucestershire).

Top right: as previous, XPL. Note general birefringence of this clay-rich soil, and moderate birefringence of the dirty coatings.

Centre left: high biological (earthworm) activity produces a very homogeneous A horizon with faunal channels in this Bronze Age grassland (pastoral) soil on the Chalk. PPL, length of frame is 5.225mm (Earls Farm Down, Wiltshire).

Centre right: as previous, XPL. Note lack of coatings.

Bottom left: a strongly heterogeneous colluvial soil comprising fragments of brown soils and calcareous brown soils formed through Bronze Age cultivation (erosion). Dark (calcareous and organic) infills probably relate to subsequent Iron Age and Roman ploughing exposing more calcareous (chalky) soils which were eroded to form chalky colluvium which overlies this horizon. PPL, length of frame 5.225mm (Bourne Valley, Sussex).

Bottom right: as previous, XPL. Note birefringent calcareous infills and impregnation.

survives some evidence of Bronze Age cultivation of such soils. This comes from a buried podzol on Bagshot Sands (Eocene) at Ascot (Bradley & Keith-Lucas 1975) and from the soils on Folkestone Beds in the vicinity of the West Heath barrow cemetery (Scaife 1982; 1983; 1985).

It is worthwhile noting the evidence for former cover loams on heathlands (Limbrey 1975) as, for example, on Blackheath. Data from soil mapping, grain size and heavy mineral analyses indicated that the plateau area of the heath had a 'cover loam' which had been eroded away prior to podzolisation (Macphail 1979; 1983). This was possibly not a Late Devensian event and it is tempting to suggest that forest clearance caused erosion of this fine cover, initiating and accelerating the acidification and podzolisation of the acid sandy substrate beneath. As noted in earlier sections, this event could be either Early Flandrian or Bronze Age in date. Palaeo-magnetic dating of colluvial silts may answer this question.

The Iron Age and Romano-British periods

It is possible that increased population pressure in these periods caused arable agriculture to be renewed in an intensive way on the Chalk using terrace/strip lynchet agriculture (Fowler & Evans 1967) and resulting subsequently in massive colluviation (fig 2.9 lower) (Kerney et al 1964; Bell 1981b; 1983). Improvements in technology may also have contributed to the major woodland clearance of areas of Clay-with-flints and plateau gravels (Waton 1982). Such increased clearance and arable activity was reflected in increased alluvial sedimentation during the Iron Age, as dated by wood debris from the River Windrush, Berkshire (Hazleden & Jarvis 1979), and near the Thames at Farmoor, Oxfordshire, where flood plain deposits cover Iron Age archaeological sites (Robinson 1981).

It may be surprising to suggest that not all sandy areas were cleared of woodland by the Iron Age, but at Keston Camp on the Blackheath Beds, Kent, the area was wooded until the construction of the camp (Cornwall 1958; Dimbleby 1962). Here, and at a number of other sites (Scaife & Macphail 1983), a fully developed humo-ferric podzol had formed not under heath, but under primary woodland, which on poor parent materials produces progressively more acid leaf leachate, the disappearance of earthworms, loss of clay in the upper soil, and eventual podzolisation of the profile. Surrey is rich in hillforts on heathlands but as yet no environmental data are available for the Lower Greensand. However, the presence of woodland soils beneath undated

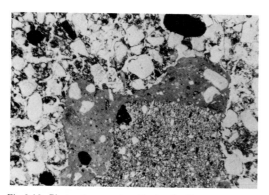 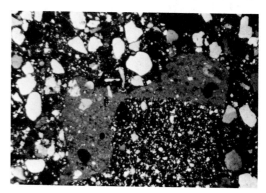

Fig 2.10. Photomicrographs of 'urban' soils.
> Left: a fragment of mortar comprising a calcareous cement (mortar) and brickearth (silty clay soil) temper, derived from a decayed Roman building. The surrounding 'dark earth' soil contains much fine charred organic matter, charcoal (hence dark colour) and ashes from domestic fires and the destruction of buildings. Silt (from brickearth), stones (eg from *opus signinum*) and calcite (mortar), from previous huts and buildings, have also been biologically mixed into the dark soil matrix. PPL, length of frame is 5.225mm (Southwark, London).
> Right: as previous, XPL. Note very dark fine soil in the 'dark earth', and the high birefringence of the calcareous mortar.

agricultural colluvium on fine-sandy Hythe Beds at Wotton Common (see case study below) may indicate that woodland remained longer on these areas than on medium sandy Folkestone Beds. Areas where *Tilia* woodland had remained the dominant woodland element, especially on areas of well-drained Greensand soils, may have been cleared in response to the need for more agricultural land. Such clearance is widely seen throughout southern England with the decline of *Tilia* in the pollen record. This *Tilia* decline, unlike the *Ulmus* decline, is not synchronous and indeed dates spanning the period from the late Neolithic (Isle of Wight) to the Saxon period (Epping Forest) have been recorded (Scaife 1980; Baker *et al* 1978). This decline is frequently associated with evidence of renewed or intensified agriculture (Turner 1962).

It is worth noting that there is increasing evidence to suggest that 'dark earth' deposits at Southwark dating from the 2nd to 4th centuries AD occur through the collapse or destruction of insubstantial buildings (Macphail & Courty 1985). Such materials as brickearth (fig 2.10) were imported from the City of London to make clay floors and clay walls and fragments of this material were later re-used as temper or as a fine soil medium for probably insubstantial daub-walled houses. It is believed that the collapse or destruction of the latter produced deposits which, when biologically reworked, produced the 'dark earth' now typical of some urban Roman sites. This interpretation is of significance, because if it is correct the presence of these ubiquitous and substantial deposits at Southwark may infer a larger urban population and activity than is currently estimated in the late Roman period generally.

The Saxon to medieval periods

Bell (1981a) suggests that in the post-Roman period the chalklands were less favoured for cultivation and consequently some areas reverted to grassland. Cornwall (1958), however, found deep deposits of hillwash dating from the 4th to 14th centuries on the North Downs at Lullingstone, Kent. Expansion of agriculture on to the clay areas apparently began during the Saxon period as a result of improved technology (Bridges 1978). Certainly in the medieval period when the numbers of occupation sites increased on the Weald Clay the population had to cope with difficult heavy textured soils affected by poor drainage. In some areas, ridge and furrow agriculture may have been used to offset this poor drainage (Bridges 1978). Evans (J G, 1975) has hypothesised that clay soils were most probably well drained under the natural woodland cover but early agriculture – of which there is as yet little or no direct evidence – caused the surface soil horizons to slake and soil porosity to decrease, thus worsening soil drainage. Such effects have been discussed by Duchaufour (1958).

It is probable that there was an expansion of medieval population on to the heathlands. At Wotton Common, podzols were apparently converted to brown earths by marling (Bunting & Green 1964; Macphail 1979; see case study). It is also possible that ridge and furrow at Ockham Common which may date to the period (David Bird & Ann Watson, pers comm), was dug to throw more fertile B horizon soil on to the bleached surface horizons (Macphail 1982). Evidence of medieval utilisation of heathlands in the New Forest, Hampshire (Dimbleby 1962), may even indicate that further deterioration of the heathland soils (Eide 1982) was produced by continued agriculture.

Case study An investigation of the soils and vegetation development on the Hythe Beds, Lower Greensand, at Wotton Common, TQ 125455

Resulting from detailed field and laboratory investigations, this special study can be regarded as demonstrating the asynchroneity of podzolisation on Surrey heathlands. It thus has clear implications relating to the Iron Age hillforts on the north-western Wealden Greensand, but is also relevant to anthropogenic usage of these areas throughout the later prehistoric period. A soil and vegetation study of the area was carried out in the 1970s (Macphail 1979). Subsequently a further soil pit was dug (in October 1982) and more soil thin sections, soil pollen and other results studied by the authors.[2]

Soil

The pedological findings[3] reveal that the lower plateau slopes at Broadmoor are characterised by weak podzols developed in fine sandy colluvium, which in turn bury eroded argillic brown earths formed in a more loamy Hythe Beds parent material. The podzolic nature of the upper soil is recognised by its chemistry (Macphail 1979) and microfabric while its colluvial character is demonstrated by the inclusion of transported micro-aggregates (Mücher 1974; Kwaad & Mücher 1977; 1979) – the latter comprising fragments of the lower sequum. The truncated buried soil itself is an argillic brown soil formed in glauconitic sands and contains a primary phase of clay coatings which indicate soil development under woodland (Slager & van der Wetering 1977). These limpid clay coatings are in turn covered by a second phase of dusty clay coatings which are followed by massive infills of coarse coatings or agricutans (Jongerius 1970). This sequence is evidence of woodland clearance followed by intensive soil disturbance, including agriculture (Slager & van der Wetering 1977; Kwaad & Mücher 1977; 1979; Courty & Federoff 1982; Fisher & Macphail 1985). A very similar micromorphological sequence was also identified from a soil in an unenclosed area of Severell's Copse. The data therefore indicate a history of soil development under woodland (see *Pollen* below), which was followed by clearance and probable agriculture. The latter probably produced a metre of weathered colluvium of sufficient antiquity to be weakly podzolised.

The presence of modern podzolic brown earths on Wotton Common can be related to short-lived 19th century ploughing (*Plan of the Manor of Wotton* 1860), while the brown earths of the enclosed area of Severell's Copse and farmland south of Broadmoor probably resulted from 14th century marling (Bunting & Green 1964) of originally acid or podzolic soils (Macphail 1979). However, the major period of erosion and colluviation described above cannot be dated. Nevertheless, the dominant character of the coarse infills in the lower sequums from the two soil pits and the weak nature of podzolisation in the upper soil horizons may indicate that this was a medieval event probably contemporary to the marling and cultivation of soils of the enclosed area of Severell's Copse.

Pollen

Soil pollen analysis from Broadmoor[3] has elucidated the vegetational changes which occurred concurrently with pedogenesis and which led to the present podzolic character of the area. Dimbleby (1961; 1962) has illustrated that pollen falling on to the surface of soils of suitable (acid) characteristics becomes incorporated into the developing soil profile. If these soils remain acidic, which therefore negates soil faunal (primarily earthworm) mixing, the pollen becomes broadly stratified in the profile through gradual downward movement. The sequence of vegetation change in the soil profile is described here upwards from the point at which pollen is preserved in the soil.

21–27cm: The earliest vegetation illustrated is that of *Quercus* and *Corylus* woodland with a substantial representation of heathland ericaceous elements (*Erica* and *Calluna*).

15–21cm: Dry heathland is dominant. Pollen of *Calluna* with some *Erica* is present in an environment of few trees within the area of the pollen catchment. A small quantity of cereal-type pollen is indicative of some arable agriculture during this phase.

6–15cm: *Calluna* declines markedly and *Pinus* woodland becomes dominant. Some *Castanea* is in evidence. Arborescent heliophilous shrubs are present of which *Sorbus* type (including *Crataegus*) is the most important.

0–6cm: *Pinus* becomes subordinate to *Betula* in these uppermost soil levels. The *Betula* is representative of the contemporaneous *Betula* woodland growing on the site.

The sequence therefore illustrates that the site sampled and presently dominated by *Betula* woodland has had a more complex history than expected. Pollen of *Quercus* and *Corylus* marks the earliest phases of soil acidification/degradation producing conditions acid enough for the preservation of pollen. Dimbleby (1962) has frequently shown that this marked representation of scrub and elements of 'full' deciduous woodland are representative of transition from brown earths to podzolic soils. Such a change has been induced by anthropogenic activity initiating soil deterioration, acidification and consequent preservation of pollen. With the development of typical podzols, a dominant ericaceous flora (*Calluna vulgaris* and *Erica* spp) became established which is analogous to many areas of Surrey heath existing today. A *Pinus* plantation during the 19th century is well illustrated. This was subsequently felled, and colonisation by pioneer *Betula* woodland took place.

NOTES

1 We are grateful to Sue Hamilton, who kindly commented on the text for us. An attempt has been made to explain the more technical terms used in this paper in the glossary which follows. In addition to the references quoted in the text, the reader is referred to the following works:

Environmental archaeology: Dimbleby 1978; Evans, J G, 1975; Simmons & Tooley 1981; Gallois 1965
Soils: Jarvis *et al* 1983; Keeley & Macphail 1981; Nortcliff 1984
Vegetation: Lousley 1976
General reading: Symposia of the Association for Environmental Archaeology; British Archaeological Reports, International Series, nos 94, 146, 173 and 181.

2 We wish to thank David Bird, Jill Macphail and Ann Watson for helping to dig the 1982 soil pit at Wotton Common.
3 Details available from the authors.

GLOSSARY

Allerød: cool temperate interstadial *c* 11,800–11,000 years bp in the Late Devensian (glacial).

Anthropogenic: originates from or is influenced by man.

Argillic: clay enriched; a horizon with 'argillans', clay coatings, through clay translocation under a forest vegetation.

Base(-rich): pedologically, soils containing calcium, sodium, magnesium and potassium: eg rendzinas on the Chalk are base-rich because they contain much calcium carbonate.

Chronozones: specific periods in the past with particular climatic, vegetational and human characteristics.

Coleoptera: beetles.

Cryoturbate: to disrupt by freezing and thawing (of soil water).

Deflation (zone of): zone of dry air in front of an ice sheet affected by the erosion and transport of fine (silt, sand) unconsolidated materials (eg loess).

Edaphic: relating to the soil; here concerning vegetation.

Gley: pertaining to the characteristics of hydromorphism or waterlogging (in soils); usually giving zones of soil affected by depletion or concentration of iron and manganese.

Head: a heterogeneous lower slope mineral deposit caused by down-slope creep movement of soils and sediments through freeze/thaw acting under gravity.

Heliophilous: light-loving; here, sense of forest trees as opposed to shade-tolerant vegetation.

Humo-ferric: in podzols iron (and aluminium) and organic matter ('humus') are translocated (leached) by soil water in acid conditions into the B horizon forming a humus and iron-enriched (hence humo-ferric) zone.

Illuviation: the process of enrichment of a B horizon, eg as above by iron and organic matter; or in argillic soils by translocated clay.

Interstadial: within the Pleistocene, major glacial periods were interrupted by major interglacial periods; minor 'warm' interruptions are called interstadials.

Lithology: composition, structure and classification of rocks.

Loess: post-Tertiary wind-blown deposit; commonly comprised of silt.

Palynological: pertaining to pollen.

pelo(-sols): non-calcareous clay soils with smooth-faced soil structures (peds) in the B horizon because of soil swelling (when wet).

Periglacial: cold but non-glacial climate; severe cold suffered by zones marginal and far removed from ice sheets in Quaternary; geomorphological processes pertaining to this cold climate.

Phyto(-geographical): pertaining to plants; distribution of plants in relation to their geographical environment.

Pingo: circular hollow caused by the collapse (melting) of expanding, intrusive frozen water or mud which forms a high (up to 100 ft) dome over the permafrost layer in unconsolidated sediments under periglacial climatic conditions.

Plagioclimax: biotic succession through the intervention of man; eg burning and grazing on heaths, grazing on downland.

Podzol: acid soil commonly formed on poor parent materials: contains no burrowing earthworms and consequently has a surface organic horizon of raw humus (MOR); the bleached upper soil is depleted of clay, iron and aluminium, whereas the B horizon is enriched in iron and aluminium, sometimes with organic matter, forming a black pan; the soil is often associated with a thin iron pan.

Rendzina: base-rich (see *Base-rich*) shallow humic soil, rich in calcium carbonate, formed on chalk; contains many earthworms.

Seral: pertaining to sequences of plant communities which reach a climax.

Sequum: individual stage or period within a sequence.

Soliflual: combined freeze-thaw (solifluction) and (melt) water (colluvial, alluvial) geomorphological processes.

Stagnogleyic: soil with characteristics of gleying or hydromorphism caused by impeded drainage or surface waterlogging.

Taxon: an individual (plant) type.

BOTANICAL GLOSSARY

Alnus: alder.
Betula: birch.
Calluna: heather; 'heath'.
Castanea: sweet chestnut.
Corylus: hazel.
Erica: erica; close relative of heather; 'heath'.
Fraxinus: ash.

Ilex: holly.
Pinus: pine
Quercus: oak.
Sorbus: a palynological grouping of Rosaceous family, mainly shrubs, eg *Crataegus*, hawthorn.
Tilia: lime.
Ulmus: elm.

The Upper Palaeolithic and Mesolithic in Surrey

ROGER ELLABY

The Upper Palaeolithic

Modern man, *Homo sapiens sapiens*, arrived in Britain about 40,000 years ago. He brought with him a range of flint tools based, for the first time, on the production of blades and accompanied by burins or engraving pieces testifying to an increase in the manufacture of sophisticated artefacts in bone, antler and wood. While this would mark the beginning of the Upper Palaeolithic, its close, about 10,000 years ago, ushered in a distinctive industry characterised by diminutive flint points – the microliths of the Mesolithic.[1]

For this 30,000-year period however, Surrey, like most of Britain, is poorly represented, with positive evidence for the presence of Upper Palaeolithic hunter-gatherers being derived from only five isolated, but diagnostic, pieces of flintwork which at best can be interpreted as casual hunting losses. This seeming paucity of occupation is no doubt due to the extreme conditions of the last (Devensian) glaciation which persisted, with only minor ameliorations, throughout the whole of the period. In all probability occupation, or rather exploitation, occurred only in the summer months as hunting forays from bases deeper within the continental landmass to which Britain was still attached. The principal quarry would have been the larger tundra-loving herbivores including bison, horse and reindeer. While these visits may have been brief and seasonal they were also episodic, with the initial phase, the Earlier Upper Palaeolithic, falling before *c* 25,000 bc, ie at a time before a progression to the maximum advance of the ice sheets at around 16,000 bc. With a subsequent rise in temperatures the second phase, or Later Upper Palaeolithic, began perhaps as early as the 12th millennium bc but was probably hindered in its full flowering by a return to colder conditions in the final centuries of the Late Glacial.

Belonging to the Earlier period are two Surrey finds. The first, and oldest, is a broken and rolled unifacially worked 'leaf point' from the Earl of Dysart's gravel pit at Ham (fig 3.1; Jacobi 1980a, 18–19; now in the Museum of London) which may be compared with other British examples of Aurignacian-type spearheads (eg Mellars 1974, fig 7) and could date, on continental evidence, to around 36,000 bc (Jacobi 1980a, 84). The second piece is the 'Font Robert' tanged spearhead from Peper Harow Park, Godalming (Winbolt 1929), which is similar to specimens of late Perigordian (Gravettian) points from Germany, Belgium and northern France and possibly dates to the Kesselt climatic amelioration of *c* 26,000 bc (Jacobi 1980a, 24–7).

Perhaps the oldest representatives of the Later phase are individual shouldered points (Jacobi 1980a, 39) from Bunkers Field, Wallington (fig 3.2; Brighton Museum and Art Gallery), and Wandsworth (British Museum, Sturge Collection) which find similar companions within the Hamburgian industries of the North European Plain and would date, at the earliest, from about the 12th millennium bc. These pieces could, however, belong with a later Federmesser industry dating to after 10,000 bc (Jacobi 1980a, 85) which includes the better known Cheddar and Creswell points. Also occurring in this technology (eg Mellars 1974, fig 8) are convex-backed and pen-knife points, the latter being exemplified in the isolated find from Pyrford (fig 3.2; Jacobi 1980a, 43; Ashmolean Museum, Oxford).

Of two further pieces listed as being possibly Later Upper Palaeolithic (Bonsall 1977a, 431), the long backed blade from the Weydon Pit, Farnham (illustrated in Moir 1929; Oakley 1939, 50) is lost and therefore cannot be re-evaluated. The second, a tanged point from Bunch Lane, Haslemere, has suffered the same fate and, illustrated without scale (Swanton & Woods 1914, 3), can only be argued to be a 'Bromme'-type spearhead of *c* 9000 bc (Jacobi 1980a, 77, 131). Also arguable as belonging to the Later Upper Palaeolithic is a collection of material from Horsell (Bonsall 1977b) and a large backed blade from upcast glacial gravels at Leatherhead (P Nicolaysen, pers comm; O'Connell & Poulton 1983, 9).

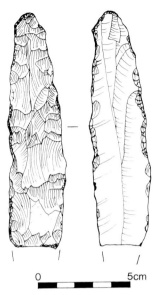

Fig 3.1. Earlier Upper Palaeolithic 'leaf point'; Earl of Dysart's gravel pit, Ham (Museum of London, accession no A18989).

Suspected of being a final development of the Upper Palaeolithic industries in south-east England, while at the same time signalling the Mesolithic, is the combination at a single site (Avington VI, Berkshire: Froom 1972a; Jacobi 1980a, 78) of a stemmed point (Ahrensburg Point) with obliquely backed and triangular microliths, scrapers and long blades. The apparent switch from Upper Palaeolithic single piece to Mesolithic composite missile heads tipped and/or barbed with microliths may be seen as a result of hunting strategies adapting from open country to a woodland environment at the end of the last glacial period. The rising temperatures that allowed the forests to spread permitted, for the first time in millennia, permanent occupation of hunter-gatherers in Britain, for which Surrey has provided considerable evidence.

The Mesolithic

HISTORICAL BACKGROUND

During the year 1857, Mr John Shelley of Redhill amassed a large collection of flint flakes and implements from a field near Redhill railway station. Among these pieces was a number of large

Fig 3.2. Later Upper Palaeolithic artefacts: left, shouldered point from Bunkers Field, Wallington (Brighton Museum and Art Gallery, accession no R2497); right, 'pen-knife' point from Pyrford (Ashmolean Museum, Oxford, accession no 1968. 1874–9).

obliquely backed points (fig 3.3) now recognised as microliths belonging to the Early Mesolithic. Housed in the Pitt Rivers and Ashmolean Museums, Oxford, these must surely be some of the earliest preserved examples of microlithic flintwork in Britain.

The Mesolithic was not in fact fully recognised until the 1920s; thus Shelley's flints and others which were collected in various parts of the county shortly afterwards were originally classed as Palaeolithic or Neolithic, between which there was believed to exist an hiatus when Britain was presumed to be devoid of population. Pertaining to this early period of research are notable accounts of Surrey collections which clearly contain Mesolithic artefacts (eg Clinch 1902a, and Johnson & Wright 1903). Whimster (1931), while fully aware of a burgeoning understanding of the Mesolithic, had little published evidence to draw upon, but Dr Wilfrid Hooper, who had been collecting microliths, or pigmy flints as they were known at the time, submitted a paper on 'The pigmy flint industries of Surrey' in 1933, a work of national as well as local significance. It assisted Grahame Clark's *The Mesolithic age in Britain* (1932) in finally quashing the old hiatus theory and placing the Mesolithic as a finite entity in man's occupation of Britain. From 1936 to 1961 the Surrey scene was dominated by W F Rankine, whose numerous publications were also of national importance. Although his work lay chiefly in west Surrey and eastern Hampshire, culminating in *A Mesolithic survey of the west Surrey Greensand* (1949a), he assembled findspots for the whole of the county (Rankine 1952; 1956).

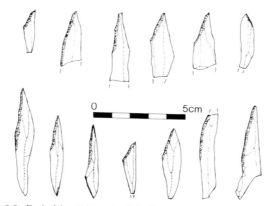

Fig 3.3. Early Mesolithic microliths from near Redhill railway station.

While the above mentioned papers remain important milestones in the general assessment of the Surrey Mesolithic, numerous articles relating to individual sites and finds have appeared in Surrey Archaeological Society publications; at the same time, however, an enormous amount of unpublished flintwork has entered museums and private collections. For details of much of this material we must be grateful for the *Gazetteer of Mesolithic sites in England and Wales* (Wymer 1977) which, with its continuing card index, provides the most recent and comprehensive survey of the many hundreds of sites and findspots within the county (fig 3.4).

THE SETTLEMENT PATTERN

The experience of casual fieldwalking suggests that it would be difficult to search any ploughed area in the county without alighting on a specimen of flintwork attributable to the Mesolithic, and recent study of around 1700 findspots in south-east England (Jacobi 1978a, 75) confirms that exploitation by the last hunter-gatherers covered terrain over all the geological deposits. Analysis, however, of concentrations of Surrey material, implying some sort of semi-permanent occupation, would show that settlement was based primarily on the free draining sands and gravels while sites on impervious clays were positioned on the faster draining slopes of ridges. In the majority of cases this predilection for the drier and warmer soils was combined with the proximity of a supply of perennial water whether spring, river or stream. Essentially this settlement pattern follows, from

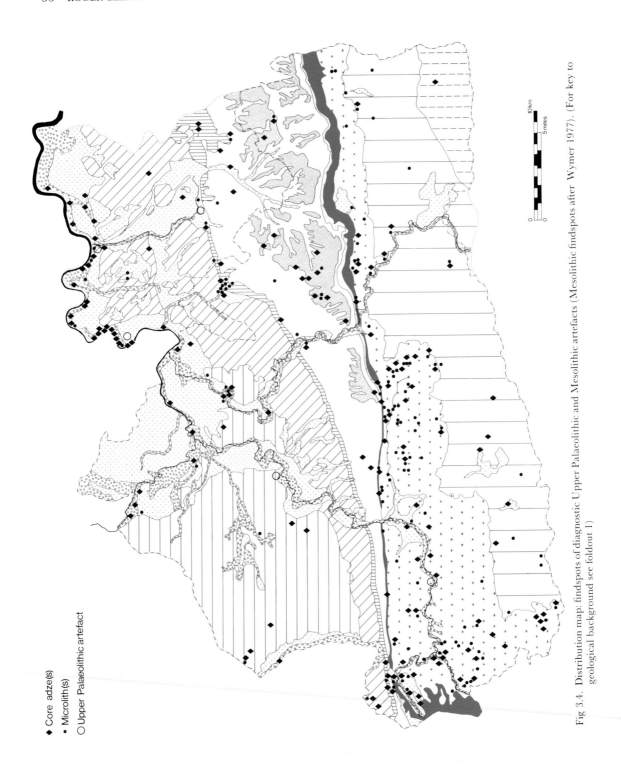

◆ Core adze(s)

• Microlith(s)

○ Upper Palaeolithic artefact

Fig 3.4. Distribution map: findspots of diagnostic Upper Palaeolithic and Mesolithic artefacts (Mesolithic findspots after Wymer 1977). (For key to geological background see foldout 1)

east to west, the roughly parallel better drained outcrops while in a generally south–north direction settlements are tied to the gravels of the Wey, Mole and minor streams draining to the Thames.

Absent from any distribution map would be a number of sites on the floodplain gravels of the Thames, as these must have been either eroded or submerged beneath alluvium. That they existed, however, may be presumed by the numerous implements taken from the foreshore and dredgings (Lacaille 1966) and, significantly, from an exposure of the gravels at Ham Fields near Kingston (Lacaille 1966, 21). Under-represented also is the London Clay, perhaps due to the difficulties of research in a largely built-up area, but the generally low-lying inhospitable soil was, in all probability, a genuine deterrent to settlement. There is, however, considerable evidence of occupation on the higher terrace deposits within this clay lowland, notably in Richmond Park and on Wimbledon Common (Lacaille 1966, 35).

The Thanet Sand, although occupying a relatively small area of the county, appears particularly well endowed, with the main concentrations occurring close to the spring line at the foot of the chalk dip slope, especially around Carshalton (Adkins 1979b, 11–12) and Ewell (Wymer 1977, 273–4). Surprisingly, few sites have been found on the expanse of sandy Bagshot Beds in the north-west of the county but a number of widely distributed core adzes (transversely sharpened 'tranchet' axes, cf fig 3.5) and thin scatters of flint on the commons is sufficient evidence to encourage further research.

The Chalk, which is largely overlaid with sandy and gravelly Tertiary deposits and Clay-with-flints, is also sparsely represented but, like the Bagshot Beds, is lacking in detailed research. Recent work in Cranborne Chase, Dorset (Barrett *et al* 1981), has shown that although not well watered (under present conditions) the Clay-with-flints was extensively exploited within the Mesolithic, possibly for the quarrying of its high quality flint (Care 1979). Suggestions that similar activity obtained in Surrey may be deduced from the spreads of Mesolithic and later flintwork discovered in the Chelsham area (Scott 1982) while recent excavation on one of these spreads, at Slines Oaks, has yielded the characteristic microliths (M Russell, pers comm). Much attention has recently been focused on the marked concentrations of discarded core adzes and picks on or close to flint rich downland, of which Chelsham may be cited as a typical example, with a marked scarcity away from these areas (Care 1979; Mellars & Reinhardt 1978, fig 4; Jacobi 1982, 17–19), but while this feature is suggestive of centres for their manufacture and distribution it may be additionally argued

Fig 3.5. Core adze from Young Street, Leatherhead. Length 18.2cm. (*Photograph: Surrey County Council*)

that these tools were, in part at least, used for the actual quarrying of raw material. The appearance of some of the more pick-like objects on these deposits (Barrett *et al* 1981, 207) would suggest that just such an industry continued into the Neolithic.

The Weald Clay, while generally assumed to have been thinly populated, has produced significant concentrations of material, particularly on the south-facing slopes of the Paludina limestone ridge at Outwood (Hooper 1933, 66) and Charlwood (Ellaby 1977b), and on the more sandy outcrops such as occur around Chiddingfold (Hooper 1933, 67). Observations on the Esso pipeline construction (Poulton & O'Connell 1981) revealed about 60 findspots across the Surrey Weald, the vast majority coming from the Weald Clay. Clearly many settlement sites remain to be discovered.

The small area of sandy Hastings Beds in the extreme south-east of the county is again lacking in fieldwork but a core adze from Dormansland (information from P Gray) points to foraging at least, and further work here would almost certainly mirror the considerable evidence across the border into Sussex and Kent (Clark 1932; Money 1960; Tebbutt 1974).

Dominating the known settlement pattern is of course the Lower Greensand, a phenomenon noted from the very early days of research (Clark 1932; Hooper 1933). Being the largest block of well-drained but well-watered terrain in the county it may be supposed that this apparent selectivity was logical where a choice of soils was available, but as outlined above this dominating pattern may not eventually prove to be real and it must be stressed that concentrations of sites, particularly on the west Surrey Greensand, are clearly biased towards the intensive fieldwork of W F Rankine and others (Rankine 1939; 1949a). Of further interest also is the fact that large areas of the Greensand and particularly those areas now covered by heathland appear to have been occupied only in the first half of the Mesolithic, say to about 6000 bc. This observation was made by Jacobi (1981, 13) on the Folkestone Beds of eastern Hampshire, a phenomenon which clearly extends, on the same division, into west Surrey. A similar pattern has been noted by the author on a smaller block of country in the east of the county where sites earlier than this threshold are to be found on Reigate Heath and Redhill Common, while the later ones occur only on the gravels and clays to the south of the Greensand escarpment. If the truth of these observations is more real than apparent then an understanding of the reasons for the abandonment of these formerly favoured lands is of paramount importance. The answer may lie in the destruction of the environment by conversion of woodland to barren heath. This could have been brought about through intentional burning to create open pasture for the attraction of game (Simmons 1969) or to increase the supply of hazel nuts (Jacobi 1978a, 83–4), an important food resource during the Mesolithic. The capacity of hazel to survive the effects of fire and hence to become locally dominant (Smith 1970) was probably recognised by Mesolithic man but persistent burning of woodland on the porous and base-poor Folkestone Sands would eventually cause a change in soil structure from a forest brown earth to a podzolised heathland (Dimbleby 1962; 1965, 88), an environment which, significantly, is not conducive to the growth of the once desired species (Curtis *et al* 1976, 58). Subsequent ignition of the fire-prone heath, a frequent possibility in the pronounced dry period of the first half of the 6th millennium bc (Evans, J G, 1975, 74), could have led to the removal of the organic fraction of the soil with consequent wind erosion and the formation of blown sand deposits (Eyre 1968, 183). These supposed deposits are a feature of the west Surrey Greensand (Rankine 1946–7b).

The implication that some, at least, of our heathlands are very ancient (Jacobi 1978a, 84) and possibly present by 6000 bc is of great interest, as also is the apparent relocation of hunter-gatherers on to the more calcareous parts of the Lower Greensand and other soils where woodland 'management' would be less damaging. It must be stressed, however, that this must remain only a theory as much work needs to be done, not only on the formation of the heathlands through pedology but also on their Mesolithic content through archaeology.

CHRONOLOGY

With the advent of radiocarbon dating it has now become possible to divide the British Mesolithic into crude stages called the Early and Later (Jacobi 1973; Mellars 1974; Switsur & Jacobi 1975), each stage being distinguished from the other mainly by differences in the characteristic component of their flint assemblages – the microliths (for classification see fig 3.7, based on Jacobi 1978b, fig 6). Within Surrey and adjoining counties, however, a third tradition provisionally called the 'Horsham' or 'Wealden' can be recognised and tentatively assigned to a place between the two main stages.

The Early Mesolithic c 8000–c 7000 bc

Coinciding with a general amelioration of the climate at the close of the last glacial episode and dating to around the end of the 9th millennium bc, there would appear to have been a considerable increase in the number of hunter-gatherer groups entering Britain, which at that time represented the extreme north-western margin of the continental landmass or, more precisely, the western upland perimeter of the North Sea Plain. The tundra had been replaced by an ever-thickening forest dominated at first by the pioneering birch and then by pine. By 7500 bc, and with increasing temperatures, the more thermophilous hazel had become a conspicuous feature of the canopy and was possibly dominant in places as a result of man's activities. However, the lack of any substantial year-round vegetable protein in these northern woodlands (Dimbleby 1978, 26) would suggest that subsistence was based primarily on meat of which the principal sources would have been wild cattle, red deer, roe deer and pig with perhaps the larger fish and fowl from the more watery environments. Among the competitive carnivores were no doubt the brown bear and, principally, the wolf, which although potentially dangerous to a lone hunter was probably more of a nuisance in dispersing game thus furthering the need for hunter-gatherers to move on in the quest for food.

Surrey and the Weald would appear to have been relatively favoured by these early settlers, the bulk of the evidence deriving from the warmer sandy soils, especially the Lower Greensand. In the cool conditions of the earliest Postglacial it may be argued that this terrain provided not only the most congenial living conditions but also supported a richer vegetation and with it a higher proportion of animal life. It is these now acid soils, however, which have destroyed the bone and antler component of hunting equipment, a distinguishing feature of the Maglemosian industries of north-western Europe and typified in Britain at Star Carr, North Yorkshire (Clark 1954), and Thatcham in Berkshire (Wymer 1962). That this component did exist within the county, however, may be presumed by the recovery of two barbed antler spearheads from the Thames at Battersea and Wandsworth (fig 3.6; Clark 1932, 18, 123, fig 2:6, 7; 1936, 118, fig 42:3, 5; Lacaille 1966, 14, fig 3:2, 1).

It is, then, towards their specific flint industry that we must look for the identification of these Early sites. The characteristic pieces are of course the microliths. While many uses have been suggested for these artefacts (eg Clarke 1976) they most probably served as the tips and barbs of hunting weapons. They consist of relatively large and simple forms, the most common types being obliquely backed points (class 1). These may be accompanied, albeit more rarely, by triangles of generally isosceles outline (class 2a), bitruncated trapeze (class 2b) or rhombic (classes 3a/b) shaped points and long convex-backed lanceolate pieces (classes 3c/d and 4).

It may be suggested that the first two shapes were used principally as barbs for light spears and arrows while the remainder represent tip pieces (fig 3.7). The processing of natural materials, eg meat, skins, bone, antler and wood, is indicated by the presence of truncated flakes, convex-edged scrapers, finely denticulated saws, burins and core adzes. Quartzitic sandstone pebbles with hourglass perforation (cf Rankine 1949b; 1951a) also appear, for the first time, in the Early Mesolithic and possibly served as the weights for bow and pump drills (Jacobi 1980b, 17). The overall visual impression of the industry is the emphasis on fine flintwork and particularly the production of elegant blades which were, in part at least, the stock from which microliths were manufactured (Rankine 1949a, 12).

While in Britain as a whole it remains difficult to detect any typological evolution of this industry over the millennium time span, there is evidence to suggest that in the south-east of the country obliquely backed points become smaller while there is an increase in the proportion of lanceolate and bitruncated points (Pitts & Jacobi 1979, 170). If correct this could imply that projectile tips of flint were replacing those of bone or antler. Interestingly artefacts of the latter materials have not appeared in succeeding Mesolithic industries (Jacobi 1982, 20).

Within the county it may be possible to isolate microliths of this Early phase from several surface collections of mixed periods but it is on only five sites that we can, with any confidence, suggest that occupation was of this lithic period alone. The surviving material from these sites is, however, limited and in no instance does it approach the considerable volume excavated from such well-known locations as Oakhanger, Hampshire (Rankine 1952; 1956, 26–7; 1960; 1961a; Rankine *et al* 1960), Iping Common, Sussex (Keef *et al* 1965) and Thatcham in Berkshire (Wymer 1962).

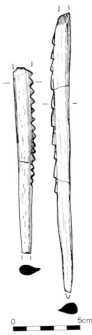

Fig 3.6. Antler spearheads from the Thames: left, Wandsworth (Museum of London, accession no A4907); right, Battersea (Museum of London, accession no A19788) (after Clark 1932, fig 2).

On the Folkestone Beds in west Surrey, two sites, Frensham Great Pond North and South, were partially excavated by W F Rankine. From the North site (Rankine 1946–7b) a typical Early assemblage of 16 microliths, all obliquely backed points, was associated with a processing toolkit dominated by scrapers, but also included a saw and an adze-sharpening flake. The South site (Rankine 1949a, 34–5) yielded a very similar industry of 10 obliquely backed points, five saws, 11 scrapers, two burins and a truncated blade. Also retrieved was a blade in Portland chert which Rankine interpreted, along with another artefact in the same material from Farnham, as evidence for folk movement from the south-west (Rankine 1949a, 40, 43–4). Other writers (Bradley 1972, 16; Jacobi 1981, 19–20), however, have remarked that the occurrence of tools of this material, and other rocks, far inland from their source is suggestive of an exchange network linking hunter-gatherer groups as far apart as Cornwall and Kent. Such a 'trade' in Portland chert can be seen to have continued into the Later Mesolithic as microliths of small scalene shape in this material were excavated from the Farnham 'pit-dwelling' site (Rankine 1951b, 94; Palmer 1970, fig 5:3, 4).

An assemblage from the third site, at Sandown Park, Esher (Burchell & Frere 1947) is again from an excavated context but this time on Bagshot Sands. The excavation yielded a very small but typical Early assemblage of large obliquely backed points with scrapers and burins.

In the east of the county an apparently Early site was excavated by T H O Phillips just before the last war in advance of sand quarrying on the Folkestone Beds at Buckland. From the Minute Book of the Holmesdale Natural History Club (Archaeological Section) dated 11 March 1938, it would appear that this was only one of four concentrations of flint 'about forty yards apart'. The details and whereabouts of Phillips' 'assemblages' from these locations are unknown but the Minutes imply that one site yielded obliquely backed points with axes, scrapers and saws. A possible sample is that in the Museum of the Croydon Natural History and Scientific Society, acquired by the late W H Bennett, an avid collector of all things ancient (Sowan 1971). The flints, which are mostly waste, include along with a few saws and burins, a number of fragmentary obliquely backed pieces, a long lanceolate point and an isosceles triangle. A second collection, that of A T Marston now in the British Museum, includes microliths of a later type and it must be wondered if these were obtained from one or more of the other locations. If this is correct then the rediscovery of Phillips' material, if it still exists, could be extremely useful in assessing the chronology of activity on an obviously favoured area.

The final site is that discovered by John Shelley, on Folkestone sands, just a little north of Redhill railway station, during the construction of cottages in the year 1857 (Evans 1860a, 70–7; 1860b, 171; 1897, 278; Clinch 1902a, 233; Hooper 1945, 13). Shelley began his collecting in the Redhill area about 1848 but the great bulk of his finds was taken from the above site. Some of the material found its way to the Pitt Rivers and Ashmolean Museums, Oxford, although at the time of writing this report only the 13 obliquely backed points depicted (fig 3.3) could be located. These pieces were apparently, at the time of their discovery, associated with a blade industry and saws (Evans 1860a, 72–3), thus testifying to their Early status. In fact the size of these microliths would suggest that not only are they the earliest collected and preserved Mesolithic artefacts from the county but they are also representative of the first settlers of the period.

The 'Horsham' period c 7000 –c 6000 bc

The distinguishing feature of the 'Horsham' period is the appearance within the microlith inventories of characteristically shaped points with hollowed (class 10) or more rarely, inversely

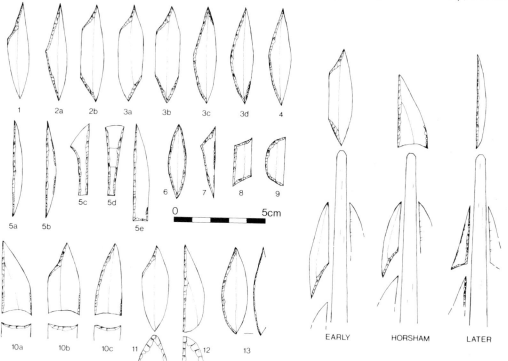

Fig 3.7. Left, classification of microlith shapes (based on Jacobi 1978b, fig 6); right, hypothetical reconstruction of Mesolithic hunting projectile heads. (The scale is only intended as an approximate guide to size)

retouched bases (classes 11 and 12). The asymmetric, and insular, hollow-based version is generally called the 'Horsham point' (class 10a) after the Sussex town near where these artefacts were first recognised (Clark 1932, 104; 1933, 64–7). Although found in small numbers throughout lowland Britain these points are most common in the Weald. Their frequent occurrence in surface collections, which we can now recognise as including specifically Later microlith shapes, was sufficient to render a collection as belonging to the 'Horsham' or 'Wealden' culture but analysis of recent and older excavated samples would show that these terms can be only realistically applied to a technology where basally retouched points are intimately associated with a restricted range of essentially Early shapes, such as obliquely backed pieces, triangles of isosceles outline and bitruncated rhombic points (Jacobi 1978b, 20). The obliquely backed pieces are, however, smaller than Early examples (Pitts & Jacobi 1979, 169), while any scalene triangles which may be present are considerably broader than the ubiquitous narrow forms of the Later Mesolithic. The overall appearance and systematic analysis of the waste material (Pitts & Jacobi 1979, 165–9) also indicates a slackening dedication towards the production of elegant blades, with knapping features standing rather closer to the Later period where blade production is certainly less significant. The basic toolkit of scrapers, burins, saws and truncated pieces remains similar to that of the Early sites but core adzes appear to be less well represented.

It was Clark (1932, 104; 1933, 65) who first postulated the derivation of the asymmetric 'Horsham point' from the continental symmetric point (classes 10b/c) and Jacobi (1981, 12), drawing upon this conclusion, has tentatively outlined the evolution of the 'Horsham' microlith inventories. While showing an increase in the ratio of asymmetric to symmetric points with time, these microliths also become more numerous with a corresponding fall in the number of obliquely backed pieces. The latter, however, appear to become partly replaced by isosceles triangles, a trend which, it may be argued, reaches its zenith in the Later Mesolithic when triangles of scalene shape become a dominant feature. On an assumption that the triangles and obliquely backed pieces were employed as barbs then the 'Horsham point' is probably an arrowhead (fig 3.7) and thus could be seen as an adjunct to the suggested increasing use of flint missile tips at the end of the Maglemosian in south-east England. Similarly the decreasing size of the microliths generally could imply a greater use of the bow, as opposed to the spear, in an ever thickening forest cover which, during the 'Horsham' period, saw the appearance of oak and elm within the canopy.

Recent radiocarbon determinations (Gillespie et al 1985) from Longmoor Inclosure Site 1 in east Hampshire, whose microlithic component falls early in the evolutionary series, suggest an introduction of the 'Horsham' technology into the Weald at around 7000 bc. This date is supported by continental data for the appearance of a similar industry in countries closest to south-east England (Jacobi 1978b, 20–1) and, significantly, immediately succeeds the late 8th millennium figures for the Early site of Oakhanger V/VII (Jacobi 1981, 11), 6km north-west of Longmoor. At the other end of the timescale the picture is perhaps less clear but radiocarbon dates (Gillespie et al 1985) for Kettlebury 103 in west Surrey, a site falling late in the evolutionary series, indicate that the 'Horsham' technology persisted into the last quarter of the 7th millennium bc.

Hollow-based points have been found in many places throughout Surrey and it may be possible to detect, from older published sources and surviving surface collections, microlith inventories of 'Horsham' or 'Wealden' type. These samples are however of dubious provenance, collected over a very wide area, or too small for any statistical analysis (Gabel 1976, 96–7). We are dependent then on the existing excavated material for the recognition of this industry, and it is indeed from west Surrey, on the Greensand between Churt and Elstead, that six sites provided data for its original identification (Jacobi 1978b, 17). To these sites, two on the Devil's Jumps Moor and four on Kettlebury Common, have since been added two at Lion's Mouth on Hankley Common and three more on Kettlebury (Jacobi 1981, 14). The majority were explored before the last war by R G and L S Venables and W F Rankine but only a few were published, with the scantiest detail (Clark & Rankine 1939, 112–16; Rankine 1944–5; 1946–7b; 1949a, 31–5). Material was however retained and, through the kindness of the late W M Rankine and R G Venables, made available to Dr Jacobi for study.

Samples of microliths from all these sites betray the same combination of obliquely backed

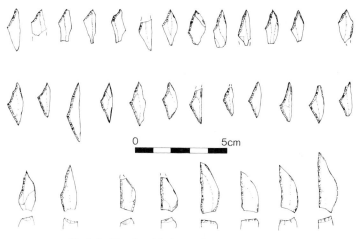

Fig 3.8. 'Horsham' industry: Site 103, Kettlebury.

points with hollow-based points and isosceles triangles but are generally insufficient to allow placement in the evolutionary series. The only exception is Kettlebury 103 (fig 3.8) which, with its high proportion of triangles and a greater ratio of asymmetric to symmetric hollow-based points, can be said to fall later in time than another Surrey site at St Catherine's Hill near Guildford (Gabel 1976; Jacobi 1981, 12) where symmetric points dominate with rare triangles and a very high proportion of obliquely backed pieces.

Arguments for a transitional stage between the Early and 'Horsham' periods arise from a further excavation near Hallam's Court, Blackheath (Janaway 1974), where only a single basally retouched microlith was found with an essentially Early industry dominated by obliquely backed points. It was not possible however to demonstrate that all the material was contemporary as the site had been much disturbed by recent activity.

The Later Mesolithic c 6000 – c 4000 bc

Radiocarbon dates from the north of England reveal that around the end of the first quarter of the 7th millennium bc a new microlithic technology had arrived in Britain, presumably via a narrowing landbridge connecting this part of the country to mainland Europe (Jacobi 1976, 71–3). The microlith inventories are characterised by the appearance of straight backed bladelets or 'rods' (classes 5a/b) and narrow scalene microtriangles (class 7) with only rare obliquely backed points. Determinations from Broom Hill near Romsey in Hampshire (O'Malley 1978; O'Malley & Jacobi 1978; Jacobi 1981, 17) suggest that similar forces were at work in southern England by the middle of the same millennium. The late 'Horsham' dates for Kettlebury 103 may indicate however, that in the Wealden district, the new technology was resisted for a further few centuries.

Industries of this 'pioneering' Later type have been excavated in the western Weald at Kettlebury Site LIX by R and L Venables (fig 3.9; Jacobi 1978b, 14; 1981, 14) and at Oakhanger Site VIII by W F Rankine (1961b; Jacobi 1981, 13). Similar surface collections have been made in the vicinity of both these sites (Jacobi 1981, 14) and, with the excavated sites, appear to represent the final Mesolithic occupation of the present-day heathlands of west Surrey and eastern Hampshire.

Both the Oakhanger and Kettlebury sites lie in close proximity to those of 'Horsham' type, implying the abrupt adoption of the new technology on favoured hunting grounds. Equally, however, they could indicate the takeover of the same terrain by incoming groups whilst ousting the previous inhabitants – perhaps to the central Weald where some of the 'Horsham' industries do indeed possess a high degree of potentially evolved microliths, such as the inverse basally retouched points (classes 11 and 12).

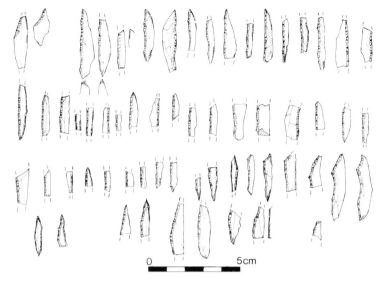

Fig 3.9. 'Pioneering' Later Mesolithic microliths: Site LIX, Kettlebury.

The suggestion that uptake of the Later technology was gradual within the Wealden district comes from collections of microliths which contain both a 'Horsham' and a 'pioneering' Later element, of which the surface-gathered material from Flanchford, Reigate (Ellaby 1985), is a typical example. No similar samples from well-stratified sites have, however, been excavated and it must be wondered if such collections represent true assemblages or are simply the remains of discrete, time-divorced occupations which have become mixed. While then we can possibly infer that a 'pioneering' Later technology had entered the county by about 6000 bc its immediate adoption throughout the Wealden district cannot be demonstrated. The earliest dates so far obtained for a purely Later industry are those centred on 5000 bc from High Hurstwood in Sussex (Jacobi & Tebbutt 1981) where rare 'Horsham'-type microliths appeared only in the very basal levels, a 'Horsham point' itself coming from well below the determinations.

Attempts to formulate an evolutionary framework for the local Later microlithic technology over perhaps 2000 years remain a very hazardous exercise and although Surrey has yielded many findspots containing an element of Later microlith types the exercise is made more difficult by the extreme paucity of large samples, particularly from well-stratified sites or from what one might suspect to be sites of short settlement duration. Radiocarbon dates for Surrey are lacking and those determinations from nearby counties, where comparable material is available, are not considered reliable when only a single sample has been assayed or doubts exist as to the contemporaneity of the associated artefacts. From the limited data available, however, it may be suggested that the dominant microliths of the late 7th/early 6th millennium bc are scalene microtriangles and straight backed bladelets or 'rods' which may or may not be associated with decreasing 'Horsham' types.

It is around this time however that Britain became an island and Jacobi (1976) deduces that all cultural contact with mainland Europe may have been lost as a result. Indeed the evidence from High Hurstwood and other southern English sites would show that by 5000 bc the microlithic industries had evolved a distinctly insular character. While the scalene triangle remains as the type artefact, the 'rods' appear to have been largely replaced by small convex-backed and lanceolate pieces (variants of classes 3c/d and 4), while other geometric microliths such as right-angled (class 5e), boat-shaped (class 6), four-sided (class 8) and lunate (class 9) appear on the scene. The rarity of the obliquely backed point would suggest that the scalene triangle, and possibly some of the other small geometrics (classes 8 and 9), are substituted for this piece as a projectile barb (fig 3.7). On this assumption the other listed points may well have replaced the 'rods' as tips.

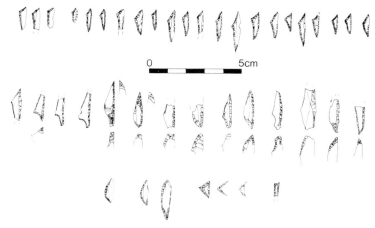

Fig 3.10. Late Mesolithic microliths: Site I, Charlwood.

Perhaps belonging to an intermediate stage of this evolution are the narrow straight and convex-backed points at Abinger Common (Leakey 1951), while similar points combined with a more exotic geometric component at Weston Wood, Albury (Machin 1976), and Wonham, Reigate (Ellaby 1977a), would fall just a little earlier than High Hurstwood. Too much emphasis cannot be placed on the Surrey sites, however, as the excavated samples from both Abinger and Weston Wood appear to contain microliths from earlier occupation(s) while the Wonham pieces were surface collected. A possible further development of the High Hurstwood industry can be observed among the microliths from current excavations at Charlwood Site I (Ellaby 1983), an industry dominated by small scalene triangles but where convex-backed tips are largely replaced by small shouldered points, often with inverse retouch (fig 3.10, middle line). Some of these points somewhat resemble and could be contemporary with, or forerunners of, the microtranchet or small transverse arrowhead (classes 5c/d; cf Clark & Rankine 1939, fig 7:98–100, fig 8:44, 59, 61). Similar to Charlwood is an inventory of microliths from Wawcott Site XXIII in Berkshire (R Froom pers comm) and, with an albeit single radiocarbon date of 4129±113 bc, it may be tentatively suggested that assemblages of this type fall towards or at the very end of a microlithic technology in Surrey and the south-east in general.

Examination of the microliths from the remaining excavated sites possessing Later types – Bourne Mill Spring, Farnham (Rankine 1936; Clark & Rankine 1939), and Orchard Hill, Carshalton (Turner 1965b) – reveals that both 'assemblages' contain elements belonging to all three stages of the Mesolithic, from long obliquely backed points at the beginning of the sequence to 'Horsham points' from the second stage and 'rods', microtriangles and small shouldered points from the Later phase. Both sites were considerably disturbed and, significantly, were positioned on or adjacent to a source of good knapping material with a spring close by; attractions no doubt throughout the Postglacial prehistoric period.

The important changes in microlith shapes which took place in the 7th millennium bc probably resulted from the acceptance of new missile heads (Mellars 1974, 87–8). Significantly these smaller geometric types appeared, both in Britain and on the continent, at a time when the forest cover was becoming both dense and deciduous and it may be wondered if the new microliths were attached to small arrows and smeared with paralysing poisons, a positive advantage in dense undergrowth. If this is correct then the larger and simpler microliths of the Early Mesolithic may perhaps be seen as the legacy of Upper Palaeolithic 'strike and follow' hunting strategies in relatively open country with the spear as the principal weapon.

A second important difference between the artefact assemblages of the Early and Later periods is the apparent reduction, in the basic toolkit, of scrapers and saws. While these pieces are characteristic of the Early Mesolithic, the saw is absent and the scraper extremely rare on the late sites at High Hurstwood and Charlwood Site I. It is too early to say whether this is truly chronological or a function of site activity but if the former it is of interest that in the Early inventories both categories may be inferred to be intimately connected with a bone and antler technology. The apparent loss of this industry after Britain became an island (Jacobi 1982, 20) may then be significant. Interestingly, on resumed contact with the continent, the flint industries of the Neolithic contain the lost artefacts while a bone industry is re-established. Both implements have of course other implied uses. The scraper is generally assumed to have been used in the treatment of skins while serrated pieces, in Neolithic contexts, have been suggested as being used for the cutting of grasses and cereals (Bell 1977, 26).

POPULATION AND GROUP SIZE

While considerable evidence for Mesolithic technology survives, and although it would seem that we are nearing the day when a crude chronological framework can be built for the whole of the 4000 radiocarbon year period, the social aspects of these last hunter-gatherers are infinitely more difficult to assess. Until evidence to the contrary can be found we can only presume that, by analogy with more recent societies practising a similar way of life, kinship bands of perhaps between 10 and 40 people comprised the principal social unit. Possibly these bands would have been only part of larger 'tribal' units with finite territorial claims, on which they relied for exchange not only of gifts and raw materials but also for marriage partners, an essential for maintaining the vigour of the population.

These small groups were, of necessity, nomadic. Presumably they exploited the food resources in the neighbourhood of a home base and, when these were exhausted, moved on. The size of these exploitation areas or 'site-catchments' is of course unknown and it is only by using data from those more recent hunter-gatherer groups in quite different environments that rough, and possibly highly inaccurate, estimates may be made of population density. If a conventional 'site-catchment' figure of 10km radius (Vita-Finzi & Higgs 1970) is applied to Surrey then, with a total area of around 2000km², seven 'territories' would result involving, at an archetypal 30 people per base (Leakey 1981, 99), 210 individuals. Such a number of adjacent contemporary 'territories' within a given area cannot, however, be considered realistic, as when resources became depleted there would be no new area in to which to move. On this basis a figure of seven must therefore be reduced and quite simply it would be possible to argue, given four millennia in which to produce the observed quantities of flint debris, that at times no more than a single band was exploiting the Surrey countryside. These estimates must of course be used with extreme caution and while it may be quite valid to suggest an extremely small population, seasonal large increases exploiting, for example, runs of salmon on the Thames and tributary streams can equally be guessed at.

Archaeological evidence for individual settlement size is particularly scanty being mainly due to incomplete excavation, spread of material by ploughing and hillwash, and intermittent occupation on favoured areas over long periods of time. Jacobi (1981, 13–15) has recently studied potentially single occupation sites on the Greensand of eastern Hampshire with results that suggest considerable variation in human numbers involved. The smaller sites occupying 10m² or less could represent stopping places for small hunting groups perhaps at a kill site or to renew projectiles, while the larger spreads of debris occupying anything up to 100m² or more are suggestive of base camps inhabited by variable numbers of family units according, possibly, to the season. In Surrey probably the only site with evidence for numbers is Charlwood I where four pit groups containing contemporary artefacts, and appearing to delineate an oval 'enclosure' of approximately 120m², suggests four family units or perhaps 20–30 persons in all.

DWELLINGS

While rare examples have been claimed for a few English counties, Surrey is completely lacking in evidence for the flimsy temporary structures which one might assume to be the summer dwellings befitting a small hunter-gatherer family. By their very nature such huts or tents, possibly of light timbers clothed with vegetation, would leave little trace, shallow stake holes being quickly lost to either root disturbance, worm action, leaching or erosion. With the so-called 'pit-dwellings' or 'winter houses', however, Surrey would appear to be well endowed but in all cases there remains a doubt as to whether the excavated features are indeed dwellings or even Mesolithic. Perhaps the most convincing example is from Weston Wood, Albury, on the Lower Greensand (J Harding, pers comm; Harding 1967) where a shallow pit approximately 3.7m in diameter and 30cm deep had been dug through a layer of natural ironstone. Traces of holes for the stakes supporting an overhead structure were found about 0.75m apart around the perimeter, with a wider gap marking the entrance. Towards the rear of the pit was an oval trench 0.75m deep while outside the entrance was a hearth. This building somewhat resembles the claimed post-built Mesolithic house at Broom Hill, Hampshire (O'Malley 1978), which was constructed over a pit of similar depth but with an interior hearth. The main problem with Weston Wood is that sherds of Late Neolithic pottery occurred at the same level and within 2m of the shelter while three petit tranchet arrowheads, probably of similar date (but see below), are depicted among the microliths from the 'Mesolithic horizon' (Machin 1976, 109). Proof, then, that this structure is Mesolithic is unfortunately lacking.

The four features excavated at Farnham and claimed to be 'pit-dwellings' (Clark & Rankine 1939) also present problems in that they were dug to depths considerably greater than either Weston Wood or Broom Hill. Although the pits had apparently been truncated by the plough, original depths of a metre or more can be envisaged, with Pit IV being cut through the gravel and just into the clay beneath. It may be suggested that pit floors of such depth and immediately underlain by clay would have been subjected to a fluctuating water table, and hence flooding, especially if used as winter quarters.

Hints that these hollows may have resulted from Mesolithic quarrying for flint are given by the observation that they were filled not with the gravel originally extracted but a sandy loam which had presumably silted into the pits, along with a large number of flint implements, after their abandonment (Clark & Rankine 1939, 67). Had they been used as dwellings the gravel would probably have been piled around the edges and subsequently redeposited, like the flints, into the fill. The recovery of 15 core tools in the form of adzes, axes and picks from the relatively small area of excavation hints just as strongly at quarrying as at the use of these tools, particularly the adzes, for carpentry in the construction of post-built houses (Jacobi 1982, 19).

The 'pit-dwelling' at Abinger Common (Leakey 1951) cannot be demonstrated conclusively to have been dug within the Mesolithic. It would appear that the flints in the filling had probably washed down the sides of the pit from the adjoining land surface (Leakey 1951, 15) and among these pieces was a large implement combining end scraper, side scraper and hollow scraper. Hollow scrapers, of which several were found in the level immediately overlying the pit along with a fragment of a polished axe, would appear to belong more firmly to the Neolithic (Smith 1974, 105). Also included in the pit filling were scrapers of discoidal and square ended type, a flake with a lustred edge and a fabricator. All these pieces could equally, and perhaps more plausibly, be of Neolithic age. In fact the inventory of flints within the pit filling shows no real difference to that in the levels above which contained, as well as Mesolithic material, a few certain pieces of the Neolithic and possibly the Bronze Age.

While doubts then must remain as to the Mesolithic origins of the pit, its use as a dwelling is equally contentious, and Jacobi (1981, 17) has argued that such a use would hardly be consistent with its steeply sloping sides reducing to a floor area of as little as 0.75m². In seeking parallels to such a feature perhaps the closest would be the similar sized 'pit-dwelling', also on the Lower Greensand, at Selmeston, Sussex (Pit I; Clark 1934a), from which large numbers of Mesolithic flints were excavated. The bulk of this material, however, appears to have silted into the hollow only after its secondary use for a Late Neolithic hearth which, interestingly, was probably nearer the base of the pit than originally stated, the latter being clearly truncated by ploughing. It would be difficult to deny that, even if of the very latest Mesolithic origin, the pit would have silted completely in the 1000 years minimum elapsing before the introduction of Peterborough pottery, sherds of which were incorporated in the hearth. It would seem possible then that the digging was carried out shortly before the fire. Its purpose is unknown but a suggestion of burial or ritual deposition of some kind could be based on the flimsy evidence of a very decayed piece of bone from near the base of the pit. Such practices are not unknown in post-Mesolithic contexts, as evidenced within the ditches of several causewayed enclosures where complete carcases of animals were laid and subsequently buried (Megaw & Simpson 1979, 82–4). At Epsom, again in a probable Neolithic context and at the bottom of a pit over 2m deep with sides sloping to a base area similar to the Selmeston and Abinger pits, was found the skeleton of a calf lying on its back (Frere 1944–5). A similar burial, but this time of roe deer, was found in a considerably smaller feature at the Whitehawk causewayed enclosure near Brighton (Curwen 1934, 102).

ORGANIC REMAINS

Apart from the fragment of a sharpened implement fashioned in bone (a metacarpal of either sheep or roe deer: Rankine 1936, 43, 42, fig X; Jacobi 1978b, 15; 1982, 21) from Pit 13 at Farnham, all of Surrey's potentially Mesolithic tools in organic materials derive from the Thames where waterlogging has permitted their survival. Most of these pieces, principally antler axes, sleeves and hammers, have been assessed by Lacaille (1966, 13–21) but their lack of context and the observation that the majority of these artefacts could be of the Danish Ertebølle culture (possibly a source of the first pottery and farming practices in south-east England) or even later (Lacaille 1966, 41; Jacobi 1982, 20) leaves us with only two pieces which may, with confidence, be attached to the indigenous hunter-gatherers. These are the barbed antler spearheads mentioned earlier from Battersea and Wandsworth, while possibly Mesolithic are the two unbarbed bone points from Battersea and Mortlake (Lacaille 1966, 15, 14, fig 3:3, 4) which may be compared with similar pieces from the Early Mesolithic site at Thatcham in the Kennet valley (Wymer 1962, 351–3, fig 13:9).

Of food remains, carbonised hazel-nut shells have been found only in Pit II and the swallowhole at Farnham (Clark & Rankine 1939, 67, 70) while at Charlwood Site I small fragments of calcined bone, some of which are possibly of roe deer (G Done pers comm), were found in four pits associated with charcoal and a homogeneous flint industry attributed to the Late Mesolithic (Ellaby 1983).

The only other organic object which has been listed as possibly Mesolithic (Wymer 1977, 288) is the dugout canoe from the bed of the River Wey at Wisley and now in Weybridge Museum. Its lack of associated Mesolithic artefacts, however, throws considerable doubt on such a dating as recent work has shown, through radiocarbon dating, that similarly found logboats can be of any age from prehistoric to medieval (McGrail 1979, 159). Joining such a list would be other Surrey finds at Walton (probably later than the 1st century AD; Blake 1966), Weybridge and Kingston, and a wooden paddle from Send (Gardner 1912). Even the best known boat quoted as being Mesolithic, that from Friarton, Perth (Geikie 1880), has recently been questioned by McGrail (1979, 160) owing to its dubious stratigraphical position. Britain is thus left with not a single craft of certain Mesolithic date, physical evidence for navigation resting solely on the wooden paddle from Star Carr (Clark 1954, pl 21, fig 77).

THE MESOLITHIC/NEOLITHIC TRANSITION

No unambiguous or reliable radiocarbon dates have been obtained for the Mesolithic of south-east England within the first half of the 4th millennium bc (Jacobi 1982, 21–2), and a similar situation obtains for the earliest farmers who are suspected of making their appearance during this period (Smith 1974, 103). It would seem then that within or just a little before this crucial half millennium subsistence changed, or began to change, from hunting and gathering to stock and crop raising. That farming was introduced from the continent is generally assumed, but whether the indigenous population was overwhelmed by newcomers is another matter. It remains equally possible that the new idea was taken up by the hunter-gatherers from continental traders with domesticated animals and seed as barter. People quite possibly already familiar with plant and animal manipulation would have readily accepted these items.

Presumably the traders or newcomers originated from the adjacent European seaboard but evidence for the initial contact is slight and inconclusive, resting on the antler axes from the Thames (but see above) and, arguably, the appearance of the ultra-narrow transverse missile tip or microtranchet. The larger petit tranchet (class A; Clark 1934b) which could be said to have even closer parallels in north European late hunting/early farming communities has not, however, been found clearly associated with Mesolithic material, and recent analysis of British flint arrowheads (Green 1980) would suggest that isolated examples are more likely to be of Late Neolithic/Early Bronze Age date.

Evidence for imported domesticated animals in the south-east English Mesolithic remains with the broken but worked 'metacarpal of a very small domestic sheep' from the base of the Later Mesolithic Pit 13 at Farnham, but its lack of a clear association with specifically *latest* microlith shapes and the possibility that it could equally be of roe deer (see above) would seemingly put an end to speculation. However, on the premise that the manufacture of bone implements may only have been reinstated with the arrival of the first farmers (after an apparent absence in the Later Mesolithic: Jacobi 1982, 20) it may be possible to reopen the discussion and suggest that the Farnham tool is indeed of a late date and of a sheep bone as originally identified. Even more speculative would be the suggestion that the calcined bone fragments from Charlwood Site I, associated with seemingly late microtranchet type microliths, are also from domesticated fauna.

The increasing use of such animals, possibly the first of farming practices, presumably lessened the need for the hunting of wild species and consequently the microliths disappeared from the flint inventories. It may be for this reason, then, that the recognition of the earliest 'pure' farming sites is made difficult and further impeded by the lack of other distinctive artefacts such as leaf arrowheads – the mark of long established communities defending, or competing for, the best agricultural resources (Jacobi 1982, 22).

NOTE

1 I would like to thank museum staff and private individuals inside and outside the county who kindly allowed access to material, and in particular Roger Jacobi and R G Venables for the Kettlebury microliths, Peter Gray for the Dormansland adze, Jean Macdonald (Museum of London) for the Ham 'leaf point', Caroline Dudley (Brighton Museum and Art Gallery) for the Wallington point, Andrew Sherratt (Ashmolean Museum) for the Pyrford point and Ray Inskeep (Pitt Rivers Museum) for the Redhill microliths. I am indebted to David Williams for redrawing the Thames antler spearheads, and to Pat Ashworth for her valuable assistance with library material. Finally, I must thank Roger Jacobi with whom I have collaborated over many years and on whose published work on the Upper Palaeolithic of Britain and the Mesolithic of neighbouring counties I have heavily leaned. Interpretations and opinions expressed remain however my own responsibility. Figs 3.1–3 and 3.7–10 are the work of the author.

Neolithic Surrey: a survey of the evidence

DAVID FIELD and JONATHAN COTTON

'Surrey is unfortunate in not having produced in years gone by men like Sir Richard Colt Hoare and Frederick Warne of Wiltshire and Dorset to record its Prehistoric Past. It is true that its antiquities are neither so numerous nor so conspicuous as in those two counties, but for all that it is no mean hunting ground for ancient remains. Not only has very little record of these things been made . . . but many of our prehistoric monuments have been treated with scant respect . . . It is time for Prehistoric Surrey to wake up!' Dr Eric Gardner (1924)

In common with a number of the Home Counties, the archaeological evidence for the Neolithic period in Surrey is disappointing. Only a handful of C14 dates exist and there are few field monuments or excavated sites of significance. Instead, the bulk of the material available for study comprises artefactual evidence in the form of seemingly diagnostic surface concentrations of flintwork contained in the public and private collections that are scattered around the county. Consequently, our method of approach in preparing this survey was to inspect as much as possible of this latter material at first hand, and to combine the information obtained with a re-examination of the previously published sites and finds. The limitations of such a method are obvious, but it does at least have the advantage of providing an insight into the relative density and distribution of settlement activity during the period.[1]

Prior to Dr Gardner's anguished plea, penned over 60 years ago and quoted above, little research had been attempted on the later prehistoric periods within the county; indeed, many of the chronological and typological divisions now taken for granted were then either in their infancy, or had yet to receive definition. However, two early papers by local collectors, A Montgomerie Bell (1888) and Frank Lasham (1893b), demonstrated the wealth of artefactual material available to fieldwalkers in the Limpsfield and west Surrey areas respectively. Lasham's paper in particular was perceptive in its recognition of a division between the roughly chipped core implements, celts and scrapers from the Chalk downs, and the generally finer artefacts to be had from the sandy Greensand ridges.

At the same time other collectors, notably the eccentric Kew antiquarian, Thomas Layton, were taking advantage of dredging and other river-works along the west London stretches of the Thames and its major tributaries to amass huge collections of material – much of it of Neolithic date – which have served as quarries for subsequent research ever since, but which have seldom been published in their own right. Coupled with this Victorian enthusiasm for collecting pre-historic artefacts, was a growing awareness of the need to identify the settlements inhabited by these prolific tool-makers. Thus papers by George Clinch (1899; 1902a), and the small monograph published by William Johnson & William Wright (1903), presented evidence of so-called Neolithic hut circles and 'pit-dwellings' in the areas around Banstead and Worms Heath, and on Shirley and Wimbledon Commons. Now discredited (eg Drewett 1970), this evidence was, in the absence of any other, sufficiently influential to have remained current up until the compilation of *The archaeology of Surrey* by D C Whimster in 1931. Pit-dwellings aside, this volume was useful in bringing together a number of finds and in providing the only distribution map so far published of the Surrey Neolithic.

Although he was primarily a Mesolithic specialist, the work of W F Rankine on the fields around Farnham and Tilford during the 1930s and beyond represented a major advance, in that for the first time considerable care was taken in plotting (and publishing) the density and extent of individual flint scatters. One of the trio of distinguished authors of *A survey of the prehistory of the Farnham district* published in 1939, he was also responsible for the discovery of the earthen long barrow subsequently excavated by Alexander Keiller and Stuart Piggott at Badshot Lea, east of Farnham (fig 4.4). The site retains the importance it assumed at the time, as the only demonstrably Neolithic monument found within the confines of the historic county.

The pace of work slowed after the war, as researchers turned to other fields of enquiry. However, the excavation of a medieval flint mine and Neolithic flint-working area at East Horsley by Commander K R U Todd in 1949–50 inspired discussion by Eric Wood (1950–1, 25–6) of the concept of the secondary Neolithic in west Surrey following initial suggestions made earlier by Rankine. Now somewhat dated, this concept was subsequently to dominate any consideration of the period following the publication of Stuart Piggott's seminal *Neolithic cultures of the British Isles* published in 1954, which itself contained much of relevance to the county.

Since the 1950s, a number of excavations have produced Neolithic material, although much of this has been found by chance on sites of later date. However, notable exceptions include the causewayed enclosure at Yeoveney Lodge, Staines, and the cursus recently under excavation to the north of Park Road, Stanwell, both of which lie on the left bank of the Thames but in modern administrative Surrey. Clearly, it will be some years before the results of these and other excavations are fully published; in the meantime, therefore, Jean Macdonald's survey of the period in Greater London, published in 1976, provides a useful interim summary of that area.

In conventional terms, the British Neolithic is distinguished from the preceding Mesolithic by the apparently sudden appearance in the archaeological record of domesticated plants and animals representative of a mixed farming economy, the manufacture and use of pottery vessels, ground and pressure-flaked flint and stone tools, and the motivation and ability to construct large communal monuments of earth, wood and stone. The period is thus often seen as one of revolution in terms of economy, technology and social structure, although the nature of the relationship that existed between the new farming communities and native hunger-gatherers is still not adequately resolved, and is a problem briefly returned to later.

Radiocarbon dates suggest that these innovations were present in this country by 3500 bc (4300 BC). In terms of chronology, the 'Early, 'Middle' and 'Late' divisions of the period proposed by Case (1969) are giving way to 'Earlier' and 'Later' terminology (Whittle 1980) spanning respectively the periods *c* 3500–2500 bc (4300–3200 BC) and 2500–1500 bc (3200–1800 BC).

Environment

The Mesolithic landscape is usually considered to have consisted of closed, mixed woodland interspersed with localised, man-made clearances. Although recent evidence suggests that the influence of Mesolithic hunter-gatherers on the landscape has been seriously and consistently underestimated in the past (eg Jacobi 1978a; Mellars 1976; Piggott 1981, 21–2), it is equally clear that incoming farmer communities faced a landscape still largely dominated by forest of mixed oak type. The general reduction of arboreal pollen noted in pollen diagrams at the junction of Zones VIIa/VIIb – particularly that of elm – has been taken as evidence for widespread Neolithic woodland clearance (Smith *et al* 1981, 152–3), although in some areas this was demonstrably localised and short-lived.

Two pollen diagrams are available from the county, of which one, that from a peat bog on the Greensand at Elstead, is unfortunately curtailed at Zone VI (Seagrief & Godwin 1960, 84–91). The other, recovered from the base of a silted-up sub-channel of the Thames at Kingston, appears to relate to the Zone VIIa/VIIb Atlantic/Sub-Boreal transition. Arboreal pollen predominates, although small but significant quantities of grass and heather pollen, together with that of weeds like *Rumex* (Dock), point to the existence of clearances nearby (Penn *et al* 1984). The presence of sherds of round-based bowls of Earlier Neolithic type might lend some weight to the suggestion that these clearances were man-made.

There is little evidence of early clearance of the chalk downland, and several studies – particularly the pollen diagrams from Wingham and Frogholt in Kent (Godwin 1962) – suggest that deforestation only began towards the end of the period. The first of two clearance phases at Brook in the same county was dated to *c* 2590   105 bc (Evans 1971, 67), followed by a period of forest regeneration subsequently cleared again during the Early Iron Age (Kerney *et al* 1964, 136). In Sussex, the evidence points to localised clearance of light woodland around settlements and individual monuments (Drewett 1978a, 23; 1980, 378; 1982, 13), although pollen analysis undertaken in the Vale of Brooks suggests that clearance did not begin there until the Middle Bronze Age (Thorley 1971a).

Within Surrey, charcoal recovered from the primary silts of the Badshot Lea long barrow was of *Corylus avellana* (Hazel), while a molluscan assemblage included snails favouring damp scrub conditions, but none favouring grassland (Keiller & Piggott 1939, 149). This episode is now dated by two C14 dates of 2530 bc and 2650 bc (BM 2273, 2274). From the secondary silts, alongside sherds of Peterborough pottery and a further C 14 date of 2470 bc (BM 2272), came charcoal of hawthorn, plum or cherry, common oak, yew and common elm. Similarly a pit containing a calf burial at Epsom, but only loosely dated to the Neolithic (Frere 1944–5, 93–4), produced a mollusc fauna thought to indicate damp woodland. The extent of these phenomena, however, remains unknown.

Away from the Chalk the evidence is less clear, although much of the sandy heathland in the west of the county may once have supported brown earth soils that have degenerated, partly due to ancient deforestation (Dimbleby 1962). This process could have begun as early as the Mesolithic (Jacobi 1981), and was likely to be under way on the Greensand by the Later Neolithic, as the Early Bronze Age turf-stack barrow at Deerleap Wood overlay a fossil soil interpreted by Barrett from the illustrated sections and descriptions as a podzol (Barrett 1976). Some 7km distant at Weston Wood, on the other hand, the sandy soils were still being exploited in the Late Bronze Age (Harding 1964). Indirect evidence of Neolithic clearance off the Chalk is provided by concentrations of broken and fragmented axes on the Greensand around Limpsfield, Peaslake and the Farnham–Elstead area, on the Thames-side gravels at Ham, and, just outside the administrative county boundary, on the brickearths in the Sipson/Harmondsworth area a little to the north of Stanwell. The presence of the cursus complex in this latter area (see below) also suggests a locally open landscape.

Mesolithic/Neolithic transition

Considerable difficulty surrounds the Mesolithic/Neolithic transition within southern Britain. Despite the introduction of new artefact types the question of whether to attribute such changes to invasion or intrusion from the continent, or to rapid indigenous development, is still open. Jacobi (1982) has argued that, following physical isolation from the continent, Britain may have experienced a technological recession, and cites the absence of a range of bone and flint artefact types as evidence. In spite of claims that much of the antler and bonework from the Thames has parallels in the Danish Ertebølle culture analogous finds can equally be found in Neolithic contexts and no clear evidence of Ertebølle contact has yet been demonstrated.

The work of Rankine and others has resulted in the recognition of a well-defined Later Mesolithic within the Weald, characterised by flint assemblages where narrow blade geometric microliths predominate. Unfortunately many of these sites are surface scatters often mixed with later material, and as Ellaby has indicated (this volume), even the excavated assemblages at Abinger Common (Leakey 1951) and Weston Wood (Machin 1976) appear to contain microliths from earlier occupations. In addition, none of the Surrey sites are yet independently dated by radiocarbon analysis, and of those which are, elsewhere in the south-east, the majority have only single determinations or are stratigraphically suspect.

The nearest sites of relevance are those at Wawcott in Berkshire where Site III has a date of 4170±134 bc (BM 767) (Froom 1976, 160), and Site I a date of 3310±130 bc (BM 449) (Froom 1972b). The latter is interesting because of its chronological overlap with the not too distant Lambourn long barrow which has a date of 4315±180 (GX 1178). Two determinations from charcoal apparently associated with geometric microliths at High Rocks Site F (Money 1960) in the central Weald, of 3710±150 bc (BM 40), and 3780±150 bc (BM 91) could, if accepted, allow interpretation of the site as a transitional period hunting encampment.

Jacobi (1973) has argued for an increasing population towards the end of the Mesolithic, and this may have led to a more controlled landscape and a highly ordered exploitation of resources. In the north of Britain several small but widespread pre-Elm decline clearances can be detected on pollen diagrams, perhaps created by deliberate firing of the forest in order to control the grazing patterns of animals (Mellars 1976). Such burning may have been a contributing factor in the degeneration of some of the sandy heathland soils in Surrey (Dimbleby 1962).

The Greensand formations have been accepted as providing ideal resources for hunting and gathering groups. For primitive farmers they would also have provided a light, well-drained, easily cultivated soil, most necessary to pioneering or experimenting settlers without plough or draught animals (Cranstone 1969, 248), and for their purposes probably the best suited in Surrey. If the Mesolithic population was increasing it is likely that clearings in the tree cover already existed and the resources of the area were fully utilised, although to impose successfully an agricultural system on to an area with a pre-existing hunter-gatherer economy would have required either the absorption, the annihilation or the removal elsewhere, perhaps to the Weald Clay, of the indigenous population. The area is too restricted for the two systems to work side by side as any farmed area would need to be fenced and protected against wild animals, thus depriving hunters of their hunting grounds and their prey of their traditional habitats.

Alternatively, the geographical restrictions of the Greensand landscape may have allowed less movement amongst the various groups of Late Mesolithic hunters and consequently encouraged at an early stage an indigenous experimentation with animal herding or plant cultivation. Such developments would be difficult to demonstrate archaeologically, without a good series of undisturbed Later Mesolithic sites containing adequate environmental data, though it is interesting to note the recent discoveries of small amounts of cereal pollen in pre-Neolithic contexts (Musty 1984, 344).

Settlement

The nature and chronology of the settlement evidence currently available consists at present of a single causewayed enclosure on the Thames river gravels, and a number of widely scattered but predominantly riverine sites producing usually isolated features containing struck flint and pottery. With one dubious and hitherto unpublished exception, no house plans are yet known, and

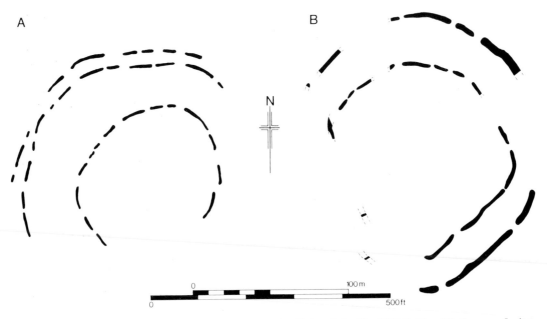

Fig 4.1. Plans of causewayed enclosures at A: Orsett, Essex (after Hedges & Buckley 1978, fig 3) and B: Yeoveney Lodge, Staines (after Robertson-Mackay *et al* 1981, fig 3).

bank and ditch enclosures of the type recently recognised at Bury Hill in Sussex (Bedwin 1981) are also lacking. However, additional information regarding the distribution of Neolithic activity is provided by the large numbers of stray finds and surface flint collections available for study around the county. The evidence for communal funerary and/or ritual monuments and flint mines is discussed separately below.

The interrupted ditch enclosure at Yeoveney Lodge north-west of Staines is the major Earlier Neolithic monument in the middle Thames basin,[2] and lies midway between the enclosures at Abingdon in the upper Thames valley to the west (Case & Whittle 1982), and Orsett in the lower Thames valley to the east (Hedges & Buckley 1978). Excavated in advance of gravel extraction between 1961 and 1963 (Robertson-Mackay 1962; 1965), the 5½ acre (2.2 ha) Staines enclosure was constructed on a spit of first terrace gravel situated in the middle of the Colne delta and some 800m north of the present course of the Thames. The site consisted of two roughly concentric, interrupted, and in places re-cut, ditches, some 20m apart (fig 4.1). Of these the more substantial outer ditch had been partially eroded by an ancient watercourse. There was some slight evidence to suggest that each ditch was originally accompanied by an internal bank, while excavation within the enclosure revealed the presence of a number of perhaps contemporary features. In view of the existence of quantities of later material from the site, however (Robertson-Mackay et al 1981), there remains the possibility that the dating of many of the internal features will be re-assessed in the final published report.

Large quantities of Neolithic domestic material were recovered, in part from the ditch-fills. Full analysis of this is awaited (but see Healey & Robertson-Mackay 1984), though in the meantime we may note the presence of substantial amounts of Earlier Neolithic pottery, flintwork and animal bone, together with some fragmentary human bone including portions of two skulls. Small piles of pottery within the ditches were interpreted by the excavator as sweepings from adjacent huts (Robertson-Mackay 1962).

Whatever the original function of the enclosure, it is clear from its size that it represented a considerable undertaking in terms of manpower, and there can be little doubt that it held a position of great local importance during the Earlier Neolithic. Its siting at the mouth of the Colne valley is suggestive of links between the Chilterns and the Thames valley.

Assignable generally to the earlier part of the Neolithic sequence are a number of more or less stratified and predominantly Thames-side sites discovered by accident during the course of other work. These usually produce features containing pottery, flint and bone, and probably represent the utilisation of riverside resources. Thus at Sefton Street, Putney (Warren 1977), sherds of shell- and flint-tempered pottery (some of it of Later Neolithic date) and nearly two and a half thousand pieces of flintwork, including leaf-shaped and possibly transverse arrowheads, were recovered from two thin sand layers sealing a twice re-cut ditch over 1m wide and 1m deep, which has been dug into the underlying natural sands and terrace gravels. Two hearths and a series of post holes were also found, apparently associated with the ditch, although the presence of Roman and medieval pottery in all but the lowest sand layer sealing the ditch, and of adjacent bomb craters, must inevitably throw some doubt on the integrity of the excavated contexts.

Across the river at Brentford in Middlesex, a number of excavations have recovered feather-sharp flint artefacts and sherds of heavily flint-tempered pottery from the upper levels of a probably water-laid sandy rootlet clay layer truncated by later Roman activity (Canham 1978a; Parnum & Cotton 1983). A small irregular gully containing part of a sandstone saddle-quern or rubber was the only feature sealed beneath it. The flintwork recovered from the area includes a single leaf-shaped arrowhead and several polished axe fragments together with a small series of apparently late microliths. Also in Middlesex, a further somewhat similar riverside site was excavated in Church Street, Twickenham, in 1966 (Sanford 1970). This revealed a small silted-up stream channel on a north–south alignment 65m to the north of the present course of the Thames. From the channel fill came a number of sharp flint flakes and cores and sherds of coarse plain undecorated pottery vessels, including a problematical decorated sherd interpreted as part of a beaker. Ox bones and a sheep or goat mandible were also found.

Further upstream excavations conducted on the Surrey bank at Eden Walk, Kingston, in 1965

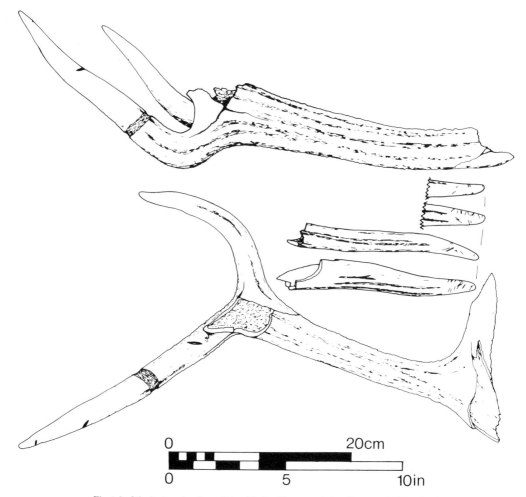

Fig 4.2. Worked antler from Eden Walk, Kingston (after Penn *et al* 1984, fig 5).

revealed traces of a large silted-up sub-channel of the Thames running beneath the modern town (Penn *et al* 1984). Evidence of Earlier Neolithic activity was recovered from the bed of the channel in the form of pottery, flintwork and worked antler (fig 4.2). The unabraded nature of the material suggested either that it had been deposited in the channel from a site on the adjacent gravel bank, or that it represented the refuse from a temporary occupation of the seasonally dry and sheltered channel floor.

Subsequent excavations during 1977 confirmed the channel sequence and recovered a further series of artefactual and environmental data (D Hinton, pers comm). A layer of organic peat sealing a deposit of late Neolithic refuse comprising Mortlake sherds, worked antler and flintwork including a tranchet derivative arrowhead, provided a C14 date of 1610±90 bc (HAR 2498). It is uncertain whether a brushwood feature associated with this refuse represents naturally accumulated flotsam or a deliberate construction.

Similar problems of interpretation occurred with another, probably somewhat earlier, brushwood deposit located during salvage work the following year at Runnymede Bridge, Egham (Longley & Needham 1979). Stratified some 2m below Later Bronze Age levels, and apparently consolidated by upright stakes or piles, this was tentatively associated with a range of Earlier

(Middle) Neolithic pottery, flintwork and two polished stone axes, together with a bone point and a semicircular piece of worked bark (S Needham, pers comm). A further scatter of pottery, struck flint and animal bone was recovered at a slightly lower level during the ensuing controlled excavation. The excavators suggest that this deposit lay within one channel of a braided river system, and stratigraphically a little above a bed of calcareous tufa of probably Atlantic age. Further excavations conducted on an adjacent contemporary land surface a little distance away in 1980 revealed a series of dug features, apparently pits and post holes, associated with a third stone axe, a fragment of a fourth, a further series of potsherds and animal and human bone (M O'Connell & S Needham, pers comm). C14 dates place these various horizons at Runnymede between c 3000 and 2600 bc (Needham 1985).

Away from the Thames, sites producing a comparable range of material evidence are rare, and tend to occur on a restricted range of lighter soil types. Groups of pits containing Later Neolithic pottery and struck flints have been found on the brickearths overlying terrace gravels just beyond the confines of the administrative county at Heathrow (Grimes 1960), Iver (Lacaille 1963), Harmondsworth and Sipson (Cotton et al 1986), while small collections of Later Neolithic sherds are known within the county from the Wey gravels at Bourne Mill, Farnham (Clark & Rankine 1939), the secondary silts of the Badshot Lea long barrow ditches (Keiller & Piggott 1939), from Wisley (Smith 1924), from brickearth over first terrace gravels at Mixnam's Pit, Thorpe (Grimes 1960), and from brickearth over chalk at Baston Manor, Hayes (Philp 1973) – the latter lying just over the Kent/Surrey border. More recently, a group of Beaker sherds has been recovered from a probably late prehistoric ploughsoil during excavations by Michael Russell just off the Clay-with-flints deposit on the North Downs at Chaldon (Russell 1982 and pers comm).

Finally, of potential significance, although not yet fully published, is the enigmatic 'shelter' located during excavations on the Lower Greensand overlooking the Tillingbourne at Weston Wood, Albury. Here, stratified some 30–40cm below the well-known Later Bronze Age site, was a roughly circular area cleared of natural carstone, and 3.7cm in diameter. An oval depression 75cm deep and interpreted as a 'bed trench' was encountered at one point within the cleared area, while around the latter was spaced a series of stake holes 75cm apart. A gap in this stake circle was taken to represent an entrance, beyond which lay a hearth. The shelter itself was unfortunately undated, although some 2m away, but at the same level and 'in a restricted area' lay a group of Later Neolithic Peterborough sherds representing parts of at least five vessels. A rim sherd of Fengate type lay within a shallow ash pit (Anon 1967; 1968; see also Ellaby in this volume and Harding 1967), while a Cornish (Group I) ground stone axe was also recovered from Late Bronze Age levels elsewhere on the site.

Contemporaneity between the pottery and the shelter cannot be demonstrated although its stake circle feature does have some affinity with Later Neolithic Beaker houses from elsewhere in Britain, of which the Gwithian Phase II house (Megaw 1976) is probably one of the best known. However, in view of the problems surrounding the shelter, not least of which is the presence of a Mesolithic flint assemblage from the same sand layer, it is perhaps wisest to reserve judgement pending the publication of the final site report.

The predilection for riverine locations, and for the lighter and warmer soils of the interior, is confirmed by the distribution of numerous flint scatters and stray finds, although such accumulations introduce the thorny problem of collector bias. Nowhere is this more apparent than on the historically productive and probably now over-searched Lower Greensand outcrop to the south of the Downs scarp. Thus nearly every area of the Greensand has yielded material relevant to our enquiry, and certain localities such as the Elstead/Seale/Tilford, Abinger/Holmbury/Peaslake and Limpsfield areas have produced very large concentrations indeed (fig 4.3). As a rule, these collections tend to be scraper-dominated, but also include large numbers of fragmentary polished flint axes and arrowheads, particularly of leaf-shaped and barbed and tanged forms. Recent study of one collection has suggested that smaller 'activity areas' can sometimes be defined within the whole, these usually consisting of clusters of scrapers (Barfoot & Cotton, in prep).

Flint scatters on the Chalk are, by comparison, fewer in number and somewhat unprepossessing in character – a factor which may have militated against their retention by collectors in the past.

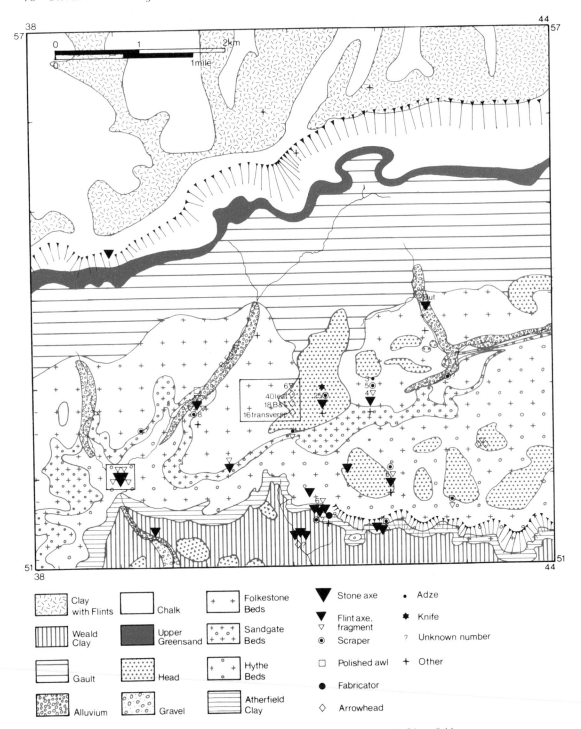

Fig 4.3. Distribution of diagnostic Neolithic flint artefacts in the Limpsfield area.

The artefacts tend to consist of crudely flaked waisted, concave and other scrapers, and numbers of coarse core-tools of pick-like form. Where axes occur they are rarely ground, while leaf-shaped arrowheads are almost non-existent – the standard form being the petit tranchet derivative and variants.

Few worked flints have been recorded from the Chalk block to the west of the Mole gap. Instead activity appears to have centred on the widespread deposits of Clay-with-flints and Tertiary sands further east, and a number of scatters have been recovered from on, or more usually just off, the former deposit in the Headley/Banstead Heath/Tadworth area. Other scatters occur around the ancient head-waters of the Wandle in the Chaldon/Coulsdon/Sanderstead area, and on the Thanet Sand outcrop at the foot of the North Downs dip slope between Croydon and Ewell.

By contrast, there is little evidence of Neolithic activity on the Bagshot Sands and on the claylands. Penetration of the Weald Clay area is apparently confined to the narrow bands of brickearth flanking the upper Mole (R Ellaby, pers comm). Fieldwork on the London Clay tends to produce similar sparse results, a point noted long ago by Johnson & Wright (1903, 128) and recently confirmed by the results of the BPA pipeline survey (O'Connell & Poulton 1983). Only on areas of perched gravel overlying the London Clay have significant concentrations of artefacts occurred in the well-known Barnes Common/Putney Heath/Wimbledon Common/Richmond Park localities, and more recently on second terrace gravels at Clapham (Densem & Seeley 1982). Close to the Thames much of the relevant evidence may be sealed beneath riverside alluvium or modern development. Several areas are, or were, available for fieldwalking, however, notably Ham (Field 1983a, 169–84), on the Surrey bank, and the Harmondsworth/Sipson/Harlington area just outside the administrative county boundary on the Middlesex bank. It is no surprise to find that, a little way back from the present channel, both are prolific localities for the recovery of struck flint.

Society

In our current state of knowledge, it would be premature to discuss the social or territorial organisation of the area, for apart from the Staines causewayed enclosure, only two other communal monuments are known through excavation – the long barrow at Badshot Lea east of Farnham, and the cursus recently discovered at Stanwell, north-east of Staines. Evidence for Neolithic burial practice is similarly somewhat slim, and comprises a small number of individual stray finds of often dubious authenticity, and some scattered human bones from the ditches of the Staines enclosure (Robertson-Mackay 1962), and from several small pits at Runnymede Bridge (1980 excavation: Rob Poulton, pers comm).

The two flat-bottomed parallel ditches discovered during chalk quarrying at Badshot Lea in 1936, and probably correctly interpreted as the side-ditches of a ploughed-out earthen long barrow, remain the most impressive Neolithic feature yet located within the historic county (fig 4.4). Excavated by Alexander Keiller and Stuart Piggott (1939, 133–49), the site of the former barrow faced up a slope of Upper Chalk overlooking the Blackwater gravels below, and was orientated just north of east. The area of the mound and much of the southern ditch had been quarried away unrecognised, while the excavated northern ditch contained a causeway towards its western end. A single undated post hole was discovered in a narrow trench laid out between the ditch terminals at the eastern end – a similar feature having been noted by one of the excavators during the excavation of a long barrow on Thickthorn Down, Dorset, a few years previously (Drew & Piggott 1936). From the assembled evidence, the excavators estimated the original length of the barrow to have been around 140ft (43m), which if correct would serve to link it with a recently defined group of Hampshire long barrows of ovoid form, whose lengths vary between 30 and 60m (Smith 1979a, xxii).

Finds from the excavation were generally scanty, and included no trace of human bones. A few sherds of possibly Earlier Neolithic pottery, together with two leaf-shaped arrowheads and a quantity of animal bones including antler, were recovered from the primary silts at the western end of the northern ditch. The animal bone has recently provided two C14 dates, of 2650 bc and 2470

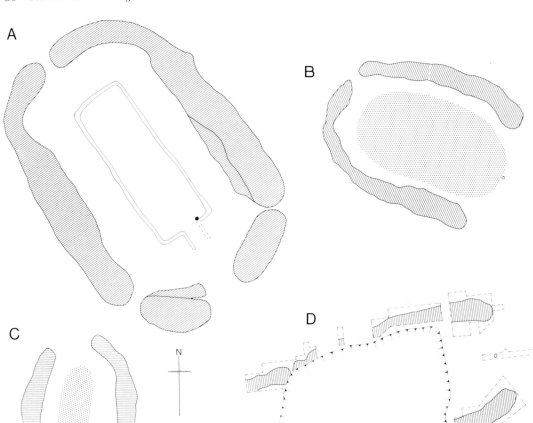

Fig 4.4. Plan of the excavated ditches of the long barrow at Badshot Lea (D), compared with examples at A: Wor Barrow, Handley, Dorset (after Piggott 1954, fig 8), B: Thickthorn Down, Dorset (after Drew & Piggott 1936, pl 16), and C: Alfriston, Sussex (after Drewett 1975).

bc (BM 2273, 2274). The secondary silts of both ditches produced a number of sherds of Mortlake ware comprising parts of at least four vessels, and an associated C14 date of 2470 bc (BM 2272) from the northern ditch, while from the upper levels of the secondary silts in the southern ditch came a few sherds subsequently recognised as belonging to a small collared urn.

The importance of this site, as was noted at the time, lies in its apparent geographical isolation from others of the same class. Discounting unproven and dubious claimants in Richmond Park (Ham Bottom and Oliver's Mount), on Wimbledon Common (the Queen's Butt: Johnson & Wright 1903, 68; Macdonald 1976, 19) and Bedford Hill, Tooting (Shore 1897, 353–4; Johnson & Wright 1903, 65), the nearest earthen long barrow lies some 25km to the west at Preston Candover in Hampshire (Smith 1979a, 14), which is itself somewhat removed from the main Wessex group still further to the west. To the east, Juliberries Grave and its two recently identified but as yet unexcavated companions in the valley of the Kentish Great Stour lie some 120km away (Clark 1982, 28), and while morphologically distinct even the long barrows at Addington and Kits Coty House (Philp 1981) – themselves part of the larger Medway megalithic group – are 78 and 88km distant respectively. The siting of these groups, however, facing gaps in the Chalk, invites a search for others in the Farnham, Guildford and Dorking areas respectively.[3]

The existence of megalithic monuments within the county remains to be established, although suitably sized boulders occur amongst the Bagshot Beds, and on some of the Greensand formations. Thus Johnson & Wright (1903, 63) drew attention to a possible Neolithic origin for the Coronation Stone at Kingston, and similar antiquity was attached by Carey (1908, 7) to a "grey wether" that may be seen close to the lane leading from the top of Shirley Common to Sanderstead'. Wood (1953–4, 45) remained sceptical of a group of at least six large stones recorded by Manning & Bray (1809, 123) at Sherbourne Lane, Albury, since removed during farming operations. A similar fate appears to have befallen two further groups of stones on the Surrey/Sussex border at Crossways and Swains Farm, Rudgwick, of which the latter group are recorded as lying to the side of Barrow Field and adjacent to the line of the former Guildford to Horsham road – now a greenway (Apedaile 1928, 233).

None of the local sites mentioned above – including the Farnham long barrow – has produced any evidence of Neolithic burial. Instead, such evidence as we possess is provided by usually questionable chance finds. At Whyteleafe, human bones were discovered 'in a confused heap' at the bottom of a dome-shaped pit about 4ft 6in high cut into the chalk, while seven similar 'graves' containing one or more skeletons were found during gravel digging at Kenley (Hogg 1905–6). Two further skeletons were found by Major Wade during the excavation of a shaft cut into the chalk on the Hog's Back, and tentatively claimed as a flint mine by Lowther (1939, 132), while a number of human bones – particularly skulls – recovered over the years from the Thames have also been attributed to the Neolithic period. One of these from Hammersmith was trepanned and partly healed (Celoria & Macdonald 1969).

The only human bone recovered from a reliable Neolithic context is that from the Staines causewayed enclosure. Here, on the floor of one segment of outer ditch lay two abraded skulls, a lower jaw and part of a forearm. One skull belonged to a female of about 19 or 20, while the other, that of a male, had a number of shatter points on the cranium suggestive of head wounds. In addition, the presence of several articulated vertebrae indicated that the individual concerned had suffered decapitation (Robertson-Mackay, pers comm).

Further evidence of seemingly irrational 'ritual' activity is provided by the burial of a calf at Epsom, mentioned earlier (Frere 1944–5) and more significantly by the construction of a narrow rectilinear feature some 21m in width and at least 4km (2½ miles) in length on second terrace gravels at Stanwell (figs 4.5, 4.6). Previously interpreted from aerial photographs as a stretch of Roman road, excavations revealed one of the ditches to have been cut by a large Later Bronze Age pit and a 'prehistoric' trackway. Subsequently several small sherds of decorated and probably Late Neolithic Peterborough pottery were recovered from the upper silts of the ditch fill, and the feature was re-interpreted as a cursus monument (Bird *et al* 1983, 188–90; O'Connell forthcoming and pers comm).

Running north-north-west from Stanwell village to an apparent terminal at Bigley Ditch, the monument – which is second in length only to the Dorset cursus – appears to bisect the double-ditched enclosures at Staines and East Bedfont, which lie 3.5km to the south-west and approximately 2.75km to the east-south-east, respectively. Re-examination of available aerial photographs further suggests that, like a number of such enclosures, the Stanwell cursus may form part of a larger complex of monuments, for in addition to the Staines and East Bedfont sites nearby, at least two other now inaccessible narrow linear enclosures, one possibly a further cursus, appear to cross its line beneath the western end of Runway 5 at Heathrow Airport (fig 4.5).

The presence of such a complex on the fertile terrace gravels, one of several now known from the Thames valley (eg Case & Whittle 1982), suggests that the Stanwell area had assumed a position of special importance for the Neolithic communities of the region. It may not, therefore, be coincidental that a number of prestige traded items occur in the vicinity (Field & Woolley 1983, 144), nor that the area appears to have provided a focus for later, Bronze Age, barrow construction, if we can interpret as such a linear cemetery of at least 10 ring ditches visible on aerial photographs between Stanwell and West Bedfont (Longley 1976, fig 12). Here then, if nowhere else within the county, it

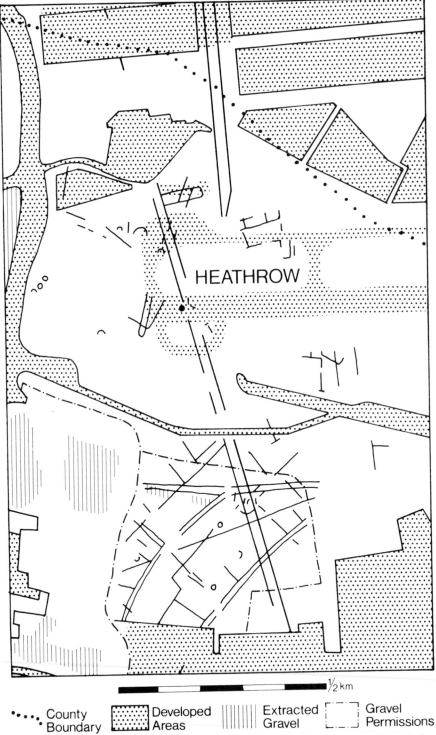

Fig 4.5. Cropmarks in the Stanwell area showing the cursus running north-west to south-east and two similar monuments intersecting it to the north of Heathrow. Later prehistoric field systems cut through the cursus to the south of Heathrow. (After a drawing by Martin O'Connell)

Fig 4.6. Stanwell cursus under excavation by Surrey County Council's Planning Department. View looking north; the large eastern side ditch, partially emptied, shows clearly to the right, while the western side ditch is just visible on the left. (*Photograph: Martin O'Connell, Surrey County Council Planning Department*)

may be legitimate to speak of an organised Neolithic landscape, and to postulate the existence of a powerful hierarchical society in control of it.

Economy: exchange

Over what area this notional society held influence cannot be known, although one element for which it may have been responsible is the movement of stone axes (*pace* Briggs 1976; 1982). Significantly perhaps, recent study of these implements within the county (Field & Woolley 1984) underlines the dominance of the Thames, and highlights the generally Later Neolithic nature of the traffic. Discussion of the flint axe trade, meanwhile, continues to be hampered by the lack of local flint mines and the difficulties surrounding the attribution of individual finds to specific known mines, while there is no evidence currently available concerning the movement of other commodities such as pottery.

In all, some 108 stone axes have now been recorded from historic Surrey by the Stone Implement Petrology Survey – 67 of which come from Surrey reaches of the Thames (fig 4.7). Of the 45 grouped implements, over half originate from sources in Cornwall, with Group I accounting for 16 and Group Ia a further three. All but four of these come from the Thames, and the predominance of Group I products within the London Basin has lead Cummins to suggest the presence of a secondary re-distribution centre in the area (1979, 7–12). Other non-Cornish axes from the county comprise 10 Group VI products from the Great Langdale–Scafell Pike area of the Lake District, including two from the recent excavation at Runnymede Bridge, four Group VII axes from Pemaenmawr in north Wales, three Group IX axes from the Tievebulliagh–Rathlin Island

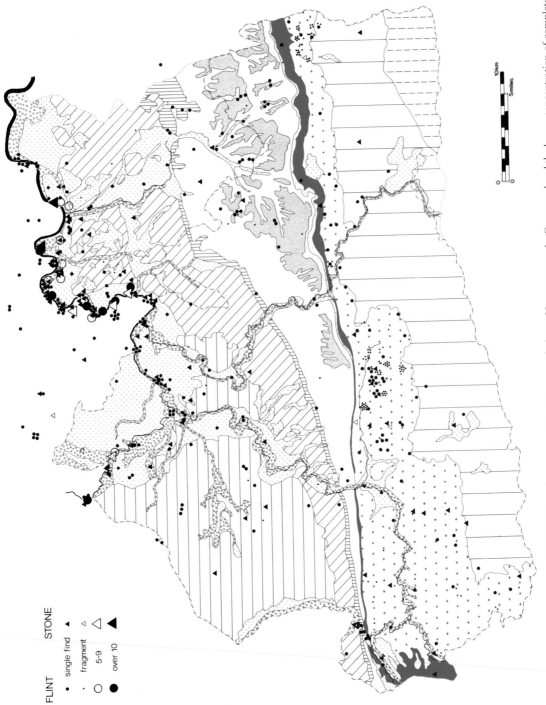

FLINT   STONE

single find	•		▲
fragment	·		△
5-9	○		◁
over 10	●		◀

Fig 4.7. The distribution of Neolithic flint and stone axes. Note the accumulations of fragments on the Greensand and the heavy concentration of complete axes from the Thames between Ditton and Battersea. (For key to geological background see foldout 1)

factories in County Antrim, Northern Ireland, two Group XX axes from Charnwood Forest, Leicestershire, and single examples of Groups XIII (Preselau, Dyfed), XVIII (Whin Sill, Northumberland) and XXIV (Killin, Perthshire). With the exception of three axes from the Cornish Group XVI, which was in production *c* 3000–2500 bc, all originate from factory sites thought to be predominantly active during the later part of the Neolithic on current evidence (Smith 1979b).

Ungrouped implements include several axes of epidiorite from south-west England and a small number of jadeite/pyroxenite and nephrite axes probably of southern Alpine origin. As well as two 'inland' finds, three jadeite axes are known from local reaches of the Thames, in addition to the butt of another recently discovered on Staines Moor (Field & Woolley 1983), a short way away from the Stanwell cursus 'complex' and the Staines causewayed enclosure.

To this list of imported exotic stones, we might add the probably transverse arrowhead of Portland Chert from Ham, now in the Museum of London, an arrowhead of jasper from Fullbrook House, Tilford (Rankine 1939, 14), and the curious bifacially worked projectile point of black 'basalt-type' rock from Holmbury St Mary (Elmore 1983b, 5).

The evidence supplied by the stone artefacts therefore suggests the existence of far-reaching contact or exchange mechanisms, particularly within the latter part of the period, and in the case of the Portland chert arrowhead, continued utilisation of a source first tapped and 'traded' in the Mesolithic (eg Jacobi 1981, 19–20).

As might be expected in a chalk-dominated region, flint axes are commoner than their stone counterparts, but are less easy to trace to source, although recent attempts have been made (eg Sieveking *et al* 1972; Craddock *et al* 1983). Unfortunately, no certain flint mines of Neolithic date have yet been discovered within the county, although claims have been lodged at various times for shafts discovered on the Hog's Back at Seale and Wanborough (Lowther 1939, 131–2, 206; OS Records) and further east at Woodmansterne (Johnson & Wright 1903, 152; Malden 1912, 246), Warlingham (OS Records; Farley 1973, 41–2) and East Horsley (Todd 1949). Of these, the last-named has the most to commend it, in that two medieval mine-shafts appear to have disturbed an area of opencast Neolithic mining activity, where flint nodules were apparently grubbed-out, worked-up and carried away (Wood 1950–1, 13).

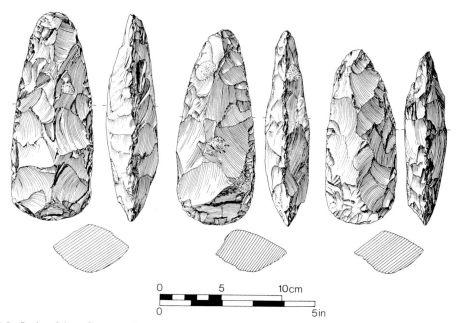

Fig 4.8. Cache of three flint axes discovered at Burrows Cross, Peaslake, in 1937 (after Bruce-Mitford 1938, 281).

Excluding the Thames finds, nearly 300 complete and fragmentary flint axes are known from the county, many from the south of the Downs being of a fine pearl-grey flint and presumably flint-mine products. Notwithstanding the recent possible attribution of small numbers of axes to East Horsley through analysis of the trace element composition of the flint (Craddock *et al* 1983), it seems more plausible at this stage to think in terms of an external, non-Surrey source for much of this high quality material. On the face of it, the South Downs mines in neighbouring Sussex offer possibilities here, and were long ago suggested as a source for the cache of three flint axes found at Burrows Cross, Peaslake (fig 4.8; Bruce-Mitford 1938). The recently published analyses appear to confirm this (Craddock *et al* 1983).

Local flint sources such as alluvial gravels and Clay-with-flints deposits seem to have continued to provide much of the raw material for artefacts other than axes, while finally we may note some slight evidence of interest in the use of the local sandstones for polishers and rubbers.

Economy: technology

Neolithic material culture from the county falls readily into three main groups, flint and stone artefacts, worked bone and pottery. However, the existence of a fourth and no doubt originally much larger group comprising wooden and leather artefacts is scarcely attested, although we

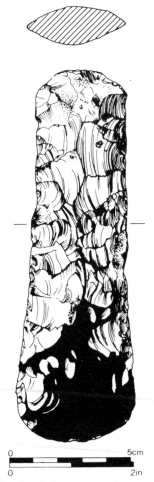

Fig 4.9. Flint axe with ground cutting edge found in the Thames opposite Hampton church. (Drawing by David Williams)

might note – with some reservations – the brushwood 'platforms' at Kingston and Runnymede Bridge, and from the latter site, the semi-circular piece of worked bark mentioned earlier (S Needham, pers comm). The well-known Erith logboat adds further corroborative detail (Spurrell 1885; McGrail 1978, 190), and while lying outside the historic county boundary, provides a reminder that some of the undated examples from the Surrey stretch of the river may date to the Neolithic.

A whole range of flint and stone artefacts, which together make up well over 90% of the surviving cultural evidence, are available for study in the various museums and private collections around the county. So far only the axes (fig 4.9; Adkins & Jackson 1978; Field & Woolley 1984) and discoidal knives (fig 4.10; Cotton 1984) have been tackled, although individual collections of surface material have received (Field 1983a) and are continuing to receive attention (eg Taylor forthcoming; Barfoot & Cotton in prep).

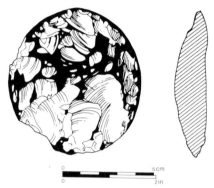

Fig 4.10. Discoidal flint knife with partially ground faces and cutting edge, found at Ewell. (Drawing by Jon Cotton)

Bone artefacts are less well represented and consist largely of antler-based tools such as 'crown' antler mace-heads (Roe 1968, 159–62) recovered from the west London Thames. However, a single (but undated) antler pick is recorded from Ockford near Godalming (A Mercer, pers comm), while evidence of actual antler-working is currently confined to the Staines causewayed enclosure (Roberston-Mackay 1962, 133) and to both Earlier and Later Neolithic levels at Eden Walk, Kingston (D Hinton, pers comm), where the technique seems to have involved 'ringing' the tines with a flint tool before snapping the weakened shaft. Finally, simple bone points are reported from Runnymede Bridge (S Needham, pers comm), and Staines causewayed enclosure (Robert-son-Mackay 1962, 133), while two bone or ivory pins with Later Neolithic grooved ware affinities are known from Putney and Wandsworth (Macdonald 1976, 26). In addition, a single antler skin-dressing comb of western Neolithic type has been recovered from the Thames at Hammersmith (Celoria & Macdonald 1969, 29–30).

Little research has yet been directed towards the ceramic group, and in the absence of a thin-sectioning programme, comment is confined mainly to style rather than fabric. The earliest Neolithic pottery so far recovered from the county is the unfortunately unassociated fine, flint-tempered carinated bowl recently discovered during excavations at Rectory Grove in Clapham (fig 4.11:1, Densem & Seeley 1982, 179, fig 5), which is referrable to the Earlier Neolithic Grimston/Lyles Hill series (eg Smith 1974, 106–9; Whittle's 'Eastern Style', 1977, 82–5). Whether it is possible to relate this vessel to the 'exiguous scraps' of pottery from the primary silts of the Badshot Lea long barrow (Keiller & Piggott 1939, 140–1) or to the few small sherds of 'undecorated Neolithic' pottery from Baston Manor, Kent (Philp 1973, 9) remains to be seen.

Still within the Earlier Neolithic ceramic tradition are the small numbers of thick-walled, round-based and usually undecorated bowls with plain or thickened rims and straightened and S-shaped profiles which have been recovered from a series of riverside sites between Kingston and Putney

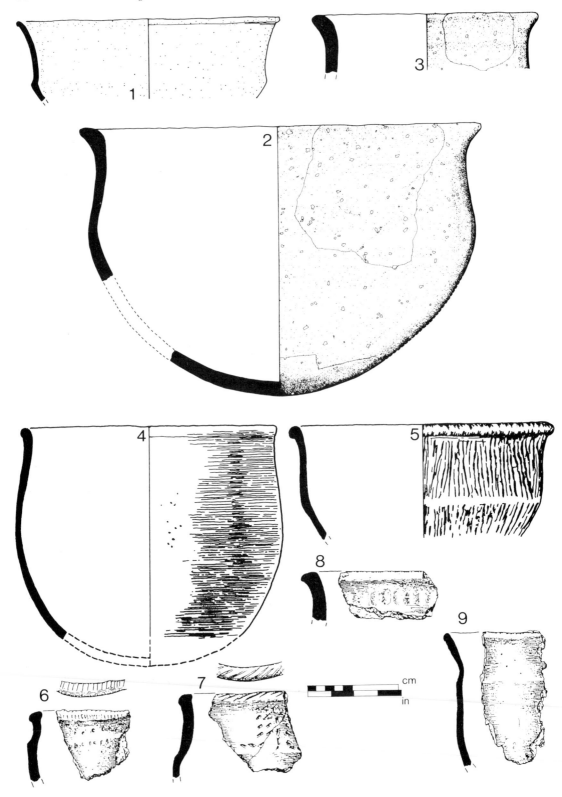

(eg Smith 1968). In most cases the fabrics are tempered with large fragments of calcined flint, while some of the vessels appear to have traces of surface wiping (fig 4.11:2–3).

Somewhat greater variation occurs at Yeoveney Lodge, Staines (fig 4.11:4–5), where flat rims and apparently closed bowls are also present. Here, the pottery is considered to have affinities with Abingdon and Mildenhall types (Robertson-Mackay 1965, 320), although comparability in both form and fabric with some of the Kingston pottery has been acknowledged (R Robertson-Mackay, pers comm). Further, thin sections of the Staines pottery have suggested the use of local clays (R Robertson-Mackay, pers comm).

By contrast, the pottery from Runnymede Bridge – dated to the earlier half of the 3rd millennium bc (Longley & Needham 1979, 266) – whilst still flint-tempered, is generally finer with a burnished brown or black-slipped exterior. Bowls are usually open or S-profiled with plain, thickened and developed rims, upon which diagonal or transverse incised decoration is common (fig 4.11:6–9). Other recurring decorative features include horizontal bands of incised chevrons, occasional rows of elongated shallow pits on the necks, squarish jabbed 'punctuation' on the necks and shoulders, and vertical and diagonal fluting on the necks and rims. Perforations below the rim are present, although lugs are scarce (S Needham, pers comm).

Unlike the Earlier Neolithic pottery from the county, which is seldom found far from the Thames, that conventionally attributed to the latter part of the period has a generally less restricted distribution, and includes sherds of Ebbsfleet and Mortlake ware, with lesser quantities of Fengate and grooved ware (fig 4.12).

With an early 3rd millennium C14 date from the type-site in Kent, Ebbsfleet ware appears to have developed out of a number of regional decorative styles (Whittle 1977, 94, *contra* Smith 1974, 112). It is known within the county from the Staines causewayed enclosure (R Robertson-Mackay, pers comm), from the Thames at Hammersmith and Mortlake, and in a somewhat more developed decorative form from Mixnam's pit, Thorpe, where two different fabrics, one flint-tempered and the other vesicular, appear to be present (fig 4.12:10–12; Grimes 1960, 181–5). Further sherds have been recovered from Baston Manor in Kent (Philp 1973).

The gradual emergence of Mortlake ware from the more developed Ebbsfleet vessels such as those found at Thorpe is thought to have occurred towards the close of the 3rd millennium, perhaps even in the Thames valley, and to have overlapped chronologically with the appearance of Beaker pottery (Grimes 1960, 195–7; Smith 1974, 112). In addition to a number of sherds from the Thames, including the eponymous bowl itself (fig 4.13), Mortlake pottery is found at several locations within the county, of which the small group reported from Weston Wood, Albury (Harding 1967) is likely to be of most interest. Associations are sparse, but include a flint scraper and polished axe fragment from the secondary silts of the Badshot Lea long barrow (fig 4.12:13–14; Keiller & Piggott 1939, fig 59) together with similar combinations of accompanying artefacts from shallow pits at Heathrow (Grimes 1960, 186–97) and Sipson (Cotton *et al* 1986) – both in old Middlesex. Finally, a bowl from Eden Walk, Kingston (fig 4.12:15) profusely decorated with cord 'maggots' and finger-tipping and associated with worked antler and an oblique tranchet derivative arrowhead, was sealed beneath a peat layer yielding a single C14 date of 1610±90 bc (HAR 2498). Flat-bottomed Fengate ware is rarer, but has been recovered from the Thames at Wandsworth and Mortlake, while a rim sherd is reported from Weston Wood, Albury (Harding 1967).

Unlike Essex, which appears to have a preponderance of grooved ware over the other Neolithic styles (Hedges 1980, 31–4), little has been recovered from Kent, Surrey or Sussex. Apart from a possible sherd from Putney (Warren 1977) the few sherds known from the county all come from the Thames, at Battersea, Putney and Hammersmith, although recent excavation of a single small pit at Harmondsworth (Middlesex) has produced over 500 sherds representing a dozen or so vessels of

Fig 4.11. Earlier Neolithic pottery: 1, Clapham (after Densem & Seeley 1982, fig 5.1); 2, 3, Eden Walk, Kingston (after Penn *et al* 1984, fig 3); 4, 5, Yeoveney Lodge, Staines (after Robertson-Mackay 1965, tav 63); 6–9, Runnymede Bridge (after Needham 1985, fig 2). Scale 1:4

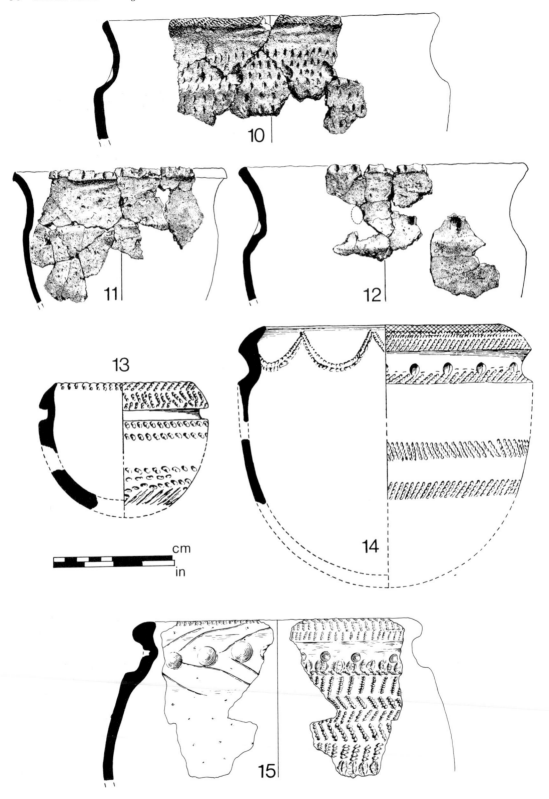

Fig 4.13. The Mortlake bowl. Height of bowl 13.8cm. (*Photograph reproduced by kind permission of the Trustees of the British Museum*)

the Durrington 'sub-style' (Cotton *et al* 1986). Another single sherd has recently been recognised in an old collection from Yiewsley, also in old Middlesex (S Needham, pers comm). The distribution of Neolithic pottery in Surrey is shown on fig 4.14.

Economy: subsistence

Pending the publication of a wide range of palaeoenvironmental data from sites excavated at Eden Walk, Kingston, Runnymede Bridge, Egham, Yeoveney Lodge, Staines and Stanwell, the subsistence economy of the period is particularly difficult to reconstruct. At present, direct evidence consists of two small faunal assemblages, some carbon-based residues on the interior walls of Neolithic sherds from Runnymede Bridge, Kingston and the Thames (one of which represented fish remains: J Evans, pers comm), quantities of hazelnut shells from Kingston and from Sipson in Middlesex (Cotton *et al* 1986) together with a number of fragments and tools of antler. Indirect evidence comprises two reported grain impressions on pottery, and a series of widely distributed artefact-types such as scrapers.

On the two sites from which reliable faunal data is currently to hand, Badshot Lea long barrow

Fig 4.12. Later Neolithic pottery: 10–12, Mixnam's pit, Thorpe (after Grimes 1960, fig 71); 13, 14, Badshot Lea long barrow, Farnham (after Oakley *et al* 1939, figs 55, 56); 15, Eden Walk, Kingston (after a drawing by S Nelson). Scale 1:3.

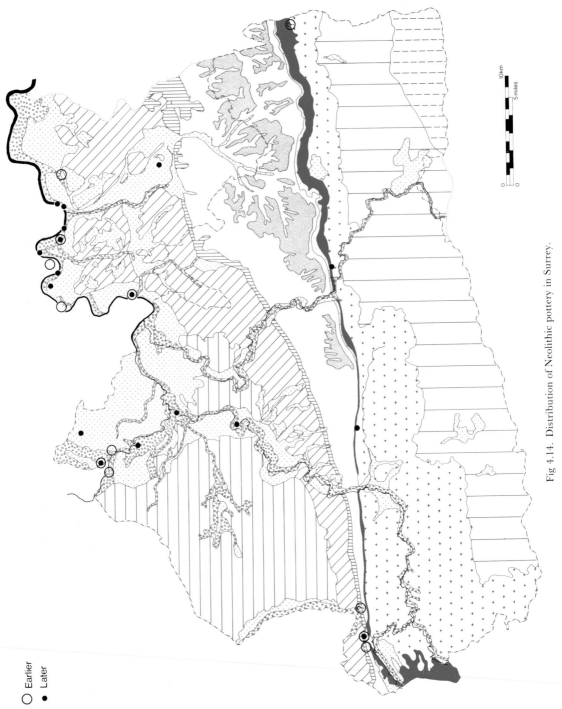

Fig 4.14. Distribution of Neolithic pottery in Surrey.

Earlier ○
Later ●

and the Neolithic levels at Runnymede Bridge (S Needham, pers comm), cattle bones were found to dominate (Keiller & Piggott 1939; Geraldene Done, pers comm). Next come pig/pig-sized fragments, followed by much smaller numbers of sheep, deer (in the form of shed antler) and dog bones, with a single fish vertebra from Runnymede. Butchery practices were recognised at the latter site, but not at Badshot Lea, although here one cattle bone from the secondary ditch silts had been gnawed, possibly by a dog (Nicolaysen forthcoming). Cattle are also present in Earlier Neolithic contexts at Eden Street, Kingston, and at Church Street, Twickenham. The latter site also provided evidence for sheep or goat, as did two small pits from Sipson and Harmondsworth (Cotton *et al* 1986). There is little that can usefully be said here regarding this evidence, beyond noting its general comparability with other Neolithic faunal assemblages. However, the almost total absence of deer from Runnymede is of interest – a situation apparently similar to the reported position at Yeoveney Lodge, Staines causewayed enclosure, where the excavator suggested that deer were not available locally, or at least were not hunted (Robertson-Mackay 1962, 133).

In addition to the two reported grain impressions, one from the Staines enclosure (R Robertson-Mackay, pers comm), and one from the base of a beaker from West Heath, Limpsfield, in Guildford Museum (Y Watts, pers comm), indirect evidence of subsistence economy is provided by a series of artefact-types such as arrowheads (hunting), scrapers (hide-processing), sickles and saddle-querns. Such artefacts have to be treated with caution, however, for arrowheads – particularly the leaf-shaped variety so common on the Greensand – could just as easily have been used in warfare, while sickles and saddle querns, even if correctly identified as such, could equally well have been used to gather and process products other than cereals (Piggott 1981, 7). If arrowheads be accepted as hunting implements, however, it is worth noting concentrations, perhaps hunting grounds, on the sandy Folkestone Beds around Tilford, Crooksbury, Blackheath, Albury and Limpsfield and on the Hythe and Sandgate Beds around Holmbury and Abinger (fig 4.15). Noteworthy also is the almost complete lack of leaf arrowheads from the Downs, compared with other types.

While, therefore, there is no reason to imagine that the conventional Neolithic mixed-farming strategy was absent from the county, we have little evidence with which to demonstrate its presence. Similarly, the local evidence allows nothing to be said of the supposed increase in pastoralism towards the close of the period (eg Smith 1974, 123).

Conclusions

A serious gap in the archaeological record needs to be filled if we are to demonstrate the transition from hunting to farming economy. While well placed geographically to solve some of the problems, there is no evidence in the county to support the view of an influx of colonists. Neither is there sufficient evidence of indigenous development. Ellaby (pers comm) prefers the latter hypothesis and has suggested that the gradual use of herding lessened the need for microliths as projectile points and that the leaf-shaped arrowhead was introduced later and reflected rivalry between communities. Thus early farming may have been an extension of the Mesolithic economy, evolved particularly in Greensand areas to cope with population pressure and based on the herding of cattle, sheep and pig, together with a small amount of hunting as much to protect herds and flocks from wild animals as for basic subsistence. Such a development would seem reasonable given the suggested Mesolithic background in controlling animal resources (Mellars 1976). Thus the biologically poorer habitats may have provided an incentive to change or to adopt new methods of subsistence earlier than in the Thames valley.

Distribution of axe concentrations aids suggestions that there was little competition between lifestyles. Clarke (1976) has demonstrated the highly productive biological nature of swamps, marshes and riverine areas, both in terms of the abundance of edible plants, shellfish and fish, and of the hunted wildfowl and mammals. C14 dating of fossil shells of the mussel *Margaritifera auriculatia* to the 4th millennium bc are of interest, though despite loose association with ground stone axes from the Thames, provide no conclusive proof that it was exploited by Neolithic man (Preece *et al* 1983). Such rich resources may encourage a more sedentary lifestyle since there is no

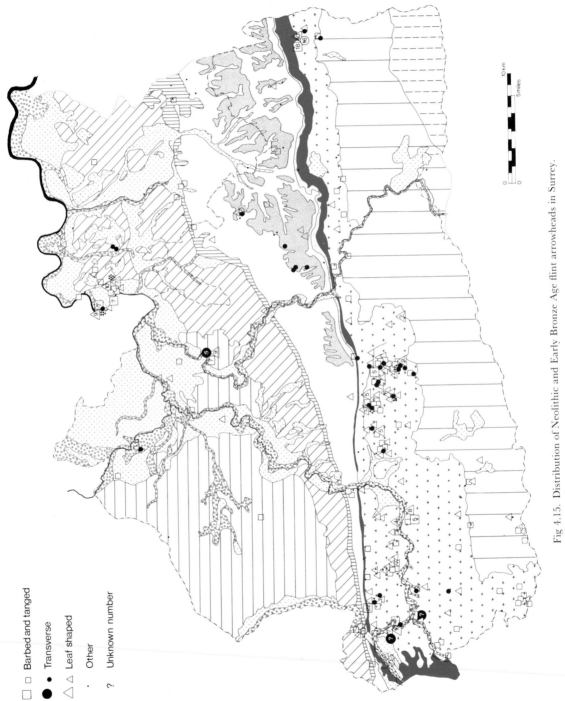

Fig 4.15. Distribution of Neolithic and Early Bronze Age flint arrowheads in Surrey.

need to move after game (Harris 1969, 9) and groups of sedentary hunters are identifiable anthropologically from north America and possible archaeologically within the Ertebølle (Rowley-Conwy 1983). The point has been made (Flannery 1969, 75) that the hunter-gatherer lifestyle was extremely efficient; thus in the London Basin, stimulus to change could be resisted for as long as the rich resources were able to support the expanding population, or until a change in the physical environment affected the resources themselves (Flannery 1969, 76).

Neolithic settlement in general appears markedly riverine with a heavy concentration of sites in the west London area, especially at confluences which effectively controlled traffic with the interior and with occasional sites along the Wey and Mole valleys and along spring lines to north and south of the Chalk. The artefact concentrations at Tilford and Crooksbury are round the upper reaches of the Wey, those at Peaslake are at the head of the Tillingbourne, while Limpsfield lies at the source of the Darent. A further accumulation can be discerned around the ancient headwaters of the Wandle. Many riverine sites may lie buried by alluvium, and with considerable development in the London area, many others have probably been destroyed. It is difficult to predict the presence of such sites and those buried at Kingston, Twickenham and Runnymede were encountered entirely by chance. The west London clusters are, however, intriguing with major concentrations of artefacts occurring at Kingston, Richmond, Brentford, Mortlake, Hammersmith and Battersea together with a number of apparently smaller sites. Investigation of these riverside sites is important. Difficulties however not only include identification but also interpretation. The effect of floods will not only have eroded banks and changed the river course, but during overbank flows may have swept away or modified occupation traces. Artefacts may be water sorted and deposited according to weight rather than cultural association (Turnbaugh 1978). A first stage however would be to determine as far as possible the ancient courses of the rivers, perhaps by a programme of boreholes, together with local contour surveys.

The earlier part of the Neolithic in the county is thus characterised by a number of small riverside sites producing coarse, plain pottery and small gravel flint assemblages. While the nature of these sites cannot yet be ascertained their location suggests a river-based economy. Monuments occur at Staines and Badshot Lea, while the Stanwell cursus may have been constructed during this phase. The significance of the Runnymede site is unclear, both pottery and flintwork being different in nature from that present at other riverside sites. It is tempting however to link it with the Yeoveney causewayed enclosure and with the cluster of flint and stone ground axes from the Staines stretch of the Thames.

The few Later Neolithic sites are characterised by the presence of Ebbsfleet or Mortlake wares. Unfortunately, much of this from the Thames is unstratified, though some was found with worked antler and flintwork at Kingston. It occurred in pits at Heathrow and at Sipson where a 'greenstone' axe was found in association, and was also recovered from the Badshot Lea long barrow ditches and the Stanwell cursus ditches at late stages of their silting, a not uncommon occurrence on British Neolithic monuments.

No pottery comes from the Chalk either in Earlier or Later contexts. Indeed, the flint sites here stand out as markedly different in nature from those elsewhere in the county and may be described as 'Campignian' in nature. The Chalk may thus be seen as an industrial area, respected for its resources, which perhaps supported groups of pastoralists whose transhumant way of life may have allowed them to exploit the flint resources and conduct exchanges at settlements along the river margins.

In addition the Chalk may be seen as dividing the county into two separate units. Sites to the north with the Thames as their focal point perhaps based their economy on rich river resources and were thus slow to adapt. To the south settlement may have developed at a swifter pace and perhaps had more in common with early agricultural settlements in Sussex than with the Thames valley. The scenario presented, based as it is largely on the evidence of surface scatters of flint, needs testing. Controlled fieldwork together with selected excavation over the next few years ought to confirm or reject many of these points.

The transition to the Bronze Age is marked by a greater increase in monuments, almost exclusively round barrows, and their location in many cases hints at a more ordered and well-utilised landscape based on stream and river valleys. It may be that the trade patterns established during the Later Neolithic in the west London area set the stage for the development and dominance of the area in metalworking in the Later Bronze Age.

NOTES

1 We would like to acknowledge the help that has been given in various ways during the preparation of this survey by Anthony Allen, Julia Arthur, Morag Barton, Carolyn Cotton, Derek Dunlop, Roger Ellaby, Geoff Elmore, Vivien Ettlinger, Suzanne Field, Ray Inskeep, Derek Jewell, Ian Kinnes, Derek Hinton, Avril Lansdell, Jean Macdonald, Ian Macdonald, Anna Mercer, Stuart Needham, Steve Nelson, Pat Nicolaysen, Martin O'Connell, Maureen Rendell, Reay Robertson-Mackay, Michael Russell, Roy Scott, Dale Serjeantson, Andrew Sherratt, Marion Shipley, Chris Taylor, Yvonne Watts, Ken Waters, Keith Winser, Margaret Wooldridge and Mike Youkee. Our thanks to them all.

2 Another enclosure 5km to the east-north-east, at East Bedfont, whilst apparently similar in terms of size and shape, awaits proper investigation.

3 Recent fieldwork in the Alton area of east Hampshire has apparently produced evidence of just such a group (Malcolm Lyne, pers comm).

The Bronze Age

STUART NEEDHAM

Introduction

'No period of Surrey archaeology has suffered more from neglect and lack of scientific investigation than the Bronze Age.' Whimster's judgement was severe, though not unduly so, and he gave no hint of optimism for the future (1931, 62). Yet now, half a century on, the tide has truly turned and the time is ripe to review afresh the early metal-using societies of Surrey and its region.[1] To Whimster and indeed later writers Surrey was overshadowed by the riches of Wessex and Sussex, these riches measured partly in the quality of the evidence recovered, partly in the good record of fieldwork. The fact that for the Later Bronze Age a wealth of metalwork from the Thames is primarily concentrated in the reaches dividing old Middlesex from old Surrey was of little consequence, for this material lay for a long time little studied and in a contextual vacuum, so that its full significance was not realised. One major factor in the lack of attention to the regional Bronze Age is probably the destruction of tangible monuments long ago, in medieval if not Roman times, in the major river valleys, which were undoubtedly the most important grounds of later prehistoric settlement. Elsewhere, although they may survive, monuments tend to be less densely concentrated or less imposing than in Wessex and so have commanded less attention. There are also certain physiographic zones with special problems: the infertile sandy heaths which seem incapable of ever having supported much settlement; the heavy clay subsoils, which we still have to view as untillable in the ard-based agricultural regime of the Bronze Age; and even the chalklands which are in parts covered by difficult Clay-with-flints and which in the west dwindle to a relatively insignificant and subordinate element of the productive landscape.

It is, however, this variability of environment across the county which promises to yield a rich understanding of prehistoric land-use. As Bronze Age sites, in particular the domestic sites, are discovered and investigated on a useful scale we may hope to perceive the importance of intra-regional variation. This process has already begun as new evidence redresses the imbalances of earlier stores of knowledge. Above all, Surrey and Middlesex may now boast a group of Late Bronze Age settlement assemblages which stand out by any regional standards.

In view of the difficulties still experienced in synthesising the fragmentary evidence for the Neolithic, the Bronze Age comes as a tonic with something of a coherent picture beginning to emerge. The current state of knowledge allows the projection of both broad outlines for the county in its regional context and a series of restrictive views of environmentally determined zones. These aspects are reflected in the two parts of this paper. In the first part material culture, settlement types, burial sites and evidence for subsistence economies and trading patterns are set against the wider chronological framework for southern Britain. In the second part, the opportunity is taken to examine the nature and development of the utilisation of the various physiographic zones which make up the county. In this latter section in particular innumerable tacit questions arise which only future fieldwork will settle.

Material culture, settlements and funerary practice

EARLY BRONZE AGE METALWORK

The definition of a Neolithic/Bronze Age transition, difficult anywhere in the country, is even more elusive in Surrey which suffers from a dearth of contextual evidence. We can begin only by looking at a series of artefact types characteristic of the transition and the ensuing Early Bronze Age. It is appropriate to look first at the metalwork itself (figs 5.1, 5.2).

Axes are by far the commonest of early metalwork forms and Surrey has a representative series

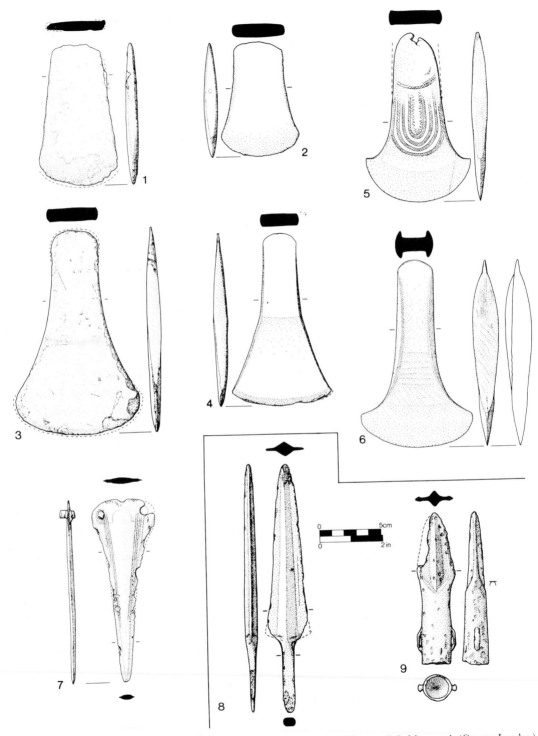

Fig 5.1. Early Bronze Age metalwork: 1, Peasepottage Forest (Sussex), class 2 flat axe; 2, St Margaret's (Greater London), class 2 flat axe; 3, Walton Heath, class 4 flat axe; 4, Chertsey, class 4 flat axe; 5, Thames at Kingston, class 4 flat axe; 6, West Drayton (Greater London), class 5 flanged axe; 7, Thames at Ankerwyke Bend, Egham, Camerton-Snowshill dagger; 8, 9, Lightwater hoard, tanged and end-looped spearheads. All 1:3

belonging to a development which may have had a duration of about a millennium in real years, beginning somewhere in the middle of the 3rd millennium BC. Amongst the copper (and presumptively earliest) British axes two main influences may be discerned, emanating from Ireland and the continent. An axe attributed to Farncombe[2] (Phillips 1967, 22, fig 4:1) belongs to a distinctive Irish type (Lough Ravel – Harbison 1969, 10–19) which is rarely found here. Another from near Crawley (fig 5.1:1) just over the county boundary represents the other strand, having a trapezoidal shape with ultimate origins in north-west Europe. To these may be added axes from Oxshott Heath and St Margaret's, Twickenham[3] (fig 5.1:2). Other copper artefacts are equally rare: just a halberd from Lambeth, another probably from the Thames (Barrett 1976, 38, fig 5:1; ÓRíordáin 1936, 312, no 5) and a tanged knife from Mortlake (Gerloff 1975, no 16).

The transition from copper- to bronze-working may have been swift in some spheres of metalwork production, occurring perhaps late in the 3rd millennium BC. Axe morphology developed along insular lines and, over some centuries, culminated in refined flat axe forms furnished with low flanges and stops and often ornately decorated. The stop bevel was first added at an early stage represented by six axes which occur in central southern England, one Surrey example coming from Walton Heath[4] (fig 5.1:3; Carpenter 1961). This local innovation was precocious, even as far as the strong Irish industries were concerned, and it was to commence the replacement of plain axes (class 3 – Needham 1983) by stop bevel forms (class 4). Class 4 axes were soon standardised to the form seen in a new find from Chertsey (fig 5.1:4), characterised by angled sides and a widely splayed blade. These are found throughout England and Wales. Subsequent and final developments in the flat axe series saw the narrowing of the blade, but this is increasingly associated with widely expanded blade tips creating the crescentic cutting edge familiar on the ensuing flanged axes. Examples of these late flat axes are known from Thames-side districts: at Sunbury, Harlington, Hounslow, Kingston (fig 5.1:5), Kew and Mortlake.[5] The hinterland of Surrey is bereft of finds and this pattern in the deposition of metalwork is accentuated in the succeeding Arreton phase.

The metalwork of the Arreton complex (Britton 1963, 284–91) represents something of a revolution stimulated by renewed contacts with the continent, particularly north-west Germany and Saxo-Thuringia. A transformation in axe design is seen in improved hafting facilities, ie the casting of substantial flanges (fig 5.1:6). An increased repertoire of metalwork types is encountered including two British innovations: tanged spearheads (fig 5.1:8–9) and lugged chisels, while new elaborate dagger types were developed, the Camerton-Snowshill[6] (fig 5.1:7) and Hammersmith types (Gerloff 1975, 99–133). Most of the Arreton types are represented in our area, some in good numbers, and they show the beginning of the dense Thames distributions that are such a well-known feature of Middle and Late Bronze Age metalwork. In this terminal stage of the Early Bronze Age the pattern of deposition may have been set by changing economic conditions. The links across the North Sea were connected with influxes of nickel-rich continental metal. It would be natural to expect the Thames to have been one of the major lines of supply from Europe, and there is much support for this in subsequent phases. This could, in conjunction with the agricultural wealth of the Thames terraces, have led to a monopoly control of the metal supply in the riverside zone and the consequent accumulation of the lion's share of surplus – surplus which could be disposed of in ritual and ceremony.

Away from the river Arreton metalwork is represented by a few axes, but most importantly by a pair of spearheads from Curley Hill, Lightwater (fig 5.1:8–9; Needham 1979a). This find is not a classic Arreton hoard, indeed these are absent from the lower Thames region; the interest lies in the association between a tanged spearhead of Arreton type and an early socketed form, almost certainly of western British or Irish manufacture. Although it had formerly been surmised using indirect evidence that these two types were contemporaneous, the Lightwater hoard was the first demonstration of this from either Britain or Ireland.

The quantity and variety of Arreton metalwork in the lower Thames region suggests that a vigorous local industry flourished here (fig 5.2), but local production could have begun earlier, its products including the Teddington dagger with its triple mid-rib which has very few parallels (Gerloff 1975, no 102), as well as the developed flat axes already described.

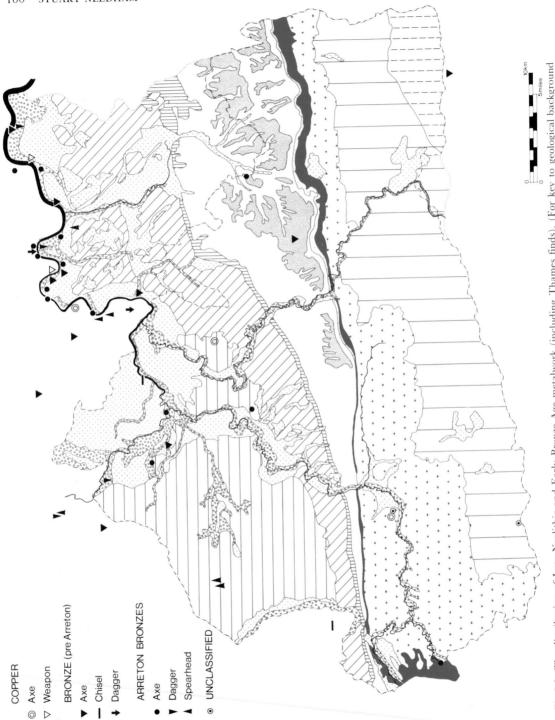

COPYRIGHT

COPPER
◎ Axe
▽ Weapon

BRONZE (pre Arreton)
▶ Axe
— Chisel
→ Dagger

ARRETON BRONZES
● Axe
▶ Dagger
◀ Spearhead

◉ UNCLASSIFIED

Fig 5.2. The distribution of Late Neolithic and Early Bronze Age metalwork (including Thames finds). (For key to geological background see foldout 1)

EARLY BRONZE AGE POTTERY AND OTHER CULTURAL MATERIAL

If earlier communities in southern England had on occasion received metalwork from the continent, the new technology did not materialise until sometime during the Beaker period. This is traditionally seen as bridging the Late Neolithic/Early Bronze Age transition, beaker pottery being the primary characteristic of this cultural complex, which had a long duration. The explanation of the introduction of beakers, metallurgy and other specialised goods varies widely, from views of sizeable population movements to acculturation in the face of a cult which employed this specific group of artefacts (Clarke 1970; Burgess & Shennan 1976). Certainly there is a case for much of the British beaker series representing a protracted insular development with regional emphases. Actual incursions from the continent may well have been few and sporadic having only a minimal effect on population growth. No single pattern need be sought: the likelihood is that Beaker cultural trappings were brought to different regions in different ways and for different reasons. For parts of the Beaker period there are undeniable links between Britain and Europe, and the Thames valley, as always, was in a prime position to be confronted by continental influences. The mechanisms by which these either became implanted in the region with new settlers, or were absorbed by native Later Neolithic communities, are likely only to be ascertainable once decent settlement assemblages are brought to light.

Surrey is not well endowed with beaker pottery and indeed most of the county is lacking in finds, few of those recorded having any known context. Some are likely to have been grave goods in unrecognised burial deposits, but there is settlement material from Southwark, Westminster[7] and Chaldon (Russell 1982), while some of the Thames material might have similar origins (eg Mortlake – fig 5.3: 4).

Although there are no associations within the region, two other prestige artefact types which occur in Beaker grave groups elsewhere may be usefully considered with the pottery, since they show comparable distributions: stone battle axes and flint daggers. All three artefact types had long currencies and their respective uses may not have been closely interlinked throughout. Nevertheless for the present purpose these three types may be grouped together. A common distribution pattern emerges, each type being overwhelmingly concentrated along the Kingston–City reaches of the Thames (fig 5.4). Outside this focus are two lesser scatters of finds: upstream along the Thames pottery has come from Oatlands Park, and flint daggers from Walton-on-Thames and Weybridge (two);[8] while on and around the North Downs in east Surrey pottery has come from Chaldon, Bromley, Limpsfield and Croydon, a flint dagger from Carshalton, and battle axes from Croydon and (possibly) the Mitcham district.[9]

The heavy shaft-hole implements which are known as axe hammers, echo the Thames-side concentration of their finer counterparts, the battle axes, but three examples occur in the south-west of the county (Field & Woolley 1984). The same pattern applies to perforated maceheads, but neither group is particularly well dated and one of the south-western maceheads may have been associated with a Neolithic axe (Field & Woolley 1984, no 47). Axe hammers are generally more crudely shaped than battle axes, the example from Ripley (Clark 1950–1) with its bulbed sides being somewhat unusual and perhaps to be linked to grooved or fluted axe hammers in south-west Scotland (Roe 1966). Finely finished types of Early Bronze Age shaft-hole implement are thus not known from south-west Surrey. This is unlikely to be due to recovery bias given the overall distributions of stone and flint implements in the county (Field & Woolley 1984, figs 8–11).

Barbed and tanged arrowheads, which are often linked to the Beaker assemblage on account of their predominant grave associations, have a very different distribution in Surrey. Some do occur in the zone of beaker pottery and prestige goods, but a larger number come from outside, particularly from the south-western hills where fieldwork has biased recovery of flintwork in general (Cotton & Field, this volume). Barbed and tanged arrowheads should not necessarily be taken to be the prerogative of beaker-using groups. Pottery associated with them in graves is by no means exclusively beaker ware; food vessels and collared urns, taken together, are associated with the arrowheads almost as frequently (Green 1980, 129–30). In day to day use the balance is perhaps likely to have been different and more utilitarian factors will have determined patterns of loss.

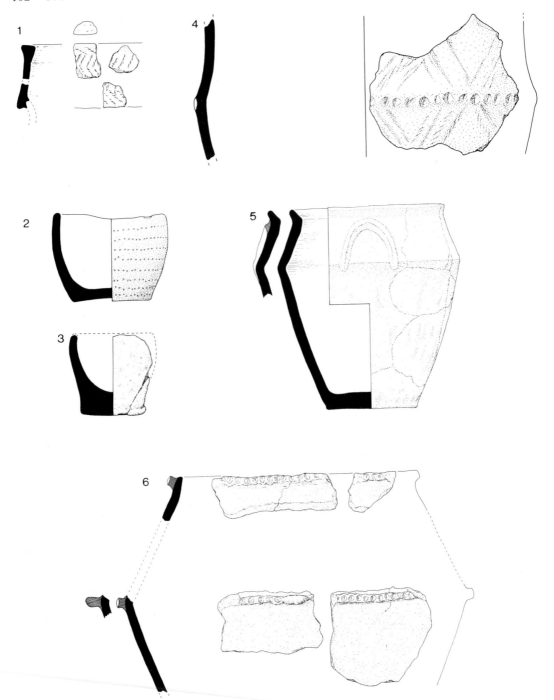

Fig 5.3. Early Bronze Age pottery: 1, Badshot Lea long barrow, collared urn sherds; 2, Thames at Mortlake, cup; 3, Cobham sewage works, cup; 4, Thames at Mortlake, beaker sherd; 5, Guildford, biconical urn; 6, The Hallams, biconical urn. Nos 1–4 at 1:3, nos 5, 6 at 1:5

A somewhat restricted zone of direct Beaker influence or infiltration seems to be implied by the present evidence (fig 5.4). This pattern is dissimilar from that of various Early Bronze Age pottery types which began during beaker currency: the relevant types found in Surrey are food vessels, collared urns and biconical urns. Some of these continued in use after the cessation of beaker wares. They are normally encountered in funerary contexts and this primary function may be assumed for most Surrey specimens.

Collared urns have a widespread distribution, as indeed they do at the national level (Longworth 1983, 82–3, fig 42); they overlap the beaker zone but also spread across to central and western Surrey (fig 5.4). Attention may be drawn to sherds of a very finely made vessel (fig 5.3:1) from the upper ditch silts of Badshot Lea long barrow, near Farnham. Although of collared urn form, the ware is of beaker quality; this is an unusual combination.[10]

Another collared urn sherd of a quite different quality comes from the Weston Wood assemblage. It is plain with a flint-gritted fabric, which stands in contrast to normal collared urn practice, and it may belong with early post Deverel-Rimbury elements on the site dating perhaps to the end of the 2nd millennium BC.

The two other principal pottery forms – food vessels and the biconical urn group – have a very localised distribution. With the possible exception of one find from Yiewsley, Middlesex,[11] all come from the upper Wey and Tillingbourne zone in west Surrey (fig 5.4). Thus while overlapping the collared urn spread, they are completely exclusive of the beaker zone. That these vessels should be focused in the west is unsurprising, since the respective types are well represented in Wessex, but it is noteworthy that beaker pottery was not absorbed through the same connections. The neat exclusivity of beakers and this 'Wessex orientated' pottery group might point to a basic if local cultural divide perhaps reflecting regional levels of aggrandisement. Other localised clusters of biconical urns occur in the south-east, notably in eastern Kent and on the Sussex Downs (Cruse & Harrison 1983, 91, fig 6), and the form is also known beyond in the Low Countries and northern France.

The Wessex orientated pottery includes two food vessels[12] of relatively simple southern types rather than of Yorkshire vase type, as well as four 'biconical' urns. Three of the urns are strictly biconical in shape and have various applied features: one from Wonersh has four lugs on the carination (Gardner 1924, pl 4b), while the second from that site has lugs interrupting an applied finger-tipped cordon in the same position[13] (fig 5.3:6) and an urn from Guildford has two horseshoe handles on the upper body in the manner of many classic Wessex biconicals[14] (fig 5.3:5). These handles are also a feature of the fourth urn, from Junction Pit, Farnham, but this has a rather unusual body profile with a high rounded shoulder and a short upright neck (Lowther 1939, pl 15).[15] Comparisons have been made with certain north French urns (O'Connor 1980, 277–8), two of which are not only very close in form but were also deposited in a similar manner – inverted and enclosed by a small stone cist. This rite is repeated, using a similar vessel, at Bircham Heath, Norfolk (Lukis 1843), where associated gold-covered beads point to an Early Bronze Age date rather than the 'Later MBA' date suggested by O'Connor (1980, 277–8).

The economic and social differentiation between south-west and north-east Surrey is enhanced by consideration of the overall metalwork distribution. The few copper pieces have a dispersed distribution which extends into the Wealden region of Surrey, Kent and Sussex, but most of this should be earlier than the pottery styles we are considering. The contemporary metalwork is of bronze, including both the pre-Arreton and the Arreton stages, and is essentially confined to our beaker zone in the Thames-side districts and the eastern block of the North Downs. There may then be a cultural background to the monopoly of the metal surplus, which was in the hands of the beaker-using groups, or alternatively the metal and other fine artefacts are all material indications of a comparatively prosperous society.

Additional pottery finds belonging to earlier Bronze Age traditions are seen in the form of two cups. At this period such cups are normally encountered in graves and taken to be accessory vessels. The lack of investigation of burial sites in the county has therefore given little opportunity for their recovery. A plain cup with a simple rim made in a sandy fabric (fig 5.3:3) was dug up casually at Cobham sewage works, not far from known Bronze Age burial finds. The form,

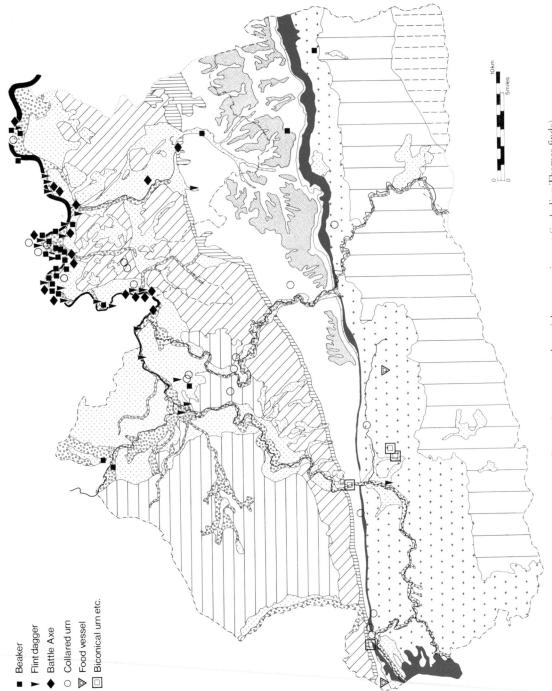

Beaker
▶ Flint dagger
◆ Battle Axe
○ Collared urn
▷ Food vessel
▣ Biconical urn etc.

Fig 5.4. The distribution of Early Bronze Age pottery and special stone equipment (including Thames finds).

although simple, is precisely matched in a cup excavated from Folkton barrow CCXLIV, North Yorkshire (Greenwell 1890, 13–14). This cup accompanied an infant cremation beneath the barrow. Another similar cup from Stancomb, Berkshire, is simply decorated with pricked impressions arranged in short vertical rows. It was not associated with a burial, but may have been deposited separately at the time of the primary interment, which was accompanied by late Early Bronze Age grave goods (Greenwell 1890, 61). Pricked ornament is also found, this time in horizontal rows, on the second Surrey cup, which comes from the Thames at Mortlake (British Museum register 1909, 5–18, 15). Again the rim is simple and the walls bowed (fig 5.3:2).

BURIAL MOUNDS

Surrey barrows have never been subjected to a concerted campaign of exploration and consequently we have only limited knowledge of their structure and associated burial rites. Although a number of the pottery vessels dealt with elsewhere in this chapter came from extant barrows and others probably from denuded ones, they were all uncovered accidentally. Grinsell's pioneering fieldwork of the 1930s first collated a list of known monuments and this must still be the basis of any assessment (Grinsell 1934). More recent fieldwork has identified a number of additional mounds, but most are not distinctive and are therefore of uncertain age and indeed function. A subsidiary problem which is particularly acute in our county is that of natural mound formation on the various sandy soils. At both Thursley, on the Lower Greensand (Corcoran 1961), and Ockham Common, on the Bracklesham Beds (excavated by the author), post-war excavations have revealed barrow-like mounds to be of natural formation. A reciprocal problem is the easy denudation of sand-built barrows either by natural agencies or, more worryingly now, by the extensive use of trackways crossing the mounds by horses and motorcycle scramblers. Extant barrows in Surrey are a small and diminishing resource and we know far too little about them.

Barrows on the gravel terraces of the Thames and major tributaries have suffered still worse degradation so that very few have survived into modern times. A notable exception was the Teddington barrow which, when levelled in 1854, still stood 12ft (4m) high and 96ft (29.5m) across (Akerman 1855).[16] Various burial deposits and artefacts were encountered in this sizeable mound

Fig 5.5. The West End Common quadruple barrow from the air. (*Photograph: Major G W G Allen, see Grinsell 1934, pl 7*)

and the primary burial appears to have been a cremation accompanied by a bronze dagger. That some ring ditches showing as cropmarks may mark the sites of former barrows is assured by many excavated examples in comparable regions, eg the upper Thames valley (see also Junction Pit below). But ring ditches are not unequivocally the remains of barrows; indeed the only two excavated in our area, at Heathrow, show that even excavation does not always answer the question of origin with certainty (Canham 1978b, Sites A and H).

In addition to the problem of natural mound formation, assessment of the Bronze Age barrow distribution is further obscured by the presence of a Saxon barrow burial tradition in the county. Saxon grave groups are known to have come from barrows at Farthing Down, Gally Hills, Merrow Downs, Walton Bridge and possibly the Hog's Back. In some cases, as in the recently excavated Gally Hills barrow (Barfoot & Price-Williams 1976) Saxon burials were primary, but the possibility of a Bronze Age foundation for some of these barrow cemeteries cannot be wholly excluded.

Nowhere in Surrey do we find the large nucleated barrow cemeteries typical of Wessex and some other regions. Most mounds appear to be isolated, but there are also small groups, both nucleated and dispersed. Nucleated groups tend to be linear and sometimes contiguous; good examples, almost certainly of Bronze Age date, are the triple mound on Crooksbury Common (Grinsell 1932, 58–60, pl 13) and the quadruple one on West End Common, Chobham (fig 5.5; Grinsell 1934, 39–40, pl 7), while the string of nine ring ditches at Stanwell looks a likely candidate (Longley 1976, 33, fig 12).

More dispersed barrow groups in the Flutters Hill area of Chobham Common (10 mounds) and Tyrells Wood on Leatherhead Downs (six mounds – Poulton & O'Connell 1984a) largely consist of nondescript 'bowl' mounds. Amongst the former group however there is a fine ditched barrow (Longcross – Grinsell 1934, 37), while the latter area yielded in 1868 'some sepulchral urns, one with impressed zigzag ornament' (Grinsell 1934, 50–1).

An important dispersed group is represented by three barrows on Horsell Common. There is no record of any excavation, but an Early Bronze Age date can be assigned confidently due to their forms. Two are bell barrows, the mounds each encircled by a level berm inside the enclosing ditch (Grinsell 1932, 61–3); the third is a disc barrow with only a small tump within the circular bank and ditch (Grinsell 1974, 101). These forms, collectively known as 'fancy' barrows, are characteristic of Early Bronze Age Wessex, and are particularly associated with the 'Wessex culture'. Fancy barrows are actually not common outside Wessex itself and in this connection it is noteworthy that Surrey examples are limited to the west of the county (fig 5.6), a distribution which coincides with the biconical urn/food vessel zone already described. It should be emphasised, however, that this is a peripheral zone which shows no indications as yet of the rich grave goods often found in Wessex. The paucity of excavated barrows may partly explain this. It is noteworthy however that the whetstone found in the one excavated Surrey bell barrow, that of Deerleap Wood (Corcoran 1963), was found on the periphery of the mound whereas in Wessex such articles are found as grave accompaniments. The Deerleap whetstone therefore, while generally reinforcing a Wessex link, could at the same time point to a difference in funerary customs. Despite its modern excavation the Deerleap Wood barrow remains somewhat enigmatic. A central turf core was partially covered by a stone capping and encased in a sand mound. No evidence for burial was found either in the form of bone remains, grave goods or a cut grave. The only other find potentially contemporary with construction was a flint fabricator which lay on the stone capping. If a burial had ever existed at Deerleap it must have been an inhumation which became completely dissolved in the acid soil.

Stone structures appear to be a recurring feature of barrows in southern Surrey, presumably due to the local availability of stone from the Greensand and Chalk. The use of the stone is varied; at Gostrode Farm, Chiddingfold, in contrast to Deerleap Wood, the stones appear to have been laid on the old ground surface as a floor described as a 'circular hearth of ironstone . . . the diameter of which extended about 10 feet' (Douglas 1793, 162). An inhumation accompanied by a pottery vessel and 'trifling fragments of corroded brass, probably the remains of a clasp or buckle' probably lay on the stone floor. At the Hallams, and at Junction Pit, inverted biconical urns containing cremated bones were enclosed by stone 'cists'. One of the Hallams urns was recorded as

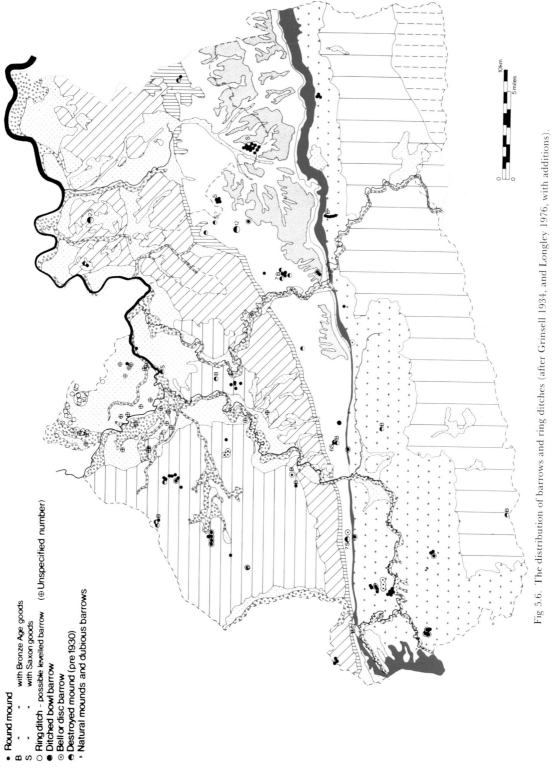

Fig 5.6. The distribution of barrows and ring ditches (after Grinsell 1934, and Longley 1976, with additions).

• Round mound
B "   "   with Bronze Age goods
S "   "   with Saxon goods
○ Ring ditch – possible levelled barrow   (⊕ Unspecified number)
● Ditched bowl barrow
⊙ Bell or disc barrow
◑ Destroyed mound (pre 1930)
× Natural mounds and dubious barrows

being 3½ ft (*c* 1m) down in the Folkestone Sand and enclosed in a cist of ironstone slabs (Gardner 1924, 15–16). The second urn from that site came from the centre of a small surviving mound. It was found fragmented but had stood on a few flat slabs of ironstone while more slabs were heaped up around and above it (Gardner 1924, 26–7). This arrangement was probably very similar to the better recorded chalk block cist protecting the Junction Pit urn (Lowther 1939, 166, fig 67). Here the cist was seen to be carefully constructed, possibly with shaped blocks protruding at the top. The floor blocks sat on a prepared clayey platform and the whole was encircled by a ring ditch suggesting the former existence of a covering mound.

The chronology of Surrey barrows is poorly documented due to the lack of critical finds. On the evidence of barrows in better explored regions the construction of most would belong to the Early Bronze Age, ending with the demise of the Wessex culture around 1400 BC. Certainly some of the collared and biconical vessels recorded from Surrey barrows could be primary interments; indeed this may be safely assumed for the Junction Pit urn.

By far the commonest funerary accompaniments in the county are Deverel-Rimbury bucket urns and these are sometimes associated with barrows. The fact that they are nominally of Middle Bronze Age date does not cause concern, since most could happily be regarded as secondary insertions into pre-existing mounds, a rite abundantly known throughout southern Britain. Nevertheless, the possibility of primary contexts for some Deverel-Rimbury pottery should not be excluded (eg Ellison 1980); radiocarbon dates now point clearly to a substantial overlap between late 'EBA' Wessex culture graves and 'MBA' Deverel-Rimbury ceramics (Barrett 1980a, 82–3, fig 2). The main obstacle to the placing of Deverel-Rimbury pottery in primary positions in barrows was thus not so much one of anachronism as one of custom. Despite the prevalent sequence, an open mind should be kept regarding the urns in one of the Whitmoor Common barrows excavated by Pitt Rivers, a bell barrow type, for they might have been primary deposits (Gardner 1924, 28, fig 3). If this were the case, and it can no longer be proven either way, then this break with the normal pattern might be accounted for by regional idiosyncrasy, by the strength of the Deverel-Rimbury tradition from an early stage here, and by the failure of Wessex burial customs to penetrate the peripheral west Surrey zone.

Finally it is worth noting a radiocarbon date of 1480±70 bc, ie around the 18th century BC after correction, which is a *terminus post quem* for the construction of a bell barrow at Ascot, just across the Berkshire border (Bradley & Keith-Lucas 1975). This accords reasonably well with other dating evidence for that type of monument.

THE DEVEREL-RIMBURY COMPLEX

The cultural complex known as the Deverel-Rimbury, defined on bucket urns and globular urns as well as a range of other material goods, constitutes a corner stone in Bronze Age archaeology because it embraces both settlement and funerary evidence. The latter component has already been introduced in the discussion of Early Bronze Age burial. Early Bronze Age beginnings for the complex are only a recent realisation, which does not however alter its basic Middle Bronze Age chronology. On circumstantial grounds the lower Thames valley is likely to be one of the regions in which Deverel-Rimbury pottery emerged earliest. Given, furthermore, the probability that funerary urns of collared and biconical styles continued in use into the Middle Bronze Age alongside the by then dominant Deverel-Rimbury assemblage, the question of interrelationships during the period of overlap becomes paramount, but not yet soluble.

There are interesting features of distribution that suggest a degree of exclusion between the users of Deverel-Rimbury and the other ceramic groups (fig 5.7). This is most obvious in the north-west of the county where two large blocks of land, centred on the Bagshot Table and the Heathrow terraces, have yielded eight Deverel-Rimbury sites each, yet no 'earlier' types of Bronze Age ceramic (except perhaps the Yiewsley 'biconical' urn). In the case of the Bagshot Table, and perhaps the higher ground of the Greensand hills, we may be witnessing here the new colonisation of uncultivated land, for there is little evidence of earlier settlement. This point is examined below. On the Heathrow terraces there is abundant evidence for Neolithic occupation (Jon Cotton, pers comm).

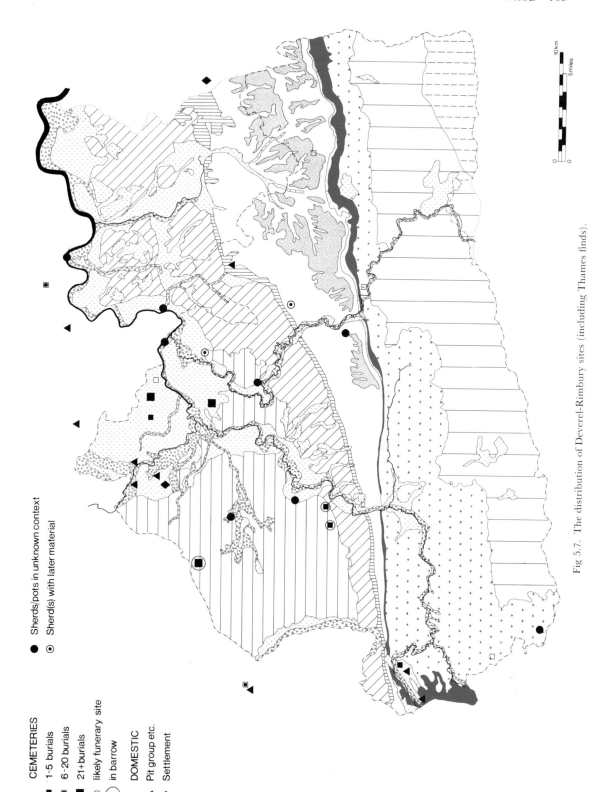

CEMETERIES

● 1-5 burials

▣ 6-20 burials

■ 21+burials

□ likely funerary site

◯ in barrow

DOMESTIC

▲ Pit group etc.

◆ Settlement

● Sherds/pots in unknown context

◉ Sherd(s) with later material

Fig 5.7. The distribution of Deverel-Rimbury sites (including Thames finds).

In north-east Surrey as far west as the Wey and south to the North Downs, a scatter of Deverel-Rimbury finds overlaps the distribution of beakers and collared urns and must essentially have replaced the beaker wares at least, which are likely to have ceased before 1600 BC.

The domestic component of the Deverel-Rimbury complex allows us to observe a fuller assemblage in broader context. From the burial evidence we can see the familiar range of burial rites which are variations on the inurned or unaccompanied cremation; the regional evidence has been discussed by Barrett and need not be enumerated here (1973, 124–7). A noteworthy aspect is the use of limited pot forms, almost exclusively buckets, thus contrasting with other regional

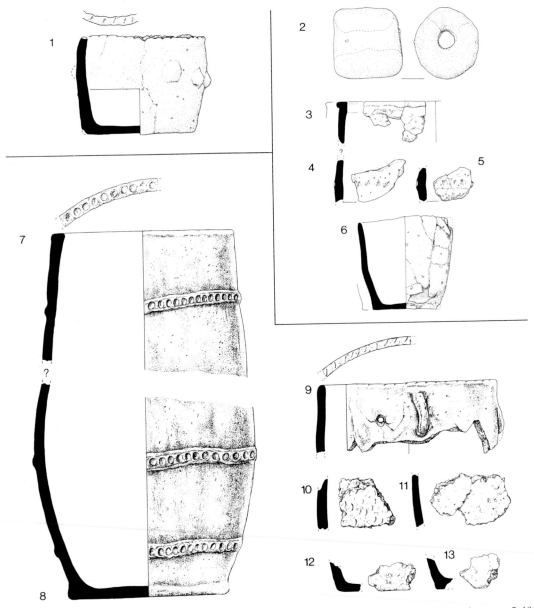

Fig 5.8. Deverel-Rimbury ceramics: 1, Stoneyfield, bossed cup; 2–6, Longsides gravel pit, loomweight and pottery; 7–13, Betchworth sand pit, pottery. No 1 at 1:3, nos 2–13 at 1:5

groups which contain a good proportion of globular urns. This probably attests the selection of pottery specifically for funerary purposes, for globular urns are now represented locally amongst the settlement assemblage at Muckhatch Farm (Johnson 1975; Barrett 1973, 121) and the likely domestic group of sherds from Osterley (Cotton 1981a).

Surrey Deverel-Rimbury material also includes a few small knobbed cups in coarse ware similar to the bucket urns, to which they were often accessories in graves. Two such cups come from the Stoneyfield cemetery, Farnham. One originally had 10 bosses, all but four of which have sheared off (fig 5.8:1; Frere 1961, pl 7b), while the other (fig 5.10:7), with four bosses, has an important bronze association discussed below (Lowther 1939, 177–9, pl 18).

Similar cups come from the Thames at 'London' and at Tagg's Island near Hampton (Celoria & Macdonald, 1969, 46; Museum of London accession no A26497). A fourth example from Kingston Hill provides something of a contrast with the standard forms, being crudely moulded and further miniaturised. A rare and close parallel for this atypical 'degenerate' form is provenanced to Brighton (Musson 1954, 111, nos 400–1, fig 6; British Museum register 1925, 12–14, 2). The Kingston Hill cup was associated with a slack-shouldered jar appropriate to 'post Deverel-Rimbury' assemblages (fig 5.12:11–12). The jar was found 'half full of ashes' and described as sepulchral; taken all together the group seems to represent the final throes of Middle Bronze Age burial practice in the lower Thames valley (Field & Needham 1986, nos 21–2).

Other material recorded from Surrey's domestic sites includes cylindrical loom-weights, a spindlewhorl, saddle querns, flintwork and even a piece of a shale bracelet (eg Johnson 1975, 12). The majority come from casual discoveries which are at best recorded as coming from pits. At Muckhatch Farm the partial plan of a roughly circular enclosure was retrieved (Johnson 1975, 22, fig 7), and other features include two post rings representing two huts, pits and linear ditches, but it is not clear yet how these components combine to make a functioning unit, or whether a sequence can be deduced. A good domestic range was also present at Hayes Common, just over the Kent border, where post holes, pits and a ditch were planned, but lacked any overall intelligible pattern (Philp 1973, 32–5). Some of the Hayes pottery is simply decorated with multiple grooves in arcs, while the standard finger tip treatment is also present. A reasonable quantity of flintwork is dominated by scrapers and piercers, but not outside the range expected for settlement sites (Bradley 1978a, 56). There is no reason why some of the flint assemblage, indeed the greater part, should not go with the Deverel-Rimbury material (contra Healey 1973, 43).

Assemblages such as these from Hayes and Muckhatch provide useful reference points for flintworking, which has received scant attention in the region. Good associations are few and only systematic metrical analysis of sizeable surface scatters will be capable of discerning the patterns for Bronze Age flintworking which have been established elsewhere (eg Pitts 1978; Fasham & Ross 1978; Pryor 1980, 106–25). Singly associated examples, such as the undiagnostic scraper found with one of the Hallams biconical urns (Gardner 1924, 27), are of limited value to such studies.

MIDDLE BRONZE AGE METALWORK

Associations between metalwork and domestic material of the Middle Bronze Age are uncommon and consequently only a general concordance can be offered. The metalwork is more susceptible to refined phasing than the pottery due to regular changes in form. Middle Bronze Age industries are characterised above all by the palstave, a developed form of flanged axe. Certain forms probably date as early as the 15th century BC and in fact overlap with the final Early Bronze Age types of the Arreton complex. Early palstaves from Farnham, Guildford, Farley Heath, Albury and Reigate (Field & Needham 1984) may be considered with an advanced type of flanged axe from Blackheath which should be contemporary (Phillips 1968).[17] The importance of this group is that they suggest the emergence of a Middle Bronze Age tradition of metalworking in southern Surrey while Arreton smiths still monopolised Thames-side production.

By the 14th century BC, in the second stage of the Acton Park industry (MBA 1), bar stop forms of flanged axe were in use alongside the developed shield-pattern palstave (Butler 1963, 45; Schmidt & Burgess 1981, 89–90). Both forms occur occasionally in our area, but from this time

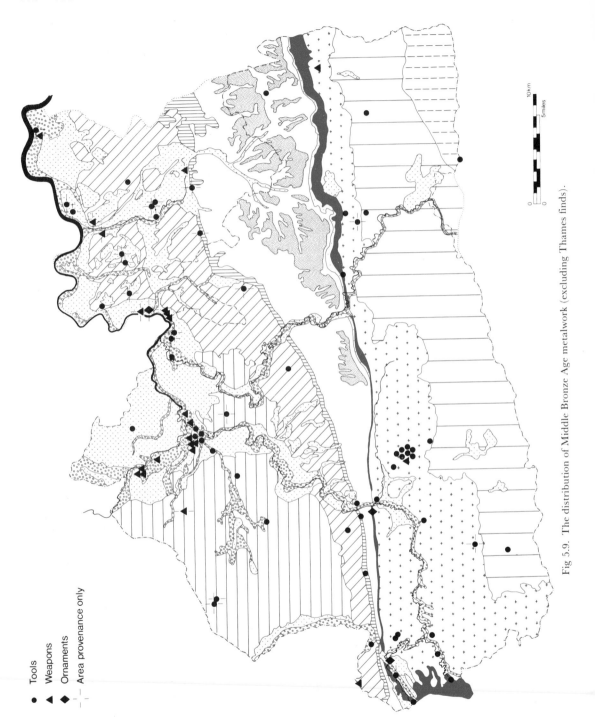

Tools

Weapons

Ornaments

Area provenance only

Fig 5.9. The distribution of Middle Bronze Age metalwork (excluding Thames finds).

onwards palstaves with midribs dominated the local series (Rowlands 1976, 30, 27, map 4). The pair of palstaves from Mitcham Junction (fig 5.10:8–9), probably a hoard, has one with midrib and the other with a more unusual shield plus long rib design. The latter is looped and the pair belong to the mature Taunton–Barton Bendish stage (MBA 2), during which the first narrow-bladed palstaves made an appearance. The county has examples of two prototypes imported from

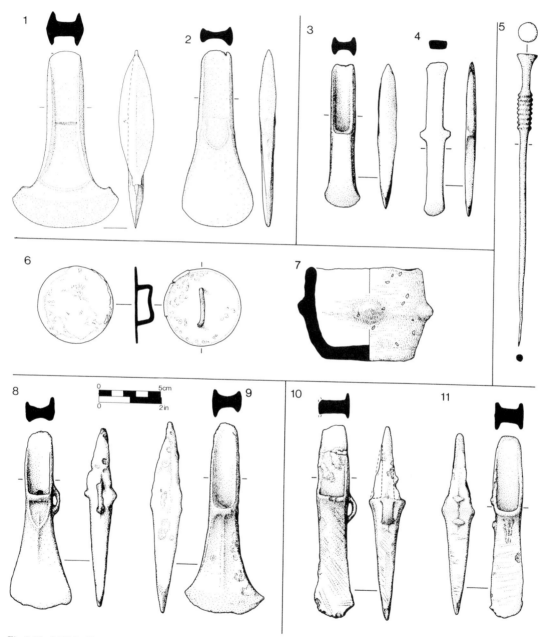

Fig 5.10. Middle Bronze Age tools and ornaments: 1, Blackheath, U-rib flanged axe; 2, Reigate, early shield-pattern palstave; 3, 4, Farley Heath, palstave-chisel and lugged chisel; 5, Thames at Kingston, multi-ribbed pin; 6, 7, Stoneyfield, stapled disc associated with accessory cup; 8, 9, Mitcham hoard, mature broad-bladed palstaves; 10, 11, near Bagshot, transitional palstaves. All 1:3

northern France, those from Weybridge and Sutton, as well as early derivatives at Winterfold and Bagshot (fig 5.10:10–11; Needham 1980a).

A more fundamental diversification in tools at this time may be seen in the addition of the socketed axe or chisel to the repertoire. The simple and lightweight Taunton–Hademarschen type seems to appear more or less simultaneously in Britain and northern Europe (Butler 1963, 74–81). Locally examples occur at Betchworth, Thames Ditton and Wimbledon. Other tool types in the Middle Bronze Age are few and miscellaneous, but include examples of the rare lugged chisel and palstave-chisel forms from Farley Heath (fig 5.10:3–4) as well as a tanged chisel from the Thames bank at Vauxhall.[18]

The bronze weapons for which the Thames is renowned begin in substantial numbers in the Middle Bronze Age. The forms are diverse and individual pieces often among the finest workmanship of the period. It is in weaponry that local metalworkers show themselves to have been most receptive to incoming novelties from the continent, in particular in the late Middle Bronze Age from c 1200 BC: swords were introduced and began to replace the traditional British stabbing weapons, the rapiers and dirks (Burgess & Gerloff 1982); the pegged form of spearhead was produced alongside the long-current looped types, although even these were modified; ferrules to furnish spear butts were used for the first time; and finally the concept of producing metal shields, for ceremony rather than practical use, was brought in.

The two earliest shields from Britain both come from the Thames valley, one of them from Hampton (Needham 1979b).[19] They can be related to the north European Nipperwiese series, but were locally manufactured implying the acquisition of new metalworking skills at this stage. These skills were developed further to produce some of the finest shields in Bronze Age Europe (Coles 1962), amongst them the lost example of Yetholm type from the Thames between Hampton and Walton.

Rosnoën swords were the initial north French response to early central European swords and are amongst the earliest types represented in Britain. The few examples mainly come from the Thames, while one comes from Limpsfield in southern Surrey (fig 5.11:4; Burgess 1968, 11, fig 7 (Lambeth); Needham 1980a, 43, fig 4). The type was superseded by leaf-bladed Ballintober weapons, which had probably appeared by about 1100 BC. These are very highly concentrated in the Thames valley, which also has a disproportionate number of early flanged hilted swords derived from the imported central European forms of Hemigkofen and Erbenheim (Brown 1982; Cowen 1951). Apart perhaps from the typologically intermediate Rosnoën swords, early swords had very different functional properties from the preceding rapiers, and they imply the acceptance of new modes of personal combat. On occasion combat may have been highly formalised or ritualised. Again the earliest ferrules, of conical form, occur locally and are exemplified by a new find from Mixnam's gravel pit (fig 5.11:6; Needham 1982, 39, fig 15). These presumably furnished the butt end of shafts carrying the modified basal-looped spearheads with triangular blades (Ehrenberg 1977, 11–12).

All the evidence points to the existence of very productive metalworking groups versed in the most advanced technological skills in the Thames-side regions. Although very rare elsewhere, three Middle Bronze Age weapons do occur in interesting locations in the heart of Surrey. The rapier and sword from Caesar's Camp, Farnham (Phillips 1967, 19),[20] and Limpsfield respectively, are from hilltop locations, while the enormous ceremonial spearhead from Wandle Park – 80cm long – must surely be a votive deposit at the head of the Wandle; it was found 9½ft deep in gravel with ox or horse bones (Anon 1899–1901, 352–3).

A few ornaments may also be referred to the Middle Bronze Age. Bignan decorated bracelets and Sussex loops with essentially south coast distributions barely affect Surrey (Rowlands 1976, maps 22, 24). The latter type occurs just to the south, at Handcross in the Weald, while decorated and plain bracelets come respectively from the Thames and the Southall hoard, Greater London (Rowlands 1976, 430, no 2010, pl 14; Britton 1960, GB 51). Pins, whether of continental inspiration as at Wandsworth and Kingston (fig 5.10:5), or of the indigenous quoit-headed form as at Hammersmith and Hounslow, are only known in the Thames-side zone (Rowlands 1976, 430, nos 2007–11; Hounslow–British Museum).

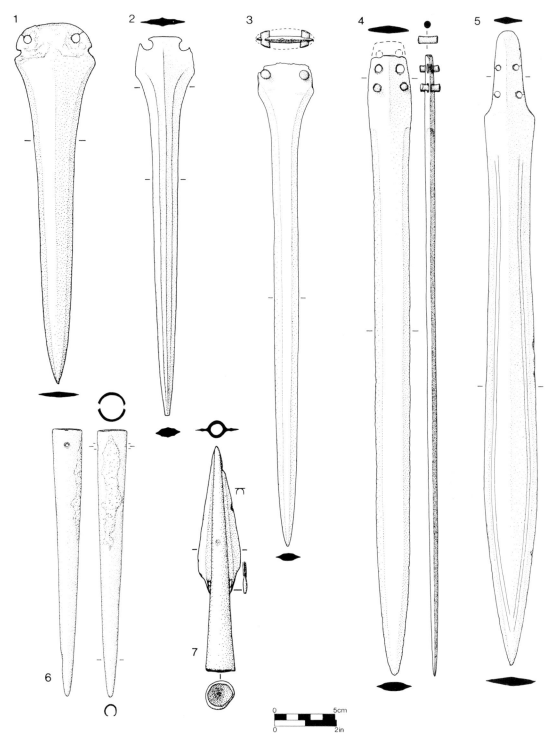

Fig 5.11. Middle Bronze Age weaponry: 1, Mixnam's pit, early dirk; 2, Caesar's Camp, Farnham, early rapier; 3, River Wey at Weybridge, late rapier; 4, Limpsfield, Rosnoën sword; 5–7, Mixnam's pit, Ballintober sword, conical ferrule and triangular basal-looped spearhead. All 1:3

These depositional patterns for Middle Bronze Age ornament types may be extended by another form, which has not generally been dated to this period. At Stoneyfield a bronze stapled disc was associated with one of the Deverel-Rimbury cups already discussed (fig 5.10:6–7). The disc has a neat openwork binding which could have clasped an ornamented organic covering (Lowther 1939, 178). The only close parallel is a stray find[21] from St Catherine's Hill, again in west Surrey (Lowther 1949b). Generalised comparisons with Late Bronze Age discs (Phillips 1967, 9) are by and large misleading.[22] On the basis of the Stoneyfield association, the Surrey discs are most likely to belong to the Middle Bronze Age rather than later. In such a context they assume some importance in representing yet another regional ornament type within the 'Ornament Horizon' (Smith 1959; Lawson 1979). If external inspiration is required for these discs, stapled forms are amply forthcoming in north European Middle Bronze Age hoards (Burgess 1976, 90, nos 22–3).

POST DEVEREL-RIMBURY SETTLEMENT: THE RUNNYMEDE–CARSHALTON GROUP 1000–700 BC

The lower Thames region has been at the forefront of the recent radical revision of Late Bronze Age and Early Iron Age ceramics. This pre-eminence is reflected in Surrey which has five key assemblages of the earliest post Deverel-Rimbury ceramics, ie 'plain-ware' assemblages (Barrett 1980b, 306). Three of these were salvaged from gravel and building works: Green Lane, Farnham (Elsdon 1982), Kingston Hill (Field & Needham 1986) and Carshalton (Adkins & Needham 1985). In contrast, recent excavations at Runnymede Bridge provide a wealth of contextual evidence (Longley 1980; Needham & Longley 1980). Weston Wood should also belong to this group of sites (Harding 1964).[23] The wide range of pottery forms, both fine and coarse wares, makes a sharp contrast with the known Middle Bronze Age assemblage, but the nature of the transition cannot yet be elucidated in any detail (fig 5.12).

Barrett recognises that the succession from Deverel-Rimbury to later complexes may have varied according to region (1980b). However, in certain zones such as the lower Thames valley he would see the early replacement of the Deverel-Rimbury by post Deverel-Rimbury elements, perhaps late in the 2nd millennium BC. Amongst this new assemblage some pot forms could be seen to be derived from Middle Bronze Age globular and bucket vessels, but there is probably also a contribution from the continental Urnfield range. In this context it is worth remembering the Urnfield pots believed to come from the Oatlands Park cemetery (Gardner 1925; Dacre & Ellison 1981, 195).[24] Their origins probably lie somewhere in the Low Countries; comparable forms may be seen for example at Temse in East Flanders (Desittere 1968, fig 93:6). Furthermore, Longley has made a number of comparisons between the Runnymede Bridge assemblage and continental pottery of Urnfield and Hallstatt date (1980, 65–74).

The new pottery forms were certainly in use in Surrey by 900 BC and external dating evidence might point to an earlier origin prior to 1000 BC (Barrett 1980b). Although in some regions Deverel-Rimbury burial practices appear to have continued well into the Late Bronze Age, no case can be made for this in Surrey where even the late-looking Kingston cremation need not be later than about 1000 BC. The Runnymede–Carshalton group of sites are spread throughout the county and we may suppose that they essentially supplanted the Deverel-Rimbury complex.

There is a comparative abundance of dating evidence for these sites, coming from metalwork associations and C14 determinations. The metalwork, securely associated only on the excavated sites, is consistently of Ewart Park types, currently dated to the 9th and 8th centuries BC. The single C14 date on grain from Weston Wood of 510±110 bc (Q-760; Harding 1964, 12), should be used with caution. Much more reliable is the coherent series of 32 dates from Runnymede Bridge which indicate an occupation span of late 9th–late 7th centuries bc (c 950–800 BC after correction). The possibility that any of these sites began earlier, during the currency of Penard metalwork (c 1200–1000 BC) has yet to be demonstrated for this region. The pottery from Green Lane appears to present a more limited and perhaps less evolved range of forms than either Runnymede or Carshalton. This difference, in conjunction with the lack of decorated sherds,[25] has led Elsdon (1982) to date the assemblage to the 11th–9th centuries BC, but in the absence of critical associations its chronological primacy should not necessarily be assumed. There could for instance have been differential development on the local as well as the regional scale with the Thames-side zone and other focal areas developing their pottery repertoires more rapidly than the hinterland of south-west Surrey.

The topographical siting of the Runnymede–Carshalton sites is a hilltop or low ridge in four of the five cases, although only at Carshalton is there evidence, in the form of a ditch and bank 150m

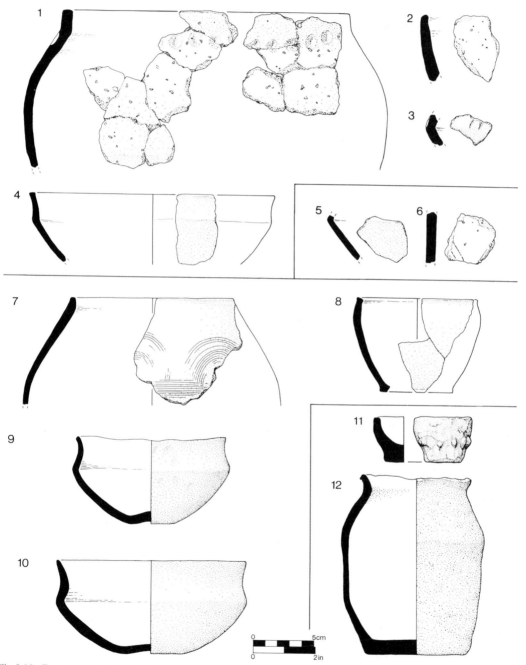

Fig 5.12. Early 1st millennium BC pottery: 1–4, Burpham; 5, 6, Green Lane, Farnham; 7, Yiewsley (Greater London); 8, Weston Wood; 9, Thames at Mortlake; 10, Leigh Hill; 11, 12, Kingston Hill. All 1:3

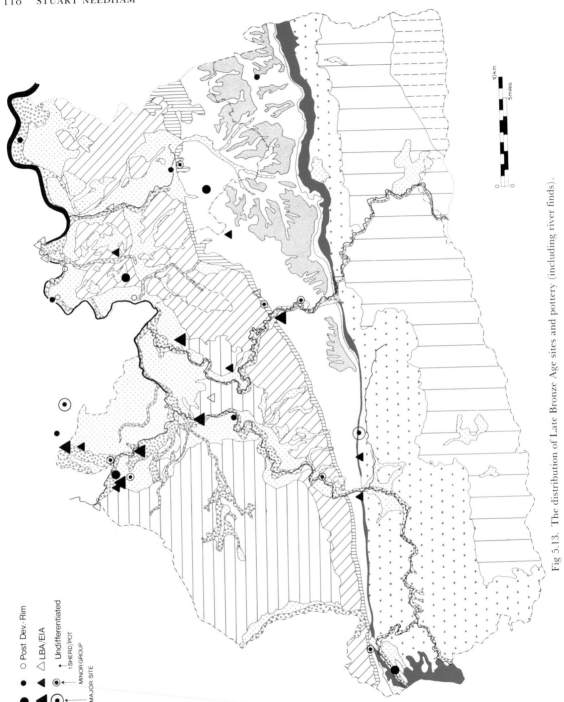

Fig 5.13. The distribution of Late Bronze Age sites and pottery (including river finds).

across, to suggest a defensive or ostentatious role (Lowther 1944–5). The big ditch at Petters Sports Field, which could have been dug during this phase, may also be part of an enclosure of unknown lay-out (O'Connell 1986).

The nearby site of Runnymede Bridge would have been defensible for very different reasons. The natural advantage of being on an island between two main streams of the Thames was enhanced by the construction of a pile-driven palisade along the ancient river bank (Needham & Longley 1980). The site of about 2ha appears to have been intensively occupied, to judge from the density of structural evidence and the amount of debris. It is probable that Runnymede and perhaps Carshalton were something more than just villages and acted as regional centres of power. The size and status of the other sites is much more difficult to gauge, although Weston Wood has been described as a 'homestead' (Harding 1964).

A rich array of artefact remains gives us some insight into the livelihood of the occupants (eg Needham & Longley 1980, 403–13): loomweights and spindlewhorls attest textile production;[26] animal bones were made into basic tools; fired clay plaques with perforations are not yet understood, but could have had some domestic function (Champion 1980, 237–8) or have controlled the draught in pottery kilns (Adkins & Needham 1985). Objects likely to have come from afar are also present, often being ornaments or trinkets: amber beads are known from Runnymede and Carshalton, while a number of shale bracelets are represented at the former site. Amongst the metalwork are continental types of razor, bracelet, pin and ring attachments, while finds of unalloyed copper and lead must have distant sources. This evidence for exchange augments that better known in the hoard and stray finds record (see below). The contemporary Thames valley hoards often include foreign objects coming either from the west of Britain or from the continent; we may note a north European socketed axe in the Kensington hoard, an Irish axe in the Beddlestead hoard, the Auvernier sword fragment in the Wickham Park hoard and various Carp's Tongue bric-à-brac in the Petters hoard.[27]

Fig 5.14.   Antler cheek pieces from Runnymede Bridge. Length of lower object: 13.9cm. (*Photograph: Victor Bowley, by kind permission of the Trustees of the British Museum*)

The abundance of metalwork and particularly of scrap for recycling, excesses from casting and unalloyed metal pieces give circumstantial evidence for well-dispersed metallurgical activity in the region. More positive evidence comes from mould finds: in bronze at Beddington and Southall, in stone at Petters and possibly Kingston Hill and finally in clay at Runnymede Bridge.[28] There is also a fragment of clay crucible from Carshalton. The survival of fragile clay mould and crucible material amidst the Runnymede occupation deposits is important in redressing the pattern of differential loss of the metalwork itself. A range of tools and weapons were cast on the site which was probably engaged in metalworking as a major specialist activity. The site was certainly well placed to control the flow of resources and finished products along the Thames and into the hinterland.

A quite different class of specialised production was also based at Runnymede. There is good evidence, in the form of trimmed antlers and a blank, for the manufacture of horse bridle equipment, in particular fine polished antler cheek pieces of two types (fig 5.14; Longley 1980, 29–30; Needham & Longley 1980, 404–7). There is therefore reason to believe that the horses present in the bone assemblage from the site were sometimes used for equitation, rather than for traction or meat (Done 1980, 79). Some horses seem to have been well cared for into old age (Geraldene Done, pers comm) and one received ritual burial in a pit.

The mainstay of the pastoral economy was undoubtedly cattle wherever pastures were lush enough. This was certainly the case in the Thames valley, since environmental evidence now points to a largely treeless landscape by the Late Bronze Age (James Greig, pers comm). Sheep and goats may have assumed more importance on the Chalk or on marginal sand environments, while greater reliance on pigs at certain sites or periods may have been governed by social as well as ecological factors (Bradley 1982, 29, 35).

Environmental evidence is beginning to yield some details of the arable economy. At Runnymede a quantity of spelt grain has been retrieved (James Greig, pers comm) and is amongst the earliest regular occurrences of spelt wheat in the country (cf Blackpatch: Hinton 1982). Meanwhile at Weston Wood the wheat in a cache of grain was very probably of the emmer variety (Harding 1964, 14). This was however outnumbered two to one by grains of barley which would probably have been more suited to the chalk and sand soils of the site's catchment area.

LATE BRONZE AGE METALWORK

The lower Thames region is very well endowed with finds of Late Bronze Age metalwork including a number of sizeable hoards (Needham & Burgess 1980, 448, fig 4, 458). These belong almost exclusively to the Ewart Park phase; the earlier Wilburton type hoards, belonging to the 10th century BC, are barely known in the region. One exception, a recent find from the foreshore at Syon Reach (fig 5.15:2–18), fits in with the overwhelming Thames bias of distinctive Wilburton types (Needham & Burgess 1980, 443–5). Otherwise only the pair of spearheads from Colt Hill, Seale (fig 5.17:4–5; Lowther 1939, 163, no 2), might possibly be referred to this complex.

The glut of Late Bronze Age hoards may be readily divided into two groups with important regional implications (fig 5.18). The difference between the two groups lies partly in the range of object types encountered, but more importantly in the overall size of hoards and the condition of the implements contained. The dominant group is that of hoards usually thought of as founders' deposits. They are well known for the scrap condition of implements, the frequent inclusion of copper ingot and the more sporadic presence of casting jets, other waste and mould fragments. They are further characterised by the frequent inclusion of metalwork types belonging to the Carp's Tongue complex: especially Carp's Tongue swords, end-winged axes, bugle-shaped fittings and other trappings (Burgess 1968, 38–9).

In Surrey these founders' hoards occur in three geographical units: Thames-side districts, the eastern North Downs and central-southern Surrey. An important feature of these zones was the acquisition of foreign implements and scrap. Analysis of the large Petters hoard has allowed some reconstruction of the mechanics of metal circulation. In this case trace elements suggest that local smiths were recycling a stock of scrap metal which had north French origins. The impurity suite of

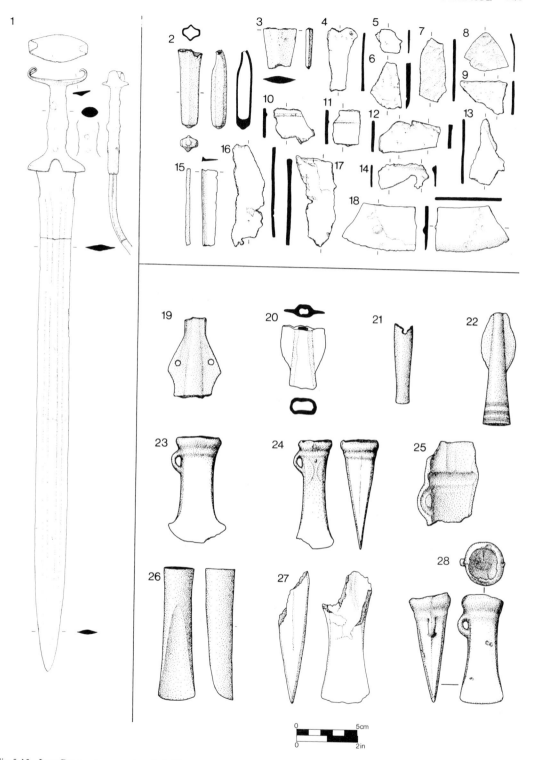

Fig 5.15. Late Bronze Age metalwork: 1, Chertsey area, Möringen type sword; 2–18, Syon Reach hoard (Greater London); 19–28, Beddington Park hoard (19, 21–26 after Flower 1874c; 20, 27 after NBI). No 1 at 1:4, nos 2–28 at 1:3

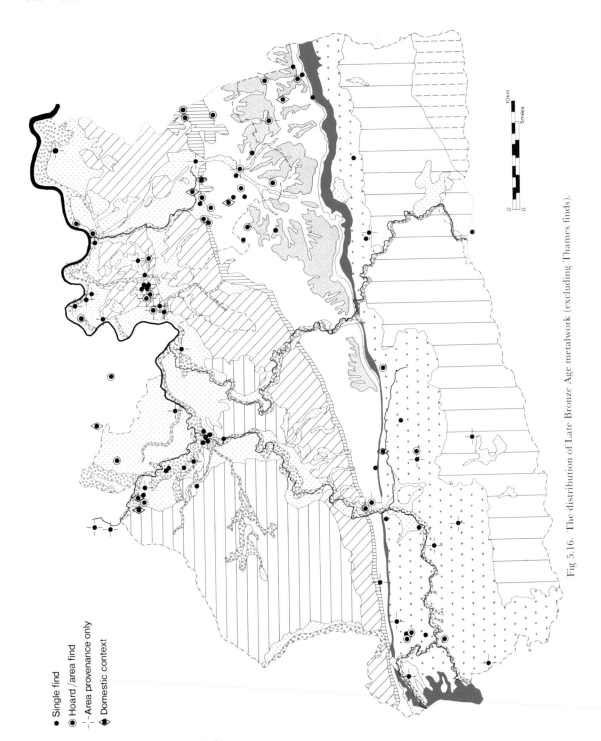

Fig 5.16. The distribution of Late Bronze Age metalwork (excluding Thames finds).

● Single find
◉ Hoard / area find
-·- Area provenance only
◆ Domestic context

the stock was however progressively altered in recycling by the addition of different, minor metal types possibly from another source area (Needham 1986).

The numerous continental pieces from the Thames may be illustrated by a newly found example from the Chertsey area, a fine solid-hilted sword of Möringen type (fig 5.15:1; Müller-Karpe 1961, 73–8) dating to Hallstatt B3, c 8th century BC.[29] A more surprising aspect of the Thames valley metalwork, is that an alien industry stemming from Wessex or beyond was apparently allowed to practise in the Egham locality alongside native smiths (Needham 1981, 52). The tradition in question produced Stogursey type socketed axes, scrapped examples of which found their way into hoards located still further east.

The picture in south-west Surrey, the zone of the second hoard group, is very different; hoards are small with two to five objects which are either axes or spearheads. These objects are usually complete so that they give the impression of being personal tool-kits or armouries, unconnected to metalworking (figs 5.17, 5.18). This evidence should not be seen to exclude the possibility of metalworking in the south-west; rather it betrays different basic customs of deposition as well as different economic conditions. In part the south-west group can be linked to the curious Broadward phenomenon, represented across the border in Hampshire, in which large accumulations of spearheads were deposited in wet environments probably as part of a ritual act (Burgess et al 1972).

THE METALLURGICAL TRANSITION: 700–600 BC

Knowledge of iron, and even of ironworking technology, was probably current in Europe long before the switch in metals took place. The replacement of bronze with iron for tools and weapons may have been due to political factors as much as economic or technological ones (eg Champion 1975, 140–2). The transition was under way by the 7th century BC in Britain as attested by mixed iron/bronze finds of Llyn Fawr metalwork, equivalent to Hallstatt C in Europe. The continuing strength of the bronze industry in this phase may be an illusion due to the difficulties of recognising specifically early ironwork when unassociated (Burgess 1979, 273). Comprehension of this transitional phase is also complicated by the possibility of overlap between the Llyn Fawr and pre-existing Ewart Park industries.

The Surrey bronzes of characteristic Llyn Fawr material (Burgess 1968, 42–4) are mainly axes and swords, plus a few miscellaneous tools: sickles, chisels and razors. Their distribution is heavily biased towards the Thames, with only rare finds away from the river: a socketed axe from St Catherine's Hill (Phillips 1967, 13, 24, fig 6:4) and a Hallstatt C sword from Charlwood (Lowther 1957). The only local association is the probable hoard of four Sompting type socketed axes from Kingston (Evans 1881, 126, fig 142).[30] There is no cultural association for the metalwork, as yet, but a tentative correlation may be advanced on the basis of external sites and ceramic sequences. The assemblage from Petters is best viewed as belonging to this stage. The major group of pottery was stratified above a Ewart Park hoard (O'Connell & Needham 1977); it is more advanced than that from the classic Late Bronze Age sites described above and it is directly associated with five C14 dates which give a corrected date range centred on the 7th–6th centuries BC (O'Connell 1986).

Other important assemblages of this type are those from Heathrow Runway 1 extension, Mixnam's Farm, Brooklands old land surface, Caesar's Camp, Wimbledon, Hawk's Hill and St Catherine's Hill.[31] The relevant pottery, characterised above all by strong shoulders, marked carinations and plentiful use of finger-tipping, probably continued well into the Iron Age and beyond the scope of this chapter.

The Caesar's Camp pottery group should, from its stratigraphical position, post-date the rampart construction but not necessarily by long (Lowther 1945a), which would seem to place this hillfort in the transitional phase. St George's Hill has yielded Early Iron Age pottery (Lowther 1949c) and St Ann's Hill a Late Bronze Age spearhead (Chertsey Museum). These medium-sized univallate hillforts[32] overlooking the Thames terraces might perhaps be seen as the successors to the round enclosure form seen at Queen Mary's Hospital, Carshalton, which is firmly dated to the

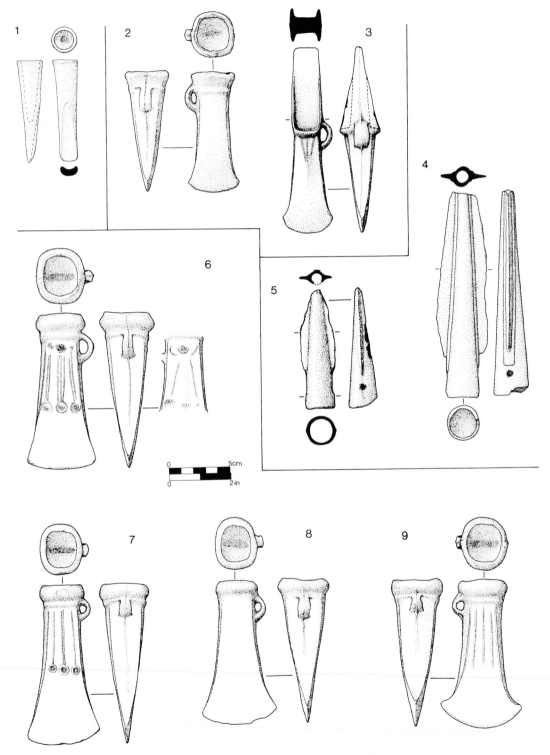

Fig 5.17. Late Bronze Age metalwork: 1, Godalming, socketed gouge; 2, 3, Stoke Hospital, socketed axe and palstave; 4, 5, Colt Hill spearheads; 6–9, Kingston, Sompting type socketed axes. All 1:3

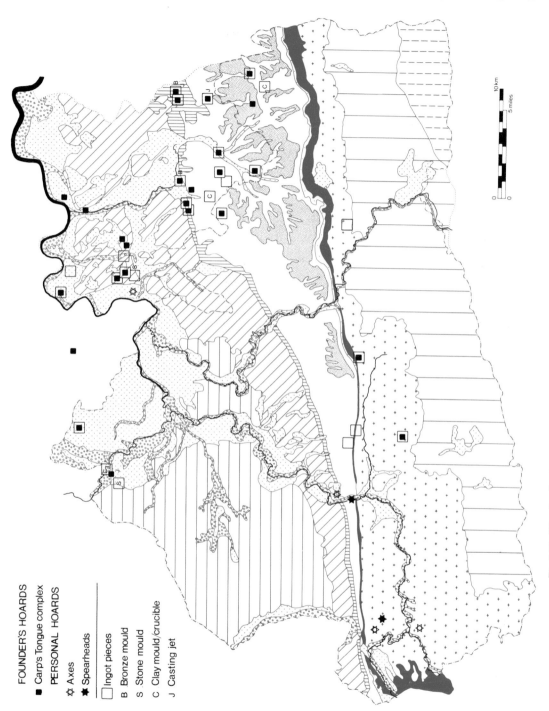

FOUNDER'S HOARDS
■ Carp's Tongue complex
PERSONAL HOARDS
☆ Axes
★ Spearheads
☐ Ingot pieces
B Bronze mould
S Stone mould
C Clay mould/crucible
J Casting jet

Fig 5.18. The distribution of Late Bronze Age hoards and metalworking evidence.

Late Bronze Age. Caesar's Camp, Easthampstead, Berkshire, has a similar topographical siting but is further back from the Thames itself. Again the only indication of its date, a haematite coated sherd (Frere 1942, 131), might point to Late Bronze Age/Early Iron Age use. The expansion of the hillfort system in the Thames valley suggests that momentous changes were taking place in social organisation as the use of bronze gave way to the use of iron. The traditional model which would have sizeable incursions from the continent at the beginning of the Iron Age is however difficult to sustain (Burgess 1979, 274–5; Champion 1975) and the changes may best be viewed as part of a widespread pattern of social upheaval and continuing technological advance amongst prehistoric European societies.

Developments in settlement patterns in physiographic zones

THE WEALD

This zone, embracing both the Wealden Clay vale and the High Weald with its variegated subsoil, is conveniently treated as a unit for the Bronze Age. It forms the southern strip of the county and spreads more extensively into Sussex and Kent. Bronze Age finds are limited but not unimportant, this poor record perhaps due in part to lack of agricultural and urban disturbance as well as little fieldwork.

The most consistent evidence for utilisation is early in the Bronze Age and is probably a continuation of Late Neolithic exploitation. The ecological effects of this phase have only recently been recognised through palynological and lithological work at Sharpsbridge in the Sussex Weald (Scaife & Burrin 1983). This offers for the first time a context for stray finds, burials and barrows. The best dated evidence is the metalwork which comprises five flat axes of copper and early bronze types from the Weald as a whole.[33] This is a good density for early metalwork comparing favourably with many regions of Britain. The date range for these axes would be c 2400–1800 BC and may represent the same period of activity as Scaife & Burrin's zone 2 of alluvial deposition, probably caused by clearance for agriculture leading to soil movement on slopes (1983, 5–7).

A small number of barrows which have been located in the Sussex Weald might well relate to this agricultural phase (eg Tebbutt 1974, 42); Money Mound for instance has been excavated and probably had origins in the Beaker period (Beckensall 1967). A similar date is likely for the 'Goldhorde' barrow opened at Chiddingfold by Douglas (1793, 162) which is sited on an isolated patch of gravel amidst Wealden Clay beds. A comparable siting probably applied to a 'British sepulchral urn' and 'flint arrowheads' found in 1839–40 to the south of Horley station, but their character is not known and Roman coins are also mentioned (Malden 1911, 200). A small assemblage of Bronze Age flintwork is known from Millfields Farm, Rowhook, Sussex, this time on a patch of sand amidst Wealden Clay (Julie Gardiner, pers comm). A number of single flints of Bronze Age type – plano-convex knives and daggers – concentrate in the Horsham–Crawley part of the Weald and succeed substantial scatters of Late Neolithic flintwork with plenty of scrapers and knives which occupy positions around the edge of the Tunbridge Wells sands (Gardiner 1984).

The Wealden area has also yielded a scatter of Middle Bronze Age bronzes suggesting continued activity. These are mainly from Sussex (Ellison 1978, 31, fig 14) with occasional additions in Kent (Champion 1980, 228, fig 1) and Surrey.[34] Late Bronze Age metalwork is sparser, but includes a fine Hallstatt C sword from Charlwood (Lowther 1957). This is noteworthy as one of few such pieces having been found away from coastal parts of Britain, the Thames and other major rivers (Cowen 1967). In keeping with this pattern however it was dredged from the Polesfleet Brook close to its confluence with the River Mole. These swords, the last to be made in bronze, belong to the 7th century BC which is the transitional phase to a full iron technology. It may therefore be pertinent that this exceptionally fine piece should have come from deep within the Weald, perhaps heralding the renewed interest in the resources of the zone, and particularly iron ore, which Hanworth recognises in the full Iron Age (this volume).

There are now indications that the Weald was not necessarily the uninhabited forest that has been envisaged for later prehistory (Tebbutt 1974). It is most interesting that prior to the Iron Age the greatest utilisation seems to fall in the Late Neolithic and Earlier Bronze Age, a phenomenon that requires consideration. Initial settlement on any tangible scale might have followed a widely observed pattern with the intake of more marginal environments springing from primary and fertile areas of Neolithic colonisation (Bradley 1978b). This generally took place in or around the Early Bronze Age. Patches of the High Weald would have offered rich soils once cleared of primary forest, and a pattern of gradual piecemeal assarting could well have built up to a moderate population density. As the Bronze Age wore on, however, a combination of localised soil exhaustion, relative isolation and an incapacity for economic growth might have stagnated the Weald while other environments saw a steady increase in population and resource control. Clearance for agriculture in the initial phase was doubtless somewhat patchy with some areas retaining their forest cover until late in prehistory, as perhaps around High Rocks in Kent (Dimbleby 1968).

THE GREENSAND HILLS

The backbone of this zone is the Lower Greensand formation which rises to a high ridge in the south overlooking the Weald. The zone is infiltrated by river terrace deposits including most of the upper Wey system as well as some flanking the Mole. Although much of the Greensand is base-poor giving rise to acidic soils, there are extensive tracts of more fertile loamy beds (Folkestone series) to augment the agricultural potential of the area. This hilly formation is most important in the west of the county where the ridge broadens considerably. It has always attracted fieldworkers, perhaps because of the ease with which intrusive flints may be recognised against the sandy soils, and this has undoubtedly weighted flint distributions.

Settlement may be inferred throughout the Bronze Age, following on from the Neolithic, although actual settlement sites are elusive prior to the Late Bronze Age. Early Bronze Age activity is indicated by pottery, flint and metalwork finds and by barrows, proven and convincing examples of which generally lie on the lower parts of the zone, though sometimes on low eminences. A fine ditched bowl barrow was discovered only recently on a promontory at Culverswell Hill[35] less than a kilometre from the long-known triple bell barrow on Crooksbury Common.

The only barrow in the zone to have been excavated in modern times is that at Deerleap Wood (Corcoran 1963). Unfortunately the opportunity was not taken to examine the environmental evidence from the buried soil (see Hanworth 1978, 61). More recent work on a barrow cemetery at West Heath, on the Greensand just to the south of Surrey, has given a picture of partial clearance very early in the Bronze Age, with grasses predominating over heather in the cleared areas (Baigent 1976). By the end of the Early Bronze Age however (C14 date of 1160±160 bc) the emphasis had changed with heather becoming more widespread and indicating deteriorating soil conditions. There may also have been some localised woodland regeneration during the intervening period. Evidence for agriculture was very sparse indeed.

Continuity of settlement through the Middle and Late Bronze Ages is suggested by pottery and a good scatter of bronze finds datable to different phases. In the Middle Bronze Age most of the bronzes are tools with just one sword from Limpsfield and two disc ornaments of local type (see above). Some of the contemporary Deverel-Rimbury pottery was associated with burials, of particular note being the cemetery or cemeteries at Stoneyfield–Snailslynch on the Shortheath Ridge which seem to have been extensive. The only indication of a settlement site of this date comes again from the Shortheath Ridge, further west at Pattersons gravel pit, where features containing Deverel-Rimbury pottery, pot-boilers and quern stones are seen as domestic (Lowther 1939, 180–3).

The more substantial group of domestic material from nearby on the ridge at Green Lane (Elsdon 1982) probably follows on directly from the Deverel-Rimbury occupation, although not necessarily without some dislocation in settlement. The shape of the settlement at Green Lane is sadly unknown, the finds having been effectively salvaged piecemeal from the quarry pit (Lowther 1939, 183–94).

Another noteworthy concentration of material comes from the Blackheath–Farley Heath district. A number of bronzes here mainly belong early in the Middle Bronze Age (1500–1300 BC) and could tie in with the two biconical urn burials from the Hallams. These finds might relate to a phase of cultivation on those heaths prior to their degradation. They are followed by a group of sites sharing a similar distributional focus in the Late Bronze Age and Early Iron Age. This includes metalwork finds again, but more importantly domestic material from three sites. Only at Weston Wood has a settlement plan, in the form of post-ring huts, trackways, working hollows, etc, been recovered (Harding 1964). The sequence on this site has yet to be elucidated, but provisional assessment of the pottery hints at early Late Bronze Age beginnings and possibly a substantial duration. The arable hinterland of this settlement situated on a low ridge of Greensand is varied. The richest deposits within easy reach would be the strip of alluvium of the Tillingbourne valley to the south and the narrow Gault Clay vale probably capped by hill-wash from the Chalk scarp to the north.

Smaller groups of pottery of Late Bronze Age or transitional Late Bronze/Early Iron Age date with other domestic trappings such as loomweights come from St Catherine's Hill and St Martha's Hill (Bishop 1971, 22, 25). These locations together with Weston Wood might suggest the regular siting of settlements on Greensand hilltops at this time. At St Catherine's the transitional looking pottery might well be contemporary with a Sompting type bronze axe found close by and datable to the 7th century BC (Phillips 1967, 13, 24, fig 6:4).

The metalwork of the Late Bronze Age in the Greensand hills zone points to the possibility of a social or economic territorial division. In the central area between the Wey and Mole valleys, two known hoards have Carp's Tongue affiliations, which may be linked most obviously to the Carp's Tongue zone of the Croydon area (see above). Furthermore, finds of copper cake outside the two hoards, from Weston Wood, Albury Down and Reigate[36] add weight to this connection. From the Guildford gap westwards, however, there is no evidence of such access to fresh metal resources, and bronze hoards have a distinct character related perhaps to those of eastern Wessex (discussed above). Hoards and single finds bear witness less to the actual practice of metalworking and more to the display of personal equipment. Besides the small axe and spearhead hoards described above there are other types as stray finds: a socketed knife and a socketed gouge.[37] One noteworthy focus of metalwork occurs in the Crooksbury–Tilford district. The small nearby enclosures, the Soldier's Ring and Botany Hill (Bishop 1971, 22), might be mentioned in this connection, although their date is so uncertain as to allow suggestions of their comparatively modern origin (Hanworth 1976). The report of considerable numbers of calcined flint pot-boilers inside the Botany Hill enclosure (Surrey County Council Sites & Monuments Record), however, recalls prehistoric burnt mounds and similar concentrations in occupation deposits as at Runnymede Bridge.

THE NORTH DOWNS

The chalk ridge of the North Downs which splits the county from east to west is capped by deposits of Clay-with-flints or Netley Heath Sands along much of its length. The gentle north-facing dip slope would have been the most important for settlement, much of it being free of superficial deposits. Along the northern foot is a spring-line and overlying Tertiary sands and gravels, which are treated as part of the North Downs zone here. To the west of the Guildford gap the Chalk becomes a very narrow ridge, the Hog's Back, which would have been rather insignificant for settlement.

Although the zone has produced a scatter of Early and Middle Bronze Age material, including pottery, metalwork and flintwork, there is little indication of the intensive occupation of the Chalk which is such a well-known feature of Wessex and Sussex. Above all, this lack of activity seems to be reflected in the small number of barrows recorded, some of which are in fact demonstrably much later in date. Barrows at Banstead, Merrow Downs and Farthing Down have all yielded Saxon burials (Barfoot & Price-Williams 1976; Saunders 1980; Morris 1959, 136–7). Against those finds may be set very sparse and inconclusive evidence for Bronze Age interment.

The earliest substantial settlement on the Downs for which we have evidence dates to the Late Bronze Age. This is preceded by some Deverel-Rimbury occupation in the area as indicated by domestic material at Ewell, on the Chalk, and Hayes, on Tertiary sands (F Pemberton, unpublished; Philp 1973, 30–52), as well as funerary urns at Chaldon (Russell 1982).

At Hayes, a short distance into Kent, pottery, flints and loomweights were associated with post holes and ditches, although no coherent settlement plan was recovered. The date of the field-system around the site is uncertain; Philp has argued that it was relatively modern and quite unrelated to the Bronze Age occupation (1973, 37–8). It had been observed earlier that the fields were rather larger than the norm for Celtic fields (Hogg *et al* 1941, 29). Nearby at Caesar's Camp, Keston, the buried soil under the period I rampart yielded pollen indicating a heavy oak forest cover with only limited clearances at most (Fox 1970). This evidence is thought to relate to the Early or Middle Iron Age, but excavations have been limited.

Back inside the county borders there is a recorded field-system of 'Celtic' type on Farthing Down on the eastern Downs (Hope-Taylor 1946–7). Hope-Taylor realised that the superimposed barrows of the Saxon period need have no bearing on the date of the field-system which could, on analogy with other regions of Britain, easily belong to the Bronze Age (*vide* Bowen & Fowler 1978).

The evidence for increased activity on this part of the Downs in the Late Bronze Age comes mainly from the markedly intensified density of metalwork finds. This might be largely a function of a new control over external supplies of metal and need not necessarily imply any notable expansion of population. It might for example reflect changed social organisation. This idea draws some support from the most important Late Bronze Age settlement known in the region, that of Queen Mary's Hospital, Carshalton (Lowther 1944–5; Adkins & Needham 1985). Here a circular enclosure of about 150m diameter was dug on an eminence on the dip slope placed centrally within the western part of the Croydon zone. The site could be regarded as a 'central-place' as far as the contemporary metalwork distribution is concerned (Needham & Burgess 1980, 450, fig 5) and a neat ecological unit is circumscribed by these finds. The enclosure is envisaged as a regional centre of power; clearly there was a greater than usual investment of labour in its construction. We should not exclude the possibility of one or more other regional centres within the Croydon zone, particularly in the east where more metalwork has been found recently (Adkins & Needham 1985). Indeed it has recently been discovered that the site of some of these finds, Nore Hill, is occupied by a promontory enclosure, again of about 150m diameter. A trial trench across the bank and ditch cutting off the promontory, has produced some finds which point to a Late Bronze Age date for the enclosure (Skelton forthcoming).

In addition to these two enclosures, Late Bronze Age settlement is attested at two sites to the north in Beddington and possibly another at Bunker's Field, Wallington (Adkins 1984). For none of these do we know anything of the nature of settlement. At Aldwick Road the material of this phase is little and scrappy (Row 1926; Gallant 1966). At the Beddington Sewage Works, Late Bronze Age settlement deposits have evidently been disturbed by a Roman villa complex since most of the relevant diagnostic pieces of pottery, metalwork and perforated clay slabs come from secondary contexts (Adkins & Adkins 1983b and pers comm). Renewed excavations on this site promise to put this material into better context.

To the west of the Croydon zone, from Tadworth to the Guildford gap, the poverty of material on the Downs might suggest a different history of utilisation. Casual finds may be somewhat diminished due to less ground disturbance in recent times, for much of this stretch is covered in woodland. Even after the long field activity of Lowther in part of this area, however, there is no positive settlement evidence prior to the Late Bronze/Early Iron Age transition. At this stage we find settlement evidence for the first time around the Mole gap with sites at Hawk's Hill, Fetcham (Hastings 1965), Ashtead Park Lane (Lowther 1946–7c) and Ashtead Quarry (Lowther 1933). The latter site yielded a small pit group of pottery probably dating earlier than the other two sites, which continue well into the Middle Iron Age. The laying out of the Mickleham field-system has yet to be dated, but sparse pottery finds hint at its use at about this time as well as later (Frere & Hogg 1944–5).

There are indications that earlier settlement will be found, though perhaps thinly spread. A bucket urn find from West Humble although presumed to be funerary may nevertheless lie in proximity to a settlement (Lowther 1939, 180). Downland enclosed settlements well known elsewhere on the Chalk (eg South Lodge, Dorset – Barrett *et al* 1983; Sussex – Ellison 1978, 36), could conceivably be represented at Headley Heath. A site now under plantation was evidently an enclosure; excavation of the ditch in 1907 yielded 'fragments of handmade pottery, with bones of many different animals and one worked flint. At a higher level was found the broken point of a bronze weapon.' Glazed pottery and hearths are described as having been found nearby, but not in the ditch (Malden 1911, 290).

THE LONDON CLAY BELT

The heavy London Clay subsoil runs in an east-west belt to the north of the North Downs and is interrupted only by the alluvial deposits of the Wey, Mole and Wandle valleys. This zone is traditionally thought to have been poorly settled in prehistory, if settled at all. Certainly this view is borne out by the sparseness of casual finds. Occasional bronzes on the Clay itself are single axe finds at Broad Street Common (near Guildford), Bookham Common and Streatham Common (National Bronze Index). All three appear to be Middle Bronze Age axes, in the former two cases blade fragments only. They might represent nothing more than casual losses during forestry operations.

Interestingly the intervening gravel and alluvium tracts reveal only a little evidence for use, despite the ease with which they may be tilled. Patchy settlement could be due to the unproductive hinterland, the river terraces being hemmed in by clay lands. The few relevant finds are treated below with the Thames valley settlement pattern.

THE BAGSHOT TABLE AND THE RICHMOND–WIMBLEDON HEIGHTS

The sands of the Bagshot Series capped with Plateau Gravels and the similar Plateau Gravels further east at Richmond and Wimbledon may be conveniently treated together: they give rise to low hilly terrain supporting base-poor and usually highly acidic soils. The zone is dissected in Surrey by the major north–south rivers, the Wey and Mole. In the north-west of the county the extensive block of the Bagshot Table spreads into Hampshire and Berkshire, split only by the Blackwater valley which forms part of the Surrey border. Minor valleys also penetrate the Table.

Across the zone finds of Early–Middle Bronze Age date are relatively well represented including a dozen bronzes and five sites with pottery which are mainly of a funerary character. The metalwork, with one exception, all belongs to the period 1600–1000 BC (late Early Bronze and Middle Bronze Age), which correlates well with the pottery which is Deverel-Rimbury with occasional collared urns. To these artefacts may be added a number of barrows which should be broadly contemporary; indeed those at Sunningdale, Whitmoor and Silvermere have yielded pottery, while the Horsell and West End, Chobham, groups have appropriate Early Bronze Age features. Although much of this evidence (the barrows and pottery finds) relates to funerary practices, it is quite unlikely that the zone served solely as a burial ground; a case can now be made for the intake of land as part of a settled agricultural regime.

The primary evidence comes from the pollen analysis of buried soil profiles beneath barrows at Ascot, Berkshire (Bradley & Keith-Lucas 1975), and West End Common, Chobham (Brenda Ware, pers comm). At both sites the barrows had been built in long-standing clearings where deforestation and soil impoverishment had led ultimately to podzolisation and the spread of heathland. At West End Common this sequence had begun with partial forest clearance, which particularly affected alder, with the subsequent establishment of hazel scrub, in turn gradually replaced by a heath cover. This progression, which was almost certainly begun well before the Early Bronze Age, refers only to the immediate environment, while a surrounding backdrop of forest continued unchanged, as indeed at Ascot. Only towards the top of the buried soil profiles at both sites is there any evidence for local cultivation. At Ascot both cereal pollen and weeds of cultivation appear. Renewed onslaught on the nearby forest attested at the same horizon suggests the cultivation of the underlying brown earth soils, as yet undegraded, but spade furrows preserved beneath the barrow mound itself could point to the sowing of already impoverished areas as well. The barrow was built before pollen-rain witnessed any woodland regeneration of the new forest clearings and therefore perhaps before podzolisation made those areas unproductive. A radiocarbon date of 1480±70 bc (c 1800 BC) was obtained on charcoal from the buried soil (HAR 478).

At West End Common there may have been a slightly longer interval between arable cultivation and barrow construction, for woodland and hazel resurgence appears at the top of the buried humus containing weeds of cultivation. Again cultivation is likely to have been concentrated in newly cleared areas rather than on the site itself, but in the absence of excavation this cannot be demonstrated either way. Less than a kilometre north of the West End Common barrows lies the valley of the Windle Brook with more fertile alluvial soil. Other barrows lie just to the north of the Windle Brook at Flutters Hill and Barrowhills, while Deverel-Rimbury pottery was found at Chobham Park Farm in the valley bottom (Gardner 1924, 16–17).

The valleys which penetrate the Bagshot Table would almost certainly have been the main axes of settlement as well as the springboards for colonisation of the more marginal land. This may also be seen in the Blackwater valley where a Deverel-Rimbury complex containing both settlement and cemetery is recorded at Yateley, in Hampshire (Barrett 1973, 125, 127). Nearby on Hornley Common lies a bell barrow, one of six barrows flanking the valley (Copsey 1963–4, 21, fig 1).

In addition to domestic Deverel-Rimbury material and the pollen evidence discussed above, other possible evidence for agriculture on the Bagshot Sands during the earlier part of the Bronze Age comes in the form of relict field systems. No systematic fieldwork has been done in the area, but one extensive field system is known to spread across Whitmoor Common where it is geographically associated with the two barrows excavated by Pitt-Rivers (Gardner 1924, 27–9). This association suggests, in the absence of independent evidence, a Bronze Age date. The major boundaries on Whitmoor Common run back perpendicularly from a small stream, up a gentle gradient to a low ridge. A series of transverse banks form some small plots, while larger areas devoid of sub-divisions tend to be higher on the slope, as are the two barrows. Fragments of other field boundary systems have been observed on other heaths, namely Smarts Heath and Horsell Common, near Woking (fieldwork by the author).

The evidence for the high ground of the Bagshot Table, the Chobham Ridges, contrasts with this picture for the lower ground in which an arable landscape was centred on the valley bottoms and the barrows were sited on flanking eminences. The dominance of infertile plateau gravels and shortage of fresh water may always have left the high ground non-conducive to agriculture except perhaps for rough grazing. A small enclosure in Albury Bottom lies beneath such terrain on Chobham Common and could conceivably represent some form of seasonally used pound for stock rather than a settlement, although there is absolutely no dating evidence for it at present. Obviously hunting could have been a major attraction on the uncultivated parts of the Bagshot Table. This might put into context the rare Early Bronze Age spearheads from Curley Hill, Lightwater (Needham 1979a), and the Middle Bronze Age side-looped spearhead from Barrowhills, Chertsey (Phillips 1967, 24, fig 6:5).

Casual finds suggest that by the Late Bronze Age settlement on the Bagshot Table had gone into severe decline, perhaps almost to the point of abandonment. The only index of this trend at present is the frequency of metalwork, since settlement scatters have yet to be discovered and the burial evidence disappears with the demise of the Deverel-Rimbury complex. However, the change seems marked; while in general the lower Thames valley experiences a glut of bronze in the Late Bronze Age, finds from the Bagshot Sands dwindle to one in Surrey plus occasional pieces outside such as a late palstave from Crowthorne, Berkshire (Reading Museum).

It may be no coincidence that the Surrey find, a peg-hole spearhead, comes from the edge of the zone at St Ann's Hill, which is occupied by a univallate hillfort. While the Bagshot Table can boast four hillforts, which should belong somewhere in the 1st millennium BC, their peripheral distribution is striking. In two cases, at St Ann's Hill and St George's Hill, the builders appear to have taken advantage of the fringe hills in order to gain commanding views over the well populated valleys of the Thames and Wey. These are part of a more extensive system including Caesar's Camp, Wimbledon, again on marginal ground, and further east the South and North Rings at

Mucking which overlook the estuary (Needham & Longley 1980, 415, fig 7). Back in Surrey, this pattern may also be followed by the Sandown Park settlement sited on the edge of Bagshot Sands overlooking the Thames (Burchell & Frere 1947). Its pottery dates the site to the transitional Late Bronze/Early Iron Age period. Caesar's Camp, Easthampstead (Berkshire), and Caesar's Camp, Farnham, lie on the northern and southern edges of the Bagshot Table respectively, but in neither case do they control particularly productive soils unless we are to think in terms of tilling of the London Clay.

None of these hillforts is dated, except in the vaguest manner by casual finds. Recent excavations across the defences at Caesar's Camp, Farnham, have however indicated a constructional sequence comprising four phases (Riall 1983). At least three of these are likely to be prehistoric and begin with two palisade phases, each followed by soil formation and potentially thus a significant interval of time. The third phase saw the emplacement of a multiple dump rampart thought to be of Later Iron Age date. Bearing in mind the use of timber framing and/or palisading at sites like Ram's Hill, Berkshire, at around the end of the 2nd millennium bc (Bradley & Ellison 1975, 29–37), the dating of the earliest phase at Farnham is wide open.

The Wimbledon heights have already been introduced in connection with the Thames valley chain of hillforts, but deserve special mention since Late Bronze Age activity is strongly attested in complete contrast to the Bagshot Table situation. This may well be due to the strategic position of the hills which command the reaches of the Thames most prolific in Late Bronze Age metalwork. Most material evidence comes from Kingston Hill and includes a good group of Late Bronze Age pottery, loomweights, bronzes and other domestic evidence (Field & Needham 1986). From the typology of these artefacts it is likely that settlement began early in the 1st millennium and there is no sign of continuation beyond the 8th century BC. On the other hand the small pottery group from the Wimbledon Common hillfort of Caesar's Camp belongs to the transitional tradition (7th–5th centuries BC) and might imply a shift of the main focus in this area. However, the pottery comes from a pit thought to be contemporary with an occupation soil which seals the rear of the rampart (Lowther 1945a, 17), which would allow rampart construction to be somewhat earlier.

THE THAMES VALLEY AND ITS TRIBUTARIES

The terraced margins of the River Thames system, including in Surrey the lower parts of the Wey, Mole and Wandle, present fertile soils which were a major focus of agricultural settlement from at least the Middle Neolithic. The terraces are easily tilled gravels or clay-loam 'brickearths' and they bound a floodplain of varied alluvial deposits. They follow the major tributaries to the south intersecting the previous two environmental zones dealt with (Bagshot Series and London Clay). On the north bank of the Thames, within the large loop between Staines and Brentford, lies an extensive tract of these fluvial deposits, in fact mainly brickearth.

This zone is by far the richest in terms of the yield of archaeological information, even if the countless river finds are discounted. This is due as much to the attention of excavators in recent years as to the high rate of casual discoveries in gravel exploitation, urban expansion and general redevelopment. Despite this, however, there is for the Early Bronze Age something of an imbalance between stray artefact finds and settlement or burial evidence. Most of the metalwork and other prestige goods comes from the River Thames itself, but a few findspots lie back on the terraces.

Two recent discoveries may point the way to locating contemporary settlement. At both Thorney Island (Westminster, Cromwell Green) and Southwark excavations have revealed beaker pottery and associated flintwork sealed beneath alluvial deposits. At Thorney Island only two sherds were found, but they came from a gully feature[38] (Feature 82 – Mills 1980, 20, fig 2). These finds and others of beaker pottery, such as that from Chiswick Eyot (P Philo, pers comm), obviously lie alongside river channels and presumably represent a continuation of the similar pattern seen in Neolithic pottery finds.

The evidence for Early Bronze Age burial in the Thames valley is even more tenuous than that for settlement when it is considered that burial sites are generally conspicuous. The dearth of barrows or their ploughed-out counterparts, ring ditches, deserves careful examination in this zone, which is likely to have been well populated. Explanation may well be two-fold according to the differential histories of the floodplain and the terraces. The terraces have undoubtedly suffered from a long history of arable exploitation which has probably destroyed barrows in antiquity. One rare survival into modern times was the large barrow at Teddington, itself destroyed last century. Where subsoil degradation has not been too severe, ditched barrows might well survive in cropmark form as ring ditches, as probably at Stanwell (Longley 1976, 33, fig 12), but even these are few and far between. Two ring ditches excavated at Heathrow in advance of Runway 1 extension were found to be rather denuded and it could not even be established that they had a funerary rather than a domestic function. Clearly other examples could have been obliterated long ago.

On the floodplain the story will have been very different. From the evidence of other areas (eg upper Thames, Fen basin valleys) it is clear that barrows were often constructed on floodplains, which, it has been suggested, would have been treated as marginal land (Barrett & Bradley 1980b, 249). This view is certainly tenable for the lower Thames where the effects of a marine transgression in the estuary during the 2nd millennium BC (Devoy 1978–9) would have created a higher flood risk on the floodplain. If barrows were built on this river margin, there is every chance that some or many will survive little disturbed under a blanket of alluvium. At Runnymede for example a silt deposit 1½m in depth accumulated during the 2nd millennium, an adequate depth to mask a barrow of average size (Needham 1985). Barrows are now known to have been partially masked in this way at Wytham in the upper Thames valley (Bowler & Robinson 1980) and more spectacularly in the Fens where sizeable cemeteries are emerging from the shrinking peat (Pryor 1982, 137–8, fig 11). Any such barrows under the alluvium of the lower Thames are likely to be superbly preserved, rich in environmental evidence and quite undespoiled.

In addition to the Teddington dagger grave, only occasional complete beakers, such as that from Ham gravel pits (Clarke 1970, no 970), may have been originally the accompaniments of decayed inhumations not recognised in the course of casual discovery. Contemporary burials lacking any fine artefacts might well not be noticed at all by the casual finder. This is less likely to have been the case when extensive urn cemeteries were disturbed and should account for the preferential recognition of Deverel-Rimbury burials in this zone.

The fact that the Deverel-Rimbury complex probably began within the Early Bronze Age (discussed earlier) does not completely negate the imbalance noted above. The larger cemeteries, best known in this area at Oatlands near Weybridge (Gardner 1924, 23–6), or at Ashford on the northern terraces (Barrett 1973) are likely to have had a long lifetime perhaps extending throughout the Middle Bronze Age (cf Kimpton – Dacre & Ellison 1981). To go alongside these and other lesser burial grounds there are tangible signs of settlement and agriculture on the river terraces.

The best settlement evidence comes from Muckhatch Farm, Thorpe, where a presumed farmstead was enclosed (Johnson 1975, 19–23). Linear ditches at Petters Sports Field, Egham, are associated with Deverel-Rimbury pottery and cut by a Late Bronze Age ditch (Johnson 1975, 12; O'Connell & Needham 1977, 123). They probably belong to a field system of a sort identifiable in cropmarks elsewhere on the river gravels. Little can be said about the small group of pottery dug up at Osterley, except that it appears to derive from a domestic context (Cotton 1981a). Other pottery finds from the river courses or close by presumably attest some form of domestic activity, but this has yet to be clarified. At Eden Walk, Kingston, a layer of pot-boilers overlying accumulated wood is suggestive of the consolidation of marshy ground, perhaps for seasonal use. The level contains animal bone and might be dated by a sherd of Deverel-Rimbury pottery (D Hinton, pers comm). Another isolated sherd comes from the Thames at Hammersmith, while small pots are known from the Thames at Tagg's Island and an unknown location. A few sherds of pottery from Westminster Hall excavations are probably to be identified as Deverel-Rimbury[38] and another small group has come to light in excavations in Staines town centre (Barrett 1984), apparently sited on the first terrace.

The distribution pattern for Middle Bronze Age metalwork has a different emphasis than that for the domestic material. Like Early Bronze Age metalwork it is overwhelmingly concentrated in the River Thames itself, with only a light scatter on the terraces. Definite land finds are almost exclusively axes.

Despite the richness of Bronze Age material from the Thames borders little can be said about the transition from Deverel-Rimbury to Late Bronze Age settlement. Continuity in exploitation is to be expected, but current evidence suggests that this does not extend to actual occupation sites. Shifts in the location of settlement need not however have been very marked.

By the end of the 10th century BC, a string of settlements using a new set of material equipment had been established along the lower Thames and its tributaries. These include the well-documented sites of Runnymede Bridge and, outside our area, Mucking South Rings enclosure (Jones & Bond 1980) and the open settlement at Aldermaston (Bradley et al 1980). The Kingston Hill material discussed above belongs with these early sites and, given its hilltop location overlooking the Thames, could easily indicate a defended site akin to Mucking. The possibility of another permanent floodplain settlement of Runnymede type has been mooted on the basis of finds from Syon Reach, Brentford (Needham & Longley 1980, 426–7). The site at Heathrow, which is in contrast sited well back on the terraces, should start within the Late Bronze Age, although probably not as an enclosed settlement (Grimes 1961; Champion 1980, 238).

At this stage we have for the first time a glimpse of the valley environment in the Bronze Age based on pollen evidence from Runnymede. The valley was by now predominantly open land with a lot of grassland which would offer rich pastures for cattle herds. There is good evidence for cereal cultivation as well, presumably on the drier terraces in field systems such as that at Stanwell associated with Late Bronze/Early Iron Age occupation (Martin O'Connell, pers comm; Poulton 1978, 241, fig 2).

There is little indication yet of continuity in settlement sites from the Late Bronze Age into the Iron Age. At Egham for example the focus of occupation seems to have shifted from Runnymede to Petters around the 7th century BC. The earliest group of pottery at Brooklands, beside the River Wey, and the Thames-side assemblage from Mixnam's Farm also belong to a terminal stage of the Late Bronze Age. On the Heathrow gravels settlement at both the Runway 1 extension site and Stanwell should belong in this period, while material from Yiewsley (Champion 1980, 237–8) and that recently excavated from Holloway Lane (Jon Cotton, pers comm), both north of Heathrow, may be a little earlier.

In the lower Wey valley a few sites may be seen to cover the Middle and Late Bronze Ages. Deverel-Rimbury material occurs in a probable funerary context at Westfield, Woking. The Deverel-Rimbury burials from Whitmoor Common lie only a short distance from the gravel terraces. The Late Bronze Age offers more substantial evidence for settlement with sites strung out along the Wey. In addition to Brooklands, already mentioned, small groups of domestic type material come from Byfleet[39] and Burpham (O'Connell 1982). At the latter site no intelligible plan could be recovered by excavation. The continuation of this Wey valley settlement into the Early Iron Age is indicated by the Wisley pottery (Smith 1924). It is noteworthy that all of the Late Bronze Age sites lie very close to the river itself. Finally, mention may be made of a pair of Late Bronze Age axes from this zone, coming from Stoke Hospital, Guildford, which is just north of the river gap through the Chalk (Lasham 1893b, 250–1, figs 11, 12).

The lower Mole terraces are astonishingly free of any Bronze Age material, a vacuum interrupted only by the Early–Middle Bronze Age funerary pottery from Leigh Hill, Cobham, and Late Bronze/Early Iron Age material from the same area (Smith 1909; Lowther 1945a, fig 4). The same is true of the Wandle valley, where three Middle Bronze Age palstaves from Mitcham (fig 5.10:8–9) are the only significant find north of Beddington (Phillips 1967, 27). It is not easy to explain this poor record of finds when compared with the lower Wey and particularly the wealth of material in the Thames valley. In the Bronze Age as in the preceding and succeeding periods the Thames determined the major axis of settlement.

Summary

The material basis for the earliest phases of the Bronze Age in Surrey and its region is, as in the Neolithic, mainly that of stray artefact finds. The introduction of metallurgy, the multiplication of potting traditions and the elaboration of stone and flint working, however, gave rise to an expanded range of material equipment which allows a Thames-side and north-east zone to be distinguished economically, and possibly even socially, from the south-west. A fundamental question now is whether this divide will find a basis in the record for settlement patterns and subsistence economies, but this requires the discovery and exploration of appropriate sites as well as the detailed analysis of well-recorded flint scatters. The recent discoveries of beaker pottery assemblages in the north-east of the county allow some optimism that this is achievable. Even the burial evidence in terms of pre-Deverel-Rimbury traditions is paltry in Surrey, and we can cite barrow morphology alone in support of a regional division with 'fancy' barrows being confined to the west. Opportunities for the investigation of barrow structures and burial rites should not be missed if they arise.

With the emergence of the Deverel-Rimbury complex and establishment of Arreton metalworking in the late Early Bronze Age, the material evidence becomes altogether more weighty and the contextual evidence more diverse. Domestic goods and funerary practices may have continued little changed through the Middle Bronze Age. Their distributions and contexts imply the consolidation of an agricultural regime across many parts of the county including the intake of marginal environments, which have consequently become degraded. There are indications, in the laying out of field systems, that land tenure was being formalised and stability might have led to farming settlements being long-lived. Some of the larger cemeteries could have grown gradually over a long period. The model here proposed urgently needs qualification through the excavation of a Deverel-Rimbury settlement site yielding economic evidence.

Although Middle Bronze Age metalwork is generally widely spread across the county, the major categories show marked distributional differences. The great majority of the fine weapons come from the River Thames or its banks where they probably result from acts of ritual deposition. These hint at a concern for religious or social position within the local communities and perhaps also indicate the continuing economic dominance of the Thames-side zone. These patterns continue into the Late Bronze Age with the addition, in the settlement record, of defended sites either on the floodplain, as at Runnymede, or on hill tops as at Carshalton or Caesar's Camp, Wimbledon. As yet these defended sites have only been identified in the Thames-side and north-east Surrey zones where their pre-eminence may have been due to an increasing need to control the rich agricultural resources and important exchange networks of the region. Although it may be premature to claim distinctions between the settlement assemblages of that area and the south-west of Surrey, hoarding practices certainly suggest a renewal of the geographical differentiation seen in the Early Bronze Age. The hoards of the south-west have been viewed as 'personal' in contrast to the 'founders' hoards' which abound further north and east.

Climatic factors and soil exhaustion probably led to the abandonment of certain marginal zones from around the turn of the millennium (1000 BC) perhaps causing Late Bronze Age communities to intensify their exploitation of the more productive lands. New field systems were probably laid out on the gravel terraces, as documented at Stanwell, and these may on occasion have necessitated further clearance of woodland. The environmental evidence for this putative phase of geographical contraction and agricultural intensification is extremely slender, indeed non-existent for most of Surrey's ecological zones. This is one of the more pressing needs if we are to understand better the Middle Bronze–Late Bronze–Early Iron Age settlement sequence in the region; hopefully we will not have to wait a further half century to see a major reconsideration of such aspects of the Surrey Bronze Age.

NOTES

1 The research behind this paper has depended on the considerate help of many museum curators in Surrey and outside over a number of years. Especial thanks are due to Julia Arthur and, formerly, Felix Holling of the Guildford Museum, and to Jean Macdonald, formerly Museum of London; also to Ian Longworth, who kindly commented on the draft manuscript. I am grateful to Philip Compton for preparing numbers 7–13 in fig 5.8; the remaining line drawings are the work of the author. Many others deserve mention for freely supplying information on sites and finds: L and R Adkins, J Barrett, D Bird, L Blackmore, R Bradley, J Cotton, K Crouch, A Ellison, D Field, J Gardiner, D Graham, J Greig, R Hanworth, D Hinton, M O'Connell, F Pemberton, P Philo, R Poulton, H Sheldon, D Tomalin and B Ware.

2 A blade fragment of a similar axe is also provenanced to Farncombe and they may have been associated (Phillips 1967, 19, 22, fig 4:4).

3 NBI – National Bronze Implements Index, British Museum. The provenance of the second axe was recorded as 'Chapel Fields, St Margaret's' and taken at one time to refer to Stanstead St Margaret's in Hertfordshire. However, its origin in the collection of George Roots of Surbiton makes it far more likely that it comes from the St Margaret's district of Twickenham where a chapel in the grounds of St Margaret's House stands on the west bank of the Thames.

4 Now in the British Museum, accession no P1980, 3-2,1.

5 Sunbury (Cotton 1981b), Harlington (Laws 1978), Hounslow (British Museum, accession no 64, 5-2, 7), Kingston (Megaw & Hardy 1938, 301, no 92), Kew (Museum of London, accession no 0 1169), Mortlake (Museum of London, accession no 0 1167).

6 The unprovenanced dagger in the Birmingham University collection (fig 5.1:7; Gerloff 1975, no 185) may be recognised with confidence as that found in the Thames at Ankerwyke Bend, near Egham, on the basis of Turner 1926, 2–3, fig 4.

7 Recent excavations at Calverts Buildings, Southwark, and Cromwell Green, Westminster, have yielded small groups of beaker sherds (Harvey Sheldon and Lyn Blackmore, pers comm).

8 Oatlands Park – Clarke 1970, 499, no 483; Walton-on-Thames – Grimes 1929–31, no 104; Weybridge – Field 1983b.

9 Chaldon – Russell 1982; Bromley – Clarke 1970, 485, no 388; Limpsfield – Clarke 1970, 499, no 973; Croydon, Pampisford Road – Frere MSS, Surrey Arch Soc Library; Carshalton – Grimes 1929–31, no 98; Croydon – Roe 1966, no 197; Mitcham district (?) – Roe 1966, no 202. The recently reported flint dagger from Warlingham (Ketteringham 1980) is of Scandinavian type and, even if an ancient import, not directly relevant to the material grouped here.

10 I am grateful to David Field and Jon Cotton for bringing these sherds to my attention; they had formerly been described as 'fragments of vessel allied to a beaker' (Keiller & Piggott 1939, 138). Clarke did not include them in his corpus (1970).

11 The small Yiewsley vessel (Barrett 1973, fig 5:1), although of biconical profile, might perhaps be better accommodated within the lower Thames valley Deverel-Rimbury assemblage (Ann Ellison, pers comm). It is flint-gritted and has a simple rim which is slightly hooked.

12 Abinger Hammer – Wood & Thompson 1966; Dippenhall – Lowther 1939, 161, pl 13:2.

13 This urn, surviving only as a few sherds, has hitherto been regarded as a bucket urn (Gardner 1924, 26–7; Barrett 1973, 132), but the evidence for its profile is unambiguous.

14 This vessel is simply provenanced to 'Guildford' in the Quex Park Museum, Birchington, Kent. It was acquired in 1938, its earlier history being uncertain, and thought to have been found some 40 years previously. It is possible that it is the 'British urn' excavated by Pitt-Rivers from a barrow on Merrow Downs above Guildford (Lane Fox 1877; Saunders 1980, 70).

15 David Tomalin agrees that this urn should be grouped with the biconical series despite its somewhat atypical profile.

16 Another barrow-like mound exists at Sunbury, behind Rooksmead Road (TQ 1003 6912); it is not modern (pace Longley 1976, 23) and could perhaps be prehistoric.

17 This axe belongs to the Bannockburn type as defined by Schmidt & Burgess (1981, 76–8).

18 Farley Heath – British Museum, accession no 53, 4-19, 19, 22; Vauxhall – British Museum accession no WG1761.

19 The shield formerly described as coming from Mixnam's gravel pit, Thorpe, is almost certainly an example remembered as having been dredged from the Thames at Hampton by Malcolm Head of Thames Water Authority. The object was spotted by Mr Head during the dredging operation, but was not recognised as an antiquity and was thrown back amongst the ballast. The dredged ballast was systematically dumped at Mixnam's pit for screening; hence the shield was retrieved at Mixnam's and this time taken to a local dealer, Oliver in Chertsey. The pit manager, Freddy Saunders, subsequently remarked on the unusual find to Mr Head, who later went to see it on display in Chertsey Museum. Mr Head was able to describe the original findspot as a narrow channel behind an island at Hampton, c TQ 146 691. He recalled 'two short swords' as having also come from that barge load. These might well be the dirk and sword in Chertsey Museum and illustrated here, fig 5.11:1, 5.

20 Another rapier has been reported from the Farnham district but its form is not yet known (David Graham, pers comm).

21 There is no evidence for an accompanying burial as recorded by Burgess (1976, 90, no 22).

22 One possibly relevant piece is a new find which was recovered with a large Late Bronze Age spearhead hoard from Bramber, Sussex (Aldsworth et al 1981, no 106). It is essentially similar but has no trace of binding, the edge instead being bevelled.

23 The pottery from Weston Wood is now at Guildford Museum and a cursory examination reveals that the assemblage, in part at least, belongs here.

24 Ellison hints that Urnfield imports such as these vessels could have had an impact on the development of British globular urns during the latter part of their currency.

25 There is in fact one sherd from Green Lane ornamented with grooved lines (fig 5.12:6) as well as parts of a plain-cordoned vessel (Guildford Museum).

26 The Late Bronze Age loomweights are generally of pyramidal type, but the Middle Bronze Age cylindrical form seems to continue in use in this assemblage.

27 Kensington – Britton 1960, GB 52.2; Beddlestead – Phillips 1967, 15; Wickham Park – Smith 1958, GB 39.2; Petters – Needham 1986.

28 Beddington – Flower 1874c; Southall – Britton 1960, GB 51.1; Petters – Needham 1981, 9–11; Kingston Hill – Field & Needham 1986; Runnymede Bridge – Needham 1980c, no 6 and unpublished.

29 This sword, when first shown to Paul Larkin at Chertsey Museum, was described as coming from a local gravel pit. Later, on submission to the British Museum by Seabys Coins & Medals Limited, the provenance was alleged to be the

River Thames between Teddington and Reading (NBI). The former information, although imprecise, is thought to be the more credible.

30 These four axes are described in the British Museum register (1849, 3-26, 1–4) as having been found 'with a gold ring of later but uncertain age'. The ring was not acquired, nor is any description or drawing known. It seems not improbable that it was contemporary with the axes, but not recognised as such in 1849.

31 Heathrow – Canham 1978b; Mixnam's Farm – unpublished, Weybridge Museum (see Grimes 1960); Brooklands – Hanworth & Tomalin 1977; Caesar's Camp, Wimbledon – Lowther 1945a; Hawk's Hill – Hastings 1965; St Catherine's Hill, Artington – Bishop 1971, 22.

32 St George's Hill, Weybridge, has a counterscarp bank detectable in places and it may, in part at least, be multivallate (Poulton & O'Connell 1984b).

33 All five come from the Sussex Weald: Peasepottage Forest; East Grinstead; Lower Beeding; Etchingham; Ore (Needham 1983). An item of late Early Bronze Age metalwork is seen in a newly found tanged spearhead from Stonepit Wood, Sussex (NBI).

34 Palstaves from Glebe House (Chiddingfold), Lagham Manor (Godstone) – probably in a secondary context – and from Copthorne on the Sussex border.

35 Surrey County Council, Conservation & Archaeology Section, Sites and Monuments Record.

36 Weston Wood – Harding 1964; Albury Down – Guildford Museum; Reigate – private possession.

37 Socketed knife, Birchen Reeds, Tilford – Phillips 1967, 28; socketed gouge, Godalming – NBI.

38 The material from the Cromwell Green and Westminster Hall sites was brought to my attention by Lyn Blackmore. The latter pottery is that described as 'probably of Iron Age' by Whipp & Platts (1976, 353).

39 A small group submitted to Guildford Museum comprising a number of sherds, a pyramidal loomweight and blocks of stone. From a market garden at TQ 0624 6014.

The Iron Age in Surrey

ROSAMOND HANWORTH

Introduction

In the last decade or so there has been a minor revolution in Iron Age studies. The old division of the period into the first three letters of the alphabet has been scrapped, together with many of the models, such as invasions, on which it was based. A new chronology has emerged and, almost the most drastic change of all, much of the pottery and trappings of what used to be called Earliest Iron Age, or Iron Age A, are now recognised as belonging in time and culture to the latest stages of the Bronze Age. This paper tries to take account of various significant ideas in circulation at the present moment and to see how the data available for Surrey fit in with them.[1] Yet it is interesting to note that even the new thinking holds to the traditional idea of geological determinism in relation to the soils on which settlement took place.

In a recent paper, Cunliffe (1982), drawing on an idea of Champion's (1976), has pointed out that both Kent and Surrey faced northwards during the Iron Age, being part of an eastern region, focused on the River Thames. If this point is appreciated, a lot of the problems of distribution of Iron Age sites fall into place. It is hoped to demonstrate here that it is not until the period after Caesar's invasions that there is any meaningful change, when settlements move to the south, and Surrey becomes part of a territory which included parts of Sussex, Hampshire and Berkshire.

The Bronze/Iron Age transition, *c* 8th–6th centuries BC

At the start of the period, in the overlap between the Bronze and Iron Ages, the distribution of major sites is heavily biased towards the River Thames and its tributaries, with only a few sites, such as Weston Wood (Harding 1964), spread to the limits of their catchment areas.[2] Earlier workers, in particular Lowther, did recognise that such sites, which we now classify as 'post Deverel-Rimbury', were greatly influenced by the Late Bronze Age. In fact it has been emphasised by Elsdon (1982) that Lowther's instinctive judgement was to place them in the early period in spite of the then current fashion for a short chronology. 'Transitional' sites, as defined in the previous chapter, are shown on the accompanying map (fig 6.1).

Recently a model has been produced (Barrett & Bradley 1980b), to show how three elements in the Late Bronze Age/Iron Age landscape might be linked together economically. A river would function as a means of transport for goods, animals, or people; the hillforts would be the collecting centres to which produce would be brought, where manufacture might take place, and where goods could be redistributed; while the farmstead sites would relate to both the others, being responsible for agriculture, and possibly other forms of production, and for exploiting the various soils to best advantage (fig 6.2). The hillforts in our case would be St George's Hill, Weybridge; St Ann's Hill, if it does exist (Longley 1976, 14); Caesar's Camp, Easthampstead (just outside the county); and Caesar's Camp, Wimbledon Common (Lowther 1945a).

With the establishment of the full Iron Age (*c* 5th century BC), many of the sites mentioned above fall out of use, mainly the ones located on the valley gravels, while those further inland carry on. It is important to emphasise that there can be no hard and fast ruling about the starting up or failure of sites in any particular period, unless they have been thoroughly investigated. For example, at Brooklands, Weybridge (Hanworth & Tomalin 1977), the Phase A material has a very limited distribution, owing to the later use to which the ground was put, and it might not have been found in a smaller excavation, in which case the interpretation could have been significantly different.

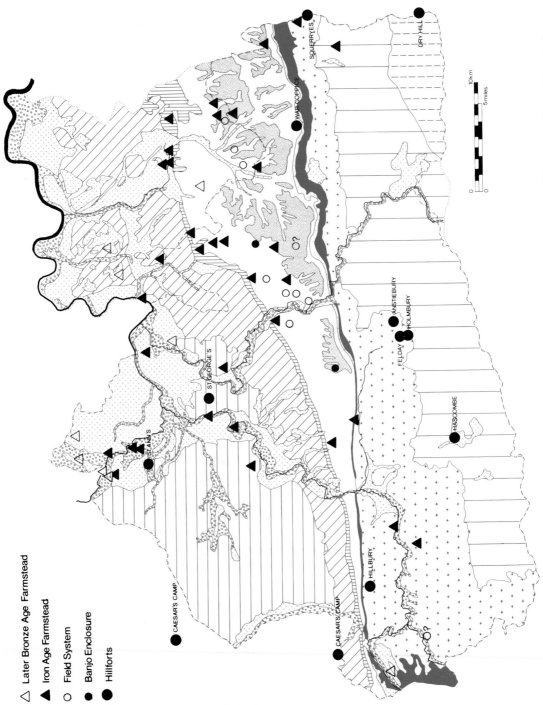

Fig 6.1. The distribution of Iron Age farmsteads, hillforts, 'banjo' enclosures and field systems in Surrey. (Note: two hillforts, Caesar's Camp, Easthampstead, and Squerryes, are outside the present county boundary, while Caesar's Camp, Farnham, straddles it.) (For key to geological background see foldout 1)

Later Bronze Age Farmstead
Iron Age Farmstead
Field System
Banjo Enclosure
Hillforts

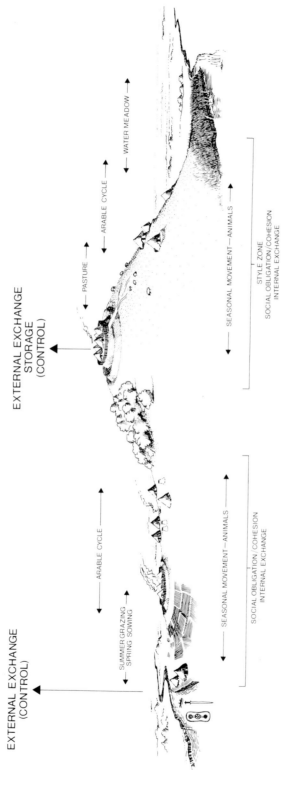

Fig 6.2. Model to show relationship between river (for transport), hillfort (for distribution and control) and farmsteads (for consumption and production). (After Barrett & Bradley 1980b, fig 6)

Distribution of sites

When considering the distribution of Iron Age sites, there are some very noticeable gaps, which seem to be determined by soil types. The north-west of the county is an empty zone, presumably because the Surrey heathlands, well known as an example of a man-made landscape caused by the exhaustion of the soil (Sankey 1975), have already established themselves. Just as noticeable is the absence of settlement, apart from the hillforts, on the greensands and clays of the south of the county. The exceptions to this in the extreme south-west are connected with the riverine distribution, which is one of the two dominant patterns now, the other being the concentration on the dip-slope of the North Downs. On fig 6.1, 43 sites have been plotted, ones where there is more than just the random scatter of a few sherds. It is noticeable that there is a concentration east of the River Mole; whether this is the true state of affairs, or represents the discovery of sites due to the development of Greater London is not yet quite clear. Workers in the Croydon area see it as somewhere where expansion took place in the Later Iron Age, and feel that there are many more sites to be discovered in their district. The sparse occupation of the Chalk between the Mole and the Wey, in spite of the important site at Hawk's Hill (Hastings 1965), may be genuine or may be partly because some large tracts are still permanent pasture, while others are inaccessible to fieldwalkers for various reasons. It is something which should be studied, but it appears probable that at that time there was no territorial division where we think of it nowadays, around the county boundary, and that Surrey east of the Mole was one region with west Kent; a point to which we shall return later when considering coins, or Patchgrove ware, both of which look as thickly spread in east Surrey as they are in west Kent.

Fortified enclosure of a settlement by earthworks was a feature of the transitional period, and such enclosed sites are at Queen Mary's Hospital, Carshalton, though this is now seen to be fully Bronze Age in date (Adkins & Needham 1985; Lowther 1944–5), and Caesar's Camp, Wimbledon (already mentioned). Others, like Hawk's Hill (Hastings 1965), Leigh Hill, Cobham (Smith 1908b; 1909), and Purberry Shot, Ewell (Lowther 1946–7a), although they start early, have no evidence of enclosure, and these sites carry on through the Iron Age, in some instances into the early stages of Roman Britain. Coombe Hill, Kingston (Gardner 1924, 8–12), is a Middle to Late Bronze Age site which goes through to the transitional period; it has been studied recently by Field & Needham (1986). Old Malden, which was enclosed, was claimed by the excavator to be an Iron Age and Romano-British site (fig 6.3; Carpenter, MS notes in Kingston Museum and OS records); the majority of the finds are with the excavator, but the pottery in Kingston Museum is virtually identical with Brooklands A, though there is very little Iron Age material lodged there.

Farming

Evidence for farming can be recovered through various means: the location of the site itself; the contents, whether animal bones, grain, or rubbish, of the deep pits which were initially dug for storage and later, if they become fouled, were used for rubbish disposal; from cropmarks of enclosures or ditches; from lynchets marking the outline of a field system; or from surviving tools; and various clues of this kind are available in Surrey.

Several sites have produced slight evidence for animal husbandry, but only at Hawk's Hill (Hasting 1965), a classic site of the Little Woodbury type (Bersu 1940; Brailsford 1948; 1949), have animal bones been recovered in sufficient quantity to be properly studied. They produced the important information that animals had not been slaughtered annually, and clearly therefore storage of fodder was properly organised and stock could be overwintered as long as was required. At the time when the report was published this constituted a breakthrough in our understanding of prehistoric farming and it is still quoted in recent general textbooks (Cunliffe 1974; Champion 1979, 352). More recently, the continuing experiment in Iron Age farming methods at Butser Hill, Hampshire (Reynolds 1979), has vastly increased our knowledge and awareness of all aspects of Iron Age agriculture.[3] Animals present in the Hawk's Hill bones inventory were cattle, horse, sheep or goat, pig and dog; there were also (less than 1% of the total), some wild species: deer, fox,

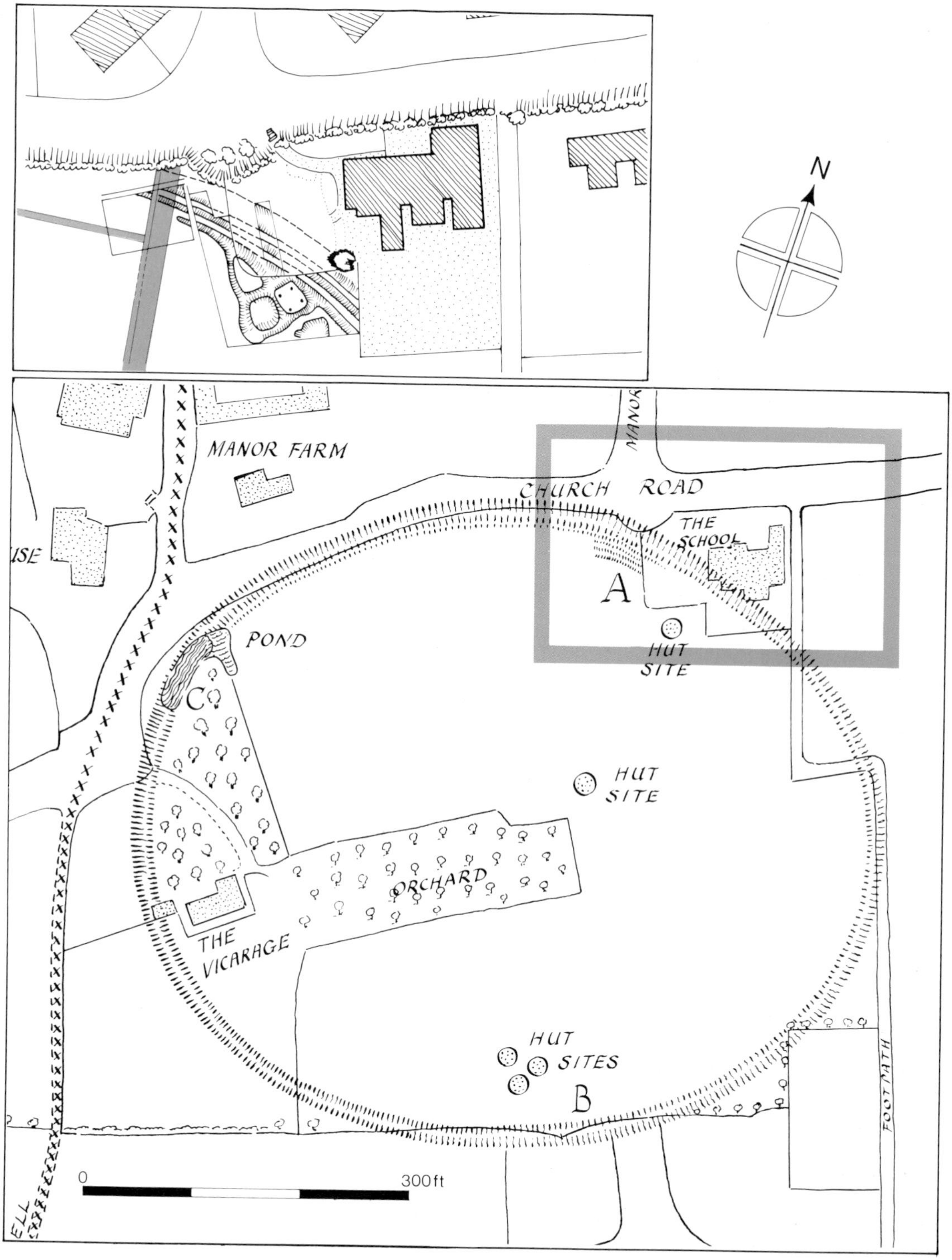

Fig 6.3. Plan of unpublished excavations at Old Malden showing (top) four-post structure and (below) five hut sites within an enclosure. The enlarged area at the top is outlined in green on the lower plan; the areas marked in green on the top plan are probably Roman. (From MS map in Kingston Museum, reproduced by courtesy of Kingston Heritage Centre)

bird, a probably intrusive rabbit and, enigmatically, a few human bones (Carter *et al* 1962). The practice of burying human bones in rubbish pits has only recently been recognised as being part of some formal ritual. It occurred at Gussage All Saints, Hampshire (Wainwright 1979, 191), and Danebury, Hampshire (Walker 1984, 442–63). The whole question is reviewed in Whimster (1981).

Horses can be recognised from parts of their gear as well as from their bones, and while there is nothing to compare in the Surrey Iron Age with the Bronze Age finds from Runnymede Bridge (Longley & Needham 1980, 27–30, figs 14–16), a harness mount was found at Burpham (D Bird, pers comm); an enamelled bronze terret came from the Thames at Runnymede and is now in the British Museum (Turner 1909); there is a harness fitting from the Thames at Battersea; and the so-called 'horn cap', if it really is off a chariot, also came from the Thames at Hammersmith (fig 6.4; Lawrence 1929).

An ubiquitous prehistoric farming structure is the 'four-poster', a group of four post holes arranged to form a rectangle. Pitt-Rivers' (1888) and Bersu's (1940) interpretation, based on ethnographic parallels, was that they represented raised granaries, and this was generally accepted for a long time. But Ellison & Drewett (1971) challenged the granary theory and

Fig 6.4. 'Horn cap' from the Thames at Hammersmith. Diameter of object 7.9cm. (*Photograph by courtesy of the Museum of London*)

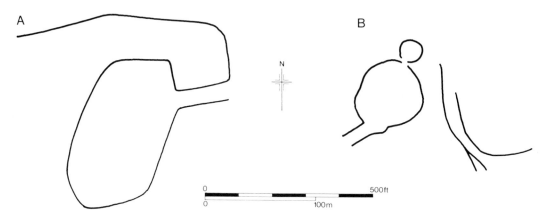

Fig 6.5. 'Banjo' enclosures at Effingham (A) and Epsom Downs (B). (After Gardner 1921, 101, and Clark 1977, fig 13)

advanced other valid possibilities, such as more general storage, watchtowers, shrines, and even platforms for the exposure of corpses. In the most recent discussion (Poole 1984, 87–110) it is clear that at Danebury there is no single overriding explanation to fit all the evidence and that the four-posters there, while many of them were probably granaries, had a variety of possible uses. At Hawk's Hill there was one 8ft square, which was probably a granary, and the same site had a group of post holes which were interpreted as a drying frame, which could have been used for cereals or hay. There is also a four-poster at Old Malden (fig 6.3), but its holes seem to be massive, and it could be interpreted as having some architectural purpose.

Cereals identified at Weston Wood were six-rowed barley and emmer, while the much later material from a pit at Hascombe hillfort included emmer, spelt, six-rowed barley and oats (Thompson 1979). The extensive use of querns (fig 6.15) must imply that a good deal of corn was being ground in local settlements. All this is in the mainstream, but one has only to consult surveys from the neighbouring counties to realise that Surrey lags behind in the study of this part of Iron Age farming subsistence. However field systems, distributed fairly evenly across the Downs, give further evidence of cereal cultivation. These are shown on fig 6.1, though two, a cropmark from Tilford and a system which the investigators had hoped to associate with the villa at Walton Heath (Prest & Parrish 1949), could belong to another period. Another, near War Coppice hillfort at Caterham, is thought to be medieval (D Graham and L Ketteringham, pers comm).

Two banjo-type enclosures (an earthwork class centred largely on Wessex), have been recognised (fig 6.5), one at Effingham (Gardner 1921), the other at Tadworth on Epsom Downs (Clark 1977). These are thought to belong to the Later Iron Age and to be principally used for stock, but recently houses have been found in or beside some of them, as appears to be the case at Tadworth.

That sheep formed an important part of the economy is well known, and Surrey produces its quota of spindle-whorls and loomweights as weaving equipment. Indeed one of the oddest sites is the oven found near the foot of St Martha's Hill, near Guildford, the dome of which appears to have been made of triangular loomweights presumably laid voussoir-fashion, their thin ends inwards to form the curve (Lowther 1935b). One might speculate, following the parallel of Wykehurst (Goodchild 1937), where a Romano-British tile kiln was built of tiles, that this 'oven' was itself a kiln made to produce loomweights. If so, it could indicate that a lot of weaving was going on in the neighbourhood. Pottery from the site is in the post Deverel-Rimbury tradition. Lowther told Audrey Henshall that he had found the impression of a textile on the base of a pot from his excavations at Purberry Shot. The cloth impression was not mentioned in the excavation report (Lowther 1946–7a), but Henshall states (1950, 135, 159) that it was a plain weave with about 18 by 16 threads to the inch. It is not known what subsequently became of the potsherd. (I owe this reference to David Field.) There is a lack of the so-called weaving-combs, only two, from the Thames at Wandsworth, being known. Although doubt has recently been expressed about whether they could be used in weaving (Hodder & Hedges 1977), others are confident that they functioned well (Sellwood 1984). All the same, it seems to the writer that they may also have been a necessary toilet article, used in the creation of the elaborate stiffened hairstyles sported by Celtic warriors. Indeed, it is difficult to imagine how they could have dressed their hair in these fantastic styles unless a comb was used.[4] Round-backed combs, of which MacGregor lists two for the north of Britain, are rare and appear to be of Romano-British date (1976, 143, figs 374–5). She too, in her section on tweezers (1976, 143, fig 276), hints at the same connection with weaving-combs.

Houses

By far the majority of houses in Iron Age Britain were circular, and seem most usually to have had as framework a setting of stout wooden posts. We know that there was much individual variety in construction, and this has been made the clearer by Reynolds' practical experiments in their reconstruction from excavated ground plans (1979). Infilling the walls could consist, for example, of withies woven through the uprights, or planks butted edge-on. A central post supporting the roof was not needed and is very seldom found; the idea of one, which dies hard, seems to stem from the experience of early excavators camping under canvas; it turns up frequently in the older literature. Rather charming period-piece reconstructions of Surrey houses are illustrated on fig 6.6. Note that the excavators envisaged the Worms Heath house as a 'pit-dwelling', which it was not (Johnson & Wright 1903).

As well as a setting of posts, excavators would expect to find ring-gullies, normally indicating eaves-drip drainage. Two gullies were identified at Brooklands, one of which had post holes lying within the gully (Hanworth & Tomalin 1977, 12, figs 4, 8), and therefore in this instance the gully has been interpreted as a bedding-trench for a stave-built wall. There were gullies at Leigh Hill, Cobham (Smith 1908b; 1909), Sandown Park, Esher (Burchell & Frere 1947); while circular post-built structures without gullies come from Thorpe Lea (Johnson 1975), Mixnam's pit (Grimes 1960, 181–5) and Weston Wood. There were five from Old Malden, one at least having a ring-gully with a hearth and central pit (fig 6.3; MS map in Kingston Museum). Other evidence for houses comes from the older excavation reports, where 'hut circles or pit dwellings' were identified at Bunkers Field, Wallington (unsubstantiated) (Major 1925; Orton 1980), and from Wisley came the report of 'regular lines of . . . dwellings, dug at fixed intervals' which R A Smith (1924) interpreted as a village. One cannot place too much faith in this, since they sound like rubbish pits. Elsewhere careful excavation has been able to identify the presence of houses from the concentrated nuclei of pottery sherds and occupation rubbish; two from Purberry Shot, where they had

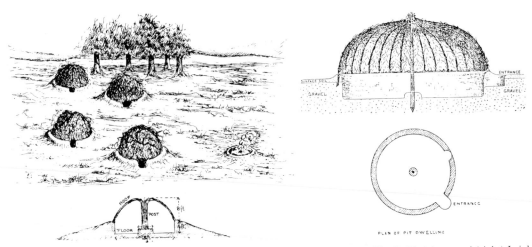

Fig 6.6. Early reconstructions of supposed Iron Age 'pit dwellings' at (left) Worms Heath, Chelsham, and (right) Leigh Hill, Cobham. (After Johnson & Wright 1903; Smith 1909, 141)

Fig 6.7. Iron sickle from Kingston. Length of object 17.5cm. (*Photograph by courtesy of the Museum of London*)

pebble floors (Lowther 1946–7a), while at Atwood, Sanderstead, there were houses of two different types, one circular, the other oval with a chalk floor (Little 1964). Such houses are likely to have had turf or clay walls, or even a frame of beams laid directly on the ground. On what must be the same site at Sanderstead, Parkinson (1968) found two rectangular structures with flint dwarf walls; the associated pottery was Iron Age/Romano-British. This is interesting because north of the Thames, in Essex, both Rodwell and Drury find rectangular houses replacing round ones in the Latest Iron Age (Rodwell 1978b; Drury 1978). A second site at Sanderstead, Kings Wood (Little 1961), datable also to the very end of the Iron Age, was unusual in that it had a cemetery just outside its enclosure. Frere & Hogg (1944–5) noted the possibility of hut sites on the edge of the field systems on Mickleham Downs, as a result of surface collections of pottery and loomweight fragments which they made during fieldwalking, but their sites have not been excavated.

An iron sickle found in a damp environment at Kingston (fig 6.7; now in the Museum of London, accession no A 1170), might have been used to cut reeds for thatching, but alternatively it might indicate that hay crops were being gathered there in time of drought, taking advantage of lusher growth in marshy land, as was done at a later date (Evans, G E, 1975).[5] The strangest evidence for what have been taken as houses comes from the so-called 'Waddon caves' in Aldwick Road, Beddington. Here a series of caves excavated out of the Thanet Sand were discovered in the grounds of what had previously been a large property (Clinch 1902b; Reid & Frere 1954). The current opinion (Muriel Shaw, pers comm) is that these caves are of recent construction, to store root vegetables or other farm produce, and that the layer of archaeological material lying at the bottom of them must represent earth from around the site, some of which got in when the caves were dug, while the rest could have been brought in by farm labourers on their boots or on the crops which they were storing. If this is so, and it is the most likely explanation available at present, then the implication is that there was in existence a substantial multi-period settlement site of some importance in the very near neighbourhood. What has been collected covers the Bronze Age, Iron Age and the whole Roman period, with a small Saxon element.

Metalwork, mainly from the Thames

The most obvious evidence for long-distance trade is the remarkable series of swords and daggers, sometimes with their scabbards, recovered from the Thames; but it now seems as though ideas were traded as much if not more than the goods. Indeed, in an important new review Stead (1984) makes it clear that imports of manufactured weapons might be more the exception than the rule.

Fig 6.8. Late Bronze Age sword from the Thames at Mortlake. Length of object 75cm. (*Photograph by courtesy of the Museum of London*)

What seems to happen over and again, is that a continental prototype would be copied and modified to British standards by local smiths, who were every bit as competent as their continental counterparts. In due course some examples of the new-style artefact were exported from Britain to the continent. Other published studies of the metalwork include those of Piggott (1950), Jope (1961) and Cowen (1967). For the Iron Age the new weapons are the great bronze cavalry swords, which come into use at about the 7th century BC (fig 6.8). Of the 33 listed for Britain by Cowen, 19 are from the Thames and of these six can be claimed for the Surrey bank, three for Middlesex, and seven just 'from the Thames'. The difficulty of regarding them as anything other than stray finds comes from the manner of their recovery. Most were found during dredging and may have been given spurious provenances to make them more attractive to prospective purchasers. Surprisingly one comes from Charlwood, from a tributary of the River Mole (Lowther 1957). Cowen thought that they were the product of a group of smiths working in the area between, say, Chiswick and Kingston.

One item which is a certain import, with a fairly secure provenance, is the well-known Weybridge bucket, which can be dated to the 6th century BC and is a type known to come from the

Alpine region north of Venice (fig 6.9; Smith 1908a; Stjernquist 1967). Originally it would have been part of a wine-mixing service; buckets were traded up to the northern barbarian countries, where they have turned up in votive deposits. The Weybridge one is the only example known in Britain. It was found by workmen sinking a shaft for the famous inclined bridge over the River Wey at Brooklands race track. Although it was not found in an archaeological excavation, its proximity to the known site makes it likely that it came from there.

Fig 6.9. The Weybridge bucket. Height of bucket 17.7cm. (*Photograph by kind permission of the Trustees of the British Museum*)

Around the 6th century BC iron daggers of the period Hallstatt D to La Tène I became fashionable for personal armament, with scabbards often made of bronze and iron (fig 6.10). Again there is a concentration of finds in the London area, this time in the five miles from Mortlake to Battersea: 10 from the Surrey bank, nine from the Middlesex bank, and a newly rediscovered one now in the Royal Ontario Museum, from Westminster Bridge (Macdonald 1978). It was thought that in Britain there was a gap in workshop tradition and perhaps also in time between the end of our Hallstatt D–La Tène I daggers, with their insular sheaths, and the appearance of La Tène swords (see eg Jope 1961, 308, 320). New discoveries and Dr Stead's researches are now suggesting that this was not the case and that British craft tradition and continental contacts continued into La Tène I (information from Jean Macdonald). Stead (1984, 47, 49) describes a number of decorated swords and scabbards from the Thames valley, including some from Battersea. There is a very fine La Tène I sword, found at Wandsworth in 1971, now on show in the Museum of London (fig 6.11; Farrant 1973). Spearheads are a group of weapon which still await study. Smiths also

Fig 6.10. Iron dagger in bronze-bound sheath from the Thames at Mortlake. Length of object 33cm. (*Photograph by courtesy of the Museum of London*)

made the brooches, of which relatively few have been found in Surrey (fig 6.12). These have been summarised by Cotton (1979; 1982). Lastly, again from the Thames, are several famous and spectacular pieces of parade ornament, for example the Wandsworth shield bosses, the Battersea shield and the Waterloo Bridge helmet. The dates of this weaponry range from mid-1st century BC to mid-1st century AD.

To revert to the exchange of ideas. Aristocratic weaponry is regularly found in graves in central and eastern Europe, but in Holland, Belgium and Britain the normal place where one should expect deposition is in fact in a river or other watery place with presumably a religious significance, as Torbrügge has demonstrated (1972).

Fig 6.11. Iron Age sword and sheath from the Thames foreshore at Wandsworth. Length of sword 71cm. (*Photograph by courtesy of the Museum of London*)

Coins

From about the 3rd century onwards, Greek coins turn up in quite significant numbers in southern Britain. For many years they were written off as losses from the pockets of collectors, but recently ideas have changed (Milne 1948; Dance 1961; Cunliffe 1974; 1981a, 29) and while some may indeed be modern losses, others are believed to be evidence for trade with the Mediterranean at this time. The Greeks used coins in dealings with barbarians who had not yet established a money economy, probably to pay mercenaries. Whether our coins got here by this or by some more indirect means of exchange, it is not possible to say. There are 17 Greek coins from Surrey, two silver, one gold, 14 bronze. Cunliffe (1981a, 29) suggests that such coins are one of the factors in the gradual familiarisation of 'natives' with standard systems of weight, measurement and value.[6]

It is now generally thought (Kent 1978a; 1981) that the first Gallo-Belgic coins to arrive in Britain before Caesar's Gallic wars, were the gold ones known as Gallo-Belgic B. At that same time potin (high-tin bronze) coins, Class I, make their appearance, and most likely represented small change. Cunliffe (1982, 45) thinks they were minted in Kent and that they represent a significant early development in the economic use of coins in Britain. The distribution of the two classes of coin is broadly across the west of Kent and the east of Surrey, but there is a concentration also around the Kew and Richmond reaches of the Thames, which has prompted Kent (1978b) to suggest an early and short-lived oppidum on the north bank of the river, possibly at or near

Brentford (Merrifield 1983, 9, fig 1). Next, for a slightly later period, Cunliffe has taken up a hint of Kent's (1981a, 40), that in fact all other coins of the Gallo-Belgic series in Britain reflect, to some degree or other, a response to the need for manpower during Caesar's Gallic Wars (Cunliffe 1981a, 34) and he maps the distribution of this second wave of coinage, while emphasising that there will have been a drift to other locations before they got deposited. An example of how such a drift would operate is the large number of coins from the temple site at Farley Heath (Tupper 1850; Lowther & Goodchild 1942–3) where they represent votive offerings. Although coins were offered up at Farley Heath, none, so far as one can tell, have been found at the Titsey temple (Graham 1936), nor is its dedication known.

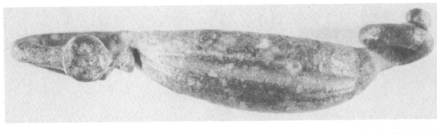

Fig 6.12. Iron Age fibula from Ewell. Length of object 3.8cm. (*Photograph by courtesy of Guildford Museum*)

Since Cunliffe's maps were drawn up (1981a, figs 12, 14), there have been new finds in Surrey covering the whole of this late stage in the Iron Age; the hoard of 20 Class II potin coins from Croydon (Shaw 1979); the two, possibly three, Class I potin coins from Hascombe (Thompson 1979); silver and potin coins from the Iron Age levels beneath Beddington Roman villa (Adkins & Adkins 1982 and pers comm); the hoard of four Gallo-Belgic E and five British Q staters from Farnham and another hoard from Frensham Manor, which included seven Roman Republican and early Imperial coins together with one silver quarter stater of Eppaticus (Graham 1986); and the massive hoard from Wanborough (figs 6.13, 6.14). Some of these finds have been made by people using metal detectors, and whilst it is gratifying that they have been notified, it is extremely worrying that such activity is increasing rapidly, in totally uncontrolled conditions which will give rise to situations very similar to the unprovenanced metalwork, described above. While some

Fig 6.13. Coins from Surrey Archaeological Society's excavation at Wanborough. Dr J P C Kent has kindly provided the identifications; types probably first known from the Wanborough find are asterisked. *Anonymous 'Pre-dynastic' issues from southern England*: 1, gold quarter-stater, perhaps inscribed T. Mack (1964) 81. 2, silver drachm, inscribed. Mack 446B. *3, silver drachm, inscribed EX. Unpublished. *Dynasty of Commius*: *4, Tincommius, silver drachm. Seaby (1987) 93c. 5, Tincommius, silver drachm. Mack 105. *6, Tincommius, silver drachm. Seaby 93B. 7, Eppillus, gold quarter-stater. Seaby 95A. 8, Eppillus, silver drachm. Mack 108. 9, Eppillus, silver drachm. Mack 305. *10, Eppillus, silver drachm. Seaby 96A. *11, Eppillus, silver obol. Seaby 96D. 12, Verica, gold stater. Mack 121. 13, Verica, gold quarter-stater, heavy standard. Mack 114. 14, Verica, gold quarter-stater, normal standard. Mack 112. Scale 2:1. (*Photographs by kind permission of the Trustees of the British Museum*)

1   2   3   4   5

6   7   8   9   10

11   12   13   14

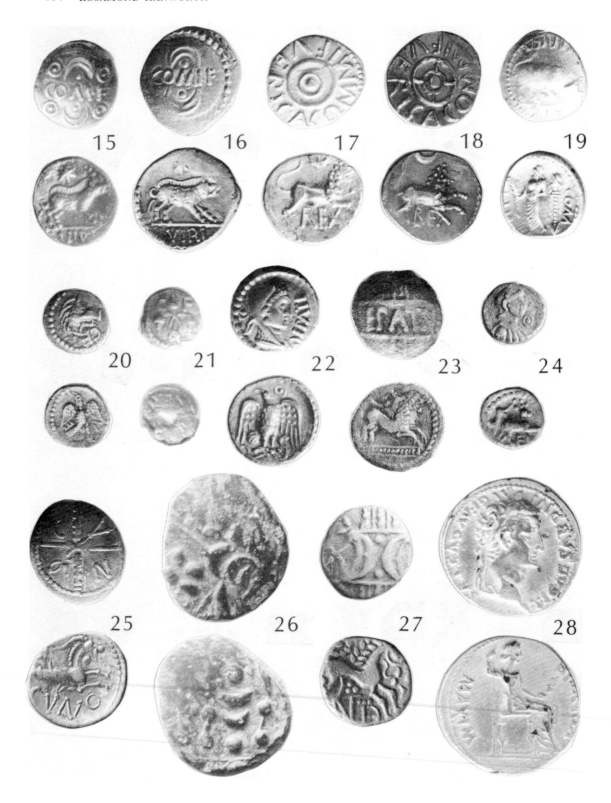

15   16   17   18   19

20   21   22   23   24

25   26   27   28

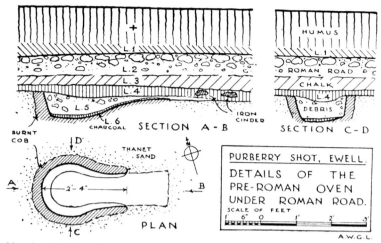

Fig 6.15. Ironworking site at Purberry Shot, Ewell (the 'oven' is a smithing hearth). (After Lowther 1946–7a, fig 4; see also Cleere 1977, 20)

metal detector users have acted responsibly and reported their finds, others have not, greatly to the detriment of the surviving evidence.

It might be thought very strange that the Haslemere hoard of uninscribed gold staters has been hitherto unknown to Surrey workers (Allen 1963). It turned up on the market in 1963 in small batches with the vague provenance of 'found in 1944 on a farm half-way between Guildford and Haslemere'. All of the first 82 coins came from only six pairs of dies. 32 would have been Gallo-Belgic imports and 50, British. None showed any signs of having been in circulation before they were buried. But there were more to come; the next batch turned up in Istanbul and was sold to the United States. The indefinite provenance, the highly unusual composition of the hoard, its unused condition, together, perhaps, with the steps taken to disperse it, have given rise to questions about its genuineness and it is not included on sites and finds records.

Ironworking

The dedication at Farley Heath was to the gods Taranis, Sucellus and their consort Nantosvelta, who are associated with ironworking (Goodchild 1938a). With so much circumstantial evidence for smiths, it is unfortunate that so little is known either here or even across into the Sussex Weald, about their workshops. The connection between St George's Hill and the ironworking site at Brooklands, Weybridge, where both processes, smelting and forging, were in operation, was made by the writer in 1977 (Hanworth & Tomalin 1977, 45) and in the same paper Potter (1977) drew attention to the deposits of good iron ore at the base of the Bracklesham Beds there, a source which might have supplied a wide area, if the parameters suggested below are correct. The other well-attested ironworking site is Purberry Shot, Ewell, where an 'oven', actually a smithing hearth, was found stratified in an Iron Age level, together with bloomery slag (fig 6.15; Lowther 1946–7a, 13, fig 4). It is very likely that much hard evidence for ironworking has been discarded unrecognised or

Fig 6.14. Coins from Surrey Archaeological Society's excavation at Wanborough. Dr J P C Kent has kindly provided the identifications; types probably first known from the Wanborough find are asterisked. *Dynasty of Commius:* 15, Verica, silver drachm. Mack (1964) 115. 16, Verica, silver drachm. Mack 115 var. 17, Verica, silver drachm. Mack 123. *18, Verica, silver drachm. Mack 123 var. 19, Verica, silver drachm. Seaby (1987) 108B. *20, Verica, silver obol. Seaby 109A. *21, Verica, silver obol. Seaby 111E. *Dynasty of Tasciovanus:* 22, Epaticcus, silver drachm. Mack 263. *23, Epaticcus, silver drachm. Unpublished. *24, Epaticcus, silver obol. Unpublished. *25, Cunobelin, silver drachm. Unpublished. *Durotriges:* 26, bronze stater. Mack 318. *Iceni:* 27, Anted …, silver drachm. Mack 420. *Roman:* 28, Tiberius, plated, ie false, silver denarius. *Roman Imperial Coinage* (**1**, 2 edn) 26. Scale 2:1. (*Photographs by kind permission of the Trustees of the British Museum*)

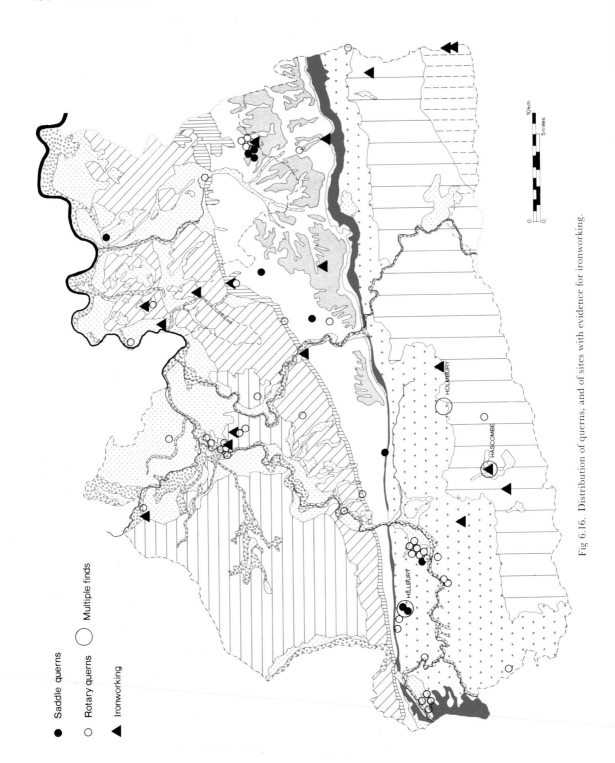

Fig 6.16. Distribution of querns, and of sites with evidence for ironworking.

unstudied. Lowther (1949c), when discussing pottery from St George's Hill, referred laconically to 'iron-working debris such as is common to all Iron Age sites'. Then again, the literature, even the recent publications, is full of references to very small pits, showing signs of intensive burning and packed with charcoal, usually interpreted as cooking-places for labourers' dinners, or to larger pits containing nothing apart from substantial quantities of burnt flints. These two types should be looked at with caution. At Brooklands we came to recognise them as constituting stages in the manufacturing process (Cleere 1972; 1977) where it was evident that the heat generated had been far higher than that required for culinary purposes, and was most likely to have been achieved by means of bellows and a cylindrical clay shaft, now only to be glimpsed as a collapsed spread. Unfortunately excavators have, up till now, expected ironworking sites to yield a high proportion of slag and other metallic detritus – a situation which is notable for its absence, as Spratling (1979) has pointed out; so that the potential of a number of sites has been overruled by cautious attitudes. Fig 6.16 shows the paucity of evidence which has been retrieved to date, some of these dots representing a single published item. But the writer's experience is that more would come from really detailed study of material lodged in museums, and the publication of local surveys and of previously unrecorded material. Such work is currently being done in several places, particularly in the Greater London area, and from it we can expect to learn some of the answers to questions about this neglected Surrey industry.

The hillforts (fig 6.17)

A hillfort is a citadel, and as such it can have very varied functions: as tribal centre, or market place, religious centre, even a 'boasting platform for Celtic nobility' (Rivet 1971), and many more. Some, like Danebury, seem to have been densely occupied and used as distribution centres, while others, like those in the southern hills of our county, appear to have been only sparsely occupied. If so, roles such as stock enclosures or refuges in times of emergency spring to mind. The origins of some stretch far back into the Bronze Age; not all were occupied at any one time, and in some instances, for example in Sussex (Cunliffe 1971), favoured hillforts are thought to have grown in power and aggression at the expense of their ultimately abandoned neighbours.

The architecture of hillforts was as diverse as their roles, but the overriding consideration was defence, and to this end all manner of banks and ditches were built – 'fence, wall, dump' (Hawkes 1971), sometimes the one succeeding the other, since a dump is the easiest way of repairing a slighted or eroded defence. The terms 'univallate' and 'multivallate' are used when describing whether a fort has more than one bank and ditch. To give but two examples, Caesar's Camp, Farnham, had a palisade in an early phase, and when this decayed, a bank was later built over the top of it (Riall 1983), while at St George's Hill, Weybridge, two banks of dump construction appear to have succeeded each other in approximately the same position, in the south-east, but on the western side there were double banks and ditches (Poulton & O'Connell 1984b; Gardner 1911).

Surrey's northern hillforts, St George's Hill, St Ann's Hill, Caesar's Camp, Easthampstead, have already been mentioned in connection with the Late Bronze/Iron Age transition, and Caesar's Camp, Farnham, might be placed into the Later Bronze Age riverside model, as it lies sufficiently close to the River Wey to qualify, but no datable material was found in the excavation, and the excavator has likened it to the southern series, to be mentioned below. Caesar's Camp, Wimbledon, which is considered by Needham to be too large to be fitted into the category of enclosed settlements, is datable also early in the period, while Queen Mary's Hospital, Carshalton, is now removed to the Bronze Age. It remains to discuss the forts in the south of the county, on the scarp of the Greensand hills, or, in the case of War Coppice, near Caterham, on the edge of the North Downs.

Long ago Boyden (1958) working from Sussex, drew attention to this group of forts ringing the Weald which tend to be sited on promontories and to share the same architecture; their defence lines are spaced widely apart, the ramparts being of dump construction revetted in front with stone, while the edge of their promontory is sufficiently steep to act as a rampart on at least one side. Recently Thompson (1979) reporting on his excavations at three of the Surrey ones,

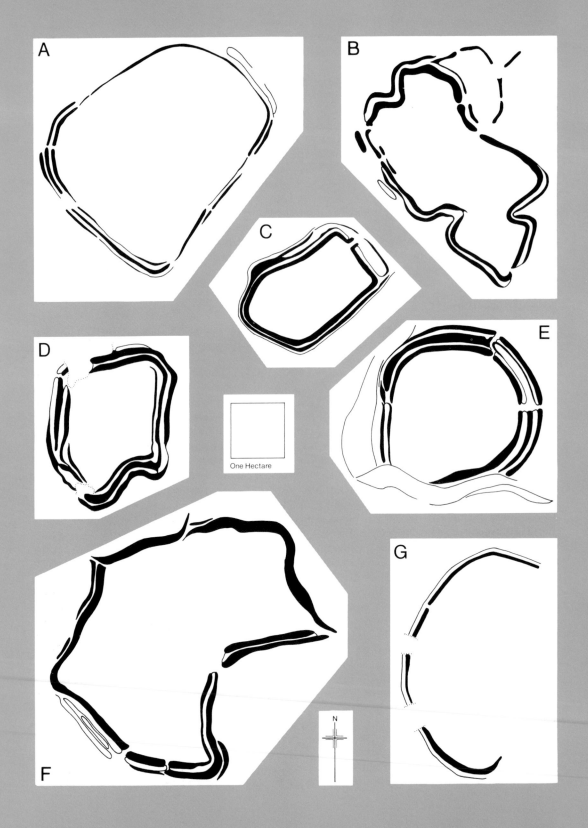

A

B

C

D

E

One Hectare

F

G

N

Anstiebury, Holmbury and Hascombe, has suggested their late dating, which is generally accepted, starting at the earliest *c* 200 BC and ending somewhat precipitately around the time of Caesar's landings, in 55–54 BC. One explanation, accepted for a long time, of their function, was that they represented a response in the 4th–1st centuries BC to a stress situation caused by population growth which meant that hitherto unproductive and marginal land had to be taken in (Ward Perkins 1939; 1944; Cunliffe 1982, 43). This sounds fine, but the evidence on the distribution maps does not bear it out, as Thompson recognised. At the present time there is no hard evidence to indicate a shift of settlement off the Chalk until the latest Belgic period. Indeed most, if not all, the evidence points to its happening in the mid-1st century AD, at a time when it can now be assumed that the hillforts had been abandoned for nigh on 100 years. This is a startling fact, and two possibilities present themselves. Either the settlement evidence on the Greensand and Weald Clay has totally failed to emerge (and it may be relevant here that the Haslemere Group who have systematically walked their area for 10 years have yet to find a single Iron Age site) or the model of stress and population growth is wrong in this context. Further research on these lines should be a priority in Surrey Iron Age studies. If we assume the evidence is there but has not yet been recognised, what factors are inhibiting it? Acid soil destroying prehistoric pottery has been advanced by Bedwin (1978, 49) for a slightly similar situation in Sussex, but this is unlikely because finds from the succeeding period have not suffered in this way; erosion off the scarp-tops has been suggested, but this could not account for the absence of evidence on the slope leading up to the scarps, part of which, in the Peaslake area, was watched for many years by the late Dr Watson. One must come back to the possibility that what the geology maps seem to be showing is correct; that during the Iron Age there was a major shift away from the over-exploited gravels and sands of north-west Surrey, but at the same time an avoidance of the Greensand and Weald Clay south of the North Downs.

To return to the hillforts. If, then, they were not a manifestation of expanding land tenure, what were they? A refuge? This is Thompson's interpretation, and seems to be the primary function. It might be thought that the forts lie a long way off from the settlement areas on the North Downs, but in fact their average distance away is a good fit to a module of 9.6km recently advanced by Johnston (1978). Drawing on the practical experience of John Budden in Sussex, he proposes that that is the distance which could be covered reasonably in four hours when driving cattle to market across country, and it should be equally relevant to driving flocks in times of emergency. But the forts could have had other functions as well. While it is possible that they are linked in some way with the expansion of long-distance trade, as has been suggested for their Kent counterparts (Cunliffe 1982, 45), in the present state of knowledge the more local redistribution of commodities seems worth investigating. What commodities? Three kinds must have been immediately available in this environment: timber, querns and iron.

TIMBER

The absence of sites around the forts raises the question whether or not forest clearance had yet taken place. Champion (1976) cites evidence from Squerryes, Westerham, from Keston, and from High Rocks, all in Kent, to suggest that wooded conditions could have survived there until very late in the first millennium BC. It is well known that the Folkestone Sand Beds had been cleared in the Bronze Age, but Dr Francis Rose (pers comm) says there is little evidence so far that the Hythe Beds scarp was ever totally cleared, and he suspects that modified primary woodland may still persist today in some areas. If the Hythe Beds had not yet been cleared in the Neolithic and Bronze Ages, then Professor Donald Pigott (pers comm) suggests a primary woodland of such species as sessile oak and beech, with an understorey of holly, and that small-leaved lime would also have been present. If, however, there had been previous intense occupation, then he would predict oak–

Fig 6.17. The principal hillforts in Surrey: A, Dry Hill, Lingfield; B, St George's Hill, Weybridge; C, Hascombe; D, Holmbury; E, Anstiebury; F, Caesar's Camp, Farnham; G, Felday (after D Field). (Note: St Ann's Hill, Chertsey, War Coppice, Caterham, and Hillbury hillforts have not been excavated and are not figured here)

birch scrub and bracken, much as parts are today. Once the original forest was destroyed, good timber would be scarce and the oak would be multistemmed scrub. Such oak under coppice treatment will provide charcoal for smelting. Indeed coppice poles are easier to handle for charcoal. We lack the relevant pollen diagrams to resolve this. If we knew more, it would greatly increase our understanding of Iron Age economy. Bearing in mind that intensive farming further north would have removed most large stands of trees, and having regard to the lavish use of timber in the Iron Age, timber here would have been a valuable asset.

In either environment hunting would be another possibility. It is generally known that wild species feature only very slightly in bone samples recovered from sites, but Thompson draws attention to the possibility that fired clay slingstones found at Hascombe were more suitable ammunition for hunting than for warfare. A multivallate hillfort, such as Hascombe, has defence lines of 30m or more in width. A light clay slingstone, weighing on average 1oz and with a tendency to shatter on impact would not seem an effective weapon (Thompson 1979, 297–8), and virtually the only other relevant site in this area at this time is a cache of fired clay slingstones from Derry's Wood, Wonersh, not far from Farley Heath (Elsley 1909).

QUERNS

Both Clark & Nichols (1960) and Tomalin (1977) have noted the very lavish distribution of querns on sites around the Godalming area at the very end of the Iron Age, and Tomalin went on to recognise that among the possible five different sources the stones display (from the Hythe and Bargate Beds of Kent and Surrey), at least two could have been located close to Holmbury hillfort, indicating a local industry. More recently Peacock (1979, 315), examining the finds from Thompson's excavations at Hascombe and Holmbury, has identified yet another source, from the Hythe Beds in the Petworth–Midhurst area, and thinks it is reasonable to regard these querns as part of an important industry. The implications of this are clear. Material was being brought to the hillforts from places up to 25 km away. Circles drawn with this radius will extend the catchment area of the hillforts into the very centre of the Weald. If relatively heavy stone objects were carried this distance, then other heavy goods or raw materials could be too. The quern distribution shown in fig 6.16 is relatively undifferentiated, covering the end of the Iron Age and the start of the Romano-British period. There is clearly a need to study this industry in detail, and there are faint indications of Niedermendig lava querns turning up on Iron Age/Romano-British sites such as Atwood (Little 1964) and the Iron Age level of Staines causewayed camp (D Tomalin, pers comm), as also at Oldbury hillfort in Kent (Ward-Perkins 1939). This carries an implication for arable farming.

IRON

This is the third commodity which should be considered as part of the stock held in the hillforts. We are not yet at the stage where we can sort out where bloomeries existed across the county, but it has already been suggested by Cunliffe that there would be centres where the ore would be processed before distribution to homestead sites for working up (1982). If, as is suggested, using the parameters just discussed, ore could have been brought in from the Weald, then it is logical to postulate that the hillforts could have been some such centres, just as St George's Hill seems to have performed that function in the north. Winbolt, having excavated Saxonbury hillfort in Sussex (1930), was in no doubt that ironworking was taking place at Hascombe where he found both slag and iron-bearing carstone, the latter in a furnace pit. Dry Hill Camp, not a promontory hillfort, situated on the edge of the High Weald, after two investigations (Winbolt & Margary 1933; Margary 1964; Tebbutt 1970), has produced no evidence of occupation debris, but slag was located in 10 places, slingstones in 26.

SEASONAL GRAZING LANDS – A SPECULATIVE APPROACH

In 1983 a hitherto unrecognised univallate enclosure was brought to the notice of members of the

Lithic Tool Research Group by a local flint collector (Elmore 1983a). Since then a bank and ditch of Felday Enclosure has been sectioned and further work is envisaged (Field 1985). It would be unwise to speculate too far in advance of detailed examination, but a few observations are necessary.

The site encloses an area of approximately 7–8ha, much larger than Holmbury hillfort (3.6ha) which lies 1.7km to the south (fig 6.17). Pottery recovered so far dates to the end of the Iron Age, probably even slightly later than that from Holmbury. The Felday defences, though the bank survives to 3m high in places, are admittedly much feebler than the norm for the southern hillforts. If it can be established that both sites were operating at the same time, then this could be an example of the pairing of hillforts, well known in Sussex and parts of Wessex, where it is observed that they seem to perform two different roles within the same economic system, one having pits for corn storage, the other being pastoral (Bradley 1971). The slight defences and larger size of Felday might suggest that it is for livestock. The two types of ground cover postulated above for the Surrey hills would not be very suitable for permanent pastoral use, but the suggestion of transhumance, made by Poulton below in this volume, is an attractive one. Seasonal movement of flocks is very well attested in prehistoric times (Bradley 1978b, 55–71), and transhumance was practised in the villages below the Greensand scarp in historic times until this century (Hanworth 1968, 5). The problem is, we do not know if the land below the spring-line on the scarp was cleared by this time (Dines & Edmunds 1954), nor whether good pasture had yet been established there, but if not, it would be a question of swine pasture which does not need grass, rather than provision for other domestic animals.

If it is once demonstrated that Felday had a function as a pastoral enclosure, then it would seem reasonable to look to the other hillforts for more evidence of pairing, as the excavator himself has suggested, and if so, a strong case could be argued for the hillforts controlling seasonal grazing lands.

To sum up then, these hillforts might be regarded as representing the frontier posts of the territory which had, as well as a defensive and possibly a pastoral role, a purpose as the bases from which expeditions could be made into the outback to fell, quarry, or otherwise obtain raw materials which could then be traded or distributed.

Ritual and religion

Since this paper was first prepared, an important new study on Iron Age religion has been published (Wait 1985). In seeking to formulate a model for religion he lists seven major areas where evidence should be sought. Two, ethnography and vernacular literature, can be left aside at this stage since they cannot as yet be more specifically applied to Surrey than has been done already. A further two have been considered above: that is, metalwork in watery places and human burial; while the other, the evidence from shrines and temples, coming as it does from the Romano-British period, falls within the next chapter.

This leaves the last two for mention here – animal deposits and sacrifices, together with ritual shafts and wells. Ross, in her paper on shafts, pits and wells (1968), drew attention to an interesting concentration in the neighbourhood of Ewell, particularly at Staneway House, now a plant nursery (Ross 1968, 264), where deposits down 10 shafts contained phenomena which she interpreted as evidence for ritual practice. In an orderly manner successive layers of large animal bone, of samian vessels, of soil containing organic matter and fruit pips and stones, of bones of cock and hare, and of a large dog had been laid down in one pit. Others had similar things, including some human bone and iron nails. Once again, the presence of samian shows that the context is a Romano-British one for a Celtic ritual. A round chalk disc from Pit 11 at Hawk's Hill (Hastings 1965, 12) might just possibly have been a votive deposit.

It would be premature to enlarge further on Celtic religious practice since in the wake of the important discoveries at Wanborough (see Bird in the next chapter) the subject is bound to form the basis for much discussion and study in Surrey in the future.

The end of the Iron Age

In archaeological terms it is often found convenient to mark the end of the British Iron Age and the beginning of the Romano-British period by Claudius' invasion of AD 43. In terms of industrial use, the Iron Age has really continued until this century, when it is being overtaken by a Nuclear Age.

With the demise of the hillforts, proto-urban settlements, termed oppida, started up over south-eastern Britain. They have been tentatively mapped by Cunliffe, with their notional territories (1981a, fig 15). We do not have one (fig 6.18), and, speculation apart, there are no likely candidates, though the ideal location would be somewhere on the banks of the Wey or Mole. But if 'Surrey' was not an Iron Age territory, none would be needed (see above). Oddly enough, a very small presence returns to Queen Mary's Hospital, Caesar's Camp, Wimbledon and Old Malden in the Late Iron Age/Romano-British transition. These finds might be connected with the burial rite of cremation which comes in at this period. Known cremations have been plotted on fig 6.19. One set of symbols represents Patchgrove pottery and fabrics allied to it; these are virtually exclusive to east Surrey and Kent, while in the west the hard black burnished fabrics which were ultimately to be produced at the Alice Holt kilns are beginning to appear. But at this point, in the south-west, the expansion of settlements off the Chalk is about to begin. Starting at Charterhouse, Godalming (Harrison 1961), it pushes out in the earliest Romano-British stage, and once again geological factors seem to determine it. It takes place on the loamy beds of Puttenham, where the soil is much less leached than other parts of the Folkestone Beds. One last point rounds the story off; all are agreed that very considerable re-groupings of people took place in the years before the Claudian invasion. Perhaps it would be fair to claim that Surrey had turned her back on the Thames valley and was finally facing south, as part of a grouping which also took in Sussex, Hampshire and parts of Berkshire, the historic territory of the Atrebates. This territory was in its

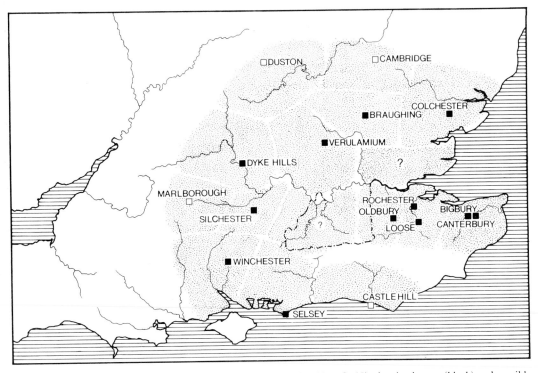

Fig 6.18. Socio-economic zones in south-east England (after Cunliffe 1981a, fig 15), showing known (black) and possible (open) settlements which could be the oppida for surrounding territories. It will be noted that the central southern territory has no identified oppidum. The area of Surrey (administrative and historic) is shown in dotted outline.

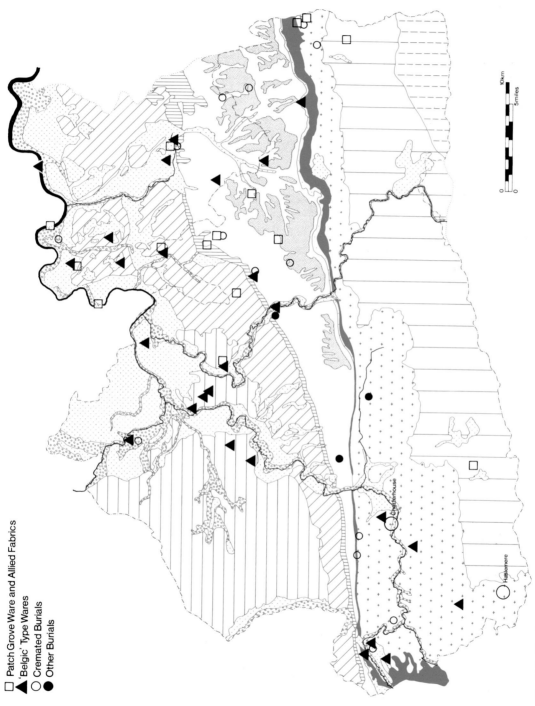

Fig 6.19. The Late Iron Age/Romano-British transition: distribution of two distinctive pottery types ('Patchgrove' and allied fabrics, and hard, burnished 'Belgic' fabrics) and of burial rites (cremation and other burials). The Charterhouse and Haslemere sites indicate expansion off the Chalk.

turn to be eroded away by dynastic and inter-tribal wars, thus providing, for example in Verica's flight to Rome, one of the causes for the Roman invasion of AD 43.

NOTES

1 In preparing the survey the writer has sought the views of many workers in the field, in libraries and in museums in various parts of the county, and is deeply indebted to them all for help, ideas and suggestions. The draft text was read by Hugh Thompson, Stuart Needham, Fred Hastings and Rob Poulton, to all of whom grateful thanks are extended for their comments.

2 Weston Wood is situated on a spur overlooking the Tillingbourne, itself a tributary of the Wey. It is a small river which has already featured in the archaeological record. See Needham, this volume.

3 The movement which advocated the testing out of various theories advanced to explain prehistoric agricultural practice by means of controlled experiment was pioneered in this country by Bowen (1961). Since the publication of that seminal paper much work has been carried out, in many other fields as well (Coles 1973) and is now a recognised and respected field for the advancement of knowledge.

4 The evidence for elaborate Celtic hairstyles comes from three sources: first the classical writers, notably Diodorus Siculus, who described them –

'Not only is their hair bright by nature, but they do their best to increase this natural peculiarity of its colour by preparations: for they are ever smearing the hair with a thick wash of chalk and drawing it back from the brow to the crown and to the nape of the neck, so that their appearance resembles that of hob-goblins and pucks – for their hair is so weighted down and stiffened by the preparation that it is just like the mane of a horse (trans J de Navarro).

These styles are also portrayed on sculpture and coins (eg Powell 1958, 66, pls 2, 5a), and further they are a prominent feature in the heroic attributes described in the later Irish vernacular epics, conveniently summarised by Ross (1970, 52). The hero Cú Chulainn is described by her as having hair

in three shades – dark at the roots, brown near the middle, and fair at the ends; clearly dyed hair. It is described as being so stiff that an apple could be impaled on the tip of each lock.

5 I owe this reference to members of Croydon Natural History and Scientific Society.

6 As attested, for example by well-made stone weights, at Winklebury (Smith, K, 1977), and Danebury. None of these latter has so far been recognised in Surrey.

The Romano-British period in Surrey

D G BIRD

There are probably more Romano-British sites on the County Sites & Monuments Record than for any other period, and it may therefore come as a surprise to find how little is known of many aspects of the Surrey area at that time. Unfortunately the evidence is biased, inevitably, towards the more sophisticated aspects such as towns, villas and roads, and this undoubtedly distorts the picture very considerably. If this veneer of sophistication is removed we are left only with evidence similar to that available for most of the other periods examined in this book. As will become clear, we know little about such aspects as the landscape in general, or the settlements in which the bulk of the population must have lived.

It should also be borne in mind that even for the apparently better known aspects, closer examination reveals that much of the evidence is seriously out of date. Most of the villas were dug before modern principles of archaeological excavation were properly established; in consequence they cannot be properly dated, nor can their development be understood, and much of the evidence which might have helped us to understand their function or economy has been lost. The larger settlements are also comparatively little known in detail because there has been little work or because of modern destruction by redevelopment, and sometimes both. It is even clear that there are still major Roman roads to be found.

Any discussion of Surrey in the Roman period will inevitably mention several names; in particular Leveson-Gower, Winbolt, Lowther, Margary (to whose memory this book is dedicated), Goodchild, Frere, and most recently Rosamond Hanworth, whose activities have now led to the formation of the Surrey Roman Villa Study Group under the guidance of John and Marian Gower.[1] It is especially on their work that the following account must be based, and if in what follows I seem to be critical of various aspects, it must be remembered that I am judging by today's standards and with the benefit of hindsight, and do not mean to belittle their achievements.

There is virtually no evidence for the immediate effect of the Roman conquest on our area. After Caesar's two famous campaigns in 55 and 54 BC, south-east Britain fell within the Roman sphere of influence,[2] and although there was to be no further military intervention for nearly a century this cannot, of course, have been obvious to the Britons at the time. The political picture at this time is confused, but apparently by the time of the conquest the Surrey area had fallen under the control of either the Trinovantes or the Catuvellauni as they drove the Atrebates to the south (Frere 1974, 60–3; cf Kent 1978b), although it is not clear how the Kentish side of the county is to be fitted into this picture. At any event, when in AD 43 the invasion finally came, the south-east was very quickly subdued; indeed it is likely that in general the population of the area welcomed the invaders: probably the 11 so-called kings who promptly surrendered to Claudius' forces did so as soon as they could be sure that the invasion had been successful and the Romans could offer them protection (Frere 1974, 82–6). No doubt one or more of these rulers controlled or claimed to control the area which included Surrey. Certainly there is little sign of a Roman military presence in the county, or any indication that the hillforts were held against the Romans.[3]

It is not clear how the south-east was occupied or administered at first. London certainly came into existence in the early Roman period, and it has normally been assumed that it was founded in AD 43 as a major supply base and army centre. Recent work, however, has suggested that this did not occur until c AD 50 (Sheldon 1978, 25–7; Merrifield 1983, 26–36). The capital's presence is now so overwhelming that it is difficult to envisage a situation in which it did not exist, and at present we are at something of a loss to explain what happened in this area in the years immediately after the invasion.[4] It seems that at least by AD 50 the first of the great roads to London were being laid out; for us those to Silchester and Chichester ('Stane Street')[5] are of interest. Roman practice was to police a newly conquered area with chains of military posts set out along roads, and it may be that the so-called 'posting stations' (see below) were first established for this reason at about this time. It is likely enough that there was a full-size fort at Staines (eg Webster 1970, fig 1) but again confirmatory evidence is lacking. Excavations in the town are said to have produced a few military objects, most noteworthy being part of an early cavalry helmet (Robinson 1976). Southwark has also produced military finds including part of a *lorica segmentata* (body armour) (Dean 1980, 369), and it is suggested that the site was a supply base from *c* AD 50 to after 60 (Sheldon 1978, 27–30).

Few sites in the countryside have produced material relevant to this discussion, but mention should be made of a harness mount from an early and regular ditch at Petters Sports Field, near Egham, although the excavator is dubious about the site being military (M O'Connell, pers comm). West of Dorking a cropmark seen from the air suggested to St Joseph the possibility of a Roman marching camp (St Joseph 1953, 82). It is well sited, and would imply campaigning along the Tillingbourne valley, which is logical enough, but the entrance appears to be too wide for a Roman defensive work.[6] The early cemeteries at Charterhouse, Haslemere (Holmes 1949) and Tilford (Millett 1974) should also be borne in mind, and Anstiebury has produced early Roman material from a layer in the fill of the inner ditch at one point (Thompson 1979, 253, 262; see also Todd 1984, especially 265, for Roman military use of hillforts). None of these finds or sites need be as early as the conquest, and some are certainly later; they could all relate to subsequent historical episodes, in particular the Boudican revolt of AD 61.[7] In London, of course, the evidence for widespread destruction by fire at this time is well known and it has also been claimed in Staines (Crouch 1978, 184), although interestingly there is little evidence in Southwark (but see Sheldon 1978, 28).[8] A good case can be made for the last battle being fought somewhere on the Silchester road (Fuentes 1983) – certainly as good a case as that which currently holds the field, for a site in the West Midlands.[9]

Administration and roads

The Surrey area now started to become Romanised within the new framework being established for Britain, apparently already centred on London.[10] The province was administered within tribal regions, each having a capital town with a great deal of local autonomy. Unfortunately it is not clear how the system worked in our area, but it seems certain that it was divided between as many as three tribal groupings and London's *territorium*. The latter was probably relatively small (Rodwell 1975, 90–4), and the claims of the Regni have been too readily accepted: both logic and what little evidence we have suggests that they are likely to have been confined to the area south of the Weald.[11] Most of Surrey, then, was probably split between the Atrebates, whose capital was Silchester (*Calleva*), and the Cantiaci, with their chief town at Canterbury (*Durovernum*), but with another major centre at Rochester (*Durobrivae*) (fig 7.1). It is interesting to speculate that the division, perhaps somewhere between the Wey and the Mole, may well have followed a pre-existing tribal boundary hinted at in earlier periods.

In no sense, therefore, did a unit like the later county of Surrey exist in the Roman period, but with the establishment of London the focal point that must have been responsible for bringing such a unit into existence was created. The established Roman road pattern was, of course, centred on the capital with, in our area, two known major highways (London–Silchester and London–Chichester) and two other probably later roads (London to the Lewes and Brighton areas respectively). A fifth road is known running north-west from near Alfoldean towards Farley Heath (fig 7.1), and it is usually accepted that it must then have continued onwards in the same direction, presumably to Staines or the probable posting station at Wickham Bushes, near Bracknell, close to the London–Silchester road.[12] The courses of the other known roads are all well enough established by the work of Margary and others (Margary 1956; 1973, 59–89 *passim*), although they have proved difficult to trace on the ground except in towns where there was regular resurfacing.[13] In Surrey, roads were usually surfaced with gravel, often on a flint cobble base. Remains of a wooden bridge to carry Stane Street across the Arun near Alfoldean have been noted (Margary 1956, 61); no doubt there were others. *Pontibus*, the Roman name of Staines, shows that there was certainly a bridge over the Thames there for the London–Silchester road – and perhaps also one over the Colne.[14] In

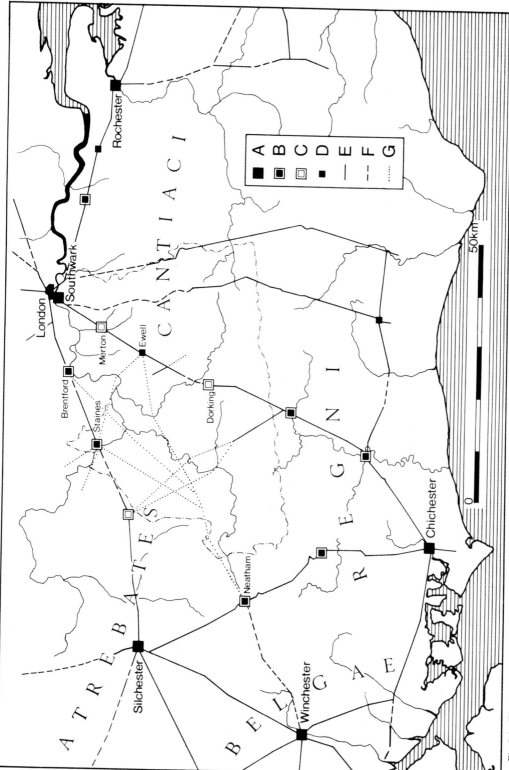

Fig 7.1. The area south of London in the Roman period, showing major sites, the tribal areas and the possible road system. The outline of the historic county and its modern administrative extension to the north of the Thames is marked. Key to symbols: A: major towns; B: minor town or posting station; C: postulated posting station; D: minor town; E: known road; F: probable course of road; G: postulated course of road, including alternatives (see text).

Southwark timber corduroys were laid where it was necessary to cross marshy ground (Sheldon 1978, 22). Milestones should have existed, at least on the major roads, but none are known in the county.

It seems certain that parts of the road system have yet to be discovered: in particular a road may be expected to run somewhere near the Chiddingfold villa, and it is likely that the London–Winchester road, which must surely have existed in some form, ran across Surrey. It has apparently been traced as far as the Farnham area, following roughly the route, though not the exact line, taken by the modern A31, from the Roman settlement at Neatham (D Graham, pers comm). From here three main possibilities present themselves: a route to Staines to join the London–Silchester road; to Ewell to join Stane Street; or between the two along approximately the line Pirbright–Chobham–Chertsey–Kempton Park–Brentford. Slight ground and place-name evidence suggest the latter, but not, as yet, convincingly. Other possible roads include one from Staines to Ewell, crossing the river at the bottom of the bend south of Kingston, and routes north-west and north-east to *Verulamium* or Brockley Hill from Staines are also likely to have existed.[15]

It may have been noticed that there has been no mention of the so-called North Downs Way (Margary 1956, 259–62). A growing number of scholars are dubious about this route, which was probably no more than a series of local tracks (Turner 1980, especially 8–9). Nevertheless, through routes probably existed north and south of the Downs, more or less along the lines of the modern A246 and A25, although they are perhaps unlikely to have been properly surfaced roads.[16] An attempt is made on fig 7.1 to draw together the evidence for the communications network, although the roads shown were not necessarily all in use throughout the Roman period: for instance the London–Lewes road is thought to date to after AD 100 (Margary 1956, 125).

Larger settlements

The major roads in the network formed part of the imperial postal system, and for this reason posting stations, *mutationes*,[17] were provided at around 20km intervals. Some of Surrey's Roman settlements probably owe their origin to the establishment of this system. As we have seen, the county was on the fringes of two or more tribal territories; in consequence there were no major towns in the area (Southwark is of course a special case, as London's suburb). A few small towns (Todd 1970) grew up to act as subsidiary market centres, in particular at Staines and Ewell, of which the former seems to have been much more town-like than the latter. Settlements of a similar size to Ewell, or at least larger than hamlets, probably existed at Croydon, Merton, in the Dorking area, and perhaps at Burpham. The evidence for these settlements varies greatly, and only Southwark and Staines have had the dubious benefit of major redevelopment schemes leading to the need for large-scale professional rescue excavations. Elsewhere small-scale digs and the records of many chance finds are our only sources of information.

Harvey Sheldon has suggested that Southwark came into existence *c* AD 50, probably as a supply base at a convenient point (a gravel island within more marshy ground) on the south bank of the Thames for the Roman bridge across to the newly founded London (Sheldon 1978, 28). One major difficulty in discussing Southwark is that a large area, perhaps as much as 4ha, along the river bank was destroyed by flooding in the 13th century, and this was room enough for a substantial earlier base (Sheldon 1978, 28–30). Southwark apparently suffered little in the Boudican revolt – though few structures of this time are known – and by the Flavian period clay and timber buildings apparently of civilian character were being constructed (Sheldon 1978, 30), probably in large numbers, as space seems to have been at a premium (indicated by houses with only narrow fronts on to the street: Sheldon 1978, 30–1). The settlement grew and prospered until around the middle of the 2nd century when it seems to have suffered a serious decline; many buildings collapsed or were demolished and were never replaced, their remains being covered with the characteristic black earth which is found over the Roman levels on many town sites. Recovery did not come for about 100 years, until the mid-3rd century, by which time the settlement had taken on a completely different appearance, with relatively few large stone buildings and apparently small-scale farming being carried out on the surrounding black earth.[18] Later anology suggests that the settlement originally existed to serve the needs of travellers and as an industrial and entertainment centre for London. So far as it can, the archaeological evidence supports this view; it also provides an all too rare insight into aspects such as the food of the population – seeds, bones and other remains indicate the presence of fig, grape, raspberry, blackberry, plum, cherry, damson, apple or pear, lentils, peas, the cabbage family, coriander, mustard, dill, millet and flax, oysters, mussels, cockles and limpets, mackerel, herring, smelt, eel, plaice or flounder, pike, dace, possibly roach, gudgeon and chubb, cattle, sheep, pig, domestic fowl and small percentages of red deer, roe deer, hare, wild boar, badger and woodcock. Dog and cat were also present (Sheldon 1978, 32–3). No doubt most of the 'native' constituents in this assemblage came from Southwark's hinterland, from farms in north Kent and Surrey.

At its greatest extent Southwark may have covered some 13ha (24 if immediately associated lands are included: Sheldon 1978, 15). By contrast Staines must have included around 4 or 5ha. This town perhaps originated as a posting station at an important river crossing, if it did not start as a settlement growing up alongside a fort placed there in or about AD 43, as already suggested.[19] The town occupies a gravel island at a suitable point for a bridge across the Thames; although the area seems to have been liable to flood there is plenty of room for a large fort, but a smaller one, say up to 2ha associated with a supply base, is perhaps more likely. Certain evidence of such a military establishment has not yet, however, been discovered. The sequence of establishment of fort, growth of associated settlement, abandonment of fort and continuation of settlement in its own right is, of course, well known in much of lowland Britain (Frere 1975, 5). The results of over 10 years work in Staines have produced a basic sequence for the town's history (as always, subject to the discovery of new evidence), starting in the early Roman period, with development up to around the middle or end of the 2nd century when there may have been some sort of disaster or decline. The town's fortunes revived in the later 3rd century and through the 4th (Crouch 1978, 184–6).[19] This is, of course, a broadly similar outline to Southwark, and also similar is the general picture of clay and timber buildings in the first two centuries and stone buildings later on.

In Staines, the various excavation sites throw light on the economy of the town: behind the Old Town Hall parts of possibly Roman wooden wharves have been found recently (Richardson 1981, 50). On the former Friends Burial Ground site there was evidence to show that cattle were brought in, watered at a pond (where their hooves left prints in the mud) and slaughtered for meat (Crouch & Shanks 1984, 16, cf 118). It is also possible that somewhere near the town sophisticated pottery was produced in the later 1st and early 2nd centuries, including mica-dusted and lead-glazed products (fig 7.10; Crouch & Shanks 1983; Arthur 1978, 298–301).

The settlements at Ewell and Croydon seem to have been less developed than at Staines.[20] Consideration of Croydon is bedevilled by the poor quality of the evidence, but the general scatter of Roman material covers a wide area and implies more than a farm or hamlet. Probably this settlement was similar to the one at Ewell, a roadside village developing in a favourable position where a made road crossed the spring-line north of the Downs. It is often suggested that Ewell originated as a posting station, but it will be argued below that the *mutatio* is more likely to have been in the Merton area. The plan (Sheldon & Schaaf 1978, fig 7) suggests that the settlement had no true centre and consisted merely of buildings straggling along the road for around 1km.[21] Much occupation debris is known (pits, pottery scatters, etc) and parts of buildings have been located, two of which, in St Mary's churchyard, have been published (Pemberton 1973a, 6–9). In so far as it is known, the outline of Ewell's history seems to be much the same as at Southwark and Staines (Pemberton 1973b).

We have already seen that there were posting stations at regular intervals along the main Roman roads. On the London–Silchester road these were apparently at Brentford (c 15km from London: Laws 1976, 187), Staines (c 30), and Wickham Bushes (c 48 and c 22km to Silchester). The last two stations on the London–Chichester road have long been known, at Alfoldean[22] (c 70km from London) and Hardham (c 53). There has been considerable speculation about the location of the first two stations which must have been in Surrey (eg Titford 1969; Neale 1973). Only excavation can resolve this problem, but at present its evidence is lacking. The most logical solution in terms of distances (matching, to some extent, especially in a short first stage, those of the London–

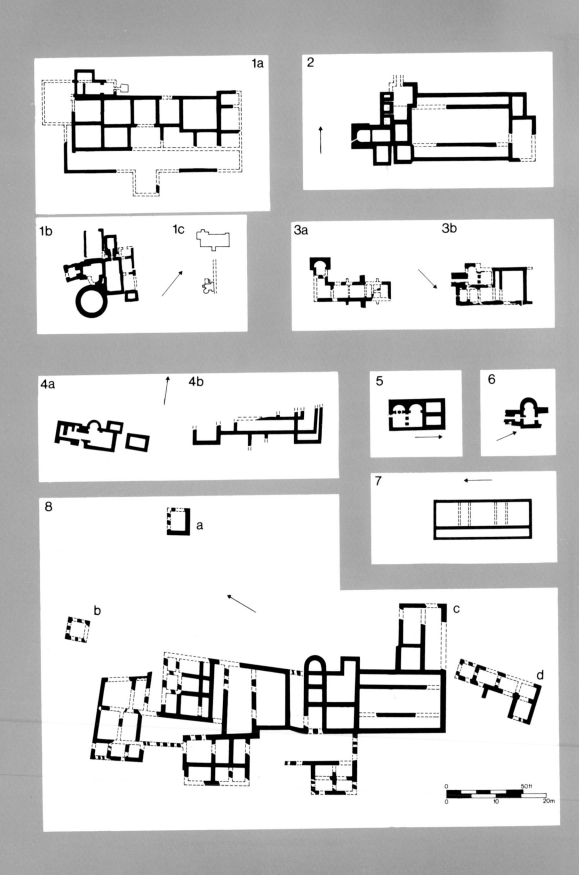

Silchester road) and of position (at major river crossings), are sites on the Wandle crossing in the Merton area and the Mole crossing in the Dorking area. If the former existed, it has probably been largely destroyed by gravel extraction and modern development,[23] while for the latter there seem to be three possible sites: Dorking town centre (Margary 1956, 67), where certainly recent work (O'Connell 1980, 51; Ettlinger 1982) has proved the presence of Roman occupation, although its extent has yet to be determined; Burford Bridge, on situation and place-name evidence alone (Neale 1973); and the Pixham area, if an eastern (with perhaps a later western) route for Stane Street is accepted. This last site, at the confluence of the Mole and the Pippbrook, is a very characteristic one for Romano-British fortified posts, and has produced a limited amount of Roman material (V Ettlinger, pers comm).

It is interesting to speculate that if the London–Winchester road existed, then there should be further posting stations between London and Neatham. No obvious candidates, however, present themselves. One other possibility should also be noted: Burpham is roughly equidistant between Alfoldean and Wickham Bushes (or Staines) and might be a small settlement between them. The site was destroyed by clay and sand digging in the last century (O'Connell 1982, 97), but the few known finds (Bird 1983) are supported to some extent by place-name evidence (Gover et al 1934, 162; cf Neale 1973, 209), and the siting, again on a major river crossing, is good.

None of the towns or settlements discussed here seem to have been sophisticated enough for any degree of formal planning[24] and they would not have had the forum and basilica complex characteristic of a large town like Silchester. Nor is there much evidence for defences. Traces of ditches have been noted at Southwark (Sheldon 1978, 47) and there is some evidence for a defensive earthwork circuit at Staines (Crouch 1978, 185). At Ewell a defence line has been postulated (Pemberton 1973b, 86) but since it links a number of disparate ditches not particularly of defensive proportions, runs at an odd angle to the main road, and effectively excludes much of the settlement area, it may be discounted. Posting stations elsewhere (eg Hardham, Winbolt 1927; Alfoldean, Winbolt 1923; 1924; and Neatham, Graham & Millett 1980) have been shown to have regular sub-rectangular defensive enclosures, although it is not clear if all were built at the same time, but none of the postulated Surrey *mutationes* have produced signs of such defences.

To round off this discussion of towns we should finally consider the negative evidence. Considerable excavation and site watching in present-day towns such as Kingston, Guildford and Reigate, have produced no evidence for Roman settlement. The religious site at Farley Heath used to be marked as a 'Roman station' on maps but the earthworks around it have been shown to be probably medieval and there is no evidence for any buildings other than the temple itself (Lowther & Goodchild 1942–3, 36–7). It is quite likely, however, that it functioned as an open-air market centre (Goodchild 1938b, 16).

The countryside

Within the framework provided by the new towns and roads and older trackways, life in the countryside probably continued much as before. It is clear that the bulk of Roman Britain's population lived in the countryside, but our evidence for their way of life is unfortunately mostly lacking. The Romanised sites, the well-known villas, were the exception, and apart from the introduction of Roman-style pottery and a few other luxuries, there is little sign that life for the native population was much altered. It is, however, now generally accepted that their numbers

Fig 7.2. Plans of Romanised buildings in Surrey. The direction of north is marked in each case. Key: 1: Ashtead, after Lowther (1930, fig opp 148); 1a, main house, 1b, bath-house, 1c, the correct relationship of the two buildings. 2: Titsey, after Leveson-Gower (1869, fig opp 219), and Fox (1905, fig 1). 3: Farnham, Six Bells, after Lowther (1953–4, figs between 50 and 51). The two buildings are shown in their correct relationship. 4: Beddington, after Frere et al (1983, fig 16). The two buildings are shown in their correct relationship. 5: Bletchingley, after Lambert (1921, 18). 6: Chatley Farm (period I), after Frere (1946–7, fig 2). 7: Broad Street Common, after Sibthorpe (1831, 399). 8: Chiddingfold, after Cooper et al (1984, figs 2, 3). The various buildings are shown in their correct relationship.

increased considerably in the Roman period (eg Taylor 1983, 106). Relatively few non-villa occupation sites have been studied in any detail, or have produced evidence for structures. In Surrey, one or two huts are claimed in the Caterham–Coulsdon area, but they are either unpublished or not very convincing (eg Little 1964, 32–3).

Inevitably then, in considering occupation sites, our attention must be concentrated on the villas, for which we have the most evidence (figs 7.2, 7.3).[25] Unfortunately, however, much of that evidence is inadequate or out of date. Only Rapsley and Beddington have been excavated recently to modern standards, and even then the latter was somewhat disappointing because much of the site had been destroyed. Current work on the villa's surroundings looks more promising. At Beddington, the bath-house had already been 'dug' in the later part of the 19th century, the period when most of Surrey's villas were recorded. At that time many informative finds were not kept (especially animal bones), and when they were retained it was rare for them to be related to the levels from which they came: indeed usually these all-important levels were not themselves recorded. A classic case is shown by the section through part of the site at Abinger drawn by Charles Darwin in 1876 (fig 7.4; Darwin 1888, fig 8); it can be seen that the work consisted, initially at least, of running a trench alongside a wall, and in the process cutting straight through at least two floor levels whose relationship to the wall was thus destroyed.[26] The same techniques were apparently still in use in the 1920s at Ashtead, to judge by a plan (fig 7.4) issued with an appeal for funds, and various of the published photographs (eg Lowther 1927, pl 4; 1929, pl 2). Such methods meant that the evidence for wooden buildings often went unrecognised.

As a result, only generalisations are possible about most of the villas, based on the finds which have been preserved or published (often relatively few in both cases), and the plans. The former can only be used to show presence, not absence (for the relevant finds may have been lost or thrown away) and as regards the latter it must always be remembered that they are likely to represent more than one phase. A useful exercise to aid understanding of what this might mean is to study the overall plan for the Rapsley site (Hanworth 1968, fig 3), and assume that there is no information to show to which phases the various walls belong.[27] Unfortunately it is rarely possible to phase the other Surrey villas, as the necessary information is simply unavailable.[28]

An attempt is made on fig 7.5 to indicate the probable dating of occupation for the villas for which reasonable evidence is available. Occupation tends to begin in the late 1st century and continue until the earlier 4th century.[29] Only Ashtead and Walton Heath seem to have begun significantly earlier in the Roman period (Lowther 1959b, 73; Prest & Parrish 1949, 59–60); the former site is also uncharacteristic in apparently going out of use by the early 3rd century. It is, of course, unusual in a number of ways (see below). The Abinger site may have been unused for a time around the earlier 3rd century, if the rather scanty coin and pottery evidence is a meaningful sample (Anon 1878; Stephenson 1916); this might explain the indications of abandonment between floor levels in Darwin's section (fig 7.4: the build-up of silt and rubble between floors). The sites at Farnham (Six Bells: Lowther 1953–4) and Chatley Farm, Cobham (Frere 1946–7) are noticeably late, but the latter is likely to be the only surviving portion of a villa largely destroyed by the Mole, and could be a late addition to an earlier building.

What these rather vague generalisations hide may be seen by looking at the picture of Rapsley built up as a result of careful excavation in the 1960s (Hanworth 1968). Five main periods of occupation were identified. No buildings were found for the first period (I), but debris in pits showed that there was occupation in the area c AD 80. In period II, dated c AD 120–200, a small timber building was constructed (fig 7.3:13), and fragmentary remains of a masonry structure

Fig 7.3. Plans of Romanised buildings in Surrey. The direction of north is marked in each case. Key: 9: Walton on the Hill, after Lowther (1949a, fig 1). The two buildings are shown in their correct relationship. 10: Walton Heath, after Pocock (1864, fig opp 1). 11: Compton, after Stephenson (1915, 43). 12: Abinger, after Anon (1878, 20). 13–16: Rapsley, after Hanworth (1968, figs 3, 6, 7, 8). 13: early building 3 (period 2), found under building 2 (=16c here). 14: building 1, at period 3. It was replaced by a building slightly to the north, as at 16d. 15: building 6 at period 3. Some of the walls survived into period 5 as at 16e. 16: the whole site in period 5: a, building 1; b, building 4; c, building 2; d, building 5 (the shrine); e, building 6.

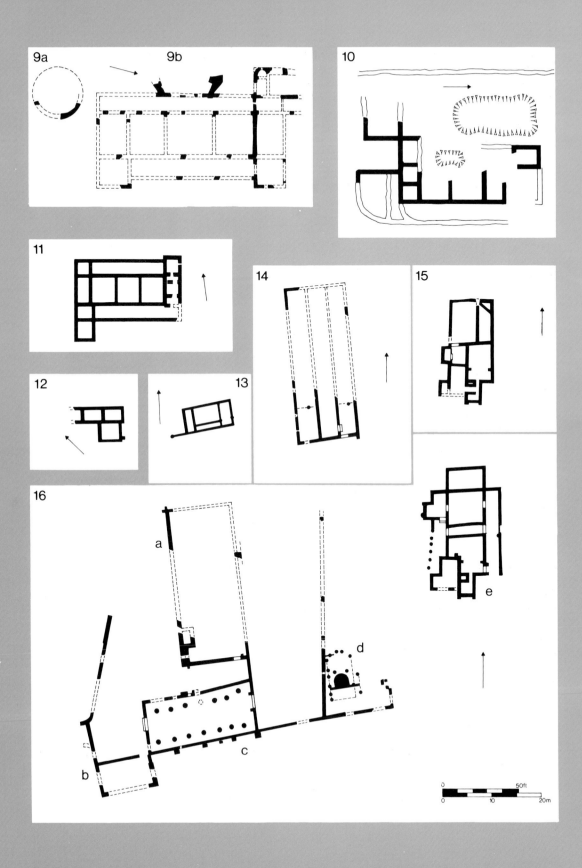

9a 9b 10 11 14 15 12 13 16

a b c d e

0   50ft
0   10   20m

were found to the south-east. Around AD 200 a fresh start was made (period III, *c* AD 200–220), and the essentials of the main complex known at the site were constructed: an aisled building (fig 7.3:14) and a separate bath-house (fig 7.3:15) were set up, divided by a fence or wall, on the baths side of which a small shrine was erected. The bath-house had two timber rooms at its northern end and a simple mosaic floor. At some point within the last 10 or so years of this third period the aisled building required urgent repairs, but its collapse could not be averted and it was rebuilt,

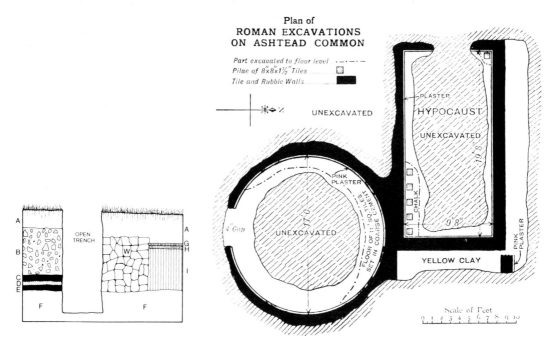

Fig 7.4. Early excavations: left, Darwin's section at Abinger (after Darwin 1888, fig 8); right, the Ashtead plan issued with the appeal for funds *c* 1925.

apparently without aisles, about 4m to the north in period IV (*c* AD 220–280). A new aisled building was constructed at right angles to it and the bath block was converted into a small house, with new rooms at the northern end and another mosaic. In the final period of occupation (V: fig 7.3:16), between AD 280 and 330, a new small building was constructed near the south-west corner adjoining the outside of the wall around the site; 'buttresses' were added to the south wall of the aisled building and three more rooms were built on to the house. This and the north-western building were destroyed by fire at the end of the occupation. It is greatly to be regretted that no other Surrey site can produce so full and interesting a picture.[30]

It can be seen from the illustrations (figs 7.2, 7.3), which include all those Romanised buildings for which meaningful plans can be produced, that there is considerable variety of size and plan in Surrey.[31] A number of villas show the characteristic 'winged corridor' front which seems to have been used to give an elegant façade to the building (rather like a Georgian refronting of an earlier structure: eg Smith, D J, 1978, 117–21). On closer examination, however, it can be seen that only Walton on the Hill (fig 7.3:9) properly conforms to the classic type, and the degree of reconstruction in the plan, based on limited evidence, is such that it cannot be taken as certain.[32] At Rapsley the evidence is instructive, for the plan suggests a failure properly to understand the architectural reasons for the winged portico front, which was clearly constructed at an odd angle. The newly discovered villa at Beddington (fig 7.2:4b) seems to be of the 'correct' winged corridor pattern, if the front-projecting walls be taken as a stepped entrance approach or similar structure. The Compton villa (fig 7.3:11; Stephenson 1915) may also be of this type if the east wing was missed because of the destruction which had obviously occurred at that corner, and the building at Titsey (fig 7.2:2; Leveson-Gower 1869) may have appeared similar. Finally, it is of interest to consider the Ashtead bath-house (fig 7.2: 1b), for there the rooms to the east suggest, to a certain extent, the possibility of the addition of a winged corridor front, parallel to the road (Lowther 1930, 132 and plan) which could have been added when the building was converted to a dwelling house – Rapsley is an obvious parallel.

There are few other links between Surrey villas as shown by their plans: the most obvious is the parallel between the main part of Titsey and the southern end of Chiddingfold, as was noted by the excavator, Cooper (Cooper *et al* 1984, 66). J T Smith (1978b, 181) has recently identified Titsey as one of a number of hall-type villas, as distinct from the more common unit type, which has blocks of separate rooms. He suggests that these halls functioned in a similar way to medieval hall houses, and imply a different social organisation to the unit type villas. However this may be, it is clear that the plan is not to be interpreted as an open courtyard as has been suggested in the past (cf Smith, J T, 1978b). Chiddingfold is clearly of interest for the very size of the complex, and it is frustrating that it is difficult to make sense of the plan (fig 7.2:8) which clearly represents more than one period. Even so, the recorded finds (Cooper *et al* 1984) suggest that the site was surprisingly utilitarian for its size.

The Walton Heath villa (fig 7.3:10) was probably also of considerable extent and its destruction at the hands of a number of well-meaning antiquaries from 1770 onwards (Prest & Parrish 1949, 59) is a sad loss to Surrey's archaeology. The mosaic and the few other recorded finds strongly suggest an unusually early and sophisticated building probably on a par with the group recognised in Sussex and Kent (Walthew 1975, 195–6). The Ashtead buildings may also have been unusually early and they are certainly very different from others in the county. The circular *laconicum* in the detached bath-house and the layout of its rooms and those of the main house are not paralleled elsewhere in Surrey and are not common in Britain generally. J T Smith has pointed out that the way the main heated room in the villa is set across the spine wall running through it is unparalleled in his experience (R Hanworth, pers comm).

Associated detached buildings are recorded at a few sites. The circular building at Walton on the Hill (fig 7.3:9a) was possibly a small temple (Lewis 1966, 86) and one or more of the odd square detached buildings (if really so) at Chiddingfold (fig 7.2:8a, 8b) may also have had a religious function.[33] The semi-circular apsed shrine at Rapsley (fig 7.3:16d), south-west of the main building, is more certain. This site has also produced the only early timber building to be recognised in the Surrey countryside, and the only true aisled buildings yet found in the county.[34]

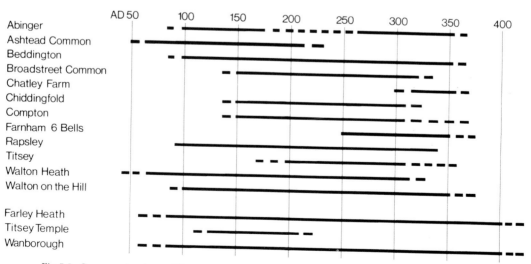

Fig 7.5. Comparative dates of Romanised buildings in Surrey. See text for comment on likely accuracy.

Little can be said of the buildings shown on figs 7.2 and 7.3 but not yet discussed. The two at Farnham (fig 7.2:3) are unusual and may well be only parts of larger structures, for photographs seem to show that excavation did not go beyond the area of the published plan (Lowther 1953–4, pls 4–8).[35] The curious 'buttresses' (fig 7.2:3a) may be simply parts of further rooms, and it is very noticeable that the best-constructed wall of the south-eastern building was at its northern end, supposedly no more than the end wall of the furnace pit! The over-large provision of baths led the excavator, Lowther, to suggest an upper storey for the house, a suggestion he also made for Ashtead.[36] This seems to be unlikely, however, over heated rooms because of the danger of fire. The building at Broadstreet Common (fig 7.2:7; Sibthorpe 1831) also seems likely to have been only part of a larger structure. It is surprisingly well appointed for so simple a plan, with possibly a mosaic, all floors at least tessellated, and a pattern along the edge of the one in the corridor. Certainly only a partial plan has been recovered of the buildings at Abinger (fig 7.3:12; Anon 1878) and Chatley Farm (fig 7.2:6; Frere 1946–7).[37] The Bletchingley bath-house (fig 7.2:5; Lambert 1921, 17–18) was probably not originally isolated, as used to be thought possible, but formed part of a villa complex.[38] When it was found, any attached timber rooms (as at Rapsley) would not have been recognised, and the recent discoveries at Beddington show how that isolated bath-house actually related to another building nearby.

Most of the villas had baths and/or heated rooms, perhaps the most Romanised aspect of these buildings. Baths are known at Ashtead (in both buildings), Titsey,[39] Walton on the Hill, Farnham (in both buildings), Compton, Beddington, Bletchingley, Chatley Farm, Chiddingfold and Rapsley. Flue tiles from both Abinger (Anon 1878, 20) and Walton Heath (Manning & Bray 1809, 644) indicate the presence of heated rooms, and baths at the latter at least seem certain. Each set of baths should have provided at least a hot room (*caldarium* – with adjacent furnace), a warm room (*tepidarium*) next door, and a cold room (*frigidarium*) to complete the range. A separate undressing room (*apodyterium*) might also be provided. The range of rooms at Compton (fig 7.3:11) is a good simple illustration with furnace at the north-east corner, and then, to the south, a hot bath, *caldarium*, *tepidarium*, *frigidarium* and perhaps an *apodyterium* if the postulated missing wing existed.[40] Both hot and warm rooms had raised floors (hypocausts), below which the heat could circulate, and flues built into the walls, at least in the former. These flues were constructed from hollow box tiles such as those made at Ashtead (see below). The same system was used to provide heated living rooms, as at Titsey (eastern end), Beddington (dwelling house), and probably at Ashtead. It is not always clear if such rooms are distinct or part of a bath complex; they may even serve both functions at different periods of a villa's life.

The majority of Surrey's hypocausts were constructed in the earlier fashion using stacks of tiles at regular intervals to support a floor. Ashtead, inevitably, has one room with an unusual system of underfloor flues made of box tiles, and another in which box tiles packed with clay were used instead of tile stacks (Lowther 1927, 152). Some of the tile stacks in the Beddington bath-house were apparently reused roofing and flue tiles (Adkins & Adkins 1983b, 327), and in general it seems likely that proper tiles for bath-houses were more difficult, if not impossible, to come by in the later Roman period. This may explain the need to construct the probably less effective channel hypocausts such as at Beddington (house) and Farnham and the later *Roman* period robbing of tile at Chatley Farm (Frere 1946–7, 85) and Walton on the Hill (Lowther 1949a, 76). At the former, Frere (1946–7, 90) suggested that the frequent rebuildings over a short period of time indicated an inability (at this later period) to solve the problems associated with bath-house construction. It is probably also significant that many bath complexes appear to have gone out of use before the buildings to which they are attached, although this is difficult to prove.

Almost all the recorded buildings had stone foundations, but the evidence is rarely sufficient to show whether the whole building was of stone or merely a stone base for a clay and timber superstructure. Usable building stone is, of course, likely to be robbed from a derelict building in a county such as Surrey,[41] so that the amount of stone found in an excavation may be no guide to what formerly existed. The type of stone varies where this is recorded, but was normally flint or greensand rubble, or a combination of both (Williams 1971, 186–7). At Abinger, Beddington, Titsey, Chatley Farm and Ashtead (apparently the bath-house only) tile is recorded in the walls, probably always used as courses to bind the stone together.[42] Tufa, probably from the Bagshot Beds, is mentioned at Beddington and Chatley Farm, and a few more special imported stones are noted below. In fact the stone, of whatever kind, must have been transported at least a few miles to most of the villas. Hanworth (1968, 31) has postulated that Rapsley had its own sandstone quarry nearby.

Window glass is noted at a few sites, in particular at Ashtead, where a large quantity was found along the front corridor (Lowther 1927, 153). This corridor had engaged half columns made from special semi- and quarter circle tiles. Roofs were everywhere of tile, when the evidence is recorded. An odd crest tile from Titsey is recorded (Oakley *et al* 1939, pl 23) and highly decorated chimney pots from Ashtead and Walton Heath (Lowther 1976, 45–6). Romano-British buildings did not have chimney stacks as such, and these, if correctly interpreted, presumably acted as vents for the hot air from the wall flues, probably those in the bath complexes.

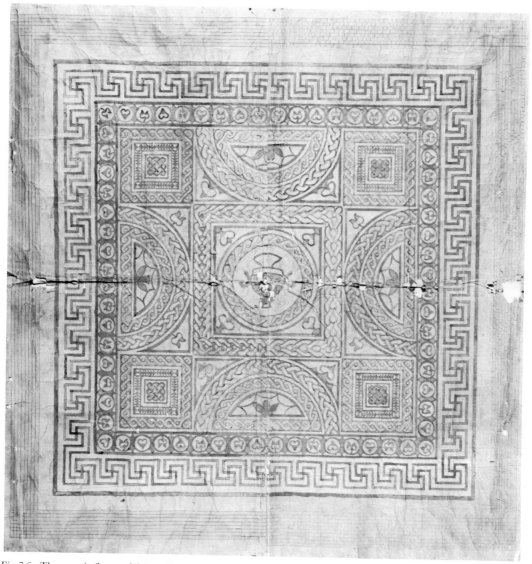

Fig 7.6. The mosaic floor at Walton Heath, a drawing made in about 1856, now in the Surrey Archaeological Society's library. There are probably a number of inaccuracies in details of the drawing.

A little evidence survives for internal decoration. The best examples are recent finds in Southwark (Winchester Palace) and at Beddington, where a large part of the plaster from a collapsed wall or ceiling was recovered. It had a pattern of squares and diamonds, in red, pink and yellow with black lines and dots (Adkins & Adkins 1982, 201–2). At Farnham plaster from the bath building had panelled designs with red, yellow and green lines on a white ground (Lowther 1953–4, 54) and Ashtead also had bands of colour on a white ground (Lowther 1929, 5). Titsey had similar garish decoration with colours including red, yellow, green, pink, white, grey and black (Leveson-Gower 1869, 228). One suspects that Romano-British interior decoration would not have been to modern taste! Floors in Surrey seem to have been more subdued but this may be because few decorated mosaics are known. The best was undoubtedly at Walton Heath (fig 7.6), where a finely executed coloured geometric pattern was laid probably in the second half of the 2nd century. At such a date mosaics were not common in Britain as a whole (Smith 1969, 77–8). The main Rapsley mosaic is also unusual because of its 3rd century date; it too has a coloured geometric design (Neal 1981, 19, 91). The same building had a simple red and (probably) white decorative scheme on the floor of another room. There was also a blue passageway, later patched in red, and some all red tessellated floors using cubes made from tiles (no doubt broken or kiln wasters).

Other Rapsley buildings had similar red floors, and they are common in Surrey's villas, although occasionally ironstone blocks were used instead, as at Broadstreet Common. This site has the only other decorated pieces of mosaic found *in situ*: a coloured rope pattern running the length of the corridor along the outer edge, and a small lozenge pattern at one end. The published plan (Sibthorpe 1831, 399) shows a rectangular gap in the centre of the central room here, and it seems likely that this once had a decorated panel. Abinger, Chiddingfold, Walton on the Hill, Compton, Beddington, Titsey and Ashtead have all produced tesserae or mosaic fragments of one or more colours other than red, so it is probable that at least some of these sites had decorated mosaics. Other flooring materials included floor tiles (eg at Titsey and Compton), *opus signinum* (a kind of pink cement, as at Compton and Walton on the Hill), possibly Horsham stone flags (at Chatley Farm), and small bricks laid in a herringbone pattern like a wood block floor (at Ashtead, and probably at Walton Heath where such bricks are recorded: Manning & Bray 1809, 645; Prest & Parrish 1949, 62).

In contrast to the many small details of their construction, we know very little about the role played by the villas in the Romano-British countryside, although clearly their very existence implies the production of a surplus which could be devoted to buildings. It is usually accepted that the great majority served as the centres of estates, normally connected with some agricultural enterprise, but perhaps also associated with some form of industry. Very little is known of the sizes or boundaries of these estates, or how they related to non-villa sites (for a useful discussion see Taylor 1983, 104–6; Wightman (1985, 119, 121) suggests that estates in Gallia Belgica varied from 50 to 100ha). Most of Surrey's villas have produced relatively little evidence to indicate their exact role in the economy of the area, but no doubt the general picture is correct. For Rapsley, Hanworth (1968, 31–2) postulated a mixed economy relying on stock raising – although unfortunately the bone evidence did not survive well on this Weald Clay site; tile-making (at the nearby Wykehurst Farm site: see below); and stone quarrying on Pitch Hill: some of the material used at Rapsley had the appearance of being 'wasters' or 'seconds' from the quarries.

The general distribution of Romano-British material in Surrey (fig 7.7), seems to follow the pattern seen in earlier periods (concentration on the spring-lines of the Downs and on the river gravels).[43] There is, however, one marked difference, which is a spread of material on to soils generally considered more difficult to work, such as the London Clay (particularly marked in the area between Farnham and Guildford). This may be connected with the coming of more advanced agricultural methods, but in the absence of evidence for site function, and the lack of agreement among specialists over when the so-called 'heavy plough' was introduced, the interpretation can only be speculative (Percival 1976, 114–16). Certainly most of the villas are sited on less 'suitable' land,[44] and their role in opening up new land – if this is the correct interpretation of the evidence – is thus of considerable interest.

In general, there is very little direct evidence for agriculture. A very few field systems which may

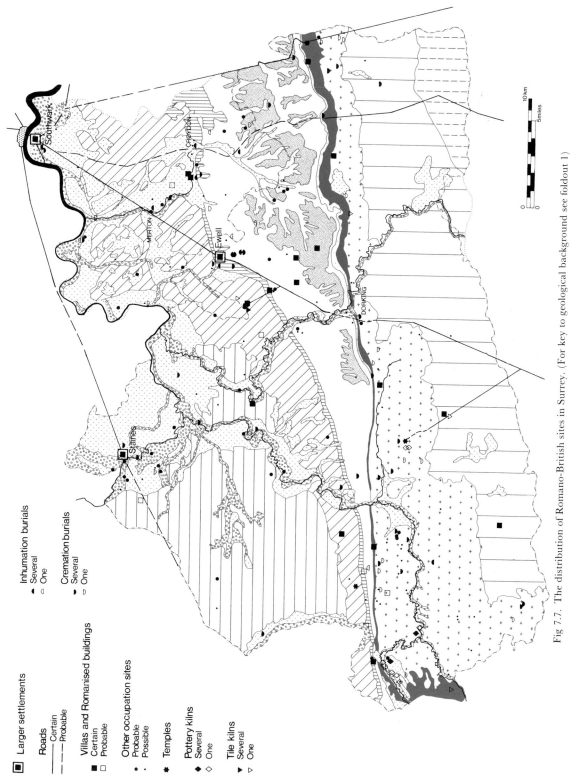

Fig 7.7. The distribution of Romano-British sites in Surrey. (For key to geological background see foldout 1)

Larger settlements

Roads
— Certain
—— Probable

Villas and Romanised buildings
■ Certain
□ Probable

Other occupation sites
● Probable
· Possible

✦ Temples

Pottery kilns
◆ Several
◇ One

Tile kilns
▶ Several
▷ One

Inhumation burials
◀ Several
◁ One

Cremation burials
▶ Several
▷ One

be, in part at least, Roman, have been suggested, such as the systems on Mickelham Downs (Frere & Hogg 1944–5), Leatherhead Downs and Farthing Down (Hope-Taylor 1946–7). Unfortunately no dating evidence could be found for another system near Old Woking recently published (Hampton & Hawkins 1983). Blair (1976a; cf Bird et al 1980, fig 2) has suggested a regular pattern of fields related to the Ashtead villa, but it seems odd that the regularity did not extend to making the axis parallel with that of the known road to the site.

There is only a limited amount of animal bone evidence recorded to help fill out this picture. Leveson-Gower's Titsey report (1869, 221) was most unusual for its day in giving any details of the bone found.[45] He mentions hare, sheep, ox, deer and 'hog'. At Farnham, sheep, ox, pig, red and roe deer are recorded (Lowther 1953–4, 55), and at Rapsley, where bone survival was poor, cattle, horse and pig were noted (Chaplin 1968). Compton has only a mention of red deer (Stephenson 1915, 49). On sites other than villas we may note the oxen, sheep, pigs and dogs at Binscombe, which also had, intriguingly, a 'small elderly and domestic fowl' and a small stallion of some 25 years of age, which had apparently been hamstrung before being killed by a collapsing building (Done 1977). Animal remains in Southwark and evidence for a cattle trade in Staines have already been noted; it is interesting that apparently the animals were not butchered at Southwark (Sheldon 1978, 33). Geraldene Done's comments on the sheep remains from the only fully published Ewell site deserve repetition: jaws aged between one and three years 'suggest the possibility of an over-wintered flock. If this was so, the healthy condition of the many teeth found (both in and out of jaws) would be an indication of a good standard of shepherding with careful culling' (Done 1973, 23; cf, for Southwark, Rixson 1978, 604).

This evidence is as yet insufficient for any conclusions to be drawn from it, for example, whether emphasis on a particular type of animal changed through time, or if different animals were favoured in different areas. Other evidence for agriculture and related activities is largely non-existent, but it must be stressed that this is because organic materials so rarely survive in the archaeological record.[46] It is very important to realise that any discussion of the economy, especially of trade and industry, inevitably centres on those materials which have survived, especially pottery and tiles, and less often metal and stone. For instance, there is no direct evidence for forestry, which must have been of prime importance, producing wood for buildings, furniture, ships and boats, carts, crates, fuel for home and industry, and so on. There can be little doubt that woodland management was a major occupation, especially in areas such as the Weald and on the London Clay. Perhaps Chiddingfold was the centre of a major forestry estate, which might explain its apparently isolated position and utilitarian appearance. Charcoal from the furnaces at Ashtead was analysed and found to be almost certainly common oak (Lowther 1929, 5–6), but there seems to be no other evidence recorded for types of wood in use. No doubt there was a specific industry for the production of charcoal for use in hypocaust furnaces and the like.

It is often assumed that major industries like tile production centres and the Wealden ironworks caused widespread destruction of woodland in their vicinities (eg Cleere 1976, 240–1; Cunliffe 1973, 123; Darvill & McWhirr 1982, 146–7). Rackham (1976, 91–5) has shown, however, that this is untrue at later times (cf Ashworth 1970, 62–3), and we may therefore suspect that it was equally untrue in the Roman period. There is no sign, for instance, that major, long-lasting Romano-British pottery industries were forced to move around to maintain an adequate supply of fuel (cf Peacock 1982, 25).

Trade and Industry

In Surrey there seem to have been relatively few industries, at least for which evidence survives or has yet been recognised.[47] The best known are inevitably those connected with pottery and tile production. A major pottery centre existed around and west of Farnham. Most of the surviving evidence is in Alice Holt Forest, just over the county boundary into Hampshire, but Lyne and Jefferies, who have considered the industry in detail (1979; see also Millett 1979), think that the main production area was around Farnham where much of the evidence was destroyed by gravel working in the earlier years of this century (Lyne & Jefferies 1979, 11; Oakley et al 1939, 221–4).

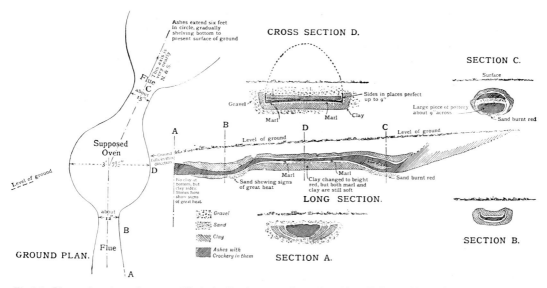

Fig 7.8. Plan and sections of a pottery kiln in the Farnham area (reproduced from Falkner 1907, 230); a very fine record for
its date.

Some kilns were recorded (eg Falkner 1907, 230; fig 7.8), and they seem to have been of the same type as those excavated and published by Clark (1950) a little to the east of the main area, at Overwey. These were double flue kilns (fig 7.9), apparently without the floor structure found in more sophisticated kilns such as those of the Nene Valley (eg Wild 1974, figs 3, 9). There have been a number of successful experiments carried out recently to reconstruct a kiln and fire reproduction

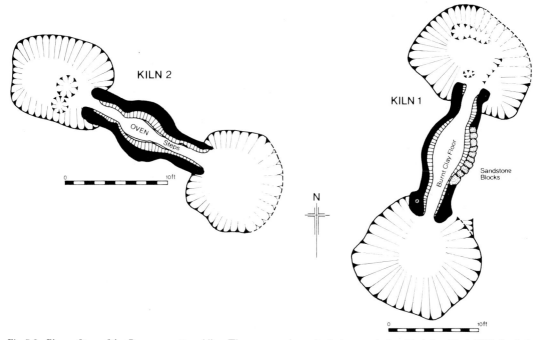

Fig 7.9. Plans of two of the Overwey pottery kilns. They are not shown in their true relationship (after Clark 1950, figs 3, 4;
cf fig 2). Some of their products feature on figs 11, 12.

pots, and to test the possibility of transport by water up the Wey and Thames to London (Anon 1978, 149–50). In fact carriage by road seems more likely.[48] The pottery produced was mostly grey domestic ware, large storage jars, bowls and the like, sometimes with simple white slip and incised decoration (figs 7.10–7.12). Frere has suggested that one special product may have been used as a beehive (fig 7.12:20; Clark & Nichols 1960, 57 n 1). The pottery started early in the Roman period, but production was at its greatest extent in the 3rd and 4th centuries.[49] It is often suggested that the Farnham Six Bells buildings were part of a pottery works, but there is no evidence to support this view. The main point of interest is the aqueduct channel identified running across the site, which might well have a connection with a pottery workshop, but had been filled in and was out of use before the buildings were erected on the site.[50]

A few other pottery kilns are known to have existed in the countryside, in particular at Farley Heath (Goodchild 1938b, 18; Lowther & Goodchild 1943, 38) and near Wisley (Gardner 1912, 131–2). There was probably also a production centre somewhere in the Leatherhead area,[51] but the kilns sometimes thought to have existed in the area of the later, medieval, Limpsfield pottery industry seem more likely to have been misinterpreted medieval kilns mixed up with Romano-British occupation material. The production centre for various types of sophisticated pottery in or near Staines has already been noted, and a full range of domestic wares is also thought to have been produced locally (Crouch & Shanks 1983).

Although exploiting the same natural resources in much the same way, pottery and tile industries seem usually to have been distinct. By far the most interesting tile production site –

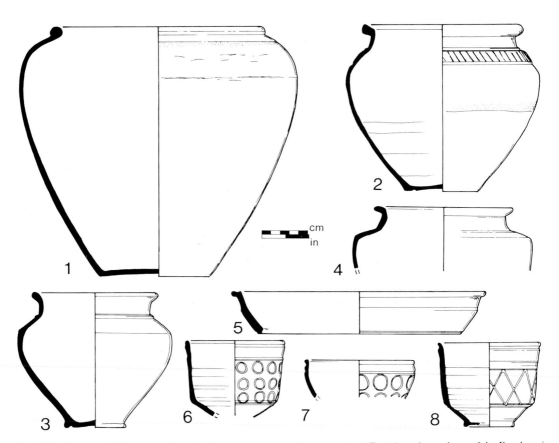

Fig 7.10. Romano-British pottery from the Surrey area; 1st and 2nd centuries AD. 1–5: early products of the Farnham/Alice Holt industry (1–3, 5, after Lyne & Jefferies 1979, 4.6, 1.10, 1.20, 5.1; 4, after Marsh & Tyers 1978, IIC.2). 6–8: lead glazed vessels possibly from a kiln in the Staines area (after Arthur 1978, 5.12, 7.8, 5.3). All 1:4

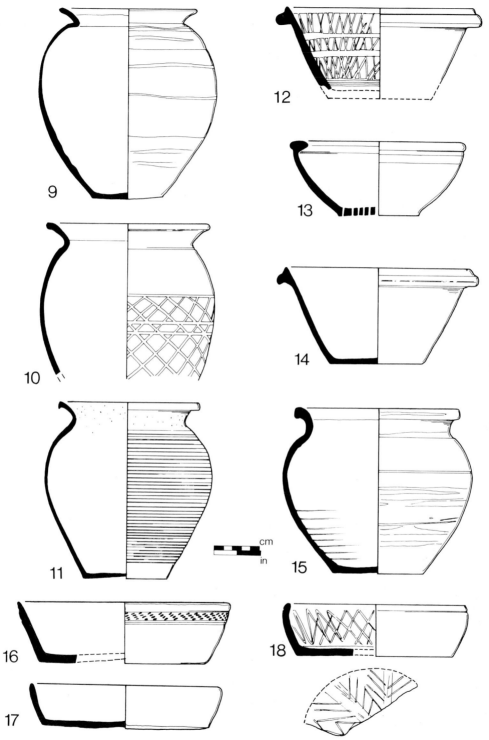

Fig 7.11. Romano-British pottery from the Surrey area; 3rd and 4th centuries AD. All products of the Farnham/Alice Holt industry (9, 14, 17 after Lyne & Jefferies 1979, 3B.8, 5B.8, 6A.1; 10–13, 15, 16, 18 after Clark 1950, nos 38, 1, 82, 94, 24, 76, 68). All 1:4

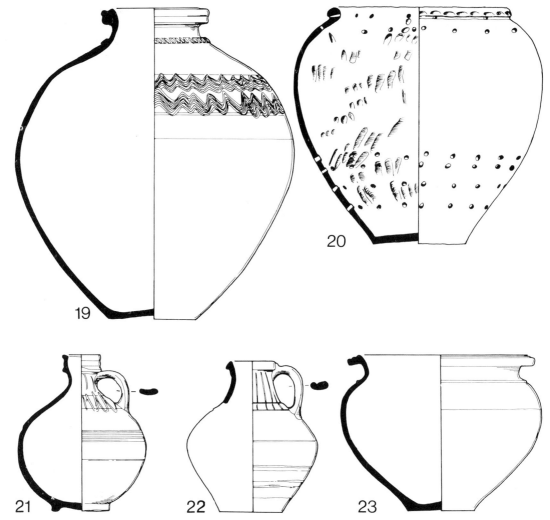

Fig 7.12. Romano-British pottery from the Surrey area; 3rd and 4th centuries AD. All products of the Farnham/Alice Holt industry (19, 21 after Clark 1950, nos 55, 91; 20 after Frere 1942–3, 52; 22, 23 after Lyne & Jefferies 1979, 8.10, 1.34). All 1:4 except 20, which is at 1:8

indeed, industrial centre of any kind – in Surrey was on Ashtead Common around the villa buildings. It is unfortunately relatively little known except as passing references in Lowther's reports on the villa (1927, 153; 1929, 1), and more recent work which has mapped some of the clay pits and located a few kilns (Hampton 1977, 31–3). The latter seem to have been simple clamps, involving no permanent structure. None the less, some of the products of the Ashtead tileries were very sophisticated, and seem to have found a market throughout south-east England and even further afield (Lowther 1948, figs 3–6; Rodwell 1978a, fig 6). Hampton calculates, from the size of the quarries, that Ashtead could have provided enough tile to roof 50 villas its own size, as well as producing the more unusual tiles (1977, 34).

In view of the lack of detailed evidence from the site, and the difficulties of dating the products elsewhere, it is not yet clear when the works were in production, but this seems to have begun early in the Roman period, and Drury has dated some of the most sophisticated products to AD 60–80 at Chelmsford (Johnston & Williams 1979, 383). The last half of the 1st century was probably the main period of production, which may not have continued long into the 2nd century. A major problem is the identification of specifically Ashtead products. Some were decorated by the use of roller stamps, but such stamps could easily have been taken by their users to other production centres; thus like the plain tiles they can only certainly be identified by analysis of the clay.[52] Nevertheless it is clear that tiles were made on the site in quantity, and probable that many different types were produced. These certainly included normal tiles, like roof and hypocaust *pilae* tiles (Hampton 1977, 33), but it is the more specialised products which have attracted attention. Box flue tiles for hypocausts were made, some of the usual type with patterns on the outer faces made by wooden or bone combs (Green 1979). There were at least two different sizes, and other types with odd cut-outs, fish-tail keys and double boxes. The designs were only incidentally decorative, as there is no doubt that they served as a key for wall plaster. This is true even of the highly decorative patterns made by means of a roller stamp which were first classified by Lowther (1948) as a result of interest aroused by his work at Ashtead. He recognised a number of different groups of decoration, each usually including a number of different dies, and these groups have not been materially altered by subsequent work. Most of the patterns were relatively simple, involving shapes based on diagonal or straight lines, but some were very complex including the famous 'dog and stag' tiles (fig 7.13) and those Lowther called 'florid.' The former include a few letters in the decoration: G. I. S. (the stops shown in proper Roman inscriptional fashion as small downward pointing triangles) and I. V. FE. A commonly suggested interpretation is that G. I. S. represents

Fig 7.13. Some products of the Ashtead tileworks: left, chimney pot or lamp column (after Lowther 1976, fig 1.1); centre, top: pattern on the 'dog and stag' flue tiles; middle: small brick for herringbone pattern floor (used with the thin long side uppermost); bottom: open lamp (from Beddington: after Adkins & Adkins 1983a, fig 11); right, box flue tile. (Drawing by David Williams) Scale 1:5.

the three names of the owner of the works, as it might be Gaius Iulius S . . . , and the rest denotes the stamp maker – Iulius (if so, perhaps a freedman of the owner) V . . . FE (cit), that is, 'made this'. Other Ashtead products were the small bricks used in herringbone pattern floors, quarter and semi-circular tiles for engaged columns, and elaborate chimney pots or lamp columns which presumably were only made to special order (fig 7.13).[53]

The early date of the tileworks and the possibility that the owner was a Roman citizen (because if he was G. I. S. he bore the *tria nomina*) are factors to be taken into account when considering aspects which suggest a military connection with the site. There are three other points to be noted: the circular *laconicum* of the bath-house is not usual on villa sites, but well known in Roman fort bath-houses (Walthew 1975, 196; Lowther 1959b, 73); the sandstone slab, fragments of which were reused in the gutter of the 'house', probably carried an inscription, again unusual;[54] and the die 8 tile, with a pattern Lowther called 'florid', has been likened to the insignia carried by auxiliary regiments of the Roman army (Liversidge 1968, 199), although it should be noted that it may not have been produced at Ashtead.[55] It may well be that G. I. S. or one of his workers was an ex-military man for it is perhaps unlikely that the tilery will have been a military establishment as such (but see McWhirr & Viner 1978, 360).

The Ashtead tileworks probably served a number of major early villas in south-east England and perhaps also public buildings in towns such as London, Chelmsford and even as far as Leicester (Lowther 1948, figs 4, 5). The villas are characterised by early sophistication including detached baths, flue tiles, small herringbone floor bricks, and mosaic floors (Walthew 1975, 195–6). Clearly Walton Heath was one of their number. It is interesting to speculate that it might have been the villa owned by the proprietor of the tilery – a continuation of the known road from the works to Stane Street would pass very close to Walton Heath. The Ashtead buildings themselves, although possessing a number of these early sophisticated features, seem in some ways to be of a lesser status, and their site cannot have been pleasant on the sticky London Clay in winter, or when the tile kilns were in full operation. On the other hand the buildings as we know them show certain contradictory elements which probably imply that earlier high quality buildings were later occupied by people of lower status (cf Lullingstone: Meates 1979, 22–3). In particular it seems clear that the specially made box tiles with integral fish-tails for bonding into the wall, and semi-circular cut-outs, must have been made on site for the building (Lowther 1927, 152–3; 1929, pl 4), and the same is probably true for the double-sized box tiles.[56] The curious use of box tiles for hypocaust *pilae*, however, implies the reuse of material because the correct types were not available.[57]

Tiles were also made in Surrey at Horton near Epsom, Wykehurst Farm, near Rapsley (Goodchild 1937), and possibly at Doods Farm near Reigate (Hooper 1945, 16–17). The first two sites have produced elaborate tile-built kilns probably to be dated around AD 150. They do not seem to have made roller-stamped flue tiles, although at Wykehurst a pear-shaped tile was one specialist product. Green's work on comb patterns (1979) may make it possible in future to recognise Wykehurst products on other sites.[58]

There is little else to mention of Surrey's Roman industries.[59] Metalworking in towns and villas is always likely to have been small-scale, for local needs only (eg Hanworth 1968, 24; cf Smith 1980, 66). No trace of larger-scale ironworking has been recognised and this all seems to lie south of the border, in Sussex (Cleere 1974, fig 1), although the Farley Heath dedication (see below) may suggest that this temple acted as a religious centre for the ironworkers.[60] Possible stone quarrying near Rapsley has been noted above, and it must have occurred elsewhere, for instance on Limpsfield Chart (Gray & Percy 1985), and to provide greensand from near Guildford for Ashtead (Lowther 1930, 138, n 1) and Chatley Farm (Frere 1946–7, 76 n 1). There may also have been quern-producing factories (Tomalin 1977, 83–5; Crawford 1953, 105).

A discussion of trade in Surrey is hampered by lack of good evidence. No doubt it is reasonable to assume that the county area was not very rich and was therefore unable to support a major town or large villas, although of course London (and Southwark) must be to some extent responsible for this situation, as also the territorial split between Atrebates (Silchester) and Cantiaci (Rochester and Canterbury). The towns will have taken particularly agricultural products, tiles from

Ashtead, and pottery from Staines and the Farnham area, which was also exported more widely in Roman Britain. So far as imports are concerned, towns and villas show the usual range of pottery including fine wares from the Continent, such as samian pottery and Gaulish colour coat vessels, and from other parts of Britain, from such centres as Oxfordshire, the Nene Valley, the New Forest and perhaps the Pulborough area. Less sophisticated products came particularly from the Alice Holt/Farnham complex. Querns from the Mayen area of Germany are recorded as well as locally produced examples, and the Rhineland also produced fine glass as found at Rapsley and Chiddingfold (and presumably the unusually large collection at Ashtead). Spanish amphorae fragments from Chiddingfold show that fish paste or oil could reach even so apparently isolated a spot. It seems that life in the villas was lived at a comfortable level. As we have seen, most of these buildings made use of local materials, but some stone came from further afield, such as the Petworth 'marble' and oolitic limestone at Ashtead, and apparently Old Red Sandstone at the Titsey temple.[61]

Death, burial and religion

Little can be said about the people who lived in Roman Surrey. There are virtually no inscriptions, even from Southwark,[62] and few burial sites have been recognised. Even fewer have received the attention that would make it possible to discuss details of illnesses, stature, longevity, etc. The cemeteries around Ewell, Staines and Southwark have received little recent attention;[63] at the last-named late inhumations within areas previously occupied must indicate a contraction of settlement in progress (Dean 1981, 53). Lead and stone coffins are known near the Beddington villa (Adkins & Adkins 1984) and in Croydon (Anderson 1877, 90–1: clearly Roman). The earlier rite was cremation and the cemeteries in south-west Surrey at Charterhouse, Haslemere and Tilford have already been mentioned. Others are known, for example at Merrow and in the Farley Heath area (Lasham 1896; Heath 1932). That this rite continued into the 3rd century is shown by recent finds at Bandon Hill, ironically coming to light in the course of grave digging in a modern cemetery (Pryer 1975; 1977). An unusual insight into the way of life is provided by a group of bone gaming counters (fig 7.14) found with a burial near Ewell: several have inscriptions which probably meant 'I shall pay back 5 denarii' (Frere *et al* 1977, 445). Finally we may note that Roman period barrows are known in several of the adjoining counties (Dunning & Jessup 1936) and a possible example has been suggested at Morden, near Stane Street (Merrifield 1975, 63).

Possible shrines associated with villas have already been noted, and there is a certain amount of evidence scattered throughout the county for religious beliefs (fig 7.15). The most noteworthy site is the Romano-Celtic temple at Farley Heath and its enclosure which unfortunately received a great deal of unskilful attention from Tupper in the mid-19th century, with a consequent loss of much important evidence (Goodchild 1938b).[64] It is nevertheless clear that the site was an important religious centre, almost certainly beginning in the Iron Age, and continuing right through to the end of the Roman period.[65] The temple was of a common type, two concentric squares in plan representing a central tower-like shrine with a portico round the outside (fig 7.15A; Lewis 1966, 19). Many interesting finds were made in the temple and within its *temenos*, the large enclosure around it. They include a priest's crown and sceptre binding (figs 7.16, 7.17), the latter being unique. It has been interpreted as showing a dedication to the Celtic deities Sucellus, Taranis and Nantosvelta, and probably also Vulcan or a Celtic equivalent (Goodchild 1946–7).[66] Small enamelled model stools from the site were probably used for part of a ritual (Bateson 1981, 47–8) and the many coins must have been votive offerings by worshippers. Certain aspects point to a link with similar temples in Normandy, including the supposed paved pond and the dedication of Neolithic axes and fossil *echini* (sea urchins). Interestingly, the Titsey temple is also one of the few in Roman Britain to have a nearby pond (Lewis 1966, 131), and fossil sea urchins and worked flints are recorded as well (Graham 1936, 99).[67] It was very similar in plan to Farley Heath, but was apparently much less important, and seems to have been one of the shortest-lived Romano-Celtic temples in Roman Britain (Lewis 1966, 51, table 6; Farley Heath by contrast was one of the most long lasting). Another rural temple has been suggested at Woodlands Park near Leatherhead

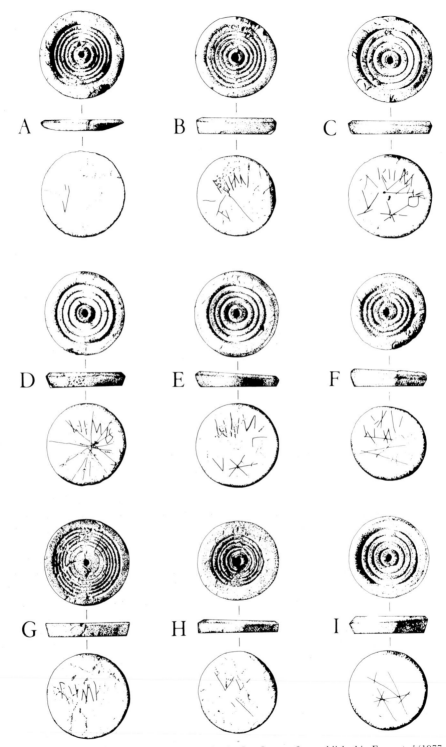

Fig 7.14. Bone counters from a burial near Ewell. Drawing by Jon Cotton, first published in Frere *et al* (1977, 447). The marks V∗ (on E, for example) should mean 5 denarii; while RIIMI (=REMI, clearest on G) could be short for *remittam*, 'I shall pay back' (Frere *et al* 1977, 445). They are presumably gaming counters. Scale 1:1

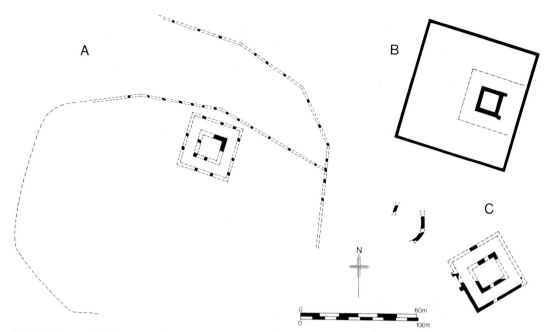

Fig 7.15. Romano-Celtic temples in Surrey. A: Farley Heath, with surrounding enclosure (after Lowther & Goodchild 1942–3, plan opp 34); B: Titsey, with surrounding enclosure (after Graham 1936, 88); C: Wanborough, with traces of associated building (after O'Connell, unpublished).

(Lowther 1963a), and a religious association for the double-ditched enclosure at the Matthew Arnold School near Staines is worth consideration (Crawford 1933, 290–2; cf Lewis 1966, 4–5). In the context of Celtic religion we should note the possible ritual shafts at Ewell (Ross 1968, 264, 271) and the groups from a pit and a well in Southwark (Sheldon 1978, 44) and a well in Staines which may represent a similar phenomenon: parts of no less than 17 dog skeletons were recovered from the latter! (Richardson 1982, 166; J Chapman, pers comm).

Other religious influences seen in the county are all from the eastern part of the Empire. Mural crowns from Chiddingfold, Rapsley and Alfoldean may be related to Cybele worship, and the bronze ibis from Chiddingfold (Bird & Hanworth 1984, microfiche 26; pl 2) suggests Isis. Rapsley's terracotta pine cones (Hanworth 1968, 36–7) presumably took the place of the real thing when unobtainable, for use in one of a number of eastern religious ceremonies. There is also a Bes figurine from Abinger (Steel 1979), a bronze Aesculapius from Walton Heath (Manning & Bray 1809, pl opp 420) and a superb Atys lamp from near Beddington (Bailey 1976) – if it is not a modern import this would be the finest lamp known in Roman Britain.[68] In Southwark the famous flagon, apparently from a temple of Isis, should be mentioned (London Museum 1930, 51) and some of the recent sculptural finds from below the Cathedral (Hammerson 1978) show an eastern influence. There is apparently no Christian material from the county as one would perhaps expect of an essentially rural area, and in this context the longevity of the Farley Heath temple is worthy of remark.

Farley Heath is in fact one of the few sites in Surrey to show activity to the end of the Roman period. Discussion of the transition to Saxon Surrey is properly a topic for the next chapter, but a few comments on the earlier period are in order. Harvey Sheldon (1975; cf 1981) has argued for a decline in our area in the period *c* AD 150–250 in town and countryside, but in fact while this may be true for towns it does not entirely square with the rural evidence (Hanworth 1975). In Surrey

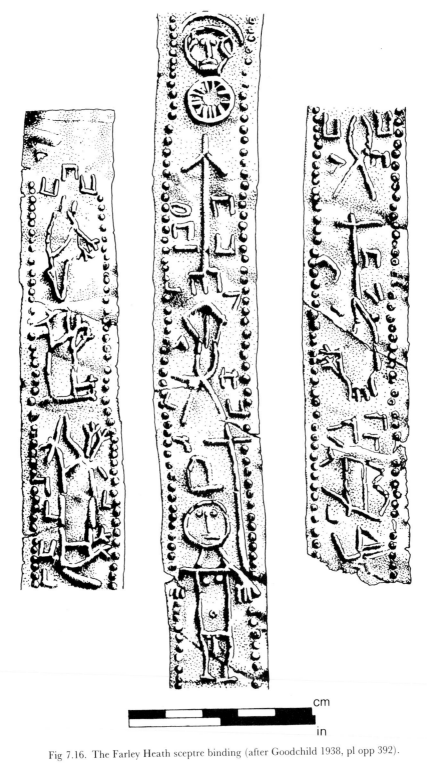

Fig 7.16. The Farley Heath sceptre binding (after Goodchild 1938, pl opp 392).

Fig 7.17. Above: the Farley Heath priest's crown. The bronze central disc and chains are shown draped over a modern leather cap. Diameter of disc: 5cm. (*Photograph by courtesy of Guildford Museum*) Below: one of the Wanborough head-dresses, after cleaning for conservation. Diameter of wheel: 3.8cm. (*Photograph by courtesy of Kent County Museum Service*)

the decline in the countryside apparently comes later, with few if any of the villas surviving late into the 4th century, the dating evidence being supported by the absence of major late buildings with quality mosaics (cf Webster 1969, 228–30). Speculation as to what this might mean is difficult in the present state of our knowledge. Coin hoards, which are traditionally held to show troubled times, are insufficient – and those that are known are rarely well enough published – to add much to the picture. For what it is worth, the Surrey examples seem to concentrate in the period from *c* AD 300 to 370.[69] It may well be that the transition from Roman Britain to Saxon England was accomplished relatively early and peacefully in the Surrey area. It is certainly still an area with high potential for the study of that transition. Indeed the foregoing discussion of Surrey in the Roman period should have made clear, if nothing else, the very many gaps in our knowledge. It is, rightly, no longer acceptable to excavate unthreatened sites, but much may be learnt from organised fieldwork and from detailed examination of material held in our museums. There are still roads to find and, above all, the villas and towns need to be set in their context. Work of this kind is being undertaken by a number of people, and if pursued with vigour should render this account out of date in only a few years time.

NOTES

1   I am most grateful to Lynn Jackson for typing the draft of this paper from a very difficult manuscript. I have also to thank many people who have discussed various aspects of the Romano-British period in our area with me over the years, in particular Joanna Bird, Tony Clark, Vivien Ettlinger, John Gower, David Graham, Rosamond Hanworth, John Hampton, Martin O'Connell, Rob Poulton and Harvey Sheldon. They cannot, of course, be held responsible for any errors that remain in this account.

2   Writers since Bede have thought to trace Caesar's route in 54 BC and the point where he crossed the Thames. Coway or Cowey Stakes near Walton Bridge has been a frequent candidate (for a sensible discussion, see Stonebanks 1972). The 1st edition (1872) of the OS 6 inches to the mile map bears the delightful legend, on the St George's Hill Iron Age fort: 'British Camp. Occupied by CAESAR before the crossing of the Thames at the Cowey Stakes.' In fact, as yet there is no *archaeological* evidence for Caesar's presence in Britain (Johnson 1983, 228), and in spite of Thompson's persuasive arguments (1979, 301–3), I feel that more evidence is required before a Caesarian date for the south-west Surrey hillforts can be entertained.

3   It may be as well to stress that only about half of the invading army were Roman citizens, and of those most were not even Italians; the term 'Roman', therefore, in the context of Roman Britain, can only be used in a somewhat loose sense.

4   Most of Surrey may have been part of a client kingdom ruled by Cogidubnus as *rex magnus* (Barrett 1979, especially 234; Bogaers 1979).

5   The name Stane Street derives from Old English words meaning a paved or metalled road – and almost invariably therefore Roman. There are, in consequence, several other Stane or Stone Streets to be found in Britain. None of the Roman names of roads in this country are known – if they ever existed.

6   David Graham has recently seen the site again from the air, and tells me that he considers it unlikely to be Roman.

7   Boudica is, of course, commonly known as Boadicea. For the name see Jackson 1979; for the date see Carroll 1979.

8   It is possible that the area of Southwark which would have been most developed and therefore most affected by the results of the revolt was destroyed by erosion by the Thames in the post-Roman period.

9   In general I would agree with Fuentes, and had independently come to similar conclusions. Surely Suetonius would have tried to concentrate his forces (and he would have been expecting Legio II, as ordered, to move towards him); to protect the most civilised and friendly part of the province – the area around Winchester and Chichester; to cover his main food supply area; and to keep open his communications across the Channel. Moreover, the rebels seem to have been mostly interested in looting and they may well have held a grudge against the resurgent Atrebates. Everything suggests a move west, not north, from London. I cannot, however, believe that it will ever be possible to be sure of the exact site of the final battle.

10   London's formal status (*vicus, municipium*, etc) at this time – and indeed throughout the Roman period – is difficult to assess. See Merrifield (1983, 61, and 61–89 *passim*), but also Drinkwater (1983, 105–8), for the suggestion that Roman usage may have been less rigorous than modern scholars tend to assume.

11   For the Regni in Surrey see, for example, Rivet (1964, fig 9), and Frere (1974, fig 1). Cunliffe (1973, fig 1) includes part of Surrey (contrast the frontispiece map), but does not discuss the tribal boundaries (contrast Todd 1973, 10–19). The problems that can arise are illustrated by Green (1976), whose gazetteer gives Leatherhead to the Cantiaci, but Ashtead (as 'Ashstead'), Ewell and even Titsey to the Regni. In fact, although our evidence is limited, it appears quite specific: the Atrebates and Cantiaci were neighbours and the Regni lay 'below' them and surely therefore south of the Weald (see Rivet & Smith 1979, 144, for Ptolemy's positioning of the *civitates*, and 445–6 for a discussion of the tribal name: perhaps originally *Regini*). Interestingly Thiessen polygons based on London/Southwark, Rochester, Silchester and Chichester tend to support this suggestion; the junction of polygons at Farley Heath may be significant, especially for its postulated market role (see below).

12 The road has yet to be definitely established; personally I expect a road to be found along roughly the line Farley Heath – St Martha's Hill (as aiming point) – Burpham – Pirbright – Wickham Bushes, although recent work by Tony Clark may indicate that the Wey crossing was at Shalford. It must also be borne in mind that Farley Heath may have been at a cross-roads, served from places like Staines, and the Dorking and Chiddingfold directions. It was clearly a major religious site.

13 For example in Staines (Crouch 1978, 180), Ewell (Lowther 1935a, 29–34; Pemberton 1973a, 4–6) and Southwark (eg Schwab 1978, 181). Recently Stane Street has been examined south-east of Leatherhead (Fasham & Hanworth 1978, 175–6: no surviving metalling but evidence for use of the plough to create the terracing for the road), and south of Dorking at North Holmwood, where the full width of the road (c 10m) survived, with metalling set on a clay *agger* (cambered bank), and an associated drainage system (Ettlinger *et al* 1984).

14 Rivet & Smith (1979, 441) discuss the name and suggest that the use of the plural may mean simply that there was more than one arch in a single bridge. The topography, however, favours more than one bridge.

15 It should be noted that the 'Roman road' seen on aerial photographs as running north from Stanwell has now been shown conclusively to be a Neolithic cursus (Bird *et al* 1983, 188–91).

16 Such routes are likely to be prehistoric in origin; they are better placed for soils underfoot and more useful than any of the routes postulated on the Downs themselves. Indeed much of the A25 route makes a perfectly good ridgeway of its own, and it has recently been suggested that the A246 route's major river crossing point at Leatherhead has a name of Celtic origin (Coates 1980). The line of this route presumably followed more or less the pre-turnpike route between Leatherhead and Guildford, much of which can be deduced from Rocque's map of 1768, passing close to each of the parish churches and, significantly, using the Thanet Sand.

17 Singular *mutatio*; often incorrectly referred to as *mansiones* (single *mansio*), which were in fact resting places about 40km apart. The word *mansio* is also used more loosely of any inn, hence the confusion.

18 The results of work in Southwark up to 1978 are summarised by Bird & Graham (1978), but Harvey Sheldon tells me that the most recent excavations have altered his theories about the 3rd century decline and the size of the late settlement. Early stone buildings are now known at 15–23 Southwark Street, and recent excavations on the Winchester Palace site have produced very interesting results. The remains of a major building of the mid-2nd century, with hypocausts and painted wall plaster surviving in quantity, and an important inscription, have been found (B Yule and M Hammerson, pers comm; cf note 62). For a summary of late Roman Southwark see Yule (1982, especially 245–8), where the various problems of the black earth are also discussed. For a technical discussion of the latter see Macphail (1981b).

19 The sequences put forward in Crouch (1978) and Crouch & Shanks (1984, 9–13), should be treated with caution, as it is doubtful if the pottery evidence will wholly bear the early date suggested for it.

20 The symbols on the Ordnance Survey Map of Roman Britain (4th edition 1978) for Staines and Ewell should be reversed.

21 The plan given by Webster (1975, fig 6) cannot be justified by the evidence (and many of the burials marked are Anglo-Saxon). The occupation site at Purberry Shot (Lowther 1946–7a) is often spoken of as though separate from Ewell, but it was probably simply part of the straggle of settlement.

22 A fascinating recent suggestion is the derivation of the older place-name, Dedisham, from *mutatio* (Coates 1981, 67).

23 Bidder (1934, 23–4) notes, as well as pottery, some 500–600 coins which seem to have been too scattered and range too widely in date to be a hoard. (For a grid reference see Bidder & Morris 1959, 51.) Recent excavations by Scott McCracken at Merton Priory have produced Roman pottery from the lowest levels (S McCracken, pers comm; see also Turner 1965a).

24 There is not enough evidence to substantiate a formal street grid in Staines, although one is sometimes claimed.

25 Surrey's villas seem to fare badly in general publications; Rapsley is frequently said to be published in *Sussex Archaeological Collections* (eg Cunliffe 1973, 147; Percival 1976, 208; Webster 1983, 253), Titsey is placed in Kent (Smith, D J, 1978, 119), Walton Heath and Walton on the Hill are conflated (Rivet 1969, 277), and so on. 'Villa' is, of course, a term which defies close definition (see eg Percival 1976, 13–15) even where much of the site has been excavated. Several possible villa sites are not mentioned in the text (eg Binscombe, Smith, C, 1977; Headley, Taylor 1960, 233; Coombe, Kingston, Whimster 1931, 231; East Clandon, Kerr 1971; Puttenham Common, Clark & Nichols 1960, 46–7).

26 This very early section drawing was not made specifically for archaeological reasons but to study earthworm action.

27 In particular, comparison of the baths area at Rapsley and Titsey is instructive; a number of different phases interpreted as one may be the origin of the theory of the Titsey 'fullery' (see note 38 below).

28 What information we are given may not be trustworthy. For example compare the plan with the perspective drawing in the first publication of the Titsey villa (Leveson-Gower 1869), especially the north wall of room K and the alignment of the north walls of rooms G and H. Compare these also to Fox's plan apparently made after later, unreported, excavation (Fox 1905, 214–15). Photographs and references make clear the bad weather conditions at Ashtead which will have made cleaning and recording very difficult (eg Anon 1929, xix; Lowther 1927, pl 3; 1929, pls 1c, 2a) and there are at least two versions of the Chiddingfold plan (Cooper *et al* 1984, 63–4).

29 The dating given relics (mostly) on the published sources and undoubtedly needs revision. There is little evidence for Iron Age predecessors for the villas; some may, of course, be new houses placed away from the old occupation sites but still relating to the same estate; there is at present, however, no evidence to support this thesis, and it would be difficult to prove.

30 It should be noted that the Rapsley plan redrawn in Cunliffe (1973, fig 28) does not match the text (84–7) which refers to the original published plan; nor did the suggested missing 'main house' to the north exist: the area was tested and

nothing found (Hanworth 1968, 6; cf Smith 1980, 68). Smith (1980) has now suggested that the Rapsley buildings represent two separate houses divided by a central wall rather than a single farmstead, and also makes a number of interesting comments on the architecture of the various buildings.

31 The plans from which figs 7.2 and 7.3 were constructed were published at a wide variety of scales and the common scale of the illustrations here can only be approximately correct. In fact the scale of the Walton Heath plan given by Page & Keate (1912, 369) is wrong, a misunderstanding of Pocock (1864), and the scales given for the Bletchingley bath-house (Lambert 1921, 17) and Walton on the Hill (Lowther 1949a, 66) do not seem quite right.

32 Lowther (1949a, 66): the rooms seem to be rather too large – compare with others on figs 7.2 and 7.3. It should be borne in mind that Lowther could only excavate between the rose beds. The evidence for the attached polygonal dining room to the west is better than for most of the villa; if it is correct, it is the only one of its kind in Surrey.

33 The Titsey temple was not necessarily associated with the villa, although this is often assumed (eg Smith, D J, 1978, 124, rather overstating Rivet 1964, 145). It is well over a kilometre away.

34 Smith (1980, 63) interprets the small early building at Rapsley as a combined house and animal shelter. The buildings at Titsey and Chiddingfold seem to be Smith's 'hall-type' villas, as noted above, and not aisled buildings. Current excavations at Beddington seem to have located an aisled building. It is noticeable that very few Surrey villas have ancillary buildings, presumably because they were usually constructed of timber and were therefore not located by the earlier excavators.

35 David Graham tells me (*in litt*) that 'additional structures were found during the construction of the surrounding council houses but for some reason were not recorded'.

36 Farnham (Lowther 1953–4, 49); Ashtead (Lowther 1930, 134). In a recent article considering upper floors in villas, Neal (1982, 153, 163) does not mention these two sites, but suggests Titsey and more particularly Walton on the Hill.

37 Ann Watson has recently located a considerable pottery scatter near the bath-house. Geophysical surveying produced promising results, but no occupation levels could be found in trial trenching (Bird *et al* 1982, 148).

38 Gorhambury is a good recent parallel for an 'isolated' bath-house actually part of a villa-complex (Anon 1983, especially plan on 116).

39 It has been suggested that the Titsey baths were actually a fullery (Fox 1905, *passim*), but Richmond (1960, 17–20) has disposed of a similar claim for Chedworth and it has been postulated above (note 26) that the small rooms at Titsey may be no more than walls of different periods interepreted as if all were of the same date. A similar site, at Bollendorf, near Trier, makes a very good parallel (Smith, J T, 1978b, 351–4; more detailed plan in Steiner 1923).

40 This is a reinterpretation of Stephenson's description (1915, 45–6); he considered the small room south of the *caldarium* to be the *apodyterium*, but as it was heated a *tepidarium* would be normal and seems more likely. The postulated *frigidarium* is marked out by a patch of large floor tiles found nowhere else in the southern 'corridor', which noticeably has what would be a matching room at the western end.

41 The chancel arch at St Mary's church, Stoke d'Abernon had, before its 19th century 'restoration', two large dressed classical stones which 'must have come from a substantial Roman building' (Radford 1961, 167). They are perhaps more likely to have come from London than anywhere closer at hand.

42 Several Surrey churches are said to have 'Roman brick' in their walls, and this is sometimes said to point to a Roman building formerly existing on the same site. These claims should, of course, be treated with scepticism: the 'brick' often proves to be much later than Roman, and even if it is Roman tile it has probably been brought for reuse from a nearby site: a few miles' trek would be worthwhile for good building material. Only St Giles' church at Ashtead has a known adjacent Roman building (which itself was apparently reusing Roman tile from the Ashtead Common villa!: Lowther 1934, 83–4).

43 The general pattern of Romano–British occupation may be more accurately reflected by chance finds than for most other periods because there is more pottery, it survives better, and it is often obviously different, and therefore more likely to be reported if found by chance. Nevertheless, detailed fieldwalking in 'dead' areas may well change the picture dramatically.

44 Morris (1982, 208–9) is surprised by the lack of fine villas on the Surrey chalklands, but he has not made allowance for the fact that much of the Chalk is covered by Clay-with-flints (and in any case he has forgotten Walton Heath). It is interesting that there seem to be no villas on the gravels around Staines, and only Beddington near Southwark/London; presumably this indicates direct farming or control of farming from the towns.

45 The bone record is also likely to be accurate, as Leveson-Gower records that he had the soil from the site 'carefully sifted' (1869, 216). Contrast the almost complete lack of any mention of bone, etc, at Ashtead (merely occasional references to 'food refuse' or 'bones', eg Lowther 1927, 150, 151; 1929, 1, 3).

46 But note the evidence for what was eaten in Southwark (see above) as a guide to what was produced locally. There is little to suggest a Roman equivalent of the important later textile industry in south-west Surrey, but in the north-east an intriguing possibility is the growing of the autumnal crocus on a commercial scale for the production of yellow dye, eventually giving Croydon its name 'saffron valley' (Gelling 1978b, 81–2).

47 In general the county has no major resources: building stone is poor and there are no large or valuable ore deposits.

48 Cf Wightman (1985, 153). The Wey required extensive work to make it navigable in the 17th century. David Graham tells me that the medieval potters of the area used road transport. Later still the potter William Smith preferred his own waggon to a canal barge (Bourne 1919, 65–6, 75, 79–84: a very useful insight into the business of arranging pottery transport).

49 The distribution maps given by Lyne & Jefferies should be treated with care; some London workers are sceptical about the early material there, and it is notoriously difficult to tell grey wares apart even with careful scientific analysis.

50 The upper fill of the aqueduct contained large quantities of 3rd and 4th century pottery (Lowther 1953–4, 48) and its destination was lost in a gravel pit to the south. The buildings were dated to the late 3rd and early 4th centuries. The reconstruction (Lowther 1953–4, pl 16) cannot therefore be correct. The concentration of villas (mostly in Hampshire) around Farnham has been linked to the pottery industry (eg Percival 1976, 162, following Rivet 1964, 140) but Peacock (1982, 132) suggests that pottery-making was seldom part of a villa economy.

51 Producing 'Surrey buff ware': Lyne & Jefferies (1979, 35 n 4 (=77); 61). The tile industry and a medieval pottery kiln (Frere 1941) suggest the Ashtead area as a likely production centre.

52 John Gower tells me that the British Museum has begun a programme of analysis on Ashtead and related products for the Relief Patterned Tiles Research Group. Stone has shown that group 2 'dog and stag' tiles were made of clay like that at Ashtead (Adkins & Adkins 1983a, 278), and Hampton found a 'waster' (1977, 32) of Lowther's group 1 in excavations there. Finds from Long Hanborough in Oxfordshire (Johnston & Williams 1979, 384) and Doods Farm near Reigate (if it was a tile kiln: Hooper 1945, 16–17 and Sites & Monuments Record information) suggest the use of the same roller stamps at different sites.

53 For most of these items there is not yet absolute proof that they were made at Ashtead, but it is highly likely. For the various tiles see Lowther (1927; 1929; 1930 *passim*); for the chimney pots Lowther (1976; prepared for the press by F H Thompson). Open lamps may also have been made (Adkins & Adkins 1983a).

54 It may be relevant to note that there was an inscription, perhaps from the bath-house, at the Beauport Park iron-working centre run by the Classis Britannica (Wilson *et al* 1971, 289). The blank area of the Ashtead stone presumably carried a painted 'inscription'; for a parallel see for example one of the altars from Busbridge – though originally, alas, from Hadrian's Wall! (Wilson *et al* 1974, 463 n 11).

55 The die 8 tile is part of Lowther's group 3, which is not recorded as being found at Ashtead; the similar die 9 is, however, known at Chatley Farm (Lowther 1948, 12). The remarkable concentration of different dies reused at Chatley Farm (Lowther 1946–7b) strongly suggests that they were robbed from a production site, perhaps Ashtead itself, but if not, obviously somewhere nearby.

56 Lowther's suggested use for these tiles as flooring along the edges of heated rooms (1930, 146–7) seems unconvincing. Note those found in the 'dwelling house' bath block, where they are said to have formed a partition between heated rooms (Lowther 1929, 4–5, pls 1c, 4), a much more likely use.

57 In room 6 (Lowther 1927, 152). Note also the peculiar box tile channels in room 4 (Lowther 1929, pl 2c), and the unbroken flue tiles noted among the debris in the ditch north of the 'house' (Lowther 1927, 150). Lowther felt that there was later inferior work (eg floors: 1929, 3; and walls: 1929, 5).

58 It is necessary, of course, to bear in mind that combs could move with their users from site to site (cf note 50 above).

59 A tantalising possibility is the production of glass in or near Chiddingfold. Could this explain the villa's position and utilitarian appearance? It must be stressed, however, that there is no evidence to support this view except that it provides an explanation of why glass working should appear in so remote a spot early in the medieval period.

60 As suggested by Hanworth (1968, 4–5); the temple is, however, well to the north of the main iron-mining area (see also Drinkwater 1983, 181).

61 Ashtead (Lowther 1930, 137–8): the Kimmeridge shale mentioned must have been the armlet in Lowther 1927, 157). Titsey (Graham 1936, 99–100), where it is also 'tentatively' suggested that a cream-coloured oolite used had come from the Pas de Calais. Old Red Sandstone is noted by Williams from only one other building in the south-east (1971, 189, appendix IIA: Badbury).

62 For recent finds from Southwark see Graham (1978, 493) and Hammerson (1978, 211); recent work at the Winchester Palace site has produced several fragments of a marble inscription referring to a military guild (M Hammerson, pers comm; Frere *et al* 1985, 317–22). It is curious that no inscriptions are known from Staines; this may reflect the lack of suitable stone. The altar from Eden Street in Kingston is usually held to be originally from elsewhere in Roman Britain; certainly it cannot have been found anywhere near its original setting (Collingwood & Wright 1965, 690, no 2217). 'A stone with an inscription which may have been Roman' was found at Wotton in the 18th century (Page & Keate 1912, 370); nothing seems to be known of its present whereabouts. Finally we may note the series of altars from Hadrian's Wall recently discovered at Busbridge, where they had been set up as part of an 18th century landscape; they have now been returned to the north (Wilson *et al* 1974, 462–3).

63 Cremation burials have been recorded at Ewell on the Bourne Hall site, and a number of scattered coins to the south-east of the settlement may indicate another burial area (Sites & Monuments Record information). A number of complete Roman pots are known from west of the railway in Staines (K Crouch, pers comm) and these almost certainly indicate a cemetery (Marsh and Dean have recently demonstrated conclusively for Southwark the link between finds of complete vessels and cemetery areas: Dean 1981).

64 Very recent work has demonstrated the existence of another religious site, at Wanborough. It too has suffered badly from treasure hunting, of the modern metal detecting variety – which in instances such as this is no different from Tupper's techniques except that its practitioners *know* that they are destroying important evidence. At the time of writing the site has been shown to have had a Romano-Celtic temple of the same type as at Farley Heath, as well as a building with a curving wall, noted previously (O'Connell 1984). The finds include bronze priestly regalia forming a nationally important group of sceptre handles and head-dresses (Bird 1986), and a very large number of Iron Age coins.

65 Iron Age because of the comparatively large number of coins of the period found there (Goodchild 1938b, 23; Lewis 1966, 49); cf Hayling Island, where Nash considers the Celtic coins to have been offerings (1980, 301). Atkins (1983) has recently gathered together information about all the known finds from Farley Heath and Titsey and their present whereabouts.

66 It was originally found by Tupper, and much later rediscovered, unlabelled, in a cupboard at the British Museum! (Goodchild 1938b, 24). It is odd that Lewis does not note Goodchild's identification of the Farley deities (1966, 48).

67 Wanborough too has a nearby pond. Curiously Lewis, who notes the various links with the Normandy group of temples at different points in his book (1966, 47, 131) does not note the *echini* from Farley Heath (Goodchild 1938b, 23) or Titsey (where Graham assumes, unnecessarily, that they were brought in with gravel loads); indeed he says that they are not found in Britain at all. A further point in common between Farley and Titsey is the presence of box or flue tiles (Lewis 1966, 43) apparently not recorded at similar temples elsewhere. Why the Surrey temples should have any link with Normandy (or the Continent in general if Titsey's oolite really was from the Pas de Calais: note 60 above) is difficult to explain!

68 I am grateful to Joanna Bird and Rosamond Hanworth, who are studying the eastern religious material, for information and suggestions. John Gower tells me that he suspects that the Abinger Bes figurine may have been imported recently.

69 The hoards vary greatly in size, from a few coins right up to 'two buckets full' and the 3800 coins from Wandle Road, Croydon (Hill 1906). Very few have been published in detail and dates are often poorly recorded (as say '3rd century' or 'late Roman'). Using Sites & Monuments Record information I have noted 22 hoards reasonably well dated; six fell before AD 200 (three in the period 160–70), the rest after 270 with five between 290 and 330 and eight between 340 and 380.

Saxon Surrey

ROB POULTON

The period and area covered by this essay have not previously received a detailed discussion as a whole.[1] The late John Morris (1959) compiled an excellent gazetteer of the pagan Saxon period, to which he appended a characteristically mordant essay, which prefigures a number of the views expressed in his brilliant, if sometimes eccentric, *Age of Arthur* (1973). The 1959 review made the earlier surveys by Smith (1902) and Whimster (1931) largely redundant. Work carried out since 1959 has made necessary a number of additions and amendments to Morris' catalogue without fundamentally altering its general balance. More importantly, however, changes in archaeological fashion, in particular the increased emphasis on settlement rather than funerary sites,[2] and new discoveries elsewhere in the country make this an opportune moment for reassessing the evidence. The archaeology of the later Saxon period has not so far received any comprehensive analysis, though in compensation the written evidence has been the subject of an important study by Blair (1982) who relates it closely to archaeological evidence.[3]

The following account is divided into a survey of the archaeology followed by a more general discussion, which relates the former to the historical and place-name evidence and attempts to set it in a larger chronological and spatial framework. The division has been made both to allow a clear appreciation of the merits of the archaeological evidence and to avoid the worst dangers of uncritically mixing the evidence from different disciplines, which a number of commentators have stressed (eg Hinton 1983). The area covered by the study is that of the old county, together with the district of Spelthorne, which now forms part of administrative Surrey.

The archaeological evidence

Many of the most important Saxon sites in Surrey are known only from the limited records made during their destruction in the 19th century. The importance of detailed and accurate recording was not then generally realised[4] and in consequence the evidence must be used with considerable caution. Neither has the balance been redressed in the modern era by the large-scale excavation (cf Barker 1982) and intensive, systematic fieldwork (Taylor 1983) which have proved so important elsewhere in England.

Dating of sites in the early medieval era is generally less precise than is possible in the periods before and after. The problem is caused by the complete absence of sites which can be closely dated either by the presence of coins or because they are referred to in documentary sources.[5] The dates given to the sites discussed below are therefore established by a consideration of the position in a typological series of the artefacts discovered. The typologies generally have few fixed points, and most of these are 5th century.[6] The cemetery sites which typically produce a wealth of finds are consequently much more easily and accurately dated than the settlement sites, which may only have a few scraps of hand-made pottery. Once the practice of depositing grave goods ceases (perhaps *c* 650–700 in Surrey), dates for mid- and late Saxon sites become very approximate.[7]

RITUAL AND RELIGION

The cemeteries (fig 8.1) in fact provide a very high proportion of all early medieval material from Surrey. They may be taken to include one or two examples of burial sites which are strictly sub-Roman rather than Saxon. A site at Coulsdon (Saaler 1970b)[8] has produced a number of apparently late Roman burials, and also an unassociated finger-ring which is probably 5th century (M Henig, pers comm). Some skeletons found at Eashing, one with a late Roman pin, have been suggested as post Roman by Morris (1959, 147). Similar burials in the late Roman tradition have been shown to be made after the introduction of 'Saxon' grass-tempered pottery at Kelvedon, Essex (Rodwell & Rodwell 1975, 29).

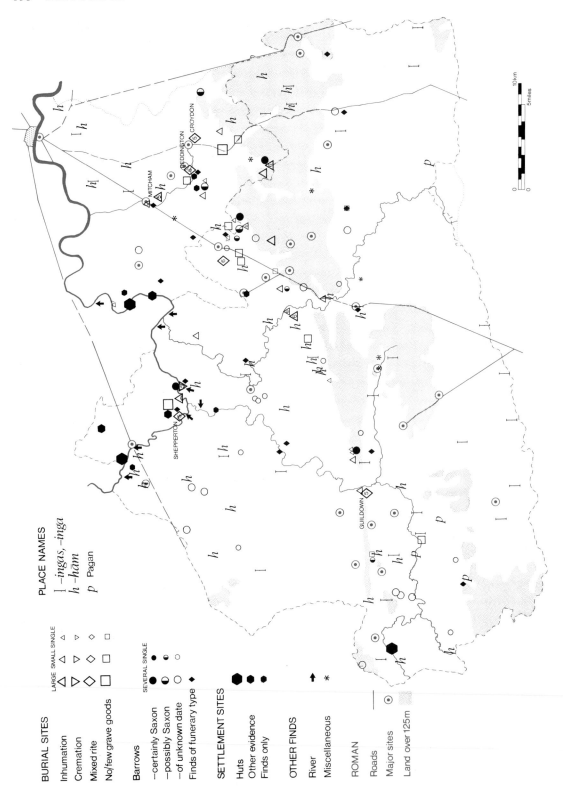

BURIAL SITES

PLACE NAMES

l -ingas, -inga
h -hām
p Pagan

	LARGE	SMALL	SINGLE	
Inhumation	◁	▷	◇	☐
Cremation	▷	▷	◇	☐
Mixed rite	◇	◇	◇	☐
No/few grave goods	☐	☐	☐	☐

Barrows

	SEVERAL	SINGLE
—certainly Saxon	●	●
—possibly Saxon	◖	◖
—of unknown date	○	○
Finds of funerary type	◆	

SETTLEMENT SITES

Huts ⬣ ⬣ ⬣

Other evidence

Finds only

OTHER FINDS

↑

✳

Miscellaneous

ROMAN

Roads ——

Major sites ◉

Land over 125m

CROYDON
BEDDINGTON
MITCHAM
SHEPPERTON
GUILDOWN

10km
5miles

The Saxon cemeteries proper may be divided conveniently into those where burial began in the 5th century and those where it began in the 6th century. The former category includes a group of three lying in the valley of the River Wandle. The best known of these is Mitcham (Bidder & Morris 1959) where part of the site was systematically excavated in the 19th and early 20th centuries. At least 230 graves are known, and a similar amount may have been destroyed unrecorded. All the known burials were inhumations, most of them aligned east–west. A pedestalled bowl and a military-type buckle are the principal evidence for the origin of the site in the early 5th century, but there are very few certainly 5th century graves[9] and the great majority of finds are of the 6th century, with only a handful of the 7th century. The evidence suggests that it would have been the burial place of a community of, at most, 50–100 people. To judge from the quantity of finds the cemetery at Croydon (Shaw 1970) may have been of comparable size. Unfortunately none of the 19th century discoveries were scientifically excavated though they include 5th century items such as a strap distributor and an elaborate *buckelurn*. Most of the material is, as at Mitcham, 6th century, including an exceptional number of swords, with a few 7th century finds such as the 'sugar-loaf' shield boss (cf fig 8.6). The size of the third cemetery, at Beddington (Flower 1874b), is unknown but again may have been considerable. It includes both inhumation and cremation burials, mostly of 6th or 7th century date, but with one item, a cast saucer brooch paralleled at Mitcham, of 5th century date.

Further cemeteries with their origins in the 5th century are known in the Shepperton area. The finds were all made in the 19th century but it is clear that large cemeteries at Upper West Field (Longley & Poulton 1982) and Walton Bridge Green (Shurlock 1868) were then destroyed. In both cases the limited evidence, principally of pottery but including a well furnished warrior burial at Upper West Field (fig 8.2), suggests that burial began in the 5th century. At Upper West Field both inhumation and cremation are attested; at Walton Bridge Green only cremation urns are known, but if the site at Windmill Hill, where inhumations (almost certainly Saxon) were uncovered in the 19th century, was on the Middlesex rather than the Surrey side of Walton Bridge, a single mixed rite cemetery seems likely.[10]

All the 5th century burials so far mentioned were in river valleys. The exception to the pattern is the cemetery near Guildford, occupying the high ground at Guildown (Lowther 1931) overlooking the site of the late Saxon *burh*. Here one or two brooches (fig 8.3) and some pottery are of the 5th century, but most of the grave goods are 6th century.[11] Thirty-five pagan burials were found, mostly inhumation but with some slight evidence of cremation. Further discoveries have also been made lower down the hill in the Mount Street area. Guildown probably represents both the western and southern limit of pagan cemeteries in Surrey.[12] During the 6th century the gap between Guildown and the early cemeteries in the Wandle valley is filled by a number of burial sites situated on or close to the dip-slope of the North Downs. The larger sites amongst these include that at Ewell (Lowther 1935a) where scattered discoveries cover a large area[13] and overlie part of the Roman settlement; at Hawk's Hill (Smith 1907), near Leatherhead, in a

Fig 8.1. Early medieval Surrey: archaeological sites (c 425–700) and place-name evidence. The dates within the 'burial' symbols indicate the century in which burial begins. Some of those with 'no/few grave goods' could be earlier or later than c 425–700. Comparison between the different distributions plotted on this map, and comparison with fig 8.12, prompts many interesting thoughts, a number of which are discussed in the text. The Saxon sites seem to bear some relationship to the known Roman roads, though not a close one: but they have a quite different distribution to the major Roman sites. If the contrast is real then the more prosperous Roman areas were able either to prevent Saxon settlement or keep it at a distance. -ham place-names are found in the same general areas as early Saxon occupation, but, again, the correspondence is not a close one. On the other hand -ingas place-names are mostly in areas without Saxon burials and hence probably originate after the end of pagan burial (or specifically refer to places without significant numbers of Saxons?). Comparison with the 'primary units' on fig 8.12 might suggest that the easternmost of these units (and the Spelthorne area) was controlled in the 5th century by Saxons who expanded westwards in the 6th century, but never arrived in significant numbers in the two westernmost divisions of the county. (Roman sites and roads after O'Connell & Poulton (1984, fig 15); place-names after Dodgson (1966) and Dodgson (1973) (simplified); for the barrows cf fig 5.6 – note especially that there is no certain or even probable example of a Saxon barrow on the Bagshot Beds, Greensand or Wealden areas, and it seems probable that the 'unknowns' in those areas are all of Bronze Age date.)

topographically similar position to Guildown, where over 100 burials, including those at Watersmeet (figs 8.4, 8.5; Cotton 1933)[14] near the Mole, have been discovered; and at Farthing Down where excavation (Hope-Taylor 1950a) has shown that a flat-grave cemetery exists in addition to the richly furnished barrow burials (Flower 1874a).

The sites of several barrows have now been excavated and shown to be of Saxon date. The mounds are generally low, without an encircling ditch, and not always easily distinguished on

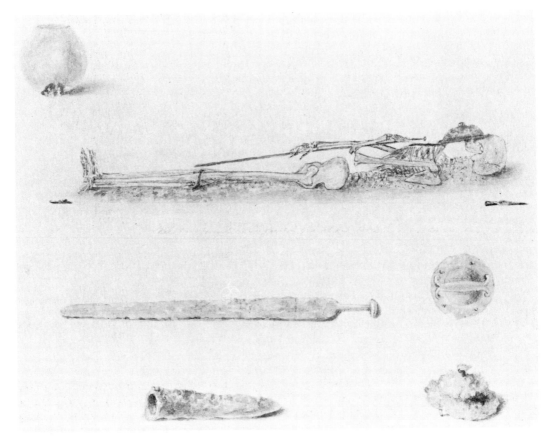

Fig 8.2. A warrior burial at Upper West Field, Shepperton. The water colour (Guildford Museum) bears the date 1868 and shows a Saxon burial of the early 6th century, accompanied by sword, spear and shield, of which only the iron boss (fig 8.6) survived. The wood of the spear had also decayed completely, but its length – 1.78m (5ft 10in) – could be deduced from the presence of both the iron spear-head and ferrule. (*Photograph by courtesy of Guildford Museum*)

morphological grounds from grave mounds or from the simpler type of Bronze Age barrow. The excavated examples, such as Gally Hills (fig 8.7; Barfoot & Price-Williams 1976), Beddington (Brock 1874) and Farthing Down, frequently have comparatively rich grave goods. At each of the three sites mentioned a male occupant of exceptional stature (1.93–1.98m [6ft 4in–6ft 6in]) was discovered and in each case a late 7th century date is likely (Evison 1963).[15]

The barrow burials bring to the fore a number of problems connected with the pagan burials as a whole. Hope-Taylor's discovery of a flat-grave cemetery at Farthing Down emphasises that the barrows are not necessarily isolated monuments. A similar relationship evidently existed at both Beddington and Guildown and also probably at Merrow.[16] Since no Surrey cemetery has been fully excavated it is clear that any generalisation from the evidence must be made with considerable

Fig 8.3. Brooches from the Guildown cemetery. The brooches are (right) a large cruciform from grave 116; (centre) four smaller cruciforms, the upper trefoil-headed pair from grave 78, the square-headed one with zoomorphic designs (bottom left) from grave 113, and the unstratified example of similar appearance but with geometric ornament (bottom right); (left) three pairs of round brooches, the upper set of saucer brooches with rosette type ornamentation from grave 210/213, the middle set of applied brooches with five-pointed stars from grave 116, and the lower set of applied brooches, one with a cross in a circle and the other with a six-pointed star, from grave 123. Length of right hand brooch 12cm. (*Photograph by courtesy of Guildford Museum*)

caution. That said, the barrow burials do seem to be a comparatively late phenomenon, and may well come after the dates generally accepted for the conversion to Christianity. It seems possible that they indicate a group of people, perhaps military leaders, of high social status, who retained a conspicuous paganism in the face of the widespread conversion. Equally a number of cemeteries, in which the dead were buried with only occasional or no grave goods, may belong to followers of the new religion. Such sites include the burials found at Shepperton Green (Canham 1979) and the hundred or more burials found at Russell Hill (Farley 1973).[17]

Before leaving the subject of pagan sites, some mention must be made of the many finds of early medieval metalwork from Surrey reaches of the Thames, and from the Wey. Most of the finds are of weaponry, and it has been suggested (Morris 1959, 132) that they represent material lost in skirmishes at river crossings. However in view of the numerous find-spots involved and the prestige character of a number of items it seems likely, quite apart from the suggestion that spears would float, that deliberate deposition, either as votive offerings or as grave goods accompanying a burial, is the correct explanation.[18] The finds are of both the Saxon and Viking periods and it was evidently a pagan ritual common to both groups.[19]

The archaeological evidence which reflects the practice of Christianity is fairly weak. In a recent authoritative survey (Taylor & Taylor 1965; Taylor, H M, 1978, especially 766–72) only two churches in Surrey, St Peter's, Godalming, and St Mary's, Guildford, are said to be pre-Conquest in date on primary grounds. By this is meant that indubitably early Norman work is clearly stratigraphically later than presumed Saxon work. The architectural features evident include a

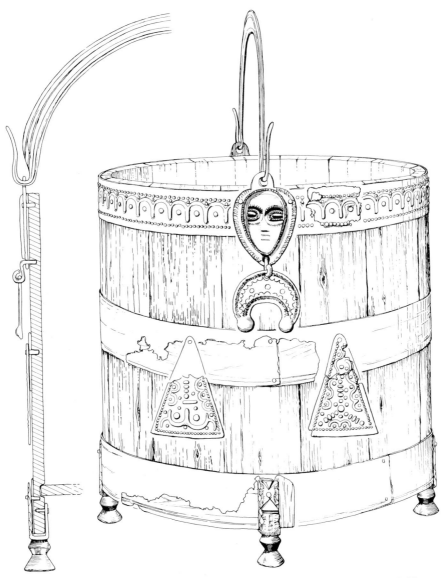

Fig 8.4. Wooden bucket with bronze attachments from Watersmeet cemetery, near Leatherhead. New reconstruction based on surviving fragments, drawn by David Williams. This is one of the most sophisticated examples of an early Saxon bucket (see also Cotton 1933, fig 2). Scale 1:2

tower with pilaster strips and double-splayed windows at Guildford (fig 8.8), and the reduced east gable of the nave, pierced by circular double-splayed windows, at Godalming. On this type of architectural evidence alone (that is, secondary grounds) the Taylors accept Saxon workmanship at Hambledon, Stoke D'Abernon, Thursley and Witley, as well as for historical and archaeological reasons the plan of the early church at Kingston upon Thames (Finny 1927). The most interesting of these is perhaps, the church at Stoke D'Abernon which has been claimed (Radford 1961) as a 7th or 8th century *Eigenkirche* (proprietory church), with its aisleless nave, stilted apsidal chancel and western gallery to provide for the lord's special seat (cf Taylor & Taylor 1965, 523–4). In addition to the churches listed by the Taylors, the church of St Nicholas, Compton, is surely in much of both

Fig 8.5. Close-up of bronze plaque from the Watersmeet bucket, showing a human face in relief. Length of object 4.9cm. (*Photograph by courtesy of Guildford Museum*)

its form and fabric characteristically late Saxon, while at Hascombe and Wonersh churches of a late Saxon character have now been demolished, but are known from drawings and descriptions (Blair 1982, 269).[20]

These churches represent only a small proportion of those built before the Conquest. Domesday Book names many places with churches, but it is known to be erratic in its listing and the existence of an independent contemporary survey of Kentish churches indicates the large number of omissions there (Sawyer 1976b, fig 1). In Surrey there are also gaps: Domesday Book does not

Fig 8.6. Iron shield bosses in Guildford Museum. Saxon shields were circular, with the iron boss projecting from the centre, and attached to an iron handle through the thickness of the wood. The examples, in chronological order, are, bottom left, from the Upper West Field cemetery, Shepperton (cf fig 8.2); bottom right, from Farthing Down, near Coulsdon; and top, from near Ewell (Lowther 1963b), a 'sugar-loaf' shield boss of late 7th century date (Evison 1963). Length of 'sugar-loaf' shield boss 14.8cm. (*Photograph by courtesy of Guildford Museum*)

mention churches at Guildford, Hambledon or Thursley, where we have architectural evidence for their presence, and it is equally difficult to imagine a place such as Reigate/Cherchefelle (Hooper 1945) not possessing a church. However, Blair (1982, 249) has recently suggested that in the main Domesday Book is a useful guide to church provision in Surrey. It should also be emphasised that whether or not it is architecturally pre-Conquest, and whether or not it is referred to in Domesday Book, a parish church, as was the case with St Mary Magdalene, Reigate (Poulton 1980), is a strong indicator of the location of an early settlement.

So far excavation has made little impact on understanding the early development of Surrey churches, though useful work has been carried out at Kingston (Finny 1927), Guildford (Holling 1967) and Wotton (Fowler, D, 1976). In some ways the most important piece of work, though of very low quality, was the discovery and excavation of a church at Tuesley (Malden 1911, 41). It

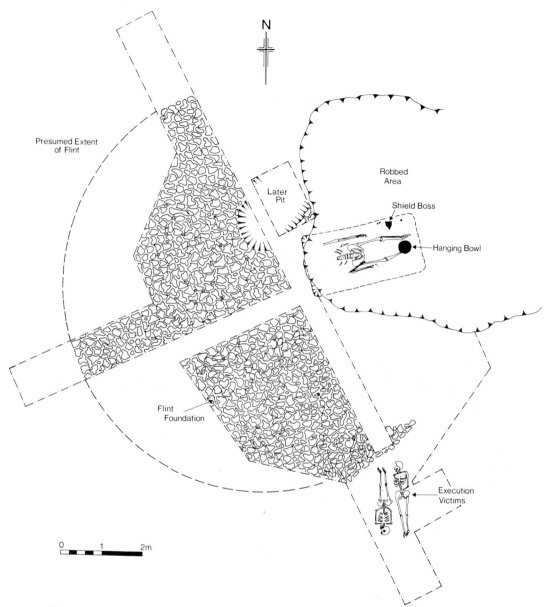

Fig 8.7. Plan of Saxon barrow at Gally Hills, Banstead (after Barfoot & Price-Williams 1976, fig 1).

was a small, simple two-cell building 4.27m (14ft) in width with a nave 6.40m (21ft) long and a chancel 3.35m (11ft) in length,[21] with many 'ancient interments in the area'. The site lies in 'minster field' which should make safe its equation with the old Minster at Tuesley, which probably preceded the establishment of the church at Godalming in the valley below.[22] The sequence suggests the establishment of the church at Tuesley at a very early date and its relationship to the pagan god Tiw's clearing (Gover *et al* 1934, 200–1) is clearly of considerable interest. A parallel case of the replacement of a pagan shrine by a minster church has been suggested for Wing in Buckinghamshire (Davis, K R, 1982, 35). At Tuesley we can identify the site

Fig 8.8. The late Saxon tower at St Mary's church, Guildford. The shallow pilaster strips are a typical late Saxon architectural device. It is evident that these pilasters can have no structural purpose since they are constructed in flint rubble which would have required shuttering to build (Jope 1964, 112–14, pl 4b). The crenellated uppermost stage of the tower is a later addition. (*Photograph by Nigel Barker, Surrey County Planning Department*)

of an early minster with some confidence, but none of the four sites mentioned in early charters, at Chertsey, Farnham and Woking (Gelling 1979), and Staines (Jones 1982) can be identified with certainty, though the parish churches now standing at all except Chertsey[23] show their probable locations.

The only material evidence, other than architectural, which relates to pre-Conquest Christianity is two sculptural fragments with interlace carving: one from Kingston church (Finny 1927) is a fragment of a cross, while the other, from Reigate church (Hooper 1945, 50; Malden 1911, 240, n 218), may be either a cross fragment or part of a coffin lid.

SETTLEMENT

Excavation, most often as rescue, or even salvage, work, has recovered evidence for a variety of settlement sites. These, however, represent only a very small fraction of those that must have existed, a point which is obvious even from a comparison with the number of burial sites. The sites may be broadly divided into those which are rural and those which refer to towns or nucleated settlements.

It is a major weakness in the early Saxon archaeology of Surrey that no settlement with associated cemetery has been excavated. The value of large-scale modern excavation has been well emphasised by work at Bishopstone, Sussex (Bell 1977), Mucking, Essex (Jones & Jones 1975), Chalton, Hampshire (Champion 1977), and Cowdery's Down (Millett & James 1983), to name some nearby sites. This type of work (cf Rahtz 1976) has shown that typical village and farmstead sites consist of loosely organised groups of huts which may be of two types: rectangular timber-framed buildings whose modal size is 10.0m by 6.0m, which are often referred to as halls and assumed to be higher status buildings; and sunken-featured buildings – *grubenhäuser* – consisting of a sunken area, roughly rectangular and about 3.5m by 2.5m in size and 0.75m deep, with post holes at either end to support the roof structure. This pattern should be borne in mind in interpreting the rather more fragmentary evidence from Surrey. The earliest site is that at Ham (Frere & Hope-Taylor 1950–1) where salvage recording of a sunken-featured building, evidently part of a group, revealed a 5th century carinated pedestal bowl (Myres 1977, **1**, 247, and **2**, fig 201:1044) amongst the pottery, loomweights and animal bones recovered.[24] Similar work at Farnham (Oakley *et al* 1939, 255–9) also produced a sunken-featured building, this time of 6th century date. The difficulty of recovering such evidence, even in a controlled excavation, is emphasised by the finds of pottery and bone combs at the causewayed camp at Yeoveney, some of which probably came from a sunken-featured building which was virtually ploughed out (Robertson-Mackay *et al* 1981). At that site, as at Clapham (pits – Densem & Seeley 1982), Stanwell (pits and gullies – Poulton 1978; M O'Connell, pers comm) and Weybridge (finds only – Hanworth & Tomalin 1977, 46–8), the pottery was principally grass-tempered, probably of 6th–8th century date. Similar pottery has also been recovered at Shepperton Green (Canham 1979), where, however, occupation, represented by a series of pits and gullies and a single *grubenhaus*, continued down to the 11th or 12th century.[25]

Later rural sites are in fact even less well known than the earlier. At Battersea beam slots and a number of pits containing late Saxon pottery were excavated principally from alluvial deposits (McCracken 1977b) while at Croydon (Drewett 1974) the rather limited late Saxon evidence of ditches and pits suggests a minor settlement at that time. A particular problem in dealing with the archaeology of this period is the difficulty in dating the pottery, especially shell-tempered wares, some of which must surely have an origin in the late Saxon period, though the forms appear to develop little before *c* 1200.[26] I have omitted discussion of sites producing such pottery except where there is other good reason for supposing a pre-Conquest date.

The weakness of the evidence for rural settlement stems both from a lack of opportunity and the failure to develop a research policy. Most of our earliest nucleated settlements (towns) still remain centres of population, and in consequence opportunities have been plentiful and even occasionally grasped. It is therefore possible to say something a little more coherent about urban origins and developments in Saxon Surrey (cf O'Connell & Poulton 1984). In Staines (Jones 1982) a series of excavations has produced sufficient evidence to suggest that the site of the Roman town, effectively occupying a gravel island, never became entirely deserted in the period before its re-emergence as a medieval borough. However, the limited nature of the discoveries, mostly ditches and pits, suggests that it did not retain any urban character.[27] The earliest known reference to a market occurs in 1218 when the market day was changed and it would seem that it was the 12th century which saw the creation of the main elements of the medieval and later urban topography.

The principal written sources for towns in the late Saxon period are the Burghal Hidage (Hill 1969; Biddle & Hill 1971) and Domesday Book. In Surrey only three[28] places mentioned in those documents need discussion. Eashing (*Escingum*) was the site of a *burh* established probably by Alfred in the period after *c* 880. The site has now been identified on the ground (Aldsworth & Hill 1971; Gower 1983) where a cliff overlooks the present bridge across the Wey (fig 8.9). Its strong defensive position and isolation from major routeways suggest that it may have been intended to act purely as a fort without any commercial importance. As such it may have been very short lived and replaced as the *burh* by Guildford.

The Domesday entry for Guildford notes that 'King William has 75 sites whereon dwell 175 men', and it was therefore a considerable town of some 750 people (Lloyd 1962) by 1086. The town was certainly in existence by the 10th century since a mint is attested by silver pennies of Ethelred

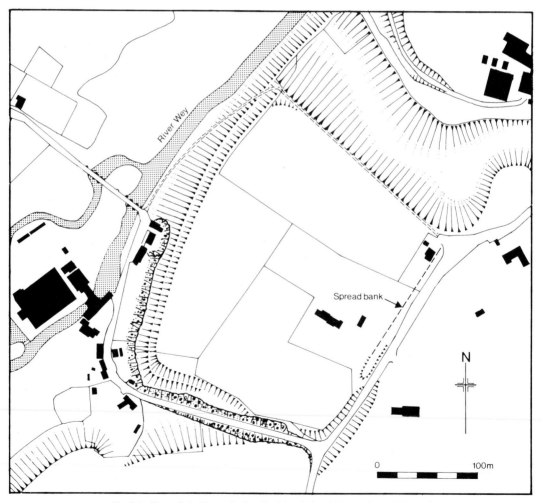

Fig 8.9. Plan of the Saxon *burh* at Eashing (after Aldsworth & Hill 1971).

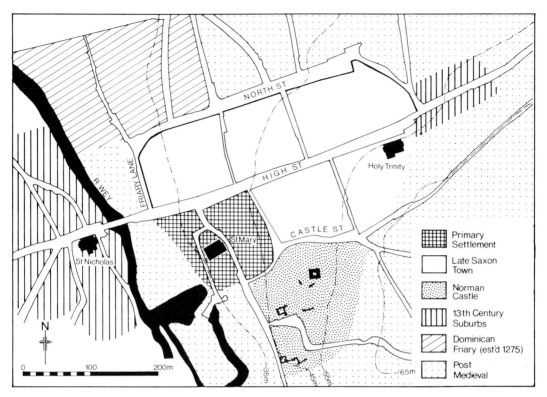

Fig 8.10. Stages in the development of Guildford (after O'Connell & Poulton 1984, fig 19).

(and perhaps Edward the Martyr; Guildford Corporation 1957, 5, 32–3), but exactly when and by whom it was founded is in some doubt. Haslam (1984a, 262–6) has suggested that it forms one of a group of *burhs* established by Edward the Elder as commercial centres to replace or complement sites of purely defensive importance, such as Eashing.[29]

A careful examination of the town plan (O'Connell & Poulton 1984, 43–6) makes clear its origin largely as a single act of late Saxon town planning. The plan (fig 8.10) is typical of the Wessex *burhs*. A main thoroughfare (High Street) has side streets at right angles to it, whose lines are followed by those of the long narrow plot boundaries either side of High Street, the whole set within a defensive enclosure, with, perhaps, even a wall street to provide access to the defences (O'Connell & Poulton 1984, 44). The area near the late Saxon church of St Mary does not however fit easily with the rest of the town plan. The regular pattern of plot boundaries is not discernible and it seems possible that this area was the site of an earlier settlement, perhaps that mentioned as a royal residence in the will of Alfred (*c* 880).[30]

The third site indicated as urban by written records is Southwark. It is listed in the Burghal Hidage as *Suthringa geweorche*, the defensive work of the men of Surrey, at a value of 1000 hides, which should correspond to *c* 2225m of man-made defences. A line drawn around the area of Roman settlement, which was almost entirely surrounded by marsh, would be of about the right length for the Saxon defences (Sheldon 1978, especially 13 and fig 4). Borough High Street probably preserves the line of the principal Saxon route, but beyond that it is difficult to deduce the earlier plan of the town with any confidence from that known later. Some useful archaeological evidence is now emerging, though, with pits and wells at 15–23 Southwark Street perhaps marking the position of 11th century tenement strips along an approach road to the bridge (Densem 1984). The Domesday entries show that it had a waterfront where fish (and presumably other items) were

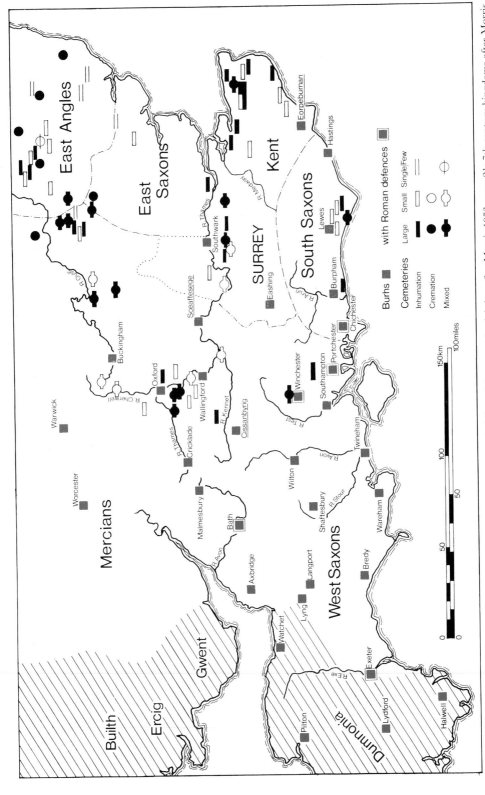

Fig 8.11. Aspects of the development of southern England in the Saxon period (later 5th century burial sites after Morris 1973, map 21; 7th century kingdoms after Morris 1973, map 23; *burhs* after Biddle 1976, fig 3.3).

landed, but, as always, it may be expected that Southwark lived very much in the shadow of London (Dyson & Schofield 1984).

There has been much recent discussion of how we are to identify late Saxon towns (eg Biddle 1976, 99–100) and a number of commentators have stressed the need for a flexible approach (Hill 1978, 177–8; Haslam 1984b, xiv–xvii), in which full use is made of the archaeological and topographical, as well as the historical, evidence. In the medieval period 10 towns existed in the area considered in addition to Guildford, Southwark and Staines (fig 8.12). Some at least of these seem *a priori* likely to have developed as market centres or settlement foci before 1066. For most of them such evidence is lacking (O'Connell 1977) but at Kingston and Reigate there is at least some information. Between 902 and 958 six kings were crowned at Kingston. It was certainly therefore an important royal residence, but it perhaps also had some of the characteristics of the late Saxon *burh*. The church has Saxon origins (Finny 1927), a plot boundary of late Saxon date was found off Thames Street (Hinton 1977), Domesday Book refers to 'beadles' who ought to be town function- aries, and there are signs of rectangular planning in the area east of the medieval bridge (undated); in addition it now seems that Kingston, like Staines and Southwark, was surrounded by water or marsh in the late Saxon period (M Shipley, pers comm). The distribution of the Wessex *burhs* (fig 8.11) does seem to have a weak point between Sashes and Southwark which Kingston would have been well placed to fill. It might even be wondered whether the *Suthringa geweorche* (above) need necessarily have been at Southwark, since the place-names are not certainly linked (D Bird, pers comm).

At Reigate the evidence for its origins is almost entirely archaeological. The modern and medieval town looks as if it developed around the Norman castle, a view supported by archaeologi- cal evidence (Williams 1983). Domesday Book, however, indicates a comparatively wealthy manor in this area, rubricated under *Cherchefelle*. There seems no doubt that the parish church of St Mary Magdalene, isolated from medieval Reigate, originally belonged to Cherchefelle with the probable implication that a settlement existed around the church. Recent excavations (Poulton 1986) have produced evidence that not only confirms this view, but also suggests that Cherchefelle may have acquired urban or proto-urban characteristics in the Saxo-Norman period. The site revealed plot boundaries delimiting a complex of rubbish pits and remains of minor industrial activity, together with a very large quantity of Saxo-Norman pottery. The most likely explanation seems to be that there was an ordered expansion of an earlier settlement around the church in the Saxo-Norman period. This development was brought to an abrupt end by the establishment of the new town of Reigate in the late 12th century.

MISCELLANEOUS

A few sites manage to escape the broad confines of the religious/ritual and settlement categories and are considered here for the sake of completeness. The question of the routeways and roads used by the inhabitants of early medieval Surrey is not one which has received serious consideration, apart from naive assertions as to the exclusive use of Roman roads or rivers by Saxon colonists (they were not able, apparently, to make an intelligent choice according to circumstances). It is a subject which eminently deserves careful local study, relating the known later pattern to archaeological finds, place-name evidence, tenurial boundaries and topography, aided, perhaps, by techniques such as hedgerow dating[31] and selective excavation (cf Pelteret 1984). Several studies have pointed the way. Turner (1980) has recently considered the evidence for a North Downs ridgeway, and found it nugatory during the Saxon period except for the Hog's Back, with a suggested continuation along the dip-slope to join Stane Street at Ewell. In the Wealden areas of the south-east of the county careful study, using a number of methods outlined above, has demonstrated the existence of a number of trackways in the Saxon period (Moss 1972; Ellaby 1977c). This is some evidence to correct the inference of an uninhabited (and untamed) Weald often made from the virtual absence of reference to places in it in Domesday Book (fig 8.12). Certainly communication across the Weald between Surrey and Sussex was important, as finds from the early cemeteries (Welch 1980) show, and very probably the Roman roads were chiefly

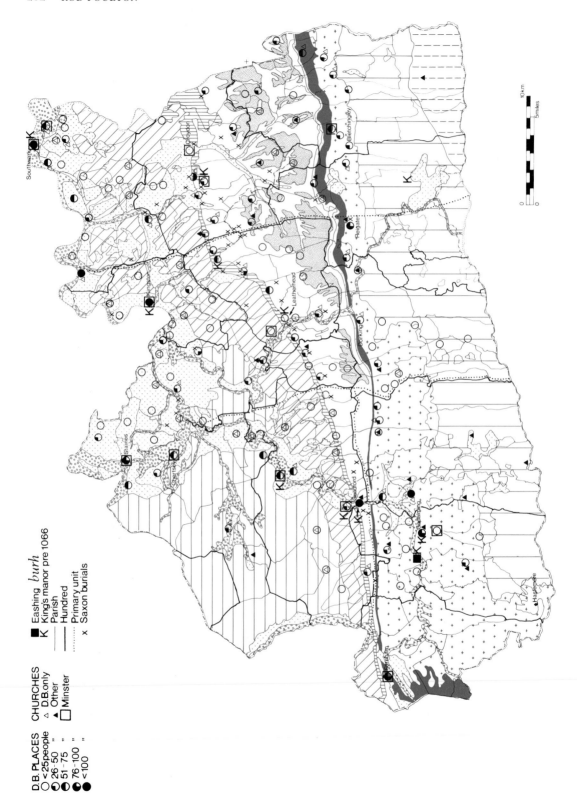

D.B. PLACES
<25people
26–50   "
51–75   "
76–100 "
<100   "

CHURCHES
△ D.B.only
▲ Other
☐ Minster

■ Eashing *burh*
K King's manor pre 1066
— Parish
⋯ Hundred
⋯⋯ Primary unit
x Saxon burials

utilised, as Copley (1950) has indicated for Stane Street, by a study of grave goods and place-names, such as the 'Poling' names found on both sides of the border.

Trackways are by their nature very difficult to date and this is even more true of boundary banks and ditches. This is certainly the case with the many parish boundary banks of which fragments survive, though occasionally other evidence indicates their early origin (cf figs 8.12, 8.13). An example is that between Epsom and Ashtead with a bank surviving 1.3m high and ditch originally 1.5m deep, both together being originally 10.0m in overall width, which, from its relationship to the meeting place of Copthorne Hundred (Nail 1965), is almost certainly of Saxon origin. At this point also a number of trackways converge and must also have existed from this early date. Other hundred meeting places are also foci for trackways (eg Blackheath: Knox 1963). A Saxon origin has been argued with some cogency (Clark 1960) for the massive (up to 3.0m high and 16.0m wide) boundary bank which still marks the border between Kent and Surrey, where it is crossed by the A25 road. Clearly it was designed to control this route and only makes sense at a time when Surrey still retained a separate identity as a kingdom or sub-kingdom, before the unification of England in the 9th century.

Discussion

The historical evidence for the period c 400–600 is lamentably weak and academic dispute correspondingly strong.[32] In bald outline it would seem that in the later 4th century the province of Britannia came under increasing pressure from barbarian raiders, Picts, Saxons and Irish. Britannia was not alone; and, with virtually the entire frontier of the Western Empire under stress, the emperor Honorius, in 410, asked that it should look to its own defence. A partition of the Empire was not intended but nevertheless happened. In the 420s[33] the province's leaders decided to call in Saxon federate troops to provide defence against the Picts. Later the Saxons rebelled and had obtained control of considerable areas by the 440s. Prolonged (though, perhaps, sporadic) war followed until, c 500, the British achieved a signal victory at the battle of Badon. This effectively confined the Saxons to the east, but renewed warfare after 550 led to their conquest of virtually all of what was later to become England by c 600 (fig 8.11).

The literary evidence nowhere refers directly to the present area of study and it is only on the basis of archaeological discoveries that we can understand the course of events. Saxon settlement in Surrey began in the earlier part of the 5th century, but it was not until well on in the 6th century that it spread beyond a limited area in the north of the county. This northern distribution has been explained in terms of groups of *foederati* whose settlements were placed so that they could defend Roman London at the points where the major approach roads cross its nearest agricultural land (Morris 1959). Indeed the presence of federate troops has been widely accepted as an explanation for the pattern of 5th century Saxon settlement over England as a whole (fig 8.11). For an individual site the case has been argued most convincingly for Mucking (Jones & Jones 1975) and it is interesting to note parallels between that site and ones in Surrey. Both Ham and Mucking are

Fig 8.12. Late Saxon Surrey: population, places and parishes. This map should be closely compared with fig 8.1. The parishes are shown as they appear on earlier 19th century maps and must be closely similar to those established throughout Surrey by c 1200. There are good grounds for believing that the ecclesiastical units were based upon the manors (estates) described by Domesday Book and early charters, and the present map shows a frequent 1:1 relationship between named Domesday places and parishes. In Surrey, as elsewhere (Goodier 1984),[47] pagan burials occur much more frequently on parish boundaries than would be expected by chance, which suggests that in many cases the estates must have been established by, at latest, the 6th century. The symbols showing Domesday population (probably heads of household: multiply by five to get an approximation of the total population) are located to the medieval nucleated settlement, but the population was, in most cases, probably spread over a rather wider area and Domesday Book cannot be assumed to prove the existence of a nucleated village by that date. These points are very obvious in the case of Farnham where the whole hundred was assessed under one head, although it is certain that a number of settlements existed in the late Saxon period. The places named on the map are the medieval towns; the frequency with which they were king's manors indicates the importance of royal influence. (Churches after Blair 1982, fig 32, with alterations; minsters and provincial territories after Blair 1982, fig 4) (For key to geological background see foldout 1)

Fig 8.13. Saxon burials at the Goblin Works, Leatherhead, under excavation in 1985. The ranging rods are aligned north–south. The east–west burials are of pagan date, while those aligned roughly north–south are later execution victims (cf fig 8.7). The site, like a number of others (cf fig 8.12 for the pagan burials, and Aldsworth 1979, 97–9 for the later burials) is very close to the parish boundary (in this case between Leatherhead and Ashtead). (*Photograph by P White*)

sited on gravel terraces overlooking the Thames, and both have produced early 5th century carinated pedestal bowls, as has Mitcham. Finds which may indicate the presence of federate troops are military-type metalwork,[34] principally belt fittings, of which there are examples from both Mitcham and Croydon. It must be stressed, however, that overall the evidence is weak, with the number of early 5th century artefacts or burials at any one site well below double figures. So far as London is concerned it is very difficult to be sure of its importance in the 5th and 6th centuries, but the paucity of material evidence suggests that it had ceased to function as a heavily populated market and port, though it may have remained an official and administrative centre (Dyson & Schofield 1984, 285–6; Vince 1984). In sum, the federate explanation of the origin of Surrey's earliest Saxon settlements *could* be correct, but it would be almost equally probable that the federate troops were defending the main routes by which would-be colonists arriving in the Thames estuary would attempt to move inland – or even that the settlements were those of the earliest such colonists. Guildown is the only settlement found beyond the northern group, and strategic considerations may also have determined its location. The Saxons there were well placed to protect and control an important river crossing on the border between two of Blair's (1982, fig 4) postulated early political entities (see below and fig 8.12).

One of the most interesting points here is the degree to which contact between Saxons and Romans occurred and the extent to which there is continuity between late Roman Britain and Saxon England. Place-names derived from Latin words (see below for British words), will obviously indicate a degree of intercourse, but the difficulty is to know whether their survival represents anything more than a random phenomenon (cf Hinton, D A, 1981, 58–9). The number of these in Surrey is not large, but they have a similar distribution to that of the 5th century cemeteries. Particular mention may be made here of *eceles hamme* near Bisley (Blair 1982, 253–5) and St Martha's Hill, near Guildford (perhaps derived from *martyrium*: Morris 1959, 143), both of which suggest the possibility of the survival of Christianity into the 5th century and beyond. Disc brooches (Dickinson 1979) and the quoit brooch style (Evison 1968) have both been explained as fashions adopted by German immigrants under native influence, and examples of both have been found at a number of Surrey cemeteries, in particular Mitcham. The most tantalising, and potentially the most significant, piece of information comes from the Croydon cemetery where in addition to the large number of Saxon objects four whole Roman pots were found. Such items would normally be funerary and open the possibility that the Saxon cemetery was successor to a Roman one.[35] Sites where settlements persisted from the Roman into the Saxon period are very hard to find. The most likely candidate is Staines, though the evidence for 5th century occupation is very tenuous. At Ewell, as elsewhere,[36] Saxon material is known from a Roman site, but does not necessarily imply continuity since nothing yet discovered is earlier than the 6th century. The extreme rarity of evidence for direct settlement continuity remains the most striking feature of the distribution maps (fig 8.1).

Despite this it is as well to remember that the mass production of pottery and other items during the Romano-British period, and the distinctive material expression of its civilisation, especially in towns and villas, too easily persuades us to forget the truism that technologically there was little superiority over neighbours or successors, and that in consequence there was no easy escape from the environmental constraints which limited development in the ancient world as a whole. It inevitably follows that while, in the modern jargon, 'systems collapse' (Rahtz 1982) will fit the end of the Roman era, a broad underlying continuity in agricultural practice is *a priori* likely and is now beginning to be demonstrated in a number of ways and places (Fowler, P J, 1976; Taylor 1983; Williamson 1984). This is partly a matter of intelligent adaptation to the environment and the strong contrasts between Wealden Clay and sandy heathland, or gravel terrace and chalk down, must always have been reflected in man's reworking of the Surrey landscape. Interest in this subject has focused around the possibility that some of the estates (manors) which are first attested in written sources in the late Saxon period reflect arrangements made in the Roman or pre-Roman periods (cf fig 8.12). The best evidence from Surrey for this is in Spelthorne, where significant correlations seem to exist between Saxon cemeteries, Roman settlements and parish (formerly manor) boundaries (Canham 1979, 110–13; Longley & Poulton 1982, 184–5). Naturally this falls some way short of conclusive proof of the antiquity of the land units, but stronger and more direct evidence came from the excavation of the causewayed camp at Staines to show that surviving field boundaries were created, at latest, in the Romano-British period, with the possibility that the Neolithic causewayed enclosure influenced the precise demarcation of the manorial and county boundary (Robertson-Mackay *et al* 1981, 110–16). It will be noted below that the artefactual evidence suggests that in the early Saxon period the 'Surrey' border was near the River Darent; there is a similar distribution pattern in the Iron Age (Hanworth in this volume), but if continuity is implied then it was broken by *c* 700 (see below) with the establishment of the enduring boundary. Presumably it was at a similar period that the large estate which originally extended both sides of the border was divided (Blair 1982, 66). Clearly one of the greatest difficulties in assessing this potential continuity is that the early Saxon pattern has been considerably altered and obscured by later developments. The multiple estates (see below), which Jones (1976) has seen as an essentially British institution, were common in Surrey and perhaps occupied some 30% of the county's acreage (Blair 1982, 62–73), but we cannot now be sure that they were always primary units.[37] What we can, however, be sure of is that transhumance, using the Wealden Clay areas for summer grazing, was fundamental to the early Saxon economy. It must surely have been of considerable antiquity, and perhaps provides the best explanation of the distribution of settlements in the Iron Age (cf Hanworth, this volume).[38]

Evidence which will directly support contentions of continuity of agricultural practice is never likely to become abundant. However the principal assumption behind the theory, that there was also a high degree of continuity of population, is rather more amenable to discussion. The assumption is indeed only likely to prove false if the Saxon colonists occupied the county in very large numbers, displacing or exterminating the British people. Before discussing numbers, it seems worth remarking upon the value of funerary evidence for this purpose. Notwithstanding the strictures of prehistorians about identifying intrusive peoples by archaeological methods (Clark 1966), in this case the literary and archaeological evidence are in such close harmony that we need have little doubt that the vast majority of the burials were of people who were ethnically Saxon. It is unfortunate, though, that so few of the interments received osteological examination when found, as the Saxon skull type is often quite distinct from the Romano-British. Keith (in Lowther 1931, 46–7) was in no doubt that he could distinguish the 6th century burials from the later ones on this basis, while Whimster (1931, 177) notes that at Mitcham a greater element of the Celtic type than was usual in skulls from cemeteries in this county was found, but on whose authority he does not say. It is appropriate here to note that the different tribal groups within the Germanic peoples are not so easily distinguished. Bede's division of the country into Anglian, Saxon and Jutish areas must be read in the light of our knowledge that these groups had already become mixed on the continent (cf Welch 1978, 19–20), but nevertheless is broadly reflected in the archaeological evidence with exclusive cremation burial marking predominantly Anglian areas, and the Jutes of east Kent distinguished by their artefacts (Hawkes 1982, 70–2). In Surrey we are dealing with Saxons who mostly inhumed their dead, though the significant number of cremation burials and some finds suggest Anglian influence.

As well as showing the ethnic origins of the dead, the funerary evidence enjoys the further advantages of being comparatively well dated and of being very hard to miss even in large-scale construction or mineral workings. Additionally, early references to finds of 'spears, swords, human bones and other *exuviae* of battle' (Edwards 1801, 25) can be safely taken as references to Saxon burials. In this case, then, the distribution map is much more likely than most to reflect the pattern of settlement in antiquity rather than accidents of modern discovery. This means that in the 5th century the Saxons in Surrey must have been very few and virtually confined to a limited area in the north-east. The 6th and 7th centuries saw expansion to the south and west, but for the most part only in small family groups, and certain areas, including the whole of the county south of the Downs, seem not to have received any colonists. Indeed the pattern of settlement is surely the product of agreement between Briton and Saxon, not the result of the traditional conquest by fire and the sword. This view is strengthened by Blair's (1982, 33–42, fig 8) recent analysis of the territorial divisions suggested by late Saxon charters and Domesday Book, from which he concludes that in the early Saxon period the county was divided into four major land units (fig 8.12). These exhibit some striking variations in the number of Saxon sites discovered within them, of which the most interesting, perhaps, is the virtually complete absence[39] of such from his proposed Godalming (south-western) unit. This area has produced much evidence for its vitality in the 3rd and 4th centuries (see Bird, this volume), and it may therefore be suggested that it continued in the 5th–7th centuries as an area in British hands after others were ceded to the Saxons. If so then the Chertsey/Woking area also stayed British, with the two eastern divisions and the Spelthorne area under Saxon control (or, at all events, heavily settled by Saxons). A similar partition of Sussex has been suggested (Cunliffe 1973, 132–9).[40]

There seems at first sight no good reason to reject the obvious interpretation that large parts of the county remained in British occupation. That these areas were eventually controlled by English-speaking peoples is not of course in question; but this is a matter of change in ownership (or even simply of language) not population. Two formidable problems must, however, be discussed before the explanation can be accepted. Most obvious is the complete absence of archaeological evidence for native settlement in the early medieval period. At present it is not possible to point to any site and say it represents a 5th or 6th century British as opposed to Saxon occupation – but we should remember that without the burials Saxon remains would be very few also. Indeed what would distinguish a British from a Saxon settlement site? It seems likely that the rapid decline of trade and industry following the collapse of the Roman economy left the British without tradition or skill in making many items, and they may therefore have learnt techniques from the Saxons quite early. Equally, the colonists will have adjusted quickly to British ways well adapted to the new environment, including, perhaps, the rectangular post-built house type

(Cunliffe 1978, 223). In the slightly longer term, as Hills (1978, 313) suggests, intermarriage and political control will have caused large numbers of the indigenous population to assume a Saxon 'colouring' whatever their antecedents. And, finally, it may just be worth noting that Keith (Lowther 1931, 46–7) initially classified what proved to be the later (? 7th–11th century) burials at Guildown as Romano-British.[41]

The only other source which might indicate areas in British occupation is the place-name evidence. Two types of name are involved: names such as Walton (the Welsh, ie British, farm), which specifically refer to British settlement; and names such as Crutchfield where the first element is derived from a Celtic word (in this case meaning 'hill' or 'barrow'). The first type of name is found only in the northern part of the county almost entirely in or adjacent to areas which show good evidence for intensive early Saxon settlement. This is entirely logical since the places are likely to be so named because they represent enclaves of (? prolonged) British survival in predominantly Germanic-speaking areas. The distribution of Celtic place-name elements is less coherent, and it is difficult to see in it anything more than a random survival of parts of British place-names.

The overwhelming majority of our place-names are, however, purely Old English in origin. Most place-name scholars assume, as the basis of their study, that this means, in the words of Margaret Gelling (1976a, 203) 'if therefore we consider the anglicisation of the place-name stock in this country as part of the sequence of evidence which extends from the Roman to the Norman conquests, we may suggest that there is a consistent relationship between the degree of transformation of the place-names and the numbers and social status of the people speaking a new language. To bring about a change of language in most of the place-names, the numbers of the newcomers must be relatively high, and the social status of the majority of them relatively low.' It is not easy to reconcile this with the suggestions already offered on the basis of archaeological discovery. Is there any way out of the conflict? There are various possibilities. There seems little doubt that population declined between its height in the 2nd or 3rd centuries and a low sometime in the earlier part of the Saxon period due perhaps to declining birth rate, war and barbarian raids, and plague (cf Cunliffe 1978, 225; Morris 1973, 503–4). It nevertheless remains difficult to envisage large areas of empty or virgin landscape, and the alternative is that there was large-scale movement and colonisation by Saxons after burial with grave goods ceased to be the normal rite. Precisely when the funerary ritual altered is difficult to say. Morris (1959, 156–7) has suggested c 600, but there can be little doubt that a number of important pagan-type burials under barrows occurred well on into the 7th century, and that these were not necessarily isolated (see above). Whatever date is favoured it remains difficult to envisage mass migration at this period, and even if it occurred there still remains a long period of British survival and control after the disintegration of the Empire.

The final, and most likely, possibility is that the interpretation of either the archaeological or the place-name evidence is wrong. The validity of the archaeological distribution map has been discussed above; if the arguments advanced there are correct then the place-name evidence must reflect a widespread change of language from Celtic to Saxon, without change of population. Further consideration of how this may have occurred must be left to those better qualified to discuss it. However, the subject cannot be left without some mention of the pagan place-names in Surrey, and in particular their extraordinary prevalence in the south-western part of the county. It seems odd that this should be the same area we have identified as persisting in British hands; the explanation can only be that the shrines were established after artefacts ceased to be deposited with burials and/or that naming for this characteristic occurred only when it became exceptional, and that where and when paganism was the norm places were not named for their religious associations (cf Gelling 1977, 104–5). This need not rule out Gelling's (1979, 151) further suggestion that the *monasterium* at Farnham was established 685–8 to mop up a persistent enclave of paganism.[42]

Turning now to economics and the organisation of society it is apparent that most of our evidence is non-archaeological, and comes late in the period. The dim outline of the early Saxon period may be perceived beneath later alterations and it would seem that within the large political units already noted a well-organised system of agricultural estates existed. The multiple estate was inevitably of considerable importance because the absence of money will have led to an emphasis on self-sufficiency. Place-name evidence (Rumble 1976) indicates the specialist units which existed within the estate, such as the goat farm (Gatton), the horse enclosure (Merstham), the place where beans were cultivated (Banstead), and the market place (Chipstead). This very specialisation may itself have tended to the break-up of the federation, which was certainly aided by the revival of trade and markets in the 7th and 8th centuries. At the same period settlement shift seems common (Arnold & Wardle 1981) and may be interrelated. If settlement sites were normally contiguous with their cemeteries (see above), then relocation occurred very commonly in Surrey. At the same time, or slightly later, a more profound transformation began, the establishment of permanent farming communities on the Wealden Clay, and the break up of the transhumance economy. Brandon (1978b) has recently discussed how place-names may record this process in the *Andredesweald*, showing how the early medieval settlers used *-feld* (perhaps indicating common pasture – Gelling 1976b, 836, 926–7), *-fold* (enclosure) and *-leah* (clearing) and other suffixes to describe their settlement of the Weald.[43] The developments outlined above were far from complete by the time Domesday Book was compiled. The whole of Farnham Hundred could still be assessed under one head, and the dependence of the Weald upon areas to the north remained so strong that only two places within it were even named. Nevertheless these changes partly prompted, together with the economic upsurge in late Saxon England, the establishment of new market centres (see above) and indeed a general tendency towards the nucleation of settlements (Blair 1982, 146).

Superimposed on, but related to, this secular organisation was an ecclesiastical one. The major subdivision of the county for administrative and legal purposes was the hundred and the basis of the ecclesiastical organisation was a system of minster (mother) churches whose areas of control were identical with, or closely similar to, those of the hundreds. Within these regions spiritual needs were served by a series of local (daughter) churches. Provision of these was by no means uniform, and the system was complicated by lords who founded churches on their own manors. Towards the end of the period a move towards more regular provision of churches was made, while simultaneously the minsters were losing control over their daughter churches; it was not however until *c* 1200 that these developments were completed (Blair 1982). In sum the familiar medieval pattern of village, manor and parish owed much to developments in the late Saxon period, but was by no means fully established until well after the Conquest.

From an early date Surrey was, and remained, part of the West Saxon bishopric. Politically however the area long formed a frontier zone, and especially in the 7th and 8th centuries, fell variously under the control of Wessex, Mercia and Kent. It is by no means certain when Surrey first emerged as a separate kingdom or sub-kingdom, but the earliest record is in the Chertsey foundation charter of 672–4 (Whitelock 1979, 479, no 54), where it is apparent that it had recently been transferred from Kentish to Mercian control. The name, *Sudergeona*, the southern region, implies that it had once formed part of a larger whole, perhaps an original kingdom of Middlesex extending on both sides of the Thames (Gover *et al* 1934, xii–xv). Any such kingdom must have ceased to exist by the early 6th century, as no historical record survives of its existence.[44] Such problems apart, it would seem that the enduring (until 1894 anyway) boundaries of Surrey were established quite early. In the pagan period the eastern boundary may perhaps have extended as far as the Darent or Medway (Morris 1959; Hawkes 1982), since the grave goods found in the cemeteries of north-western Kent have close affinities with those from Surrey burial sites. However it seems likely that the present boundary was established fairly early (perhaps soon after 568: Clark 1960) and was marked by the bank visible either side of the A25 near Westerham. The southern boundary may not have been so closely defined, especially if a large part of the Wealden Clay was open pasture land.[45] Much of the western boundary was evidently established by 685–8 since the charter of that date (Whitelock 1979, 484, no 58) appears to grant an estate at Farnham identical with the later Farnham Hundred. Finally in the north the Thames must always have been an obvious boundary and the Chertsey foundation charter confirms its early establishment.

The region thus defined had much that was distinctive in its character. In terms of agriculture and tenurial organisation it shares characteristics of both the 'champion' and 'wood pasture' zones without fully belonging to either (Blair 1982, 357–8). Grave goods (eg Bidder & Morris 1959, 78–131) and the variety in funerary rites point to the same conclusion; at different times the area falls under the influence, but never domination, of different regions, without ever sharing the wealth evidenced in Kent or East Anglia. It looks as if from the beginning the county was relatively poor and backward, and this was emphasised once London was re-established as a prosperous port (at latest by the late 7th century), with its tendency to stifle development in its hinterland. Certainly this, together with Surrey being an entirely inland county, must be largely the explanation of the relatively feeble and late development of urbanism within the area (cf O'Connell & Poulton 1984 with Haslam 1984b *passim*). The Norman Conquest effected no alteration in this dependence of the county upon the city.

'Possibly', 'perhaps', 'it may be'; the persistent, necessary, repetition of these tired phrases has probably strained the patience of the reader almost as much as that of the author. But they accurately reflect the present state of knowledge of early medieval Surrey. Much of the archaeology we have is the product of an inadequate record of 19th century destruction. Discussion of any aspect of the Saxon county is bedevilled by uncertainty and, in some cases (eg economics and industry), a complete lack of useful archaeological evidence. The time is ripe for the development of research strategies aimed at testing the strength of the thin threads of speculation with which the arguments presented above have been stitched together. At the moment the questions must remain broad. Can we find evidence for settlement in the 'British' areas? Do the numerous 6th and 7th century cemeteries have adjacent settlements? If not, where are the occupation sites? Are they part of a dispersed settlement pattern largely replaced by nucleated centres? When and why does this occur? Such work must involve intensive fieldwalking, which has in many parts of the country radically altered the distribution maps and with them our understanding of the past. Such work, though never easy in the peculiar conditions of the Surrey landscape, has now been undertaken in a number of areas, but little has yet been published. Even negative results[46] may be of considerable importance, especially if they are closely related to local topography and soils, and historical and place-name evidence.

Two further points may be stressed. First, much of the known evidence still requires to be adequately published despite its antiquity. Second, it is important that whenever specific threats emerge the opportunity is taken to obtain new information. Even since the foregoing essay was completed in 1984 major new cemeteries have been excavated at Tadworth (S Nelson, pers comm) and at the Goblin Works, Leatherhead (excavated by the author: fig 8.13), while further work has taken place at the 6th–12th century site at Shepperton (by the author: see above), and work in the Binbury area of Staines has produced evidence for its pre-Conquest development (P Jones, pers comm). Discoveries such as these may well help to refine the questions posed above; only by actively looking for the answers to such questions (cf Collingwood 1939, ch 11) will a new and better synthesis emerge and replace the present one sooner rather than later.

NOTES

1 I should like to thank the following: Julia Arthur for help with the Saxon material in Guildford Museum; Pat Ashworth for her forbearance in allowing me to disrupt the library at Castle Arch; Martin O'Connell for discussion of the Saxon towns, and allowing me free use of the material collected for O'Connell & Poulton (1984); and John Blair for allowing access to his PhD thesis – its forthcoming publication as a Surrey Archaeological Society research volume will be an immense step forward in the study of Saxon and medieval Surrey. Finally I am especially grateful to my wife for never showing the least interest in any of this.

2 The change might be measured by comparing *The arts in early England* (Baldwin-Brown 1903–21) with *The archaeology of Anglo-Saxon England* (Wilson 1976). Since Surrey has many cemeteries but few excavated settlement sites it scarcely appears in the latter work. Both works are, however, invaluable for study of the period.

3 Certain aspects, such as towns (O'Connell & Poulton 1984; O'Connell 1977) and church architecture (Taylor & Taylor 1965; Taylor, H M, 1978) have been assessed recently. Good, easily accessible, editions of two of the most important elements of the written evidence are now available: Domesday Book (Morris 1975), on which see also the commentary by Lloyd (1962), and the pre-Conquest charters (Gelling 1979, ch 7). In view of this I have not normally given precise references to Domesday Book or individual numbers for pre-Conquest charters.

4 There were some honourable exceptions, as for example the sites at Mitcham (Bidder & Morris 1959) and Upper West Field, Shepperton (Longley & Poulton 1982).

5 There are, of course, a limited number of sites elsewhere in England which can be directly dated, for example Sutton Hoo (Bruce-Mitford 1972) and a few churches (Taylor & Taylor 1965; Taylor, H M, 1978, ch 1).

6 For recent discussions of how dates are arrived at see Morris (1974; cf 1959, 148–52) and Wilson (1976, 8–13).

7 Jones' (1982) careful assessment of the pottery evidence from Staines indicates the difficulties of chronology.

8 I am grateful to John Clark for bringing the find to my attention. The principal reference only is given when sites are first mentioned; thereafter only specific points are referenced. For fairly complete bibliographies for most sites reference should be made to Morris (1959).

9 Eg grave nos 38, 61, 66, 133, 199, 200, 205a, 205b and 221 (Bidder & Morris 1959). Welch (1976) is very sceptical about the claimed early 5th century beginnings of Mitcham. It may be accepted that the evidence in total is weak, but the attempt to discredit the very early date for the pedestalled bowl on grounds of its association with a pair of applied brooches does not succeed. Myres' (1975) defence of its early date is not easily overcome and it seems most probable that both pot and brooches were deposited in the early 5th century.

10 The Windmill Hill site is referred to by Douglas (1793, 94) as being on the approach road to Walton Bridge, but without specifying on which side of the Thames. I have been unable to trace the place-name on any early map, though an area on the Middlesex side is now known as Windmill Common. Meaney (1964, 168) states that the OS considered that Walton Bridge Green used to be known as Windmill Hill. If the place-name is any guide Walton (see above) should not have a *Saxon* cemetery. A further cemetery at War Close (Meaney 1964, 168) in Shepperton is possible, but the evidence is very weak; when part of the area was deep ploughed in 1960 nothing of interest was encountered (Surrey County Council, Sites & Monuments Record antiquity no 550).

11 See also Evison (1965), Myres (1977) and Welch (1975).

12 Possible exceptions are a barrow burial at Puttenham (Grinsell 1963, 84) and the skeletons at Eashing, one with a late Roman pin, which Morris (1959, 147) has suggested may be post Roman.

13 Some of the excavated finds (Lowther 1935a, 18–19, figs 3, 4) do not have associated human remains, but their character and distribution suggests that bodies were originally present.

14 Again no bodies were discovered but the finder reported that the weapons and other grave goods were found lying in a line in groups (SCC antiquity no 147).

15 The only other certainly Saxon barrows where grave goods survive, at Merrow (Saunders 1980), could be of similar date. It is possible that other late 7th century burials, such as that found near Ewell (Lowther 1963b, fig 5) were originally covered by barrows.

16 For Merrow see SCC antiquity nos 515, 521, 1836 and 2277, and Saunders (1980).

17 Morris (1983, ch 5) gives a good discussion of 'final phase' cemeteries and makes clear the innumerable problems of interpretation they pose; problems which this essay probably avoids too readily. To take one example: the sites at Russell Hill and Shepperton Green could with almost equal probability be suggested as the cemeteries of British people at a period contemporary with the normal pagan Saxon cemeteries at Farthing Down or Beddington, and Upper West Field, respectively.

18 The character of the finds clearly rules out erosion from settlement sites, but erosion from cemeteries such as Upper West Field (near the Thames in a stretch where finds are recorded) is a possibility. The problem has received the most acute discussion in the context of finds of Bronze Age date (cf Needham & Burgess 1980, 442–9).

19 East *et al* (1985, 3–6) take a rather different view in reporting the recently discovered, and magnificent, Viking sword from near Chertsey (now on display in Chertsey Museum). They consider that the far greater numbers of Viking than Saxon swords from rivers indicates that the ritual was not a pagan Saxon one. I take the view that all the various types of material from rivers should be considered together. In passing it may be mentioned that their case for the sword (found in gravel extraction) deriving from a buried river channel is much strengthened by the fact that it came from a point where the county boundary loops away from the present course of the Thames. Normally such departures occur where a meander formerly existed, as recently demonstrated near Runnymede Bridge (S Needham, pers comm).

20 Many other churches have been claimed at various times as displaying Saxon workmanship. Some of the more likely candidates include Betchworth (Malden 1911, 170), East Horsley (Malden 1911, 351–5) and Great Bookham (Renn 1967).

21 There are no visible remains, but the site is marked on the ground in a garden belonging to the nearby convent at Tuesley Court.

22 The discussion of churches of minster status is greatly indebted to the recent lucid analysis by Blair (1982).

23 At Chertsey none of the excavations on the abbey site have produced any material that need be earlier than 12th century (apart from re-used Roman tile). It seems reasonable to suppose, however, that the site of the pre-Conquest abbey is not far away (Poulton forthcoming).

24 I am grateful to Professor Frere for discussing the discoveries at Ham with me.

25 I have omitted the turf-walled structure (one of five) excavated at Croham Hurst by Drewett (1970), which produced a C14 date of 805±95 AD from a fire pit, from the discussion as the excavator was very doubtful about the authenticity of the date. Even so, there seems no obvious reason for contamination of the sample, and the prehistoric flint assemblage (itself of mixed dates) was only loosely associated.

26 The subject is discussed by Phil Jones in the context of the excavation at Reigate Old Vicarage (see below; Poulton 1986).

27 The extent to which late Roman Staines was truly urban in character is doubtful in view of the dark earth deposits (cf Reece 1980) frequently found in excavations. Judgement on this must await the full publication of the excavation work.

28 The 46 burgesses mentioned in the Domesday account of the manor of Staines were almost certainly based in London (Campbell 1962, 131).

29 That Guildford replaced Eashing seems almost certain, though when is more problematic. O'Connell & Poulton (1984)

consider that it must be after *c* 919, following Hill's (1969) dating of the Burghal Hidage. More recently however Davis (R H C, 1982) has suggested that it should be dated to the later 9th century, which strengthens Haslam's (1984a, 262–6) arguments for a reform under Edward the Elder.

30 Archaeological evidence is needed to confirm the plan and development sequence. Excavation underneath the late Saxon tower at St Mary's has revealed that it may have had a timber precursor (Holling 1967), while late Saxon pottery was recovered from a site in the High Street (Holling 1964; I am grateful to Phil Jones for drawing my attention to the probable date of this material).

31 Doubt has recently been cast upon the accuracy of hedgerow dating (Hall 1980). A hedgerow date on its own proves nothing, but taken in conjunction with other evidence it may be a useful guide.

32 It would be extremely difficult to summarise briefly the many facets of this debate. Accessible works with full discussion of the issues and bibliographies include Alcock (1973), Morris (1973) and Johnson (1980). Dumville (1977) is extremely important, and urges caution in the use of the Celtic sources.

33 The sequence of events is tolerably clear but precise dates are not easily given, since our principal source, Gildas (Winterbottom 1978), gives none. See the discussions in the works cited in note 32 and also Morris (1966) and Muhlberger (1983).

34 Hawkes & Dunning (1961) first drew attention to this material and their work has generated much comment, for which see Hills (1978).

35 Cf Smith (1902, 262) who considers that the Roman pots were accessory vessels in Anglo-Saxon graves.

36 Examples include a potsherd and knife from Ashtead villa, pots from a Roman settlement site at Betchworth and potsherds from an Iron Age fort apparently re-used in the Roman period at Bunkers Field, Carshalton (see Morris 1959 for all these). See Blair (1982, 46–7) for the possibility that St George's Hill and Holmbury hillforts were re-used in the Saxon period.

37 Blair (1982, 62–73) inclines to the view that they are secondary to the creation of his provincial territories, but accepts that this is virtually unprovable. It is interesting that they seem much more frequent in the Weald, perhaps due to late development there allowing us to see what was obscured at an early date elsewhere in the county.

38 The hillforts on the Greensand, in particular, might be explained in this fashion. Thompson (1979) rightly points out their isolation from other evidence of settlement, but his attempt to confine them to a single period of construction in response to Caesar's invasion surely fails on his own dating evidence. Cunliffe's (1974) explanation of their origin as due to population pressure and conflict for resources may be the correct one, if it is remembered that the resource was the summer grazing grounds of people whose permanent habitations were further north. For the uses to which the hillforts were put see Hanworth, in this volume.

39 See note 12.

40 The best example of an area ceded to the Saxons may be the Ouse–Cuckmere district (Welch 1978, 23–7). Welch also notes (1978, 27) that Cunliffe's views really require much more archaeological evidence to support them. Since this may be a long time coming, it may be more useful to take this as a working hypothesis and test it against the place-name and documentary evidence.

41 Mourant (1962) has also suggested that the relatively high proportion of people with blood of type O (predominant in Celtic areas) in Surrey indicates considerable British survival. I am grateful to E N Montague for drawing my attention both to this reference and to Edwards (1801) quoted above.

42 However if it is accepted that the minster church was the basis of ecclesiastical organisation in early Christian Surrey, then what is remarkable about Farnham is not so much its establishment as the persistence of the control of a large area from a single centre into a much later period. The reader will have noted the complete absence of reference to *-ingas* (Dodgson 1966), *-ham* (Dodgson 1973) or other place-name forms (Gelling 1976b) as indicative of the chronology of Saxon settlement (though see fig 8.1). The most recent work by place-name scholars has accepted that the chronology of place-names can only be established relative to the archaeological distribution maps. Since all the elements so far identified as useful could be used in place-name formation over a long period, it follows that the place-name evidence has no independent validity for determining the progress of Saxon settlement. On the other hand its value in indicating the economic and social character of the period is enormous and still to be fully appreciated (see eg Brandon 1978b; Rumble 1976; and Gelling 1978b for a very readable general account). Some aspects of this are discussed below.

43 Brandon does however tend to regard the time when the place was named as the time when the clearing or whatever was established and hence sees the whole process as the work of Saxon colonists. Chiddingfold and Rapsley, both the sites of Roman villas, are excellent reminders that the *-fold* or *-leah* may be of much greater antiquity.

44 Morris (1973, 616) considered that the name Surrey cannot have come into general use until after 661, the date which he assigns to the Tribal Hidage, a document that does not use the term Surrey. This is difficult for two reasons. Firstly, Davies & Vierck (1974) date the Tribal Hidage to the 670s, by which time Surrey is attested in the Chertsey foundation charter. Secondly, the authors of the *Place-names of Surrey* (Gover *et al* 1934, xi) consider that the *ge* element is itself indicative of a date very early in the Saxon period. Morris' (1973, 322–3) further suggestion that Surrey would be counterbalanced by a 'Norrey' north of the Thames is not in contradiction to that already advanced above; but his suggestion that the very rich Taplow burial is that of King Taeppa of Norrey whets the appetite for a similar discovery in Surrey. Bird *et al* (1975, 141) have advanced the suggestion that Surrey is simply the southern region relative to London, and need not belong to any larger whole. Gelling (1976b, 841–2), on the other hand, accepts the idea of a Middle Saxon kingdom of which Surrey was formerly a part, but argues that the Chertsey foundation charter implies that the *regio* of the *Sunningas* (now in Berkshire) was part of Surrey at that date.

45 Brandon (1978b, 151–2) notes the artificial appearance of the county boundary and the marked similarities of place-

names on both sides of the border and suggests that originally the whole area was settled from the Sussex area. This seems unlikely in view of the vital importance of pasture land on the Wealden Clay to the economy of the Surrey estates.

46 Do negative results necessarily imply the absence of settlement? Or might they mean that in certain areas settlement drift was not the norm? Or that although settlements existed, the pottery which is the principal evidence recovered from fieldwalking either never existed or does not survive?

47 Goodier (1984) has demonstrated for England as a whole that while there is a statistically valid association between 6th–7th century pagan burials and parish boundaries, this is not the case for the 5th century burials (though in Surrey the few examples are mostly close to parish boundaries!) and suggests that this implies that the estates were not closely defined until the later period. However, there are surely other possibilities. If the 5th century burial sites *are* those of federate troops then their settlements may be sited in relation to military needs, not local tenurial arrangements. Excavated settlement sites which begin in the 5th century have nearby cemeteries (eg Mucking); those which do not begin until the 6th century may not (eg Chalton). If detailed research and/or further excavation should prove the truth of this dictum then burial on boundaries may be a ritual development of the 6th century, the existence of which proves nothing about the anterior existence of the boundaries.

Archaeology of Surrey, 1066–1540

D J TURNER

Introduction

In order that the material should be comparable with that from earlier periods and be kept within the confines of a single chapter, the archaeology of medieval Surrey is discussed under the headings of fortifications, religion and death, rural settlement, towns, housing and, very briefly, industry. Moated sites are discussed both from the point of view of defence and as evidence for settlement but many subjects of interest and importance have, perforce, been omitted. Documentary evidence is referred to where it is relevant to the archaeological but no attempt is made to produce a fully integrated account of medieval Surrey – this would take a much broader canvas than that available. Within the areas discussed, examples and conclusions will have to stand in place of a fully detailed argument for the same reason.

Information about the field of medieval archaeology has been made increasingly available over the last decade in a number of accessible works (notably Platt 1976; 1978; 1981; 1983; Beresford & St Joseph 1979; Clarke 1984; Steane 1985), one or more of which should be consulted for additional background material to the topics covered in this chapter.

Medieval archaeology, of a sort, began quite early in Surrey at Southwark (fig 9.1). One of the first excavations to be recorded after the formation of the Surrey Archaeological Society was that of the medieval abbey at Chertsey (Pocock 1858) while by far the most important 19th century excavation in the county was that of Waverley Abbey by Cooper, Horncastle and Brakspear between 1899 and 1904, published with exemplary speed and in exemplary detail (Brakspear 1905). In the same period a number of lengthy accounts of medieval churches were published.

Following this pattern, medieval archaeology in Surrey remained very much a question of church architecture and monastic sites right down to the late 1940s, Marshall's account of the Cheam pottery kilns (Marshall 1924) being one outstanding exception. D C Whimster's volume on the archaeology of Surrey published in 1931 covered only the periods before 1066.

Material evidence is only one source for reconstructing the past and some historians would argue that, in medieval studies, it is not the most valuable or the most illuminating. They would regard archaeological evidence as a source only of background information or illustrative material but they would be mistaken. There are many pre- or proto-literate aspects of medieval society that can only be illuminated by archaeological methods. There are many gaps in the documentary record, particularly at the local level, and many parts of society did not participate in the record-making process at all.

Castles and other private fortifications

When William, Duke of Normandy, had completed his conquest of southern England, he was faced with four particular problems. First, he had to administer his new kingdom; second, he had to reward his followers; third, he had to guard against insurrection by the Anglo-Saxons; and, finally, he had to guard against rebellion by his fellow Normans. All of these problems were met, to a certain extent, by the new king taking all the land of the kingdom except church land into his own hands – by right of conquest – and then distributing much of it between his followers as military tenancies or fiefs – so much land in return for so much military service when required. To prevent his barons becoming too powerful they were granted scattered rather than compact fiefs but, for the defence of the realm and of the crown, they were encouraged to build castles in imitation of the royal example. The vast majority of castles were first built during the century between the Conquest and the accession of Henry II.

To start with, earthwork and timber fortifications were a sufficient answer to the cavalry of

Fig 9.1. The 'excavation' of Winchester Palace, Southwark, in 1828.

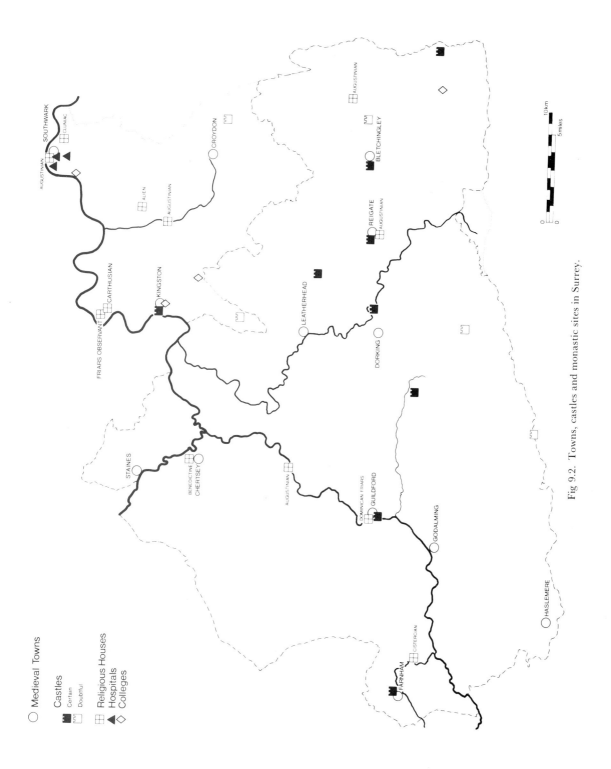

Fig 9.2. Towns, castles and monastic sites in Surrey.

Medieval Towns

Castles
  Certain
  Doubtful

Religious Houses
Hospitals
Colleges

SOUTHWARK
CLUNIAC
AUGUSTINIAN
CROYDON
ALIEN
AUGUSTINIAN
AUGUSTINIAN
BLETCHINGLEY
REIGATE
AUGUSTINIAN
CARTHUSIAN
KINGSTON
FRIARS OBSERVANT
LEATHERHEAD
DORKING
STAINES
BENEDICTINE
CHERTSEY
AUGUSTINIAN
DOMINICAN FRIARS
GUILDFORD
GODALMING
HASLEMERE
FARNHAM
CISTERCIAN

10km
5 miles

mailed knights which were the main threat in 11th century warfare. Royal castles were sited to overawe key towns and to keep vital areas in subjugation – Guildford is Surrey's exemplar. Whole areas of Saxon towns might be flattened to make way for them, as at Oxford and Winchester, but at Guildford the royal castle seems to have been built alongside the Saxon town on a ridge commanding both the river crossing and the possible approach to the Thames valley through the river gap.

The chronicler Ordericus Vitalis attributed the failure of the English to resist the Normans to their lack of castles. Although documentary sources such as the *Anglo-Saxon Chronicle* suggest the presence of perhaps half a dozen castles in England before the arrival of William's army, it is clear that private fortresses were not common in late Saxon England. Excavations at Sulgrave, Northamptonshire (Davison 1977), and Goltho, Lincolnshire (Beresford 1981, 7–9), have shown that some private ringworks were constructed before the Norman Conquest but such earthworks appear to be rare. Such thegnly defences are not to be distinguished from Norman ringworks without excavation and pre-Conquest earthworks of this type have yet to be identified in Surrey.

The majority of the earliest Norman castles were simple enclosures. Where there was no Roman wall or natural feature to utilise, the rampart and ditch had to provide all-round cover producing the simple earthwork castle known to the archaeologist as a ringwork. Specialised forms developed, among them, most importantly, the motte-and-bailey and the ringwork-and-bailey. In Surrey a small number of earthwork castles were built by the Normans, most of them still surviving in some form or another. Castles were built at Bletchingley, Reigate, Guildford, Farnham, Walton on the Hill and Abinger (fig 9.2). The first two of these were ringwork-and-bailey castles, the last four of motte-and-bailey type. Enigmatic earthworks, often claimed as lesser castles of uncertain date, have been noted at Ockley, Godstone, Chessington and near the county boundary south of Cranleigh. To these have recently been added two possible ringworks at Botany Hill and Soldier's Ring in Seale parish (Hanworth 1976). The proximity of the last two named to each other, however, makes their identification as medieval castles as dubious as was their previous identification as Iron Age earthworks. These minor works are virtually without documentation and have as

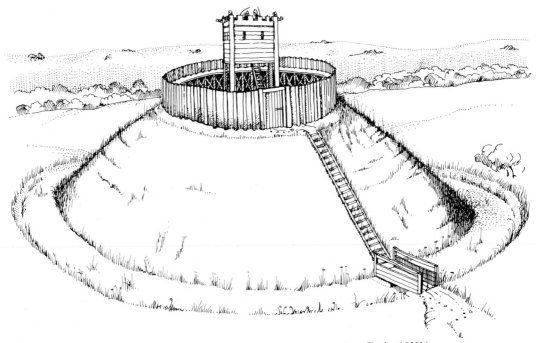

Fig 9.3. Reconstruction of Abinger motte (after Hope-Taylor 1950b).

yet received only scanty archaeological attention. One earthwork that has been regarded as a castle, at least since the time of John Aubrey, is that known as Thunderfield Castle, near Horley, but this should perhaps be better classified as a moated site (Turner forthcoming a).

There is reason to believe that the primary earthwork at Bletchingley was erected soon after 1066 (Turner 1986b). The royal motte at Guildford should also be early; the castle at Reigate (like Bletchingley, a ringwork-like enclosure with an outer bailey) was probably built in the 1090s; the motte at Abinger was dated by its excavators to around 1100 and that at Farnham to the mid-12th century.

The most easily recognised form of Norman earthwork castle is undoubtedly the motte or motte-and-bailey. Research has shown that this type of castle was the result of a complex series of influences from a number of continental sources interacting, in some areas, on local traditions (Davison 1969). The royal castle of Guildford was initially of this type and smaller mottes were built a little later at Walton on the Hill and Abinger by feudal tenants who were not tenants-in-chief. Footings of a timber tower were excavated on the motte at Abinger in the first modern excavation of such a site in England (Hope-Taylor 1950b). Around the edge of the top of the motte were found the sockets for a stockade and its bracing supports (fig 9.3). In the centre were the post holes dug to take the vertical timbers of a watch tower. It seems that Abinger's motte was crowned by a tower on stilts very similar to that shown at Dol on the Bayeux tapestry (fig 9.4). The building had replaced a previous structure that had collapsed. Hope-Taylor also found traces of the bridge across the moat which showed that the approach may have resembled that of Rennes as shown on the tapestry (fig 9.4). The castle only had a short life before it was abandoned, the site never being refortified. Blair (1981b, 146–8) deduces that Robert of Abinger was established in his Surrey manors in the 1090s or early 1100s and that either he or his son William may have built the motte. Hope-Taylor dated the motte to c 1100 on the basis of pottery found but pottery dating is far from being an exact science.

The motte at Abinger stands adjacent to the church: a juxtaposition typical of the relationship between lordly dwelling and proprietorial church found in late Saxon and Norman times. Where the proprietorial church accompanies a Norman motte, questions are raised as to whether or not the proprietorial relationship pre-dates the motte and the position of the church determined that of the motte. At Abinger, it seems at least possible that military considerations determined the position of the motte and the church followed. The Domesday church at Abinger may have been on a different site.

As the king and baronage tightened their grip on the country, their resources increased and they were able to construct permanent buildings in stone which could offer a greater degree of comfort and security. Over a period of time, certain elements of the motte-and-bailey and ringwork castles were replaced by stone, usually in a piecemeal fashion. Timber palisades along the crest of the ramparts surrounding a ringwork or bailey tended to rot away and were sometimes replaced by crenellated stone walls with a platform or rampart walk on the inside to enable the garrison to man the walls when the castle was under attack. The large outer bailey at Farnham was given a stone curtain (Thompson 1961, 13) as was the inner ringwork at Reigate, although this has long since been reduced to the point where nothing remains above ground and we depend for our scanty knowledge of it upon late documentary evidence (Hooper 1945, 46–7). Recent excavations have shown that the massive earthworks around the inner ward at Bletchingley were never equipped with stone defences (Turner 1986b): this probably indicates that the de Clares soon came to regard Bletchingley as more a house than a castle.

The place of the motte became taken by the stone tower, donjon or 'keep'. There were two main types: the shell keep and the tower keep. In the former, which was relatively inexpensive, the stockade around the flat top of a motte was simple replaced by a stone wall. The stone wall provided a tough shell against which timber and stone-walled buildings were set. A polygonal keep of this type was built on the motte summit at Guildford in the early 12th century but did not survive for long – today only fragments remain. It was replaced, possibly before the Anarchy, by a small tower keep that still stands (Clark 1872, 12–22; Malden 1911, 554–9; Brown et al 1963, 658–9; Renn forthcoming).

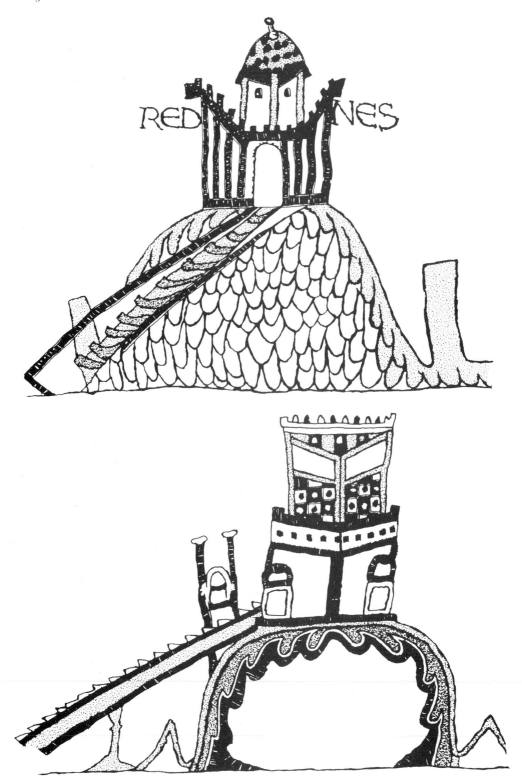

Fig 9.4. Rennes and Dol mottes after the Bayeux tapestry.

Tower keeps were dedicated to defence (Renn 1960) but also provided a status symbol of considerable vigour. Among their characteristics were walls which might be as much as 6 or 7m thick. The walls of such keeps were made of a skin of ashlar or masoned stone encasing a core of rubble and mortar. The entrance was usually at first floor level, approached by an external staircase at right angles to it and sometimes covered by a forebuilding which frequently was added as an afterthought. The keep at Guildford is a relatively modest example of the type. It is built partly on the foundations of the shell keep and to one side of the motte so that the tower actually rests partly on the motte while one end is founded on the solid chalk at the bottom of the surrounding ditch, thus obtaining much needed stability.

Farnham Castle, a large motte associated with a masonry tower and other defences from the start (Thompson 1960b; 1961; 1967), was built by Henry de Blois, Bishop of Winchester, and was incomplete at the time of the Anarchy. It appears to be the successor of a castle at Barley Pound on the Winchester monks' manor of Crondall in Hampshire (King & Renn 1971).

Henry II established firm control over the barons and began to build improved stone castles of great strength. From this time on, Surrey's castles decline in importance and the county lacks examples of the technical developments that took place in the 13th century elsewhere in Britain. Only the totally destroyed examples at Kingston[1] and Lingfield and the fragmentary remains of Betchworth Castle,[2] plus minor alterations at Reigate, Farnham and Guildford, represent developments before the addition of the great brick tower to Farnham in the 15th century.

Military requirements changed in the 13th century. Projecting round towers were probably added at this time to the masonry curtain walls that had been built around the two wards of Reigate Castle and a new gateway was added to the outer ward at Farnham. The gateway of a castle was a potentially weak point and probably one of the first parts of the original timber castles to be replaced in stone. Early stone gatehouses were plain utilitarian structures with thick walls and plain arches which did not add anything to the offensive potential of the castle: they simply made it more difficult to get in. In the 13th century the principal entrance was often strengthened by building projecting stone towers, one on either side of the gateway. The gatehouses thus formed were often residential and sometimes palatial. The new gatehouse to the outer ward at Farnham is a small example of this type.

In the 14th and 15th centuries, the defence of castles was usually secured by quadrilateral fortifications and a combination of water-filled moats, strong angle towers, mural towers, gun ports and an aggressive gatehouse. Surrey has, or rather had, one castle of this type established at Starborough, near Lingfield (Malden 1912, 302). Licence to crenellate was granted to Sir Reginald Cobham in 1341. A drawing by Hollar survives to show that Starborough Castle had four towers and a gate after the fashion of Maxstoke, Warwickshire, and was almost certainly less symmetrically organised than the later Bodiam, Sussex (Turner 1986a). The castle was dismantled in 1648 after being garrisoned by Parliamentary troops at the outbreak of the Civil War. Dismantling, which appears to have been pretty thorough, was, as with Reigate, probably intended to prevent the site from becoming a rallying point for Royalist sympathisers. Some traces of the towers and gatehouse remain on the edge of the moat and surviving stones were built into a battlemented gothick summerhouse in 1754.

By the late 14th century, however, the great age of the medieval castle in England was drawing to a close. Changes in society and social demands made defence a secondary consideration. Later castles show increasing attention to domestic planning. Fireplaces, lavatories and small private rooms were required at Farnham, where remodelling in the 14th century was of an entirely domestic nature.

The castle tradition lingered on in quasi-fortified gatehouses such as those built in Surrey, by Bishop Waynflete at Farnham (1470–5) and Esher (1475–80) (Thompson 1960a) and by Cardinal Moreton at Lambeth (RCHM 1925, 85–6). Both the gateways by Waynflete were in brick and were probably inspired by the great brick tower at Tattershall Castle in Lincolnshire – Waynflete was a native of that county and was friend and executor of Ralph, Lord Cromwell, Tattershall's builder. The gatehouses were built on the lines of false keeps with false machicolations – more prominent at Farnham than at Esher – between octagonal corner turrets and shallow mouldings below the crenellated parapets of the turrets. The four-centred entrance arch at Farnham with its portcullis slot is off-centre and dovetailed into the base of the right-hand turret. At Esher, where the gatehouse is all that remains of 'a stately mansion of brick' built by Waynflete between 1450 and 1480 (Nevill 1880, 214), the entrance is central. The gatehouse at Farnham is more severe than that at Esher and has no string courses below the false machicolations: the force of the elevations, despite the segment-headed windows inserted in the 18th century, is military in its effect while the string courses at Esher lighten the structure to prettiness.[3] The accounts of the bishopric of Winchester show that the entry tower of Farnham was largely built between 1470 and 1475: the first time that moulded brick was used in Surrey. It is an impressive example of the bricklayers' art.

By Tudor times, artillery was sounding the knell of castles, although in England they had one final hour of activity during the Civil War before the Parliamentarians acquired an adequate siege train.

Moated sites

Castles provided a measure of security. a sense of magnificence and a symbol of power for the nobility and the crown. The Plantagenet period saw the development and widespread use of the cheaper trappings of security and status provided by the moated house or homestead (Aberg 1978). A wide ditch was dug, usually enclosing a rectangular or near rectangular area, the removed earth piled up into the centre and the homestead built on top of this. Where the moat was dug around a homestead that already existed, the removed earth was piled up outside the ditch. The sites of approximately 150 of these, many of them long since damaged or destroyed, have been identified in the county with the greatest concentration lying on the clay lands of the Weald in south-east Surrey (Turner 1977b plus more recent discoveries – fig 9.5). The status range of medieval moated sites was broad, from freeholders so humble that they cannot now be identified confidently in any document to the royal manors of Rotherhithe and Sheen (Brown *et al* 1963, 989–1002) and the royal hunting lodge at Guildford (Crocker 1977; 1980).

Moated sites have received considerable attention in the Midlands and Yorkshire and half a dozen have been excavated in Surrey since the pioneering work at Leatherhead around 1950 (Renn 1983). More lost sites occasionally come to light but some of the provisionally listed ones will probably eventually be rejected or remain for ever dubious and the total for the county is unlikely to rise much above 150 – far less than in neighbouring Sussex and Kent.[4]

Most moats seem to have been designed to enclose a house and associated structures. It is not completely clear, however, that their principal function was actually defensive. A now badly mutilated moated site at Tolworth Manor was described in a survey of 1327 undertaken after Hugh le Despencer had been hanged for supporting Edward II. The survey records the moated manor house with a gateway and drawbridge, two halls, six chambers, kitchen, bakehouse, brewhouse and a chapel. Outside the moat were two granges (barns), two ox-houses, a stable, pigsty, garden and a watermill known as Brayest Milne (Manning & Bray 1814, 17).

The fact that the important barns, which must have contained large quantities of valuable produce at certain times of the year, stood outside the moat is a strong hint that by 1327 the moat was not seriously defensive in function, but more, perhaps, of a status symbol, unless it had been constructed to assist the drainage around this low-lying site. If defence against even casual marauders had been intended (and defence against serious military attack could hardly be expected) then surely it would have been important to protect the granary and some stock.

Moats seem to appear during the period 1200–1325 but this is not the only time during which defence against violent marauders and local undesirables could have been thought worthwhile. The moats were not formidable defences, they were psychological barriers and one must conclude that there was a considerable element of fashion, of 'status symbol', involved: a fashion that declined sharply after the time of the Black Death. The concept lingered on, however, and a moat appears to have been made at Oatlands, Weybridge, in the 15th century (Cook 1969).

Nothing has been found during the investigation of any moated site in Surrey to alter the accepted view that moats were not usually constructed before the 13th century (Le Patourel &

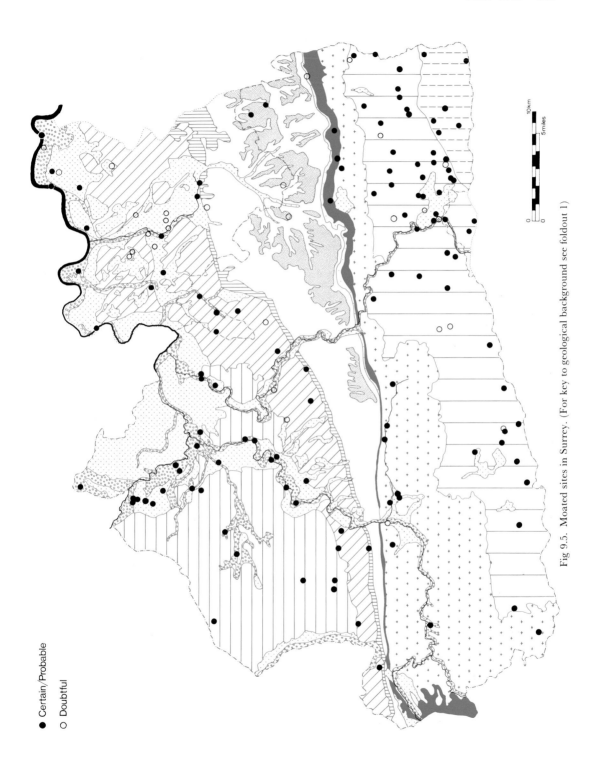

Certain/Probable

Doubtful

Fig 9.5. Moated sites in Surrey. (For key to geological background see foldout 1)

Roberts 1978, 51). From the national and local distribution, it can be seen that their construction was greatly dependent on the presence of heavy clay soil. It would seem that, while in some cases their function may have been social prestige, the need to drain the house site and aspects such as fish rearing were also frequently involved.[5] It is interesting that some moated sites, such as that at Hedgecourt, near Felbridge, occur in very low-lying situations where it would be difficult to build a house today. Several of the farms and manor sites thus 'defended' may have been established before the time of the climatic deterioration in the 14th century. Those enclosures where careful arrangements were made to lead water through moated sites (as at Moat Farm, Hookwood (Turner 1977a) and Flore Farm, Godstone) could also reflect the need to be able to flush out the ditches in the dry seasons that must have occurred even in a deteriorating climate.

One of the first moated sites to be excavated in England was that of Pachenesham Manor, Leatherhead, excavated from 1948 to 1952 by Captain A W G Lowther, one time Honorary Secretary of the Surrey Archaeological Society, and A T Ruby. The building that was partly surrounded by this moat has many puzzling features and it is not surprising that the excavators delayed preparing a final report on the site. Following the deaths of both men, their interim reports and site notes were edited into a final report by Derek Renn (1983). The site comprised an overall enclosure of about 0.15ha (one-third acre) surrounded by a large and impressive ditch except to the south where the ground falls away to the Rye Brook. Dr Renn suggests that the use of a naturally sloping site for a manor house defended by curving ditches may be earlier than the more common angular moats on level ground. A similar arrangement can be seen at Castle Hill, Chessington.

The building within the moat at Pachenesham incorporated a number of confusing features and its chronology is far from clear. It is documented that Eustace de Hacche 'made new' a hall at Pachenesham in 1292 but the archaeological evidence does not demonstrate categorically that the main building excavated in 1949 was that hall. It was a modest building, comparable in size with excavated centres of sub-manors and not convincingly appropriate for the caput of a royal household knight who had been overseeing the building of Caernarfon Castle only a few years previously (Renn 1983, 30). The excavators at Pachenesham were commendably enterprising in exploring the approach road to the site and the medieval road beyond (Ruby 1950; 1951). Too few investigators pay attention to such important environmental detail.

Attempts have been made to classify moats by their setting in the landscape but, since the basic idea behind the moat seems to have been to keep it filled with water, the scope for classification by site location is limited. The morphology of moats seems to defy analysis as they can be almost any shape (Taylor, C C, 1978; McLees 1982). By far the majority, however, appear to enclose a rectangular, or near rectangular, island, although today it is often difficult to be certain what the full medieval plan was because of partial infilling or later adaptation as landscape features.

The majority of moated sites in the county are simple square, rectangular or sub-rectangular enclosures of 0.4ha (1 acre) or less: there are few of the more complex enclosures found frequently in the Midlands and elsewhere (fig 9.6). The site known as Thunderfield Castle seems to be of this type and there appear to have been complex water channels around Chertsey Abbey and Lambeth Palace. However, in the latter cases, it may be thought questionable whether the channels can really be defined as moats. It is evident that a more detailed analysis of morphology, distribution and associated tenure is needed if we are to understand these sites.

Only one Surrey moated site so far excavated has a moat that encloses a large area. This site, Lagham Manor, which is wholly exceptional in enclosing over 3.7ha (9 acres), has a number of features that makes it more akin to the earthwork castles or ringworks than to the normal moated site, but it appears not to have been constructed until late in the 13th century (licence to crenellate 5 February 1262 – Cal Pat Rolls, 1258–66, 199) and never to have been regarded as more than a

Fig 9.6. Comparative plans of selected moats from 19th century 25in OS plans. A – Lagham Manor, South Godstone; B – near South Park, Bletchingley; C – Moathouse Farm, Ewhurst; D – Wildwood Copse, Alfold (formerly Albury detached); E – Cudworth, Newdigate; F – Thunderfield Castle, Horley (formerly Horne detached).

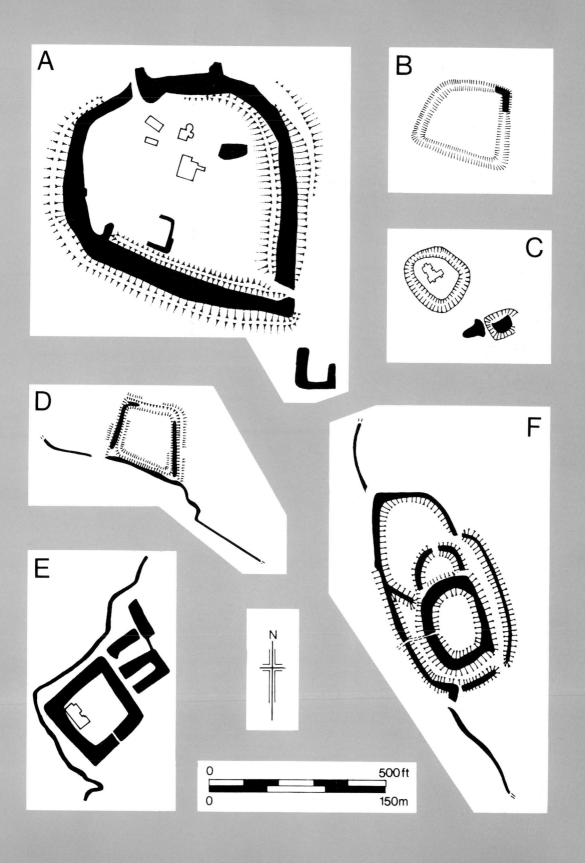

A

B

C

D

E

F

N

0   500ft

0   150m

fortified manor house (fig 9.6). At the time of the licence, Lagham was the seat of Roger de St John who was appointed one of the nine councillors by the three 'electors' of Simon de Montfort's short-lived constitutional scheme that followed the Battle of Lewes. It must be counted a possibility that Roger de St John had a more grandiose scheme in mind when he set out such a large moat around his Surrey manor. In 1316 it stood within a park of over 120ha (300 acres) (Lambert 1929, 106) the boundaries of which can still be easily traced on the ground.[6]

The site has impressive banks and is fed by surface drainage and a very small stream which flows around the south-west corner. As it now appears, the width of water in the north and east channels varies from 10.4 to 18m (34–59ft) and it is from 1 to 2m (3–6ft) deep over at least another metre (3ft) of silt. The south channel is now dry but the old water level can be seen on the banks, showing that it was from 15 to 22m (49–72ft) wide. The average width between the outer and inner bank crests on the north, east and south sides is about 32m (105ft) and the greatest height of the banks is 4.5m (15ft) above the silt level in the south. The north, west and east channels were dug into the clay but, because of the slope across the site, the south channel runs between two built banks, the original level of water in the channel being higher than that of the field outside (Ketteringham 1984).

Many moated sites still retain internal buildings, some from the late medieval period (eg Burstow Lodge; Cogman's Farm; Crowhurst Place) but more often from the post-medieval centuries (Charlwood Place; Lagham; Cudworth). Where such buildings survive, of course, continuous occupation since medieval times is indicated and the chances of extracting meaningful information by archaeological means is greatly diminished. The deserted sites (Wildwood; Lake; Send Old Hall) offer much greater prospects of advancing knowledge by excavation.

Some of the medieval moats in Surrey were utilised in landscape gardens (eg Loseley) in later centuries as occurred elsewhere in the country (Taylor 1974 *passim*). Other moats may have been dug specifically for landscape gardening (Great Fosters) but this is difficult to establish ineluctably.

The religious life

The importance to men and women in the Middle Ages of their churches and the rites, festivals and feasts connected with them cannot be over-emphasised. Of the monastic churches, most are in ruins and, in many cases, hardly a stone is left above ground. The humble parish church, however, has often survived – although, alas, more often greatly altered in Surrey than in most other counties. Despite the over-restoration of the majority of Surrey's parish churches, the county can boast one or two unique distinctions. For example, the Chaldon wall painting is unrivalled; at Compton there is one of the oldest pieces of ornamental ecclesiastical woodwork in Britain; at Walton on the Hill there is one of the finest lead fonts; and at Stoke D'Abernon there is the oldest remaining memorial brass in England.

Even where the church has been 'restored' out of all recognition, its site is often that of the original. Careful consideration should always be given to the site of the church. Continuity with earlier sanctuaries is more properly a matter for early medieval studies than that of the centuries after the Conquest, as is the siting of the early minster churches, but the period between 950 and 1150 saw churches and chapels spread throughout England. Side by side with their erection went the recognition of parochial status (although not necessarily yet the close definition of parish boundaries). Both were the fruits of countless haphazard impulsive legal and political decisions.

The progress of church development, architecture and decoration has been frequently described. In order to understand the complexities of a parish church which has been altered and added to over 1000 years, however, it is important to realize that it has had a number of changing functions throughout its life. Changes meant that former features were obliterated or covered over.

For example, many churches saw the lengthening or rebuilding of the chancel in the 13th century, as at (Old) Woking. One reason for this was that monasteries had frequently appropriated proprietorial parish churches by then and they rebuilt the chancel to bring it more in line with monastic practice which was to make more room for the choir and for ceremonial processions. The priest now entered the church through a door made in the south of the chancel. He, and perhaps a deacon, sat in specially made graded stone seats in the choir called *sedilia*.

A second common and major structural change was the addition first of a south aisle and subsequently of one to the north. The addition of aisles was frequently done in the 12th and 13th centuries to provide space for the swelling population. Squints or passages were constructed, as at Guildford, to allow people in the aisles a clear sight of the altar where Pope Innocent III had enjoined, *c* 1200, that there should be a more magnificent rendering of the office of the mass.

In some cases enlargement by aisle-building may simply have been the result of pious expenditure by a local magnate – this need have had no relationship to the growth, stagnation or decline of the local population but it is rarely possible to demonstrate conclusively that this is so in any particular case. Subsequently, the decline of the prosperity of a church sometimes led to the loss of aisle or chapels. Little Bookham provides an example of this in Surrey.

Further developments took place in the later Middle Ages when there was a multiplication of altars. The chancel walls were pierced and aisles or chapels were built north and south, each with its side altar. Here masses could be said for the souls of founders or benefactors. Kingston church, for example, although perhaps not typical for Surrey, had at least three chantries by the end of the Middle Ages – not to be confused with the four subordinate chapels of East Molesey, Thames Ditton, Petersham and Sheen and the 'Free [chantry] Chapel of St Mary Magdelene' (Lovekyn Chapel) (Heales 1883a, 48–57; 1883b).

The elucidation of the complex building sequence of a church is no longer only the province of the architectural historian. Where the opportunity arises the archaeologist may be called upon increasingly to assist, often working above as well as below ground level (Addyman & Morris 1976; Rodwell & Rodwell 1977). Church archaeology in Surrey has, however, been comparatively modest. There is undoubtedly much more that could be done, particularly in the investigation of lost or abandoned church sites or even of churches rebuilt in the 19th century on or adjacent to the medieval site (Blair 1978; Turner forthcoming b).

Archaeological work was undertaken on a modest scale before the Second World War at the chapel of West Humble (Hart & Braun 1941) and the Saxon church at Kingston (Finny 1927), while the Saxon minster site at Tuesley was 'excavated' nearly a century ago (Malden 1905, 447 n l). The then Ministry of Works excavated a chapel at Preston, Tadworth, in advance of obliteration, as well as the nearby manorial chapel at Preston Hawe, some 30 years ago but the results of these excavations have not been published. It is only in our own generation that 'church archaeology' has really come into its own. In addition to those already noted in the preceding chapter, excavations have been undertaken at Old Coulsdon (Ketteringham 1977), Putney, Streatham and Watendon (Saaler 1967). By far and away the most thoroughgoing and rewarding exercise has been the excavation of St Mary's church, Barnes, following a catastrophic fire in 1978 and in advance of rebuilding (McCracken 1980; 1981; 1983 and pers comm).

Investigation of the fabric and foundations of the medieval part of the church showed that two, or possibly three, phases of construction had been involved (fig 9.7). The first stone building had consisted of a small rectangular church of uncertain size with walls almost entirely of small flints set in regular courses on shallow foundations. This phase was dated to *c* 1150 by an infilled Norman doorway in the south wall. The early church was extended *c* 1200 to the east to create a small chancel with three lancet windows and having walls which were faced with large chalk blocks and were set on deeper foundations. The west end of the church was also extended, most likely at the same time or possibly as a separate third phase of building. Four layers of medieval wall decoration were discovered, the upper three consisting of double red lines on lime wash designed to create the impression of ashlar blocks. The centre of each of these blocks contained a small, six-petalled flower. The earliest layer of painting consisted of a single red line motif imitating ashlar but without the flower. The single red line decoration was confined to the first phase church; the double red line covered this and extended over the walls of both the eastern and western extensions. The church experienced several post-medieval changes but has now been rebuilt in a way that preserves as much as possible of the medieval fabric.

One fundamental feature in the history of any region of England is the number and character of

I Mid 12th century

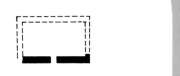

II Early 13th century

III Late 15th century

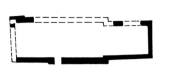

IV Late 18th century

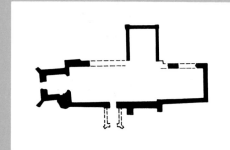

V Late 18th century

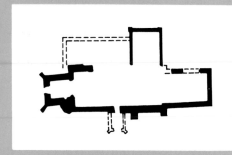

VI Mid 19th century

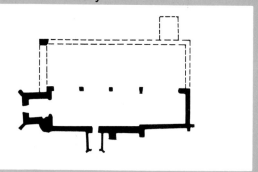

VII Early 20th century

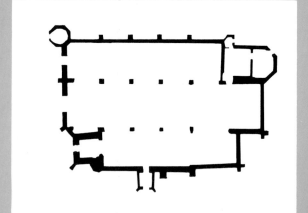

VIII Late 20th century

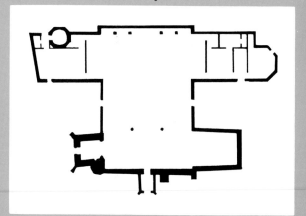

0   10   20m

Fig 9.8. Encaustic tiles from Chertsey Abbey (after Eames 1980).

its monastic foundations (fig 9.2). The premier monastic order was that of St Benedict of Nursia, founded in the 6th century and introduced into England by St Augustine, though several centuries elapsed between his coming and the final regularising of the monastic life according to the Rule of the founder. All pre-Conquest foundations in England were of the Benedictine order.

The first monastery in Surrey was indisputably that at Chertsey. It was established in or near AD 666 by Bishop Earconwald and endowed soon after with extensive lands by Frithuwold, sub-regulus of Wulfhere of Mercia. The church was destroyed by the Danes and refounded as a Benedictine abbey before the Conquest. It was rebuilt again from c 1110 to a plan similar to that which can be seen today at Romsey Abbey, Hampshire (fig 9.8). Chertsey provides a good example of how badly Surrey monasteries have survived the passage of time: this is undoubtedly the consequence on the one hand of the shortage of decent building stone in the county and, on the other, of the high population density in post-medieval times.[7]

Fig 9.7. St Mary's, Barnes. Plans showing the historical development of the church (after J Scott McCracken, unpublished).

The later monastic orders (apart from the Friars) were usually the offspring of successive efforts to reform and tighten up the observance of the Benedictine Rule. The first of these was the Cluniac Order, originating *c* 912. All the houses of this order were directly dependent on the mother house at Cluny, near Mâcon, though in England the bonds were gradually relaxed. There were 32 Cluniac houses in England at the Dissolution: one in Surrey, at Bermondsey.

Bermondsey Abbey was situated where today Tower Bridge Road crosses Abbey Street. In the 1920s, Morton established the topography and architectural development of the abbey from records, particularly from drawings made by Buckler, the early topographical draughtsman (Morton 1926). In the 1950s, Professor Grimes was able to excavate the site of the north side of the presbytery and to confirm Morton's conclusions. Inevitably he found that the remains, consisting largely of robbed foundation trenches, had been badly disturbed in post-medieval and modern times (Grimes 1968, 210–17).

Nevertheless, Grimes was able to distinguish several phases of construction and to show that the early monastic church was evidently in the tradition of the mother church of La Charité and of its sister foundation at Lewes, although smaller than both. It had parallel apses at the east end with outer spaces forming projecting wings or transepts on each side (fig 9.9). The main transepts, 15.25m (50ft) to the west, contained two apsidal chapels represented by solid chalk foundations. The north wall of the presbytery, linking both transepts, survived as a robber trench. Buckler had located the west end of the church which can now be seen to have an overall length of about 94m (310ft), compared with 133.5m (440ft) at Lewes.

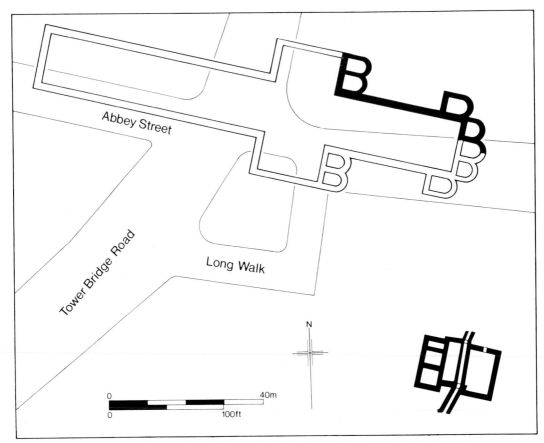

Fig 9.9. Plan of excavations of Bermondsey Abbey (after Grimes 1968 and Beard 1986).

At some later stage, or stages, the apses at Bermondsey were replaced by a square end which had the same width as the original presbytery. The north side of the presbytery itself was completely remodelled and a new buttressed north wall built some 3.9m (13ft) north of the original presbytery wall and crossing the original transept – presumably new transepts were built further west at a position suggested by Buckler's drawings. This must have involved some remodelling of the claustral buildings but it cannot be said how this was done.

After the Dissolution, the church was used as a quarry by Sir Thomas Pope who built a large house to the south and used the area of the church as a garden. Nothing remains above ground today and we must turn to surviving Cluniac ruins such as Castle Acre Priory in Norfolk to obtain some idea of what Bermondsey may have looked like. (Since 1984, further excavations, this time of the infirmary by the Museum of London, have been in progress at Bermondsey Abbey – Beard 1986.)

The Cistercians were far more numerous in England than the Cluniacs: their houses numbered 100 at the Dissolution. In Surrey there was only one, Waverley Abbey, but this was the premier Cistercian house in England, founded in 1128 by monks from L'Aumône in Normandy. The 'reform of Cîteaux', commonly dated to 1098, was to lead in the following century or so, to a rapid spread of religious houses which appealed to the original simplicity of the Benedictine Rule.

The first church of the Cistercians at Waverley, as revealed by excavations (Brakspear 1905), truly reflected the austerity of early Cistercian philosophy. It had an unaisled nave, a short, square-ended presbytery, and short transepts, each with one east chapel. The very slightly later first church at Tintern, the first Welsh Cistercian house and also colonised from L'Aumône (Williams 1970, 15), was similar. The second church at Waverley, which totally replaced the first, was much grander, although still severe: an aisled cruciform plan with three east chapels to each transept and a square east end with five chapels in it. This church was begun in 1203 and completed in 1278.

The reform of Cîteaux tried to remove certain accretions, customs and unhelpful developments which had crept into contemporary monasticism. The appeal to the original Rule of St Benedict meant rejecting the whole system of feudal administration – including the possession of manorial bakeries, mills, fairs, courts and serfs. At first the monks also gave up emoluments such as tithes and other proceeds of appropriated parishes – 'the only permissible source of income for Cistercians was hard manual labour in their fields' (Lekai 1953). It was, however, a short-lived ideal.

The Cistercians were to become an important force in early medieval agriculture, industry and trade. It is probable, for example, that the monks of Waverley Abbey were responsible for the construction of the series of medieval bridges that span the River Wey between Farnham and Guildford. The similarity of the bridges (Renn 1975) suggests that they were built as a group for a common purpose – groups of similar bridges are rare. Their architecture lacks datable detail but there were at least four stone bridges on the Wey below Waverley Abbey in 1223 and 'certain stone bridges' were damaged by flood 10 years later.

Of another famous monkish order, the Carthusians, all England had only eight houses and Surrey one, at Sheen. The history of the foundation in 1414–15, dissolution in 1539, refounding in 1556 and final dissolution in 1559 has been told a number of times in histories of the Carthusian Order and of Richmond but, until recently, its location was not precisely known. This was changed in 1977 when John Cloake published a detailed paper which used documentary, graphic, cartographic and topographical evidence to build up a strong argument for the precise location of the monastery and for a conventional Carthusian layout with the church on the south side of a cloister of cells. The Ancient Monuments Laboratory of the Department of the Environment undertook both magnetic and resistivity surveys over the site in August 1983. While neither survey technique provided especially convincing results, one magnetic anomaly along the proposed eastern line of the cloisters did correspond to the dimensions of a single cloister cell (McCracken 1984a).

From monks we pass to Canons Regular, of which there were three orders, but the transition is slight and the distinction becomes negligible. The rule which governed the most important of them was attributed to St Augustine of Hippo but the letter or tract which contains its principles needed a great deal of codification and comment to reduce it to a Rule. The Augustinian Order, which came to England in the first decade of the 12th century, eventually numbered some 170 houses of canons and nuns, of which five were in Surrey, Southwark and Merton being the most important. The Austin Canons were known from their garb as the Black Canons.

One Augustinian house that survived the Dissolution relatively intact was that of St Mary Overie, Southwark, refounded for Canons Regular in 1106 by William Pont de l'Arche and William Dauncey (Knowles & Hadcock 1971, 174). At the Dissolution, this church was rededicated as the parish church of St Saviour but it has seen many vicissitudes in the subsequent centuries and now owes more to Sir Arthur Blomfield than to the Canons Regular. It does retain, however, its immaculate retrochoir in austere 13th century style reminiscent of the architecture of Salisbury Cathedral.

The Austin priory of St Mary, Merton, is located today beneath and on either side of Station

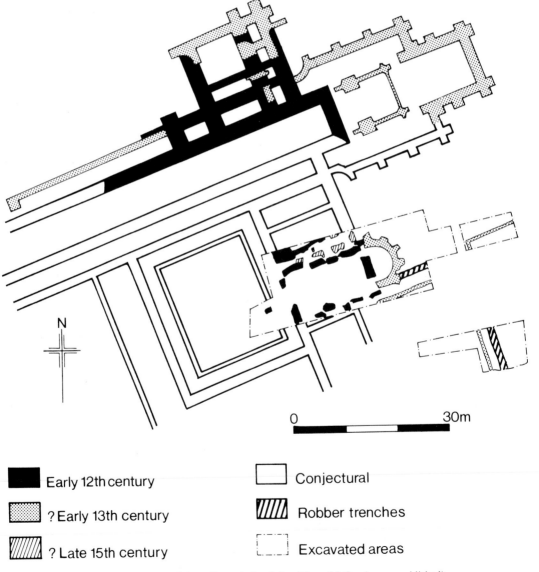

N

0   30m

■ Early 12th century

▨ ?Early 13th century

▨ ?Late 15th century

☐ Conjectural

▨ Robber trenches

⌐⌐ Excavated areas

Fig 9.10. Merton Priory. Ground plan (after J Scott McCracken, unpublished).

Road. The remains of the priory were until recently covered by factory, road and industrial storage areas. Excavations in 1976–8 were centred on the site of the former Merton Abbey railway station (McCracken 1977a) while excavations in 1983 examined an area further east where the priory infirmary had been situated (McCracken 1984b) (fig 9.10). Current excavations in advance of redevelopment are on a more comprehensive scale.

The documentary history of the priory has been treated at length by Heales (1898) but this contributed little to our knowledge of the buildings themselves. The site was first excavated in 1921 by Colonel Bidder (Bidder & Westlake 1929) who uncovered fragments of the church, chapter house and cloister. Bidder distinguished two major building periods: a stone church of 12th century date with a square east end and transepts; and a 13th century phase which includes the lady chapel at the east end of the church. Lionel Green has subsequently argued, largely on the basis of documents not used by Heales or Bidder, that the eastern limb of the church should be dated to the 12th rather than 13th century, although the lady chapel can still be ascribed to the latter (Green 1977). Green proposes four construction periods, including an initial one of temporary structures: (1) 1117–24, wooden chapel and other temporary structures; (2) 1125–31 or later, main stone church built; (3) 1154–c 1175, eastern limb of church built; (4) c1225–50, repairs following the collapse of the tower, lady chapel built. These datings by Green apply only to the church and not to the chapter house and associated buildings where excavations took place in the late 1970s.

Archaeological excavations of monastic churches often show that the interiors and the ground outside were honeycombed with graves. Excavation of the entire area of the Merton chapter house between 1976 and 1978 revealed 35 graves and seven disturbed burials (Waldron 1985). The usual practice in Augustinian houses was for priors to be buried beneath the chapter house floor, lay persons within the church and canons within a canons' cemetery east of the chapter house. The graves in Merton chapter house were of four types: graves lined with greensand blocks, including decorated stone; graves that once held stone coffins; graves holding traces of wooden coffins; and graves having no sign of stone lining or coffin. Those graves having a stone lining generally tapered from west to east and all had a 'niche' in which the head rested. Two graves at the extreme east end appear to have held stone coffins as impressions of the coffins, now robbed, remained in the clay subsoil. Four graves were found at the west end of the chapter house in which nails from wooden coffins remained and in one of these graves two silver pennies of c 1476 were discovered.

All the burials lay east–west with the body resting on its back and with the hands along the side of the body or crossed at the waist. No grave furniture was found although all graves that were well marked had been robbed at some time. It is possible that the burials began at the east end of the chapter house and that burial continued towards the west. The stone-lined graves were at the east end and in the centre of the chapter house; lesser graves (wooden coffins) were found at the west end. Two graves were placed directly over earlier ones. Most graves had been robbed, presumably at the Dissolution, and some graves had had the burials completely removed. It was not possible to identify any of the burials (S McCracken, pers comm).

One of the skeletons recovered from the chapter house was that of a woman, presumably a benefactress (Waldron 1985). Examination by Dr Waldron of the skeletons showed a high incidence of a spinal defect thought to be associated with rich living. The defect was three times as common among the skeletons examined from Merton as it is among the general population today, possibly lending archaeological support to the late medieval criticism of the life style of the monastic clergy which led, in part, to the Reformation.

A small area of the canons' cemetery, immediately to the east of the chapter house, was also excavated. Only nine single graves were examined but two others were located and not excavated and one 'burial pit' was excavated. The burial pit, approximately one cubic metre in extent, contained disarticulated bones from at least 17 individuals, at least three of whom were females. These may represent reburial of bones disturbed during reconstruction within the church (S McCracken, pers comm). None of the graves in the canons' cemetery showed signs of having stone lining or of having held a wooden coffin. No grave goods were discovered and the manner in which graves cut into one another suggested that none of the graves were permanently marked.

The excavations also revealed that the construction of the chapter house at Merton involved two main phases, not one as thought by Bidder (Bidder & Westlake 1929, 61–2). The original early or mid-12th century structure was rectangular, 17.5m (57ft) east–west by 9.5m (31ft) north–south. It was of poor construction with 1.0m (3ft 3in) thick walls on weak foundations. Sometime later, but probably before c 1200, the east wall of the chapter house was taken down and an apsidal wall with five external buttresses was constructed. This extended the chapter house an additional 5m (16ft) to the east. Floor levels within the chapter house had been badly disturbed and no floor tiles remained *in situ*. Fragments of a number of decorated tiles were, however, recovered from the soil by the excavators (S McCracken, pers comm). The chapter house had provided a convenient council chamber that was used by kings from time to time during their visits to Merton while on perambulation. The well-known 'Statutes of Merton' were adopted here.

The ruins of the chapter house have been consolidated by the Borough of Merton who, at one time, intended to create a park with the chapter house in the centre. However, at the time of writing, there are plans to develop the site which will be crossed by a 'relief' road. There is some talk of preserving parts of the priory beneath the development and of retaining the memorial stone at present located in a small garden on the site of the north wall of the chancel.

A third Augustinian priory, that of Newark near Ripley, still stands in part although no dressed stone remains. The ground plan of the church and main claustral buildings was recovered in 1930 (Pearce 1932). Two other Austin houses, Reigate and Tandridge, were very small and nothing is known of their medieval appearance.

The friars close the list. Monks and friars were very different persons. The appearance in Britain of the friars, orders of professing priests of higher than usual education, enthusiastic preachers who built churches with spacious naves, was important in the development of 13th century ecclesiastical life.

The name of the Friary Meux brewery at Guildford preserved a faint memory that it lay on the site of the Dominican friary, although knowledge of the exact location of the buildings had been lost since its dissolution in 1538. When the brewery was demolished and redevelopment of the site proposed, excavations by Felix Holling, then curator of Guildford Museum, relocated the friary and showed that the footings, at least, were well preserved. Large-scale excavations in 1974 and 1978 resulted in the recovery of much of the ground plan of the friary, many artefacts of note and a large number of medieval burials (Poulton & Woods 1984).

It was clear from the excavations that, despite notable changes in the character of the wall foundations from place to place, the friary buildings were conceived as a single plan with only the chantry chapel and chancel extension forming later additions. The mendicant friars in England have left a common architectural legacy (Martin 1933–4, 13) and that of the Dominican order has been surveyed by Hinnebusch (1951). The general view of Hinnebusch has not been changed by subsequent excavations on the sites of some 14 Blackfriar houses (eg Drury 1974; Lambrick & Woods 1976).

The ground plan of Guildford Friary could be used as a type site of the English mendicant tradition. There are unusual features but these are either minor or explicable in terms of the special needs of the site, or both. For example, the cloister is on the north side of the church because the house is on the north side of the town and the arrangement allowed the church to be as close to the town as possible. An unaisled, square-ended choir (to which a chantry chapel was added) was separated from an aisled nave (unusual in having only a single aisle) by the usual walking place with tower above (cf Hinnebusch 1951, 140; Martin 1933–4, plan opp 22). The cloister abutted the nave with its eastern alley leading to the walking place, and the east range, probably containing the dormitory on the first floor, had the chapter house midway and projecting from it. The north range housed the kitchen, probably with refectory above; the west range could not be excavated. Presumably the lack of site restriction enabled a more idealised layout to be achieved than at friaries on more confined sites. The house was nevertheless clearly a modest one. Although its church was larger than either of the parochial churches in the town, there was no second cloister and the structure itself and its component parts were small in comparison with other friaries (Poulton & Woods 1984, 22–42).

Some 65 formal interments were excavated from the site of Guildford Friary in 1974 and 1978, principally from the nave and churchyard, together with scattered bones representing many other burials totalling 113 individuals in all. The bones have been fully studied (Henderson 1984) but even a sample of this size is not large enough for satisfactory statistical or demographic conclusions to be drawn. No chronological sequence could be established and the samples were biased in that on the one hand probably only persons from the upper levels of society were buried in the nave and, on the other, one of the cemeteries appears to have been that of the friars themselves. Some additional interest lies in individual burials among the collection. For example, the examination of a lead coffin (the parallels for which are from the 14th century) found in the nave, revealed a name, Margareta Daubeny, and study of the skeleton showed that she was aged about 20 and may well have died in childbirth.

The standard form of interment was for them to be east facing, single and supine in graves dug to an average depth of 75 cm (2ft 6in). Where the evidence survived, the head was normally facing straight upwards and when tilted to north or south this was as likely to represent post-mortem change as to have been the original position. Three distinct positions for the arms were noted: hands crossed upon the chest; hands crossed over the pelvis; or with arms laid by the side. The original presence of wooden coffins, long since decayed, could be deduced from the soil stain or iron nails surrounding the body.

The precinct of Guildford Friary was some 4ha (10 acres) in extent, larger than average for the order which lies at around 2–2.5ha (5–6 acres) (Hinnebusch 1951, 70). This cramped norm may be the result of urban siting for, where the friary lay outside the built-up area as at Guildford or Llanfaes, Anglesey, with 12ha (30 acres), the extra space was welcomed and used for orchards, gardens and meadows (Hinnebusch 1951, 206; Martin 1933–4, 9; Girling 1981). Until 1475, owning land away from the precinct was forbidden to the Dominicans but, by the Dissolution, Guildford Friary had acquired a modest estate of more than 14ha (35 acres) at Woking, Worplesdon and Stoke (Palmer 1887, 19–20).

Rural settlement

In Surrey, where land use has been increasingly intensive since the end of the medieval centuries and much is now submerged below modern housing, motorways and airports, it is not easy to distinguish the medieval villages in their ancient contexts of fields, woods and waste. Features which could have helped – the corrugations of obsolete field systems, the earthworks of abandoned settlements, the hollows of disused tracks – have mostly been built over or bulldozed and ploughed away. The relationship between field systems, enclosure and settlement is particularly in need of more research. Notable steps have been taken by Bailey & Galbraith (1973), while Blair (1982, ch 3) has summarised the evidence available to date. Although it is unsatisfactory to consider settlement separately from farming, its economic base, there is no space here to discuss the archaeological evidence for agriculture.

Much thought has been devoted by geographers to the classification of medieval settlements on the basis of size, compactness, shape and regularity (Roberts 1982; 1985). There are considerable difficulties in such morphological analysis, however, because of the problem of determining the actual medieval size and shape. Documentary records seldom mention the shape of places they are recording. Occasionally, as in parts of the east Midlands and Cambridgeshire, they mention groups of houses some distance away from the centre of the village as clearly definable units called 'Ends'. On the map today, some Surrey examples of this can be recognised – West End, Chobham, for example, and the two 'Ends' of Ockham (a village which, today, consists only of 'Ends').

Village plans may have changed radically in the post-medieval centuries and, even if there is an extant 16th century estate plan to show the shape of the village in Tudor times, there can be no guarantee that the village was the same shape two or three centuries before. Only with much careful archaeological work of a kind that has hardly yet begun in the county could there be any hope of recovering with certainty the ground plan of a village in the Middle Ages. Nevertheless, there are hints from work in towns such as Reigate and Kingston that, in some cases, there may have been considerable stability from the 12th to the 19th centuries in such matters as street layout and plot boundaries.

Whether such stability extended to smaller communities is uncertain and there may sometimes have been dramatic changes amounting to full-scale migration or replanning. Fieldwork in Norfolk (Wade-Martins 1980) and Hampshire (Cunliffe 1972) has shown that the locations of settlements bearing the same name have moved round the countryside and that settlement shift may have been quite a common phenomenon. Abandoned moated sites and other earthworks suggest that similar forces may have been at work in Surrey. Some Surrey villages probably experienced migration – Ockley, Godstone and Haslemere are examples. Reigate, before it found stability and quasi-urban status from the late 12th century on, was moved and experienced a change of name (see preceding chapter) and there is some reason to think that Kingston was once centred at a site further north. Other villages suffered extinction at an early date – for example, Civentone was suppressed when the new borough of Bletchingley was formed in the late 12th century.

With these reservations in mind, it can still be claimed that there appear to have been two basic village shapes in Surrey: the assemblage of houses and enclosures can be linear, forming one or more rows, or non-linear, forming an agglomeration. The simplest shape was a single row of houses, with holdings at the back of them, facing on to one side of a street or green. A more usual shape was the village with houses facing one another across a street, or across the junction of two streets (West Clandon; Great Bookham). The church or manor house is often at one end of a street village, inhibiting growth in that direction. As the village expanded, it grew along the street, the holdings extending outwards in long strips using the street frontage as a base. In some streets there are traces of a strict regularity of layout (Great Bookham). The planning involved may have gone further than determining the topography – a regularly planned village usually went hand-in-hand with an ordering of the agriculture and tenure. Such settlements may have been regulated by customs and obligations imposed at the time the layout was established.

Agglomerations, by their very nature, are harder to describe objectively. A few Surrey villages (Buckland; Brockham) are compact settlements centred on a village green, while others appear to have grown up as loose settlements around or on the edge of much larger areas of common pasture. Dunsfold is of this type and retains its green-edge character. Charlwood is of the same type but infill and enclosure have removed all the once extensive common land.

Where settlements have more than one green, major road junction or group of buildings, they have been termed 'polyfocal' (Taylor 1977). A number of suggestions have been offered to explain this type of nucleation. The simplest is that different foci of settlement grew up as a result of differences in ownership, land tenure and social grouping. Another possibility is that they reflect a situation that may have been much more widespread in the early medieval period, namely a completely dispersed settlement of small and scattered hamlets or farmsteads. In many areas, this pattern has been obscured by the process of 'balling' into nucleated villages. It is increasingly coming to be held that the hamlet and its associated infield–outfield system was an early form of settlement all over Britain, and this type of pattern has been identified in south-west Surrey (Baker & Butlin 1973, 655–6; Yates 1961) and in the Weald.

Amid this settlement pattern, especially in the Weald, moated sites are found in many locations but, as far as can be seen at present, there is little correlation between the form and size of moats, their relationship to other forms of settlement and their status or function. However, there may have been a distinction between moated sites within a village, within a community of a dispersed 'green-edge' village and in even more remote parts of the parish. The first were usually capital manors, the last probably originated as sub-divisions of manor land and the middle group may have had a variety of origins.

The distribution of moated sites in Surrey (fig 9.5) shows that they were spread widely across the county. There are concentrations of particular interest in the south and south-east of the county around the headwaters of the Arun and the Mole on the Weald Clay (fig 9.11). It is clear that, in Surrey, moated sites existed alongside other forms of medieval rural settlement – villages, hamlets and unmoated farmsteads – and that there are great variations between parishes in the incidence of moated sites.

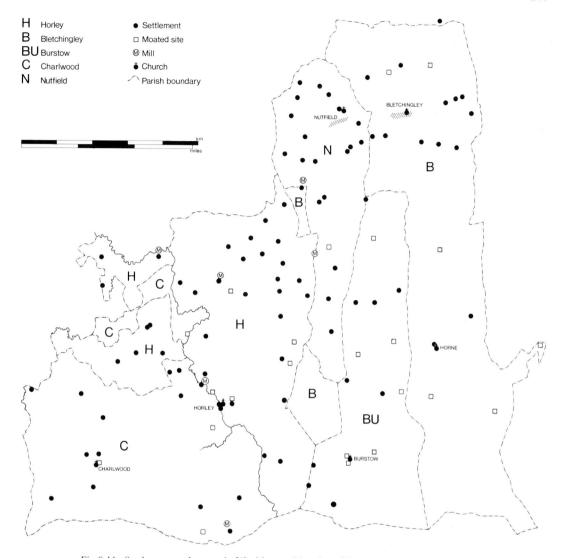

Fig 9.11. Settlement and moats in Wealden parishes from Bletchingley to Charlwood, *c* 1325.

It would be wrong to assume that the majority of the moated sites in south-east Surrey were manor houses. Many do seem, however, to be associated with the more important holdings in this area of reputed medieval assarting or colonisation (eg Horley Lodge) or with longstanding holdings (eg Lake) but, equally, many important (Bures) or longstanding (Kinnersley) holdings are not moated while a number of quite minor and possibly short-lived holdings were.[8] The research is being complicated by the realisation that some apparently quite important holdings (eg Cogman's Farm, Burstow – Gray 1982) seem to be wholly without documentation. The problems are, at present, some way from being resolved.

Less concentrated groups of moated sites once existed and partly survive in west Surrey, located mainly close to rivers and tributary streams. The moats of west and central Surrey have recently been studied by Christopher McLees (1982) who concluded that here the majority of moated sites do represent manor houses although far from every manor house was moated. However, as only a small percentage are located by or in an existing village, the majority probably represent migrated or secondary manorial centres. Moats in north-east Surrey have almost all been destroyed and are known only from map or casual documentary references. Their distribution in this quarter of the county is almost certainly under-represented on the map (fig 9.5).

One of the most important qualities of moated sites, especially isolated and deserted sites, is that they actually reveal where specific medieval occupation took place. Deserted unmoated farmsteads or manor houses are much harder to locate although they may from time to time be discovered by chance or careful fieldwork as at Alsted (Ketteringham 1976), Brooklands (Hanworth & Tomalin 1977) and Woodlands Field, Salfords (Ellaby 1984). In fact, one of the outstanding problems concerning moated sites is the lack of comparable earthworks on soils incapable of readily supporting a moat although it should be noted that, in the documentation concerning a number of unmoated royal manors, there is mention of ditches, banks, hedges and palisades (Brown *et al* 1963, 895–1021). Almost by definition moats may be expected on impervious subsoils and not on porous soils, but, if the function of moats were defence or prestige, one would expect to find comparable phenomena on porous soils whereas the number of comparable earthworks that are not moats is very small. Sites such as those at Preston Hawe, Tadworth; Alsted, Merstham; and Henley Wood, Chelsham, are remarkable for their rarity and are actually on soils that would probably support a moat.

The earthworks at Henley Wood, Chelsham (Ketteringham 1980), enclose approximately 4ha (10 acres) in all and comprise a stirrup-shaped enclosure surrounded by a pentagonal outer enclosure. The banks of the outer enclosure are inturned at one point to bound a trackway that approaches the entrance to the inner area, which is on its straight side. Within the inner enclosure there was a well and at least one flint-walled building. Pottery found in 1974 dated from the 12th to 14th centuries and included sherds from a Saintonge jug. The history of Chelsham appears to be poorly documented and, despite the apparent importance of the site in Henley Wood, it has not proved possible to identify it satisfactorily in any record. Nevertheless, the study of such sites is well worthwhile as it is of the utmost importance to accept that we will never understand moated sites if we do not also study contemporary unmoated sites.

To summarise the settlement evidence: in common with much of south-east England, medieval Surrey contained villages, hamlets and isolated farmsteads. Rarely, if at all, in the county would the traveller have encountered the classic 'Midlands' situation of nucleated villages separated only by their open fields.

The declining village, 1300–1500

Deserted villages are not the phenomenon in Surrey that they are in some Midland counties (Beresford & Hurst 1971). This may be, in part at least, because later emparkment and landscaping or later rebuilding and re-occupation has covered many erstwhile traces of abandoned medieval settlements. The dearth of Decorated and Perpendicular church architecture in the county suggests a 'poor folk and a few' in the later Middle Ages and one or two shrunken and rudely repaired churches (Wotton; Little Bookham) indicate reduced congregations over many generations. However, the published gazetteers of deserted villages contain a number of sites that were probably never deserted and also sites that may never have been villages.

In some cases, a solitary church may suggest vanished homesteads as at Tatsfield, Chelsham and Wotton. Many single farms of today may also be the only surviving descendants of once prosperous hamlets or villages (Tillingdown; Chivington; West Humble). Nowhere in Surrey, however, do we see the earthworks of deserted homestead sites and village streets which can be readily identified in many other parts of the country. In Surrey, of course, there is little land that has remained undisturbed as permanent pasture for six centuries, and so such traces as may once have existed have been ploughed or landscaped away or have been built over in more recent, more prosperous times. But, equally important, much of Surrey was a landscape of scattered farms and hamlets and it is not easy to demonstrate the existence of a village in medieval times in any given location.

Industry and communications

The industries of medieval Surrey have not been so fully studied as the castles, churches and houses. Their remains are less easily recognised and often less easily interpreted. The glass industry in the Weald has been investigated (Kenyon 1967; Wood, E S, 1965; 1982) as has the iron industry and, while the latter is largely a post-medieval phenomenon (Straker 1931), an early iron working and forge site has been examined at Alsted (Ketteringham 1976, 17–31).

The industry that has received by far the greatest attention from medieval archaeologists in Surrey is the manufacture of pottery. The typological chronology of vessels provides vital assistance in the dating of archaeological horizons and the distribution of wares is an invaluable indicator of trade (Peacock 1977; Davey & Hodges 1983) and kilns are known from many parts of Surrey. They have been found in towns at Kingston (Canham 1970), Farnham (Cole 1982) and Southwark but more frequently in rural contexts: for example at Ashtead (Frere 1941), Cheam (Marshall 1924; Orton 1982), Earlswood (fig 9.12; Turner 1975) and Limpsfield (Prendergast 1973; 1974) in east Surrey and at Ash (Holling 1968) and a number of places near the Hampshire border (Holling 1971) in the west. In late medieval times, the white-ware kilns of north and west Surrey became important sources of supply to the growing markets of London but current research seems to indicate that neither the products of the prolific kilns of the Limpsfield area nor the elaborately decorated wares of the Earlswood kilns reached the City in appreciable quantities (Vince 1985).

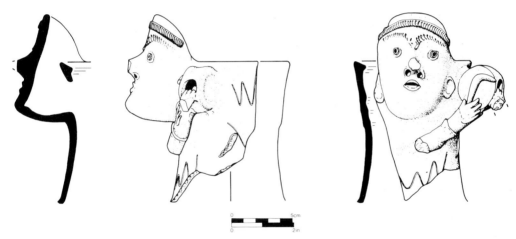

Fig 9.12. Anthropomorphic jug spout and neck from the Earlswood kiln excavated in 1975. (Drawing by Michael Russell)

A number of studies concerning aspects of Surrey pottery manufacture and trade are approaching completion and the Surrey Archaeological Society hopes soon to publish a collection of these, at which time a reasoned overview of the county's medieval pottery industries may be possible.

An impression has arisen that medieval life styles were largely immobile. Medieval society is regarded as largely static and peasants, in particular, are thought to have been tied to the land and limited in their experience of travelling to within a mile or two beyond their nearest market centre. The existence of hundreds of such rural markets, however, itself presupposes much movement. Beyond that, countrymen migrated to the towns, townsmen moved to the country away from urban poverty and guild restrictions. Rectors and vicars acted as links between rural 'backwaters' and the wider world. The higher echelons of society – kings, barons and ecclesiastics with their sprawling retinues – moved freely about the kingdom. All this implies an effective communications network.

Nevertheless, medieval roads and routes are hard to map and harder to date because they were seldom formally engineered and frequently indirect. Most of them have been overlain by modern roads although some have declined into green lanes or have been ploughed away.

Parts of the Roman road network stayed in use, as they do today. Lengths of the London–Chichester road and the London–Portslade road remained, for example, although the London–Lewes road retained its value to Surrey merely as a boundary. But the pagan English had followed a settlement pattern that drew traffic away from former routes and that pattern remained throughout the Middle Ages. In places, the Roman roads had been engineered on lines that needed constant maintenance to preserve the route and this was just not available in the Middle Ages – consequently stretches such as that through Redlands Wood south of Dorking fell totally out of use.

The concept of a national road system centring on London was slow to grow. The Gough map of *c* 1340 suggests that, by that date, London had once again become a route centre with five through roads running to distant parts of the kingdom. One ran across Surrey from London to Winchester, Salisbury, Exeter and Cornwall. It is not certain that the lines connecting the towns on the Gough map denote the actual roads, or were drawn as a cartographic convention on which a figure was placed representing the distance (Parsons 1970, 17), but the latter seems the most probable. The map omits several well-authenticated roads such as that from London to Dover along the Roman Watling Street.

Travelling monks compiled guides or itineraries to help their brethren plan their journeys, and these show how others required to travel would have dealt with the problems arising from the complete absence of maps. Guides would have been hired to assist with unfamiliar or complex links in the overall journey.

One of the determining factors for the site of towns were fords and bridging places. At London, the bridge has been there as long as the city. The Roman bridge was followed by a succession of Saxon and medieval structures: timber piled, multi-arched and finally topped with houses, shops, gates and drawbridges.

During the four centuries after 1066, the Thames was crossed by a series of bridges dictated by the needs of state rather than by commercial convenience – the proximity of royal residences and the availability of great timbers from the royal forests were deciding factors. This succession of bridges included one at Kingston by 1219, one at Staines by 1222 and one at Chertsey by *c* 1410 (Stratton & Pardoe 1982). These timber bridges have all now disappeared, at any rate above water level, but there are numerous smaller stone-built medieval bridges surviving. The string of such bridges across the River Wey, attributed to the monks of Waverley, has already been mentioned.

Towns

Following a temporary setback in the disturbed years following the Norman Conquest, the 12th and 13th centuries were a flourishing period for English towns. The growth of towns was stimulated by the development of trade and commerce both at home and abroad, especially with Flanders and the Rhineland. Many towns were protected and encouraged by the king and by the more powerful nobles and prelates. However, as Surrey was in close proximity to the growing dominance of London, its towns were inhibited in the medieval period. Beresford (1967, 490–1) describes it as 'another old-settled county with few opportunities for the medieval economy to support more towns'. Guildford, Godalming and Kingston were probably the only settlements with anything approaching true urban status apart from Southwark which was a bridgehead suburb of London (fig 9.13).

Chertsey, Bletchingley, Dorking, Croydon and Haslemere achieved little more than villages in the Middle Ages. Farnham, Leatherhead and Reigate may have come closer to urban status but even here growth was limited. For example, it is evident that the initial layout of the new town of Reigate in the late 12th century only made provision for two very modest market places, one at

Fig 9.13. Surrey town plans after Rocque's map of 1762. A – Bletchingley; B – Reigate; C – Dorking; D – Croydon; E – Leatherhead; F – Kingston; G – Godalming; H – Staines; I – Chertsey; J – Guildford; K – Farnham; L – Haslemere; M – Southwark.

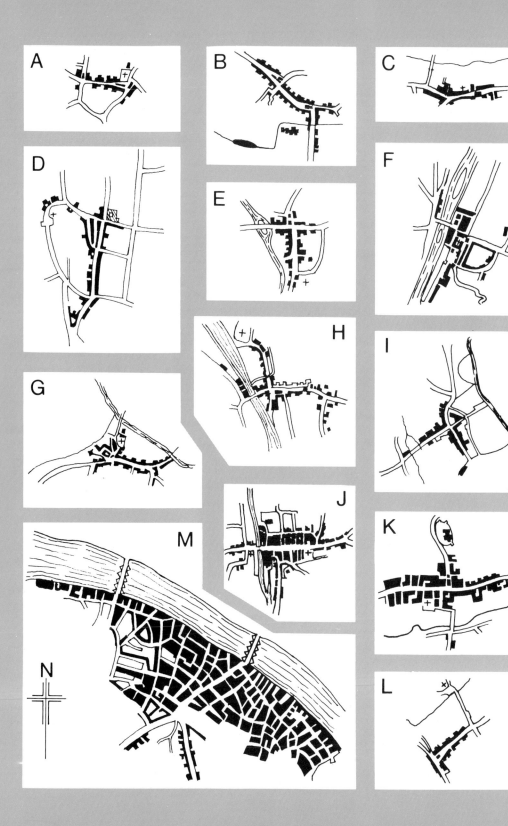

each end of the High Street. At some later stage a more generous triangular market place seems to have been established at the west end of the town but even this presents a problem in that it became overbuilt between the late 14th and 16th centuries while the whole frontage facing its northern side remained without buildings.

Nationally, urban excavation has concentrated on the successful towns and there can be little doubt that the picture obtained has been accordingly biased. Consequently work on such Surrey towns as Kingston and Reigate is particularly important. Nationally again, there has been a tendency to think of medieval England as a simple dichotomy: town and village, the urban and the rural. Reality was certainly more subtle and more intricate. There would have been at least four more or less clearly recognisable levels of nucleated settlement – the city or national centre; the regional centre; local market centres; and villages. The towns which acted as regional centres had long-distance trading contacts and a distinctly urban life and institutions. In Surrey, only Guildford and Southwark (as a suburb of London) approach this condition: the other 'towns' fall into the category of local market centres, itself embracing a broad range of settlement size.

Local market centres lacked, in general, the long-distance trading contacts of the regional centres. It is significant, for example, that little imported pottery has been found in the excavations in Kingston and Reigate, demonstrating the limitations on trade that applied. The local market centres differed from lesser villages in having traders and craftsmen whose services could be drawn upon by the surrounding villages. Villages had the majority of their inhabitants directly engaged in agriculture although there were some households pursuing specialist functions.

Local market centres tend to have few written records from the medieval period and archaeology often therefore remains the major source for detailed information. However, they rarely offer the spectacular opportunity for excavation provided in the more important towns by urban development – opportunities that by their nature sometimes draw funding for archaeology. On the other hand, they seldom provide the totally deserted areas found in some villages (but too often ignored by archaeologists).

O'Connell (1977) has reviewed the history and archaeological potential of nine 'historic' towns within Surrey. This review discussed plans and topography along with the dates of settlement and progress of 'urban' development but the survey was confined to the present administrative county and therefore ignored Southwark, Croydon and Kingston.

The number of buildings surviving in part, at least, from the earlier medieval centuries in Surrey's towns is remarkably small and the growth of the towns has to be studied mainly through their town plans. Guildford shows signs of having been founded, or at least greatly expanded, as a late Saxon planned town – possibly of the early 10th century (fig 8.10). The way in which the parishes of St Mary and Holy Trinity appear to have been carved out of the corner of the large parish of Stoke strongly suggests that Stoke – a royal manor – was there first. Kingston, Croydon, Bletchingley and Haslemere show clear market-based plans although, in the case of Kingston, the early plan is far from certain. Dorking, Leatherhead and Chertsey may also be market-based but the market at Dorking does not seem to have played a dominant part. There is nothing in Surrey that resembles the formal grid pattern of planned towns or extensions of the Middle Ages: even the 'new' towns of Reigate, Bletchingley and Haslemere seem to have consisted of little, if anything, more than burgage plots set along a street or around a market place. Leatherhead, not identified by Beresford (1967) as a 'new' town, appears to have been established along the approach to a new bridge (Blair 1976b) and its creation may have involved the suppression of a polyfocal group of settlements. The creation of Reigate and Bletchingley certainly seems to have involved the suppression of other settlements (Cherchefelle and Civentone).

The siting of Surrey's towns shows the influence of the leading landowners rather than geography. Guildford, Godalming and Kingston grew up at geographically determined locations, and at Guildford the castle followed, but Farnham, Reigate, Croydon and Bletchingley were dominated by the castle or manor place of the lord. Chertsey grew up around the gate of the Benedictine abbey. Leatherhead is at a geographical node but an act of town creation seems to have been involved. Dorking, hardly a town throughout the Middle Ages, seems to have been inhibited by the lack of a resident lord of the manor while Reigate and Bletchingley declined with the importance of their castles. Haslemere seems to have been planted deliberately to minister to the needs of a remote area.

Some urban investigations have been among the great successes of the archaeology of the Middle Ages but medieval archaeology in Surrey towns has been modest. Southwark has been subjected to more archaeological investigation than any other Surrey town but the results have been disappointing from the medieval point of view. Aspects of its medieval history can be reconstructed using documentary sources (Johnson 1969) and archaeology has added only a limited amount of information (SLAEC 1984).

The peace following the Norman Conquest allowed the bridgehead settlement and one-time *burh* of Southwark to grow and Domesday Book (Morris 1975) records at least 40 households, a minster church (and possibly also St Olaf's church), a dock and mooring places along the Thames. This settlement remained small throughout the Middle Ages but, by the 16th century, it had spread in ribbon developments eastwards as far as Horsley Down (ie nearly to modern Tower Bridge Road – Corner 1858, 157–67), west in a narrow strip along Bankside and south along Borough High Street to near St George's church (Darlington & Farrar 1950, 9–10; pls 1, 8). Beyond the built-up area, the land remained marshy and subject to flooding. Several magnates, ecclesiastical and lay, had houses in Southwark and they competed with representatives of the king, the City and the county of Surrey to exercise some control over the area.

Remains of the London residence of the Bishop of Winchester were the subject of an excavation by the London Museum in the 1960s which still awaits publication, but further excavation has taken place on other parts of the palace site. It has recently proved possible also to produce a detailed reconstruction of the palace from documentary sources (Carlin 1985). Other excavated remains include parts of medieval buildings of chalk and other types of stone; a dock known to have been in existence in 1323; an early medieval building near London Bridge that had been badly damaged by river erosion in the late 13th century; and many wells, rubbish pits, cesspits and ditches. Objects found in the excavations support the picture of Southwark presented by the written records. Leather shoes and garments have been found including a group which may have come from a workshop or leather market near Bankside. Evidence of pilgrims survives in the form of pewter and silver badges which were purchased at Canterbury and other shrines. Examination of several medieval rubbish pits has shown some of the foods which were available in the area: these include apples, plums, grapes, figs, blackberries, strawberries, elderberries, cabbages, carrots, black mustard, sorrel, peas, beans, barley, wheat, rye, oats, hazelnuts, pinenuts and opium poppies. Bones of cattle, sheep, goat, pig, rabbit, hare, and domestic fowl have been found along with oyster and mussel shells. The discovery of many bones of herring, smelt, eel, cod, plaice and dogfish confirm, as might have been expected, that fish formed an important part of the diet. In addition to objects showing some aspects of Southwark's medieval economy, many household utensils and other possessions of the populace have been recovered: as well as the inevitable pottery, a stone mortar, iron tools, bronze buckles, pins, brooches, rings, keys and coins have been found.

Documentary references to Southwark increase in the 14th and 15th centuries and it is possible to trace the development of this transpontine suburb of London which supplied the City with goods, services and accommodation. Bread, meat, fish and other foodstuffs, some of which were grown locally, were sold in its market and shops as were clothing, shoes, and various manufactured goods. Much criticism was made of some of Southwark's more notorious inhabitants – criminals, prostitutes and rebels. Large numbers of artisans provided a growing challenge to the authority of the City guilds and contributed to the vigorous commercial life of the area. Southwark had a market and the right to hold a fair was granted in 1444. There were a large number of shops and taverns which catered for travellers going to and from London, the best remembered of which today are probably the pilgrims immortalised by Chaucer.

At Guildford, by contrast with Southwark, opportunities may have been lost in the failure to excavate any but the friary site in advance of the redevelopment of the low-lying parts of the town centre close to the River Wey. Medieval archaeology in Croydon has also been disappointing. Of necessity, work there has been small-scale but it is difficult to understand why the results have been

BELL STREET

No 16

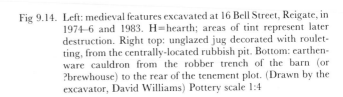

Rubbish
Pit

N

?BARN

Drying
Kiln

Robber
Trench

0   10m
0
                    30ft

Fig 9.14. Left: medieval features excavated at 16 Bell Street, Reigate, in 1974–6 and 1983. H=hearth; areas of tint represent later destruction. Right top: unglazed jug decorated with rouletting, from the centrally-located rubbish pit. Bottom: earthenware cauldron from the robber trench of the barn (or ?brewhouse) to the rear of the tenement plot. (Drawn by the excavator, David Williams) Pottery scale 1:4

so meagre – an illustration, if any more were required, of the unpredictability of such work. Work in Reigate (Williams 1980; 1983; 1984) and Kingston, spearheaded by amateurs in both cases, has produced useful and interesting results (fig 9.14). In Kingston, evidence is emerging of medieval urban industry that so far has eluded archaeologists in other Surrey towns with the exception of a malting kiln in Reigate (Williams 1984) and a pottery kiln on the edge of medieval Farnham (Cole 1982). Excavation in Kingston has produced traces of medieval potters, tilers, masons, blacksmiths, bronzesmiths, leathermakers, hornworkers, butchers and hurdlemakers in the form of finished products or waste materials. Their discovery confirms the trading and industrial aspects of medieval Kingston with craftsmen having their workshops close to the market area. As is to be expected, dirty industries – or those with a high fire risk – seem to have been situated some distance from the medieval centre, especially in the Eden Street area. Kingston provides the clearest archaeological view of a Surrey town to place alongside, for example, that derived from the documents concerning Farnham (Robo 1935). Papers by Hall (1981) and Hinton (M, 1981) have set out the conclusions of work done before 1980 and work in the town is now being undertaken by the professional team based on the Museum of London.

A number of minor problems may be susceptible to archaeological investigation in several Surrey towns. The interesting history and street plan of Leatherhead, for example (Blair 1976b), ought to be open (even after the recent redevelopment) to some archaeological testing and is one place where even 'key-hole' archaeology might prove useful.

Housing

Common to rural and urban settlements are the houses in which people lived. Inevitably, most studies of medieval domestic architecture concentrate on the readily visible features of buildings that still stand (Wood, M E, 1965) but the essential features of such survivors can also be recognised in archaeological investigations both above and into the ground.

Few houses from the two centuries or so after the Conquest are known from Surrey. Inevitably, even on excavated sites, it is the dwellings of the wealthy that provide the more substantial and readily examinable remains. In plan, larger medieval houses were originally collections of buildings, groups of halls (or communal living rooms), chambers (private living rooms), wardrobes, kitchens, barns, stables and brewhouses: all separately roofed, loosely linked together, of different dates and added to when required. With advancing date, the survival of standing buildings grows more complete and their coherence more noticeable. Nevertheless, survivors above ground from the Middle Ages of even the main hall or hall-and-chamber block are rare. Excavation and documents can help to complete the picture and allow the context of ancillary structures to be seen: the complexity of the whole reflects the social status of the owner.

The earliest post-Conquest building deserving the appellation 'house' to have been examined in the county is the masonry structure, the footings of which survive within the earthworks at Bletchingley Castle. This was partly excavated in the 19th century and thought at that time to be a keep (Malden 1900b). Re-examination and re-excavation has shown it to have been an unusual square building of two storeys with accommodation in two ranges on the lines of a structure recently excavated at Castle Acre, Norfolk (Coade & Streeten 1982, 147–56). Stair turrets at two corners provided communication between the storeys and the lower level was lit by narrow, double-splayed windows. One chamber in the upper storey (probably the hall) was heated by a large open hearth supported on a massive pillar (plan: fig 9.15). The house has further parallels in Hampshire and, possible, in Normandy, and can be dated to the reign of William I (Turner 1986b).

Castles continued to be used as residences by the crown and by the nobility. For example, to the south-east of Guildford Castle, and closely adjoining if not actually within it, there was a royal house or palace (as it was often called in the 14th century) that was a favourite residence of Henry III. Throughout his reign, the king constantly embellished and added to the structure (Brown *et al* 1963, 950–5). Successive bishops of Winchester used Farnham Castle as an occasional residence or as a staging post when *en route* from Winchester to London (Thompson 1961; Brooks 1985).

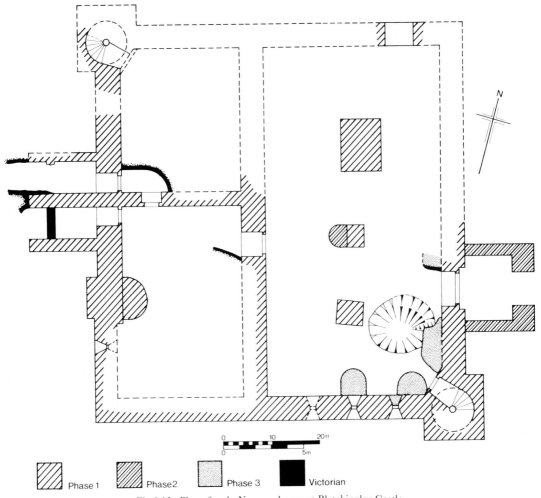

Fig 9.15. Plan of early Norman house at Bletchingley Castle.

Phase 1   Phase 2   Phase 3   Victorian

By the 12th century, three main types of hall were found in the more prosperous medieval houses (Wood, M E, 1965, chs 2–4): the first-floor hall, the aisled hall, and the ground-floor hall. Where these halls are found combined with chambers in a single building to form an integrated living unit, the term hall-house is applied. Remains of a great first-floor hall of the 14th century survive from the palace of the bishops of Winchester at Southwark (Darlington & Farrar 1950, 45–56). This measured at least 18m (60ft) by 9m (30ft). At the other end of the scale, a small first-floor hall, dated to c 1250–70 and measuring 8.6m by 4m (28ft 4in by 13ft 4in) internally, was identified by the excavator at Alsted, near Merstham (Ketteringham 1976, 6–8). Such buildings and their urban cousins were probably once common in the county and stone undercrofts still surviving or well authenticated at Guildford (O'Connell 1983), Wallington (Johnston 1932) and Southwark (Malden 1912, 126–7, 138; Wood, M E, 1965, 82, 95) may have belonged to buildings of this type. A further similar undercroft has recently been rediscovered in Kingston but has been removed from site with the intention of relocating it elsewhere in the Horsefair redevelopment.

The second type of hall followed the Saxon tradition of a barn-like structure: the aisled hall with two rows of posts or arcades forming nave and aisles. The remains of an aisle post of the 12th century hall survives at Farnham Castle (Malden 1905, 599–602; Wood, M E, 1965, 38). Alsted again provides a modest excavated example – around 1270 the small first-floor hall was replaced by a larger, but still small, ground-floor hall with a single aisle. To the hall was attached a solar block and service rooms while the kitchen remained detached (Ketteringham 1976, 9–16).

The type persisted in small numbers and became incorporated into box-frame construction, but such aisled hall-houses are uncommon among surviving medieval buildings. Fewer than 20 are known in the Wealden counties of which only three are in Surrey – Old Court Cottage, Limpsfield (Mason 1966); Forge Cottage, Dunsfold; and a further example recently discovered in Limpsfield (P Gray, pers comm).

The subdivision into nave and aisles was originally the only way to enable a wide span to be roofed but, gradually, carpenters successfully experimented to get rid of the obstructive posts and the result was a series of ingenious roofs such as the arch-braced collar beam and the hammer beam roofs. The unequalled hammer beam roof of Westminster Hall was framed up at Farnham before being dismantled and moved to Westminster for final erection. At times the service end of domestic halls retained their aisle posts even when the rest of the hall was roofed in the span: this was especially possible when the hall itself was only two bays long and only the central truss had to be roofed in the span. Such houses are classed as 'quasi-aisled' and usually incorporate a base-cruck in place of the aisle post of the central truss. Houses of this type are very rare, fewer than 10 being known in the south-eastern counties and less than 100 in England as a whole. Cogman's Farm, Burstow, is the only quasi-aisled hall known in Surrey (Gray 1982).[9]

Aisled halls were probably only erected for men of some local importance. Mercer (1975, 99–101) has suggested that the base-cruck halls are usually of manorial status associated with important local economic enterprises. Cogman's Farm stands within a moat but, so far, no documentary evidence relating to its original ownership or use has been discovered. Base-crucks are generally considered to pre-date 1400 but other features at Cogman's Farm would indicate a late 15th century date.

The unaisled ground-floor hall is a basic living unit that is also found before the Norman Conquest. Such ground-floor halls vary greatly in size but almost all were heated by an axial open hearth. Archaeology has established that open hearths were commonly made of pitched stones or tiles set on edge. Beyond the hearth was the 'upper' end of the hall where there was a table for the owner, perhaps placed on a dais as still happens in college halls. The opposite, or 'lower', end of the hall was for the servants and doors led from this end to the service apartments: a buttery for strong drinks and pantry for storing bread and table utensils. Between them, in the largest houses, a passage sometimes led to the kitchen standing by itself in a detached building as a protection against the effect of fire.

Early ground-floor halls were limited in their width by the constraints of roof construction. Enigmatic remains of such a hall survive at Walton on the Hill, incorporated in a later farmhouse, now much divided. The problems of covering large roof spans with a single truss were solved in the late 14th century and a far grander example of an unaisled hall survives from the 15th century at Croydon Palace, rebuilt by Archbishop Stafford, c 1445 (fig 9.16). A second grand hall at Beddington was probably built about the turn of the century and is covered by a hammer beam roof copied from that at Eltham Palace. From a slightly lower status comes the hall of Crowhurst Place, built c 1425 for the Gaynsford family and heavily restored and built around by George Crawley, c 1920.

The second structural element of hall-houses was the series of chambers which could be attached to one or both ends of the hall, usually (in later medieval centuries at least) in the form of a two-storeyed chamber block roofed at right angles to the hall (Faulkner 1958). These arrangements provided self-contained accommodation for the lord and his family at one end of the hall and for the service rooms and servants at the other. The principal chamber in the lord's accommodation was generally on the first floor and was often referred to as the solar. It offered privacy and sometimes comparatively luxurious accommodation, occasionally being heated by a fireplace and lit by a large window and provided with a garderobe. An especially magnificent and aristocratic example of this feature survives at Croydon, built by Archbishop Arundel, c 1400.

In houses of manorial status or similar, a series of lesser buildings to accommodate the other needs of the establishment were associated with the nucleus of hall and chamber block. That their

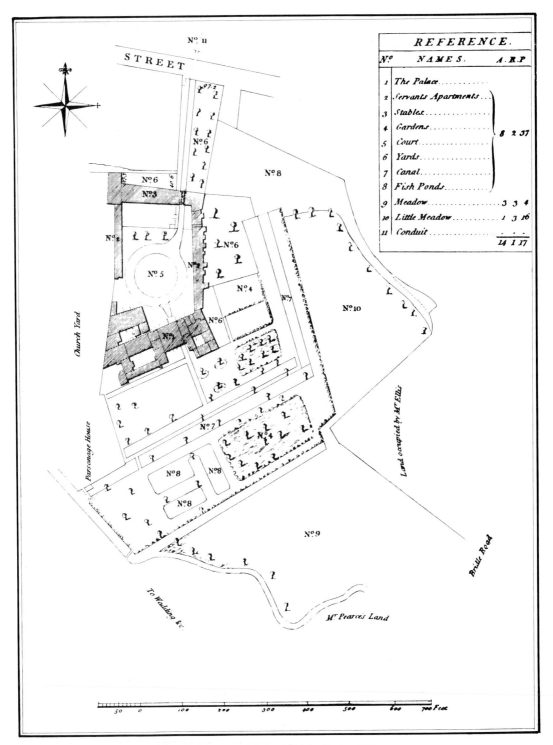

Fig 9.16. Croydon Palace in 1780 (Archbishop Stafford's hall is marked 'No 1'. Plots 7 and 8 were respectively canals and fishponds).

layout was often quite informal, even at the top of the social scale, was clearly revealed by the economical excavation of the Black Prince's palace at Kennington (Dawson 1976). Such informality was not universal, however, even in the 14th century, and there is documentary evidence that Rotherhithe, rebuilt for Edward III in the 1350s, was a courtyard house (Brown *et al* 1963, 989–94). Excavations in 1983–4 on the northern part of the Bishop of Winchester's palace at Southwark examined the foundations of 12th century buildings, the early 13th century hall and a great 13th century drain which had been built of large slabs of Purbeck limestone. It was also found that south and east of the hall lay a range of buildings that appeared to form part of a group around a courtyard. Some of these buildings can be identified on 16th and 17th century prints and continued in use until the 19th century.

Attempts to push the boundaries of knowledge back to times or levels of society from which no standing buildings have survived meet great problems. Humble medieval peasant housing, for example, is only known through the results of excavation and, unfortunately, little information has so far been forthcoming on this front from Surrey but evidence from adjacent counties gives some idea of what one might expect (eg Holden 1963; Hurst & Hurst 1964).

A building complex of the 13th century from a social level slightly below that of the manor lord has been excavated at Brooklands, Weybridge (Hanworth & Tomalin 1977, 49–76). The buildings at Brooklands, dated *c* 1175 to *c* 1300, were not heavily framed, had earth-fast posts as their main structural elements and did not follow the hall-and-chamber-block layout (fig 9.17): there were several buildings, including a detached kitchen. The house itself comprised three rooms in line, none of which could truly be called a hall but which may, nevertheless, correspond to terms sometimes found in 12th century leases – *camera* or *thalamus* (bedchamber), *aula* and *domus* or *domus privata*: the *domus* being the heated room. Close parallels to the Brooklands structure are known from Ellington, Huntingdonshire, and Newstead, Yorkshire, and buildings of this type may once have been far more frequent than can be evidenced today.

Vernacular houses of sufficient substance to be able to survive to the 20th century appear in the countryside of Surrey from towards the end of the Middle Ages. Above the level of the humblest cottage, these late medieval dwellings were generally of the hall-house type: based on a small unaisled ground-floor hall, sometimes with the cooking hearth in the hall. The smoke from the open hearth found its way out through gablets at the end of the ridge or between the tiles of the roof itself. As a consequence, the rafters rapidly became blackened by smoke and this smoke-blackening often remains behind subsequent obscuring alterations as an indicator of the origins of the house. Many of these buildings survive, in part at least, although much altered and overbuilt down the centuries with floors and fireplaces inserted in the open hall. About half a dozen common plan types can be identified (Mercer 1975).

Building stone was highly localised in Surrey but good quality wood was plentiful and so timber framing was almost universal. Such buildings were divided into a series of structural 'bays' by the principal load-bearing uprights of the frame: the bay posts. Some indication of the social status of a medieval house at the time it was built can be given by the number of bays utilised for the open hall – one, two or, occasionally, three. The number of rooms and details such as style of roof truss, spacing of studs and types of window varied both with wealth and, across the centuries, with fashion and changing technology, but the basic form of construction lasted to the 18th century in houses and into the present century in farm buildings.

The sheer numbers of such houses show that many must have been the homes of prosperous peasants. They vary in size from one to six rooms and the larger had the same accommodation as the smaller manor houses. The variation in size reflects a considerable range of wealth. The occasional multiplicity of rooms in such houses is confirmed from documentary sources. In the 15th century, the documents show that a house might be divided on the death of a peasant between his daughter and his widow and a specific mention of an upper storey might occur. By this time, many of these houses had become completely detached from their farm buildings, in itself another sign of increasing prosperity.

The systematic investigation and recording of the legacy of standing medieval houses in Surrey is a very long term task. Pioneer work was done by Ralph Nevill in the last century (1891) and

Fig 9.17. Brooklands, Weybridge. Reconstruction of the medieval house (after Hanworth & Tomalin 1977, fig 33).

during the last 30 years much has been done by Kenneth Gravett, R T Mason, P J Gray and John Baker as well as by the enthusiastic team led by Joan Harding. It is clear that some 14th and many 15th century buildings have survived in the county, although usually in a drastically altered state. Frame building and plastering does not attain in Surrey the perfection of the clothiers' houses of Kent and East Anglia but the exuberance of the buildings of Lancashire, Cheshire and the Welsh Borders was matched briefly in Surrey at the end of the 16th century. The remarkable durability of the timber and the high standard of local workmanship in the traditional restrained style, coupled with a tendency to adapt and modernise rather than to demolish and rebuild, has preserved hundreds of houses with sufficient original features to permit the layout and details of a late medieval homestead to be visualised (eg Mercer 1975; Harding 1976).

The simplest surviving medieval houses – and it must not be forgotten that the smallest houses of the period were too flimsy to have survived as more than traces in an archaeologist's trench – appear to have had two bays open to the roof with no upstairs room. Today, such basic houses are more often than not found incorporated into larger dwellings and the chambers floored over, but they can sometimes be recognised by the presence of long passing braces, archaic roof systems and a low roof line. Windows inserted for the upper rooms have been squeezed in under the eaves or inserted as dormers and the roof space itself has been used for head room.

Some medieval houses of two bays were built with one bay floored over to provide an upper room with the lower stage of the floored bay either partitioned off to provide a service room where goods could be stored or, less commonly, open to the hall as in the reconstructed 14th century example from Little Winkhurst exhibited at the Weald and Downland Open Air Museum at Singleton.[10] Slightly larger houses, of three bays in length, either had one end floored over and a two-bay hall or had both end bays floored over leaving a single-bay hall in the centre of the house. The two-bay hall gave an opportunity for a finely decorated central roof truss, often with an arched or cambered tie beam. This tie beam was sometimes supported by impressive arched braces and was generally surmounted by a crown post. The four-bay house, larger still, allowed the spaciousness of a two-bay hall to be combined with floored-over bays at both ends. The entrance in all cases could have been into a cross passage beneath the upper room at the service end of the house, thus giving maximum space in the hall, but in the two-bay hall the entrance is sometimes into the hall. Three- and four-bay houses could be further extended by the addition of a parlour wing at the 'upper' end.

The larger late medieval peasants' and yeomen's houses in Surrey thus resembled those of the lesser gentry in that they often consisted of a central open hall with floored-over service rooms (such as pantry and buttery) at one end and private rooms reserved for the owner of the house and his family at the 'upper' end of the hall. A frequent characteristic of such timber-framed houses is the projection or jettying of first floor rooms on the front – and sometimes also the end – elevations at one or both ends of the hall. Where and why external jettying developed in England is still uncertain but it probably started in congested urban areas as a device to increase the space in the upper storeys. Prestige and fashion may have caused the technique to be taken up in smaller towns and in the countryside. The technique increases the problems of construction and design and the only technical advantage would be the stiffening of the floor joists since the projecting ends of these carry the whole weight of the jetty and are placed under tension. Whatever the reason, jettying originated in the 14th century and spread throughout the country in the 15th, and still more in the 16th, century.

Where there were jettied 'wings' at both ends of the house, the roofs which would be used to cover this arrangement were of two basic patterns. They were either of three parts – a half-hipped roof over the main body of the building with lower gabled sections projecting forwards over the jetties – or a unitary roof. The unitary roof was carried on a top or wall plate that supported the feet of the rafters and was bridged between the two jetties and supported on massive braces at each end of the open hall. The roof was thus framed in one unit with a single ridge line and, usually, hipped ends. In urban or quasi-urban versions, gable ends may be found (eg Munby 1975).

Houses of this type are known as 'Wealden' hall-houses or Wealden houses. They were particularly popular in south-east England and their distribution is densest in the vicinity of Maidstone in Kent where the form may have been developed – hence the name it is given today.

The type is, however, also found outside the Wealden counties. Houses of this type seem to have reached their peak of development in the latter part of the 15th century and were common in Surrey, although not as common as in the neighbouring parts of Kent and Sussex. Charlwood parish, for example, where late 15th and 16th century survivals are particularly numerous and have been closely studied (Harding 1976; Gray 1978), contains no Wealden house.

Apart from a few manor houses, the Wealden and other jettied hall-houses were mostly built by the prosperous traders and craftsmen in the towns and by the growing class of independent yeoman farmers in the countryside. The type represents the highest level of yeoman attainment in Surrey and would have been more costly to construct than the simpler houses without jetties: it must therefore represent a conscious decision of taste and display. At this time the London market was expanding and reasonably accessible to the south-eastern counties and a class of independent farmers had been increasing in numbers and wealth, especially in the Wealden forest where the social pattern tended to produce few big landlords but many yeomen farmers. All the rooms in their houses were normally for domestic purposes: animals and farm implements were housed in separate barns and sheds.

The Wealden house is well known and well studied because of its morphological consistency but the majority of late medieval timber-framed houses are not so easily labelled. The late medieval timber-framed houses of Surrey cover a wide social and morphological range that fully bridges the divide between medieval and early modern times. Some parish surveys have been undertaken (Harding 1976; Gray 1978) but until wider synthesis is available it would be premature to accept the judgement of Nairn & Pevsner (1971, 35) that, from the 15th century onwards, Surrey yeomen rebuilt their houses 'to a pattern of timber framing as standard as any speculative builder would provide today'.

ENVOI

Four centuries after the Battle of Hastings and a century and a quarter after the Black Death, the medieval period slipped violently into the Tudor in the mêlée at Bosworth. By rebuilding Richmond Palace with such enthusiasm, Henry VII gave Surrey a social status that it had not had since the time of Henry III and more building by the crown and wealthy courtiers followed. Eventually Henry VIII built his megalomaniac extravaganza at Cuddington (Nonsuch Palace) which idiosyncratically presaged the change to Renaissance taste.

There had been no cultural break in 1485 – or even 1509. The architecture which began under Richard II and the art that went with it (Harvey 1947) was still predominant in the time of Henry VII and was to remain so until after the death of Henry VIII. It was not until the cataclysmic events of the late 1530s that an unequivocal terminus was provided to the Middle Ages in southern Britain. The monastic buildings found a new life either through conversion or through demolition and the re-use of stone. But the destruction of an immeasurable quantity of sculpture, vestments, jewellery, plate and fine architecture was truly horrific. What remained was only a fraction of what had been. The medieval period was over.

NOTES

1 In contrast to those early undocumented castles known only from their surviving earthworks, Warwick Castle at Kingston is only known from documents and maps. It was captured by Henry III in 1264 (Malden 1911, 345) and may have been erected shortly before to defend the river crossing. It is said to have occupied an area bounded by Clarence Street and the west side of Eden Street and to derive its name from its 15th century ownership by the Nevill earls of Warwick. The site is not available for excavation so conclusive evidence for its form or location cannot at present be obtained.

2 Betchworth Castle, in Dorking parish west of Brockham Green, was crenellated by licence in 1379 and again in 1448 (Malden 1900a, 87; Renn forthcoming). It is said to have been partly dismantled in the reign of Queen Anne, being ruinous, and further reduced in 1798 and 1837, the last time by Henry Hope of Deepdene.

3 It is uncertain how much of the external appearance of the tower at Esher is original and how much is due to remodelling by William Kent. The false machicolations and the diaper patterning of blue header bricks are clearly original and can be paralleled at Farnham. The horizontal bands of stone string courses may, in part, be original – they can be compared

with features at Lambeth and Queen's College – but they are not matched at Farnham and could be largely the work of Kent, as could the ogee-headed doorways, and some of the windows below their original square labels or hood-mouldings.

4 Nine moated sites in Surrey have been scheduled as ancient monuments but another 15 or more would justify being given this protection. Two hitherto well-preserved unscheduled sites (Pollingfold and East Shalford) are known to have been severely damaged by ploughing recently and one (Eastwick Park) partly built over. Two poorly preserved sites (Thorpe Lea and Pooley Green) have been totally destroyed by roadworks.

5 A number of moated sites have associated fish ponds (Flore Farm, Godstone; Court Lodge Farm, Horley; Moathouse Farm, Ewhurst) which are in various states of preservation, but the investigation and analysis of these has hardly begun in Surrey.

6 The value of Lagham greatly declined between 1316 and 1346 (IPM Ed II 1316 and IPM Ed III 1346). The estate was badly affected by the ravages of the Black Death and a graphic description in an IPM of 1350 has misled more than one author into thinking that this was a deserted village site.

7 Excavations undertaken several years ago by the Department of the Environment are now being prepared for publication by Rob Poulton.

8 At present, it appears that the widespread distribution of moated sites in the county and the lack of a discernible relationship between the number of moated sites and the number of contemporary unmoated settlements in any given parish argue against the almost traditional view that such sites are often to be associated with the assarting of the forest.

9 The only other recorded example of a base-cruck in Surrey appears to be the aristocratic example of five trusses at The Guardroom, Lambeth Palace (Alcock & Barley 1972; RCHM 1925, 86, pl 135). Base-crucks are not to be confused with eaves crucks (Gravett 1977).

10 An interesting variation has been noted by Blair (1981a) at Leatherhead in which the two bays were separated at ground floor level by a partition. The unheated bay was ceiled over while the central truss was open at first-floor level producing a 'cragloft' above. The cragloft bay was probably end-jettied and the building apparently had a simple coupled rafter roof.

Bibliography

The abbreviations SyAC (Surrey Archaeological Collections) *and* SyAS (Surrey Archaeological Society) *are used throughout the Bibliography.*

Aberg, F A (ed), 1978 *Medieval moated sites*, Counc Brit Archaeol Res Rep, **17**

Addyman, P, & Morris, R (eds), 1976 *The archaeological study of churches*, Counc Brit Archaeol Res Rep, **13**

Adkins, L, 1979a *The archaeology of the London Borough of Merton: an interim survey for the South-west London Archaeological Unit, March 1979*, SyAS, privately circulated

—, 1979b *The archaeology of the London Borough of Sutton: an interim survey for the South-west London Archaeological Unit, March 1979*, SyAS, privately circulated

—, 1980 Settlement patterns in the area around Beddington, Carshalton and Wallington: an outline of the archaeological evidence, in *The past – our future: essays presented to Keith Pryer* (ed C Orton), Beddington Carshalton Wallington Archaeol Soc Occas Paper, **4**, 8–12

—, 1982 *The development of settlement patterns in the Wandle valley from earliest times to the Saxon period*, unpublished M Phil thesis, Univ Surrey

—, 1984 A baked clay weight from Wallington, *SyAC*, **75**, 305–6

—, & Adkins, R, 1982 Excavations at Beddington, 1981, *London Archaeol*, **4.8**, 199–203

—, & —, 1983a An unusual lamp from Beddington, *Britannia*, **14**, 274–8

—, & —, 1983b Excavations at Beddington, 1982, *London Archaeol*, **4.12**, 326–9

—, & —, 1984 Two Roman coffins from near St Mary's church, Beddington, *SyAC*, **75**, 281–4

—, & Needham, S P, 1985 New research on a Late Bronze Age enclosure at Queen Mary's Hospital, Carshalton, *SyAC*, **76**, 11–50

Adkins, R, & Jackson, R, 1978 *Neolithic stone and flint axes from the River Thames*, Brit Mus Occas Paper, **1**

Akerman, J W, 1855 Notes of antiquarian researches in the summer and autumn of 1854, *Archaeologia*, **36**, 175–86

Alcock, L, 1973 *Arthur's Britain*

Alcock, N W, & Barley, M W, 1972 Medieval roofs with base crucks and short principals, *Antiq J*, **52**, 132–68

Aldsworth, F, 1979 Droxford Anglo-Saxon cemetery, Soberton, Hampshire, *Proc Hants Field Club Archaeol Soc*, **35**, 93–182

—, & Hill, D, 1971 The Burghal Hidage – Eashing, *SyAC*, **68**, 198–201

—, Kelly, E, & Needham, S P, 1981 *A Late Bronze Age founder's hoard from Bramber, West Sussex: a preliminary report*, West Sussex County Counc, privately circulated

Allen, D F, 1961 The origins of coinage in Britain, a reappraisal, in Frere 1961, 97–308

—, 1963 The Haslemere hoard, *Brit Numis J*, **31**, 1–7

Allen, M, 1984 *Land mollusca from Wen Barrow; a Bronze Age bell barrow, Surrey*, HBMC Ancient Monuments Lab Rep

Allison, J, Godwin, H, & Warren, S H, 1952 Late glacial deposits in the Lea valley, north London, *Phil Trans Roy Soc London*, ser B, **236**, 169–240

Anderson, J C, 1877 *Saxon Croydon*

Anon, 1878 Recent discovery of the remains of a Roman villa at Abinger, Surrey, *The Builder*, **36**, 19–20

—, 1899–1901 A report of the meeting held on Thursday May 2nd, 1901, *Proc Soc Antiq London*, 2 ser, **18**, 351–3

—, 1929 Report of Council for the year ending December 31st, 1927, *SyAC*, **38.1**, xvii–xxi

—, 1935 A palaeolith from Dorking, *Antiq J*, **15**, 343

—, 1936 Palaeolith from Plateau Gravel, *Antiq J*, **16**, 199

—, 1967 Weston Wood, Albury: Mesolithic settlement, in Report of the Council for the year ended 31st December 1966, *SyAC*, **64** [no pagination]

—, 1968 Weston Wood, Albury: Bronze Age and Mesolithic settlement, in Report of the Council for the year ended 31st December 1967, *SyAC*, **65** [no pagination]

—, 1978 Alice Holt, *Current Archaeol*, **64/6.5**, 148–51

—, 1983 Gorhambury, *Current Archaeol*, **87/8.4**, 115–21

Apedaile, E G, 1928 [in Notes and queries], *Sussex Archaeol Collect*, **69**, 233

Applebaum, S, 1983 A note on Ambrosius Aurelianus, *Britannia*, **14**, 245–6

Arnold, C J, 1980 Wealth and social structure: a matter of life and death, in Rahtz *et al* 1980, 89–141

—, & Wardle, P, 1981 Early medieval settlement patterns in England, *Medieval Archaeol*, **25**, 145–9

Arthur, P, 1978 The lead glazed wares of Roman Britain, in *Early fine wares in Roman Britain* (eds P Arthur & G Marsh), Brit Archaeol Rep, **57**, 293–355

Ashbee, P, Smith, I F, & Evans, J G, 1979 Excavations of three long barrows near Avebury, Wiltshire, *Proc Prehist Soc*, **45**, 207–300

Ashworth, G J, A note on the decline of the Wealden iron industry, *SyAC*, **67**, 61–5

Atkins, C W, 1983 *The Romano-Celtic temples of Surrey: Farley Heath and Titsey*, privately circulated

Atkins, J E, & Sallnow, J, 1975 Geology, geomorphology and climate of Surrey, in Salmon 1975, 1–32

Avery, B W, 1980 *Soil classification in the Soil Survey of England and Wales*, (Higher Categories) Soil Survey Technical Monograph, **14**

Baigent, J, 1976 Appendix 1: pollen analysis, in P Drewett, The excavation of four round barrows of the second millennium BC at West Heath, Harting, 1973–75, *Sussex Archaeol Collect*, **114**, 126–50

Bailey, D, 1976 Attis on a cult-car, *Antiq J*, **56**, 72–3

Bailey, K A, & Galbraith, I G, 1973 Field systems in Surrey: an introductory survey, *SyAC*, **69**, 73–88

Baker, A H R, & Butlin, R A, 1973 *Studies of field systems in the British Isles*

Baker, C A, Moxey, P A, & Oxford, P M, 1978 Woodland continuity and change in Epping Forest, *Field Stud*, **4**, 645–69

Baldwin-Brown, G, 1903–21 *The arts in early England*, 5 vols

Barfoot, J, & Price-Williams, D, 1976 The Saxon barrow at Gally Hills, Banstead Downs, Surrey, *SyAS Res Vol*, **3**, 59–76

Barker, P, 1982 *Techniques of archaeological excavation*

Barrett, A A, 1979 The career of Tiberius Claudius Cogidubnus, *Britannia*, **10**, 227–42

Barrett, J C, 1973 Four Bronze Age cremation cemeteries from Middlesex, *Trans London Middlesex Archaeol Soc*, **24**, 111–34

—, 1976 The Bronze Age, in Collins *et al* 1976, 33–41

—, 1980a The evolution of Later Bronze Age settlement, in Barrett & Bradley 1980a, 77–100

—, 1980b The pottery of the Later Bronze Age in lowland England, *Proc Prehist Soc*, **46**, 297–320

—, 1984 The prehistoric pottery, in Crouch & Shanks 1984, 31–3

—, & Bradley, R (eds), 1980a *Settlement and society in the British Later Bronze Age*, Brit Archaeol Rep, **83**

—, & —, 1980b The Later Bronze Age in the Thames valley, in Barrett & Bradley 1980a, 247–65

—, —, Bowden, M, & Mead, B, 1983 South Lodge after Pitt-Rivers, *Antiquity*, **57**, 193–204

—, —, Green, M, & Lewis, B, 1981 The earlier prehistoric settlement of Cranbourne Chase: the first results of current fieldwork, *Antiq J*, **61**, 203–37

Bateson, J D, 1981 *Enamel-working in Iron Age, Roman and sub-Roman Britain. The products and techniques*, Brit Archaeol Rep, **93**

Beard, D, 1986 The infirmary of Bermondsey Priory, *London Archaeol*, **5.7**, 186–91

Beckensall, S G, 1967 The excavation of Money Mound, *Sussex Archaeol Collect*, **105**, 13–30

Bedwin, O, 1978 Iron Age Sussex: the Downs and coastal plain, in Drewett 1978b, 41–51

—, 1981 Excavations at the Neolithic enclosure on Bury Hill, Houghton, West Sussex, 1979, *Proc Prehist Soc*, **47**, 69–86

Bell, A Montgomerie, 1888 *The later age of stone, especially in connection with remains found near Limpsfield*

Bell, M, 1977 *Excavations at Bishopstone, Sussex*, Sussex Archaeol Collect, **115**

—, 1981a *Valley sediments as evidence of prehistoric land use: a study based on dry valleys in south-east England*, unpublished PhD thesis, Univ London (Inst Archaeol)

—, 1981b Valley sediments and environmental change, in Jones & Dimbleby 1981, 75–91

—, 1983 Valley sediments as evidence of prehistoric land use on the South Downs, *Proc Prehist Soc*, **49**, 119–50

—, & Limbrey, S, 1982 *Archaeological aspects of woodland ecology*, Brit Archaeol Rep Internat Ser, **146**

Beresford, G, 1981 Goltho Manor, Lincolnshire: the buildings and their surrounding defences, *c* 850–1150, *Proc Battle Conference Anglo-Norman Stud*, **4**, 13–36

Beresford, M W, 1967 *New towns of the Middle Ages*

—, & Hurst, J G, 1971 *Deserted medieval villages*

—, & St Joseph, J K, 1979 *Medieval England: an aerial survey*, 2 edn

Bersu, G, 1940 Excavations at Little Woodbury, part 1, *Proc Prehist Soc*, **6**, 30–111

Bidder, H F, 1934 Some new material for the determination of the course of Stane Street, *SyAC*, **42**, 11–25

—, & Morris, J, 1959 The Anglo-Saxon cemetery at Mitcham, *SyAC*, **56**, 51–131

—, & Westlake, H F, 1929 Excavations at Merton Priory, *SyAC*, **38.1**, 49–66

Biddle, M, 1976 Towns, in Wilson 1976, 99–150

—, & Hill, D, 1971 Late Saxon planned towns, *Antiq J*, **51**, 70–85

Bird, D G, 1986 Wanborough, *SyAS Bull*, **209**

—, Crocker, A G, Douglas, R I, Haber, L F, Sturley, D M, & Sykes R, 1975 The archaeology and history of Surrey, in Salmon 1975, 133–76

—, —, Crocker, G, & McCracken, J S, 1980 Archaeology in Surrey 1976–78, *SyAC*, **72**, 231–53

—, —, —, & —, 1982 Archaeology in Surrey 1979–80, *SyAC*, **73**, 147–54

—, Crocker, G, & McCracken, J S, 1983 Archaeology in Surrey 1981, *SyAC*, **74**, 185–94

Bird, J, 1983 Roman pottery from Burpham, *SyAC*, **74**, 221–3

—, Chapman, H, & Clark, J (eds), 1978a *Collectanea Londiniensia: studies in London archaeology and history presented to Ralph Merrifield*, London Middlesex Archaeol Soc Special Paper, **2**

—, & Graham, A, 1978 Gazetteer of Roman sites in Southwark, in Bird *et al* 1978b, 517–26

—, —, Sheldon, H, & Townend, P (eds), 1978b *Southwark excavations 1972–74*, London Middlesex Archaeol Soc & SyAS Joint Pub, **1**

—, & Hanworth, R, 1984 The small objects, in Cooper *et al* 1984, microfiche 26–30

Bishop, M W, 1971 The non-Belgic Iron Age in Surrey, *SyAC*, **68**, 1–30

Blair, W J, 1976a Ashtead and Leatherhead: a possible Roman field-system, *SyAS Bull*, **124**

—, 1976b *Discovering early Leatherhead*

—, 1978 The destroyed medieval church at Headley, *Proc Leatherhead District Local Hist Soc*, **4.2**, 39–44

—, 1981a A small 14th century cragloft house at Leatherhead, *Antiq J*, **61**, 328–34

—, 1981b William Ansculf and the Abinger motte, *Archaeol J*, **138** (1982), 146–8

—, 1982 *Landholding, church and settlement in Surrey before 1300*, unpublished D Phil thesis, Univ Oxford [SyAS Res Vol, forthcoming]

Blake, B P, 1966 Walton-on-Thames: dug-out canoe from Thames, *SyAS Bull*, **24**

Blytt, A, 1876 *Essay on the immigration of the Norwegian flora during alternating rainy and dry periods* (Christiana)

Bogaers, J E, 1979 King Cogidubnus in Chichester: another reading of RIB 91, *Britannia*, **10**, 243–54

Bonsall, C J, 1977a Gazetteer of Upper Palaeolithic sites in England and Wales, in Wymer 1977, 417–32

—, 1977b Woking: Brockhill, near Parley Bridge, Horsell, *SyAS Bull*, **139**

Bourne, G, 1919 *William Smith potter and farmer: 1790–1858*

Bowen, H C, 1961 *Ancient fields*

—, & Fowler, P J (eds), 1978 *Early land allotment in the British Isles. A survey of recent work*, Brit Archaeol Rep, **48**

Bowler, D, & Robinson, M, 1980 Three round barrows at King's Weir, Wytham, Oxon, *Oxoniensia*, **45**, 1–8

Boyden, J R, 1958 Excavations at Hammer Wood, Iping, 1957, *Sussex Archaeol Collect*, **96**, 149–63

Bradley, R, 1971 Economic change in the growth of early hill-forts, in Hill & Jesson 1971, 71–83

—, 1972 *A Mesolithic assemblage from East Sussex*, Sussex Archaeol Soc Occas Paper, **2**

—, 1978a *The prehistoric settlement of Britain*

—, 1978b Colonization and land-use in the Late Neolithic and Early Bronze Age, in Limbrey & Evans 1978, 95–102

—, 1982 Position and possession: assemblage valuation in the British Neolithic, *Oxford J Archaeol*, **1**, 27–38

—, & Ellison, A, 1975 *Rams Hill: a Bronze Age defended enclosure and its landscape*, Brit Archaeol Rep, **19**

—, & Keith-Lucas, M, 1975 Excavation and pollen analyses on a bell barrow at Ascot, Berkshire, *J Archaeol Sci*, **2**, 95–108

—, Lobb, S, Richards, J, & Robinson, M, 1980 Two Late Bronze Age settlements on the Kennet gravels: excavations at Aldermaston Wharf and Knight's Farm, Burghfield, Berkshire, *Proc Prehist Soc*, **46**, 217–96

Brailsford, J W, 1948 Excavations at Little Woodbury, part 2, *Proc Prehist Soc*, **14**, 1–23

—, 1949 Excavations at Little Woodbury, parts 4 & 5, *Proc Prehist Soc*, **15**, 156–68

Brakspear, H, 1905 *Waverley Abbey*, SyAS special vol

Brandon, P (ed), 1978a *The South Saxons*

—, 1978b The South Saxon Andredesweald, in Brandon 1978a, 138–59

Bridges, E M, 1978 Interaction of soil and mankind in Britain, *J Soil Sci*, **29**, 125–39

Briggs, C S, 1976 Notes of the distribution of some raw materials in later prehistoric Britain, in Burgess & Miket 1976, 267–82

—, 1982 [Review of Clough & Cummins 1979], *Archaeol Cambrensis*, **131**, 150

Britton, D, 1960 Bronze Age grave-groups and hoards in the British Museum, *Inventaria Archaeologica*, GB 48–54

—, 1963 Traditions of metal-working in the Later Neolithic and Early Bronze Age of Britain: part 1, *Proc Prehist Soc*, **29**, 258–325

Brock, E P L, 1874 [No title], *J Brit Archaeol Assoc*, **30**, 212

Bromehead, C N, 1919 Excursion to St George's Hill, Weybridge. Saturday March 29 1919, *Proc Geol Assoc*, **30**, 127–8

Brooks, A, unpublished *Pollen data from Elstead, Surrey, Broxbourne and Ponders End, Hertfordshire, and Wellingham, Sussex*, Department Plant Sci, Kings College, Univ London

Brooks, P D, 1985 *Farnham Castle: the forgotten years*

Brown, M A, 1982 Swords and sequence in the British Bronze Age, *Archaeologia*, **107**, 1–42

Brown, R A, Colvin, H M, & Taylor, A J, 1963 *History of the King's Works: the Middle Ages*, 2 vols

Bruce-Mitford, R L S, 1938 A hoard of Neolithic axes from Peaslake, Surrey, *Antiq J*, **18**, 279–84

—, 1972 *The Sutton Hoo ship burial: a handbook*, 2 edn

Bryant, I D, Gibbard, P L, Holyoak, D T, Switsur, V R, & Wintle, A G, 1983 Stratigraphy and palaeontology of Pleistocene cold-stage deposits at Alton Road Quarry, Farnham, Surrey, England, *Geol Mag*, **120**

Buckley, D G (ed), 1980 *Archaeology in Essex to AD 1500*, Counc Brit Archaeol Res Rep, **34**

Bunting, B T, & Green, R D, 1964 *The soils and geomorphol-ogy of an area around Dorking. Guide to London excursions* (ed K M Clayton), 20th Internat Geog Congress, London

Burchell, J P T, 1925 The shell mound industry of Denmark as represented at Lower Halstow, Kent, *Proc Prehist Soc East Anglia*, **5.1**, 73–8

—, 1926 Further report on the epipalaeolithic factory site at Lower Halstow, Kent, *Proc Prehist Soc East Anglia*, **5.2** (1927), 217–23

—, 1927 A final account of the investigations carried out at Lower Halstow, Kent, *Proc Prehist Soc East Anglia*, **5.3** (1928), 289–96

—, & Frere, S, 1947 The occupation of Sandown Park, Esher, during the Stone Age, the Early Iron Age and the Anglo-Saxon period, *Antiq J*, **27**, 24–46

Burgess, C B, 1968 The Later Bronze Age in the British Isles and north-western France, *Archaeol J*, **125** (1969), 1–45

—, 1976 Burials with metalwork of the Later Bronze Age in Wales and beyond, in *Welsh antiquity* (eds G C Boon & J M Lewis), 81–104

—, 1979 A find from Boyton, Suffolk, and the end of the Bronze Age in Britain and Ireland, in Burgess & Coombs 1979, 269–82

—, & Coombs, D (eds), 1979 *Bronze Age hoards: some finds old and new*, Brit Archaeol Rep, **67**

—, —, & Davies, D G, 1972 The Broadward complex and barbed spearheads, in *Prehistoric man in Wales and the West* (eds F Lynch & C B Burgess), 211–83

—, & Gerloff, S, 1982 *The dirks and rapiers of Great Britain and Ireland*, Prähistorische Bronzefunde, **4.7** (Munich)

—, & Miket, R (eds), 1976 *Settlement and economy in the third and second millennia BC*, Brit Archaeol Rep, **33**

—, & Shennan, S, 1976 The Beaker phenomenon: some suggestions, in Burgess & Miket 1976, 309–31

Burleigh, R, & Kerney, M P, 1982 Some chronological implications of a fossil molluscan assemblage from a Neolithic site at Brook, Kent, *J Archaeol Sci*, **9**, 29–38

Burnham, C P (ed), 1983 *Soils of the heathlands and chalklands*, Proc South-east Soils Discuss Group, Seesoil, **1**

Burrin, P J, 1981 Loess in the Weald, *Proc Geol Assoc*, **92**, 87–92

—, 1983 *The character and evolution of flood plains with specific reference to the Ouse and Cuckmere, Sussex*, unpublished PhD thesis, Univ London (London School Econ)

—, & Scaife, R G, 1984 Aspects of Holocene valley sedimentation and flood plain development in southern England, *Proc Geol Assoc*, **95.1**, 81–96

Bury, H, 1913 The gravel beds of Farnham in relation to Palaeolithic man, *Proc Geol Assoc*, **24**, 178–201

—, 1916 The palaeoliths of Farnham, *Proc Geol Assoc*, **27**, 151–92

—, 1917 Some 'flat-faced' palaeoliths from Farnham, *Proc Prehist Soc East Anglia*, **2**, 365–74

—, 1935 The Farnham Terraces and their sequence, *Proc Prehist Soc*, **1**, 60–9

Butler, J J, 1963 *Bronze Age connections across the North Sea*, Palaeohistoria, **9**

Cal Pat Rolls Calendar of the Patent Rolls preserved in the Public Record Office, 54 vols, HMSO (1891–1916)

Campbell, E M J, 1962 Middlesex, in Darby & Campbell 1962, 97–137

Canham, M, 1970 Medieval pottery kiln at Kingston, *SyAC*, **67**, 102–3

Canham, R, 1976 The Iron Age, in Collins *et al* 1976, 42–9

—, 1978a *2000 years of Brentford*

—, 1978b Excavations at London (Heathrow) Airport 1969, *Trans London Middlesex Archaeol Soc*, **29**, 1–44

—, 1979 Excavations at Shepperton Green, 1967 & 1973, *Trans London Middlesex Archaeol Soc*, **30**, 97–134

Canvin, G, 1978 An Acheulian hand-axe from the Thames at Mortlake, *Trans London Middlesex Archaeol Soc*, **29**, 144–5

Care, V, 1979 The production and distribution of Mesolithic axes in southern England, *Proc Prehist Soc*, **45**, 93–102

Carey, A E, 1908 *Prehistoric man on the highlands of east Surrey*

Carlin, M, 1985 The reconstruction of Winchester House, *London Topog Rec*, **25**, 33–58

Carpenter, C P, & Woodcock, M P, 1981 A detailed investigation of a pingo remnant in western Surrey, *Quaternary Stud*, **1**, 1–26

Carpenter, L W, 1955 A Palaeolithic hand-axe from Banstead Heath, Walton on the Hill, *SyAC*, **54**, 136–7

—, 1956 The palaeoliths of Walton and Banstead Heaths, *Proc Leatherhead District Local Hist Soc*, **1.10**, 6–10; additional figs, *ibid*, **2.1** (1957), facing 2

—, 1960 A Palaeolithic floor at Lower Kingswood, *Proc Leatherhead District Local Hist Soc*, **2.4**, 99–101

—, 1961 An Early Bronze Age flat axe from Walton Heath, *SyAC*, **58**, 111–12

—, 1963 More palaeoliths from Walton Heath, *Proc Leatherhead District Local Hist Soc*, **2.7**, 202

Carroll, K K, 1979 The date of Boudicca's revolt, *Britannia*, **10**, 197–202

Carter, P L, Higgs, E S, & Phillipson, D, 1962 Faunal report, in Hastings 1965, 40–2

Case, H, 1952 The excavation of two round barrows at Poole, Dorset, *Proc Prehist Soc*, **18**, 148–59

—, 1969 Neolithic explanations, *Antiquity*, **43**, 176–86

—, & Whittle, A L (eds), 1982 *Settlement patterns in the Oxford region: excavations at the Abingdon causewayed enclosure and other sites*, Counc Brit Archaeol Res Rep, **44**

Catt, J A, 1977 Loess and coversands, in *British Quaternary studies: recent advances* (ed F W Shotton), 221–9

—, 1978 The contribution of loess to soils in lowland Britain, in Limbrey & Evans 1978, 12–20

—, 1979 Soils and Quaternary geology in Britain, *J Archaeol Sci*, **30**, 607–42

Celoria, F, & Macdonald, J, 1969 The Neolithic age; the Beaker period; the Bronze Age, in *The Victoria history of the county of Middlesex, vol 1* (eds J S Cockburn, H P F King & K G T McDonnell), 29–50

Champion, T C, 1975 Britain in the European Iron Age, *Archaeol Atlantica*, **1**, 127–45

—, 1976 *The earlier Iron Age in the region of the lower Thames: insular and external factors*, unpublished D Phil thesis, Univ Oxford

—, 1977 Chalton, *Current Archaeol*, **59/5.12**, 364–9

—, 1979 The Iron Age (*c* 600 BC–AD 200) A. Southern Britain and Ireland, in Megaw & Simpson 1979, 344–432

—, 1980 Settlement and environment in Later Bronze Age Kent, in Barrett & Bradley 1980a, 223–46

Chaplin, R E, 1968 The animal bones, in Hanworth 1968, 69

Clark, A J, 1950 The fourth-century Romano-British pottery kilns at Overwey, Tilford, *SyAC*, **51**, 29–56

—, 1950–1 Ancient weapons from Ripley, *SyAC*, **52** (1952), 80–2

—, 1960 A cross-valley dyke on the Surrey/Kent border, *SyAC*, **57**, 72–4

—, 1977 Geophysical and chemical assessment of air photographic sites, in J N Hampton & R Palmer, Implications of aerial photography for archaeology, *Archaeol J*, **134** (1978), 187–91

—, & Nichols, J F, 1960 Romano-British farms south of the Hog's Back, *SyAC*, **57**, 42–71

Clark, G T, 1872 Some account of Guildford Castle, *Archaeol J*, **29**, 1–25

Clark, J G D, 1932 *The Mesolithic age in Britain*

—, 1933 The classification of a microlithic culture: the Tardenoisian of Horsham, *Archaeol J*, **90** (1934), 52–77

—, 1934a A Late Mesolithic settlement site at Selmeston, Sussex, *Antiq J*, **14**, 134–58

—, 1934b Derivative forms of the *petit tranchet* in Britain, *Archaeol J*, **91** (1935), 32–58

—, 1936 *The Mesolithic settlement of northern Europe*

—, 1954 *Excavations at Star Carr*

—, 1966 The invasion hypothesis in British archaeology, *Antiquity*, **40**, 172–89

—, & Rankine, W F, 1939 Excavations at Farnham, Surrey (1937–38): the Horsham culture and the question of Mesolithic dwellings, *Proc Prehist Soc*, **5**, 61–118

Clarke, A F, 1982 The Neolithic of Kent: a review, in Leach 1982, 25–30

Clarke, D L, 1970 *Beaker pottery of Great Britain and Ireland*

—, 1976 Mesolithic Europe: the economic basis, in *Problems in economic and social archaeology* (eds G de G Sieveking, I H Longworth & K E Wilson), 449–81

Clarke, H, 1984 *Medieval archaeology*

Clarke, M R, & Dixon, A J, 1981 The Pleistocene braided river deposits in the Blackwater valley area of Berkshire and Hampshire, England, *Proc Geol Assoc*, **92.3**, 139–57

—, & Fisher, P F, 1983 The Caesar's Camp gravel – an early Pleistocene fluvial periglacial deposit in southern England, *Proc Geol Assoc*, **94**, 345–55

Cleere, H F, 1972 The classification of early iron-smelting furnaces, *Antiq J*, **52**, 8–23

—, 1974 The Roman iron industry of the Weald and its connections with the *Classis Britannica*, *Archaeol J*, **131**, (1975), 171–99

—, 1976 Some operating parameters for Roman iron-works, *Bull Inst Archaeol*, **13**, 233–46

—, 1977 Comments on the iron-working activities, in Hanworth & Tomalin 1977, 19–22

Clinch, G, 1899 Prehistoric man in the neighbourhood of the Kent and Surrey border, *J Anthropol Inst*, **29**, new ser 2 (1902), 124–42

—, 1902a Early man, in Malden 1902, 227–53

—, 1902b Prehistoric chambers discovered at Waddon, near Croydon, *SyAC*, **17**, 181–3

Cloake, J, 1977 The Charterhouse of Sheen, *SyAC*, **71**, 145–98

Clough, T H McK, & Cummins, W A (eds), 1979 *Stone axe studies*, Counc Brit Archaeol Res Rep, **23**

Coade, J G, & Streeten, A D F, 1982 Excavations at Castle Acre Castle, Norfolk, 1972–77, *Archaeol J*, **139** (1983), 138–301

Coates, R, 1980 Methodological reflexions on Leatherhead, *J English Place-Name Soc*, **12**, 70–4

—, 1981 [Review of Rivet & Smith 1979], *J English Place-Name Soc*, **13**, 59–71

Cole, G H, 1982 Excavations at Park Row, Farnham, *SyAC*, **73**, 101–14

Coles, J M, 1962 European Bronze Age shields, *Proc Prehist Soc*, **28**, 156–90

—, 1973 *Archaeology by experiment*

—, & Simpson, D D A (eds), 1968 *Studies in ancient Europe. Essays presented to Stuart Piggott*

Collingwood, R, 1939 *An autobiography*

—, & Wright, R P, 1965 *The Roman inscriptions of Britain. I: inscriptions on stone*

Collins, A E P, 1936 A Palaeolithic ovate from Abinger Hammer, *SyAC*, **44**, 137

Collins, D, 1976 Palaeolithic and Mesolithic, in Collins *et al* 1976, 1–18

—, Macdonald, J, Barrett, J, Canham, R, Merrifield, R, & Hurst, J, 1976 *The archaeology of the London area: current knowledge and problems*, London Middlesex Archaeol Soc Special Paper, **1**

Cook, A, 1969 Oatlands Palace excavations, *SyAC*, **66**, 1–9

Cook, J, Stringer, C B, Currant, A P, Schwartz, H P, & Wintle, A G, 1982 A review of the chronology of the European Middle Pleistocene hominid record, *Yearb Phys Anthropol*, **25**, 19–65

Cooper, T S, ed J L Gower & M Gower, 1984 The Roman villa at Whitebeech, Chiddingfold: excavations in 1888 and subsequently, *SyAC*, **75**, 57–83

Copley, G J, 1950 Stane Street in the Dark Ages, *Sussex Archaeol Collect*, **89**, 98–104

Copsey, H W, 1963–4 A list of barrows around the Berkshire–Surrey–Hampshire boundary, *Berkshire Archaeol J*, **61**, 20–7

Corcoran, J X W P, 1961 Excavations of two mounds on Thursley Common, *SyAC*, **58**, 87–91

—, 1963 Excavation of the bell barrow in Deerleap Wood, Wotton, *SyAC*, **60**, 1–18

Corner, G R, 1858 On the history of Horsley Down, *SyAC*, **1**, 156–79

Cornwall, I W, 1952 Appendix 2, in Case 1952, 158

—, 1953 Soil science and archaeology with illustrations from some British Bronze Age monuments, *Proc Prehist Soc*, **19**, 129–47

—, 1958 *Soils for the archaeologist*

Cotton, A R, 1933 Saxon discoveries at Fetcham, *Antiq J*, **13**, 48–51

Cotton, J, 1979 Three Iron Age brooches from the Thames foreshore at Mortlake, Syon and Wandsworth, *Trans London Middlesex Archaeol Soc*, **30**, 180–4

—, 1981a Bronze Age pottery from Wood Lane, Osterley, *Trans London Middlesex Archaeol Soc*, **32**, 18–23

—, 1981b Sunbury Weir: two bronzes from the Thames, *SyAS Bull*, **173**, 2–3

—, 1982 An Iron Age brooch from Seymour's Nursery, Ewell, *SyAC*, **73**, 169–71

—, 1984 Three Later Neolithic discoidal knives from north-east Surrey: with a note on the type from the county, *SyAC*, **75**, 225–33

—, Field, D J, & Nicolaysen, P C, 1984 Montgomerie Bell's Limpsfield collection: Palaeolithic flint artefacts in the Pitt-Rivers Museum Oxford, *SyAS Bull*, **194**

—, Mills, J, & Clegg, G, 1986 *Archaeology in west Middlesex: the London Borough of Hillingdon from the earliest hunters to the late medieval period*

Courty, M A, & Federoff, N, 1982 Micromorphology of a Holocene dwelling, in *Proc 2 Nordic Conf Applic Scientific Methods Archaeol, Aug 1981*, PACT, **7.2**, 257–77 (Counc Europe, Strasbourg)

Cowen, J D, 1951 The earliest bronze swords in Britain and their origins on the continent of Europe, *Proc Prehist Soc*, **17**, 195–213

—, 1967 The Hallstatt sword of bronze on the continent and in Britain, *Proc Prehist Soc*, **33**, 377–454

Craddock, P T, Cowell, M R, Leese, M N, & Hughes, M J, 1983 The trace element composition of polished flint axes as an indicator of source, *Archaeometry*, **25.2**, 135–63

Cranstone, B A L, 1969 Animal husbandry: the evidence from ethnography, in Ucko & Dimbleby 1969, 247–64

Crawford, O G S, 1933 Some recent air discoveries, *Antiquity*, **7**, 290–6

—, 1953 *Archaeology in the field*

Crocker, A, 1977 Guildford Park manor, *SyAC*, **71**, 278–80

—, 1980 Guildford Park manor, *SyAC*, **72**, 232–3

Crouch, K, 1978 New thoughts on Roman Staines, *London Archaeol*, **3.7**, 180–6

—, & Shanks, S A, 1983 One of the early Roman pottery industries at Staines, Surrey, *Britannia*, **14**, 253–5

—, & —, 1984 *Excavations in Staines 1975–76. The Friends' Burial Ground site*, London Middlesex Archaeol Soc & SyAS Joint Pub, **2**

Cruse, R J, & Harrison, B A, 1983 Excavations at Hill Road, Wouldham, *Archaeol Cantiana*, **99**, 81–108

Cummins, W A, 1979 Neolithic stone axes: distribution and trade in England and Wales, in Clough & Cummins 1979, 5–12

Cunliffe, B, 1971 Some aspects of hillforts and their cultural environments, in Hill & Jesson 1971, 53–69

—, 1972 Saxon and medieval settlement patterns in the region of Chalton, Hants, *Medieval Archaeol*, **16** (1973), 1–12

—, 1973 *The Regni*

—, 1974 *Iron Age communities in Britain*

—, 1978 Saxon Sussex: some problems and directions, in Brandon 1978a, 221–6

—, 1981a Money and society in pre-Roman Britain, in Cunliffe 1981b, 29–39

— (ed), 1981b *Coinage and society in Britain and Gaul*, Counc Brit Archaeol Res Rep, **38**

—, 1982 Social and economic development in Kent in the pre-Roman Iron Age, in Leach 1982, 40–50

—, 1984 *Danebury, an Iron Age hillfort in Hampshire*, Counc Brit Archaeol Res Rep, **52**

—, & Rowley, T (eds), 1978 *Lowland Iron Age communities in Europe*, Brit Archaeol Rep Supp Ser, **48**

Curtis, L F, Courtney, F M, & Trudgill, S T, 1976 The influence of Mesolithic and Neolithic man on soil development in the uplands, in *Soils in the British Isles* (eds L F Curtis, F M Courtney & S T Trudgill), 54–69

Curwen, E C, 1934 Excavations in Whitehawk Neolithic camp, Brighton, 1932–3, *Antiq J*, **14**, 99–133

Dacre, M, & Ellison, A, 1981 A Bronze Age urn cemetery at Kimpton, Hampshire, *Proc Prehist Soc*, **47**, 147–203

Dance, E M, 1961 Ptolemaic bronze coins found in Surrey, *SyAC*, **61**, 113

Daniell, G, 1856 Remarks on the burnt timber found in the bogs in the neighbourhood of Chobham, Surrey, regarded as the consequence of extensive conflagrations by the Roman troops under Caesar, *Proc Soc Antiq London*, **3**, 236–42

Darby, H C, & Campbell, E M J, 1962 *The Domesday geography of south-east England*

Darlington, I, & Farrar, J H, 1950 *Survey of London vol 22: Bankside*

Darvill, T, & McWhirr, A, 1982 Roman brick production and the environment, in *The Romano-British countryside, studies in rural settlement and economy* (ed D Miles), Brit Archaeol Rep, **103**, 137–50

Darwin, C, 1888 *The formation of vegetable mould through the action of worms, with observations on their habits*

Davey, P, & Hodges, R (eds), 1983 *Ceramics and trade*

Davies, W, & Vierck, H, 1974 The contexts of Tribal Hidage: social aggregates and settlement patterns, *Frühmittelalterliche Studien*, **8**, 223–93

Davis, K R, 1982 *Britons and Saxons: the Chiltern region 400–700*

Davis, R H C, 1982 Alfred and Guthrum's frontier, *English Hist Rev*, **97**, 803–10

Davison, B K, 1969 Early earthwork castles: a new model, *Château Gaillard Stud*, **3**, 37–47

—, 1977 Excavation at Sulgrave, Northants, 1960–76: an interim report, *Archaeol J*, **134** (1978), 105–14

Dawson, G J, 1976 *The Black Prince's Palace of Kennington*, Brit Archaeol Rep, **26**

Dean, M, 1980 Excavations at Arcadia Buildings, Southwark, *London Archaeol*, **3.14**, 367–73

—, 1981 Evidence for more Roman burials in Southwark, *London Archaeol*, **4.2**, 52–3

Densem, R, 1984 Roman and medieval Southwark, *Rescue News*, **33**, 8

—, & Seeley, D, 1982 Excavations at Rectory Grove, Clapham, 1980–1, *London Archaeol*, **4.7**, 177–84

Desittere, M, 1968 *De Urnenveldenkultuur in het Gebied tussen Neder Rijn en Nord Zee* (Bruges/Brugge)

Devoy, R J N, 1978–9 Flandrian sea level changes and vegetational history of the lower Thames estuary, *Phil Trans Roy Soc London*, ser B, **285**, 355–407

Dickinson, T M, 1979 On the origin and chronology of the early Anglo-Saxon disc brooch, in *Anglo-Saxon studies in archaeology and history* (ed S C Hawkes, D Brown & J Campbell), Brit Archaeol Rep, **72**, 34–80

—, 1980 The present state of Anglo-Saxon cemetery studies, in Rahtz *et al* 1980, 11–34

Dimbleby, G W, 1961 Soil pollen analysis, *J Soil Sci*, **12.1**, 1–11

—, 1962 *The development of British heathlands and their soils*, Oxford Forestry Mem, **23**

—, 1965 Pollen analysis, in Keef *et al* 1965, 85–8

—, 1968 Appendix C: pollen analysis, in J H Money, Excavations in the Iron Age hillfort at High Rocks, near Tunbridge Wells, 1957–1961, *Sussex Archaeol Collect*, **106**, 158–205

—, 1978 *Plants and archaeology: the archaeology of the soil*

—, & Bradley, R J, 1975 Evidence of pedogenesis from a Neolithic site at Rackham, Sussex, *J Archaeol Sci*, **2**, 179–86

—, & Evans, J G, 1972 Appendix I, in Wainwright 1972, 86–90

Dines, H G, & Edmunds, F H, 1929 *Geology of the country around Aldershot and Guildford*, Mem Geol Survey, England and Wales, new ser, sheet 285

—, & —, 1954 *British regional geology: the Wealden district*

Dixon, A J, Fisher, P F, & Goddard, P L, 1983 The Plateau Gravels of north Surrey, south Berkshire and north Hampshire, England: discussion, *Proc Geol Assoc*, **94**, 279–86

Dodgson, J M, 1966 The significance of the distribution of the English place-name in *-ingas, -inga* in south-east England, *Medieval Archaeol*, **10**, 1–29

—, 1973 Place names from *ham*, distinguished from *hamm* names, in relation to the settlement of Kent, Surrey and Sussex, *Anglo-Saxon England*, **2**, 1–50

Done, G, 1973 The animal bones, in Pemberton 1973a, 21–3

—, 1977 The animal bones, in Smith, C, 1977, 37–41

—, 1980 The animal bone, in Longley 1980, 74–9

Douglas, J, 1793 *Nenia Britannica: or a sepulchral history of Great Britain, from the earliest period to its general conversion to Christianity*

Drew, C, & Piggott, S, 1936 The excavation of barrow 163a on Thickthorn Down, Dorset, *Proc Prehist Soc*, **2**, 77–96

Drewett, P L, 1970 The excavation of a turf-walled structure and other fieldwork on Croham Hurst, Croydon, Surrey, 1968/69, *SyAC*, **67**, 1–19

—, 1974 Excavations in Old Town, Croydon, 1968–70, *SyAS Res Vol*, **1**, 1–45

—, 1975 The excavation of an oval burial mound of the third millennium BC at Alfriston, East Sussex, 1974, *Proc Prehist Soc*, **41**, 119–52

—, 1976 The excavation of four round barrows of the second millenium BC at West Heath, Harting, 1973–75, *Sussex Archaeol Collect*, **114**, 144–7

—, 1978a Neolithic Sussex, in Drewett 1978b, 23–9

— (ed), 1978b *Archaeology in Sussex to AD 1500*, Counc Brit Archaeol Res Rep, **29**

—, 1980 Blackpatch and the Later Bronze Age in Sussex, in Barrett & Bradley 1980a, 377–96

—, 1982 *The archaeology of Bullock Down, Eastbourne, East Sussex: the development of a landscape*, Sussex Archaeol Soc Monograph, **1**

Drinkwater, J F, 1983 *Roman Gaul. The three provinces, 58 BC–AD 260*

Drury, P J, 1974 Chelmsford Dominican Friary: excavation of the reredorter 1973, *Essex Archaeol Hist*, **6**, 40–81

—, 1978 Little Waltham and pre-Belgic Iron Age settlement in Essex, in Cunliffe & Rowley 1978, 43–76

Duchaufour, P, 1958 Dynamics of forest soils under the Atlantic climate, *Lectures in surveying and forest engineering*, Inst Sci Franco-Canadien

—, 1965 *Précis de Pèdologie* (Paris)

—, 1977 *Pedology, pedogenesis and classification*

Dumville, D N, 1977 Sub-Roman Britain: history and legend, *History*, **62**, 173–92

Dunning, G C, & Jessup, R F, 1936 Roman barrows, *Antiquity*, **10**, 37–53

Dyson, T, & Schofield, J, 1984 Saxon London, in Haslam 1984b, 185–313

Eames, E S, 1980 *Catalogue of medieval lead-glazed earthenware tiles in the Department of Medieval and Later Antiquities, British Museum*

East, K, Larkin, P, & Winsor, P, 1985 A Viking sword found at Chertsey, *SyAC*, **76**, 1–9

Edwards, J, 1801 *Companion from London to Brighthelmston*

Edwards, K J, & Hirons, K R, 1984 Cereal pollen grains in pre-elm decline deposits; implications for the earliest agriculture in Britain and Ireland, *J Archaeol Sci*, **11**, 71–80

Ehrenberg, M R, 1977 *Bronze Age spearheads from Berkshire, Buckinghamshire and Oxfordshire*, Brit Archaeol Rep, **34**

Eide, K S, 1982 *Some aspects of pedogenesis and vegetation history in relation to archaeological sites in the New Forest*, unpublished PhD thesis, Univ London (Inst Archaeol)

Ellaby, R L, 1977a A Mesolithic site at Wonham, *SyAC*, **71**, 7–12

—, 1977b Charlwood: Mesolithic sites, *SyAS Bull*, **136**

—, 1977c Earlswood; Salfords; Horley. Ancient trackway, *SyAS Bull*, **140**

—, 1978 Salfords: Acheulian hand-axe, *SyAS Bull*, **152**

—, 1983 Charlwood: Mesolithic site, *SyAS Bull*, **182**

—, 1984 A deserted medieval farmstead in Woodlands Field, Earlswood, *SyAC*, **75**, 195–206

—, 1985 Prehistoric and medieval occupation near Flanchford Mill, Reigate, *SyAC*, **76**, 51–60

Ellison, A, 1978 The Bronze Age of Sussex, in Drewett 1978b, 30–7

—, 1980 Deverel–Rimbury urn cemeteries: the evidence for social organisation, in Barrett & Bradley 1980a, 115–26

—, & Drewett, P, 1971 Pits and post-holes in the British Early Iron Age: some alternative explanations, *Proc Prehist Soc*, **37**, 183–94

Elmore, G, 1983a Holmbury Hill: earthwork enclosure (TQ 108 447) [printed as (SU 108 447)], *SyAS Bull*, **184**

—, 1983b Holmbury: Neolithic spearhead (TQ 109 439) [printed as (SU 109 439)], *SyAS Bull*, **184**

Elsdon, S, 1982 Later Bronze Age pottery from Farnham, a reappraisal, *SyAC*, **73**, 127–39

Elsley, F H, 1909 A find of sling bolts at Wonersh, *SyAC*, **22**, 199

Ettlinger, V, 1982 Dorking (TQ 164 495), *SyAS Bull*, **181**

—, Gower, J, & Green, L, 1984 Stane Street at North Holmwood (TQ 167 471), *SyAS Bull*, **195**

Evans, G E, 1975 *The days that we have seen*

Evans, J A, 1860a Proceedings of the Society of Antiquaries, January 19, 1860, *Proc Soc Antiq London*, 2 ser, **1**, 63–77

—, 1860b Proceedings at meetings of the Archaeological Institute, April 13, 1860, *Archaeol J*, **17**, 167–74

—, 1881 *The ancient bronze implements, weapons and ornaments of Great Britain and Ireland*

—, 1897 *The ancient stone implements of Great Britain*, 2 edn

Evans, J G, 1971 Habitat change on the calcareous soils of Britain: the impact of Neolithic man, in Simpson 1971b, 27–73

—, 1972 *Land snails in archaeology*

—, 1975 *The environment of early man in the British Isles*

—, & Dimbleby, G W, 1976 Appendix I: the pre-barrow environment, in T G Manby, Excavation of the Kilham long barrow, East Riding of Yorkshire, *Proc Prehist Soc*, **42**, 150–6

—, & Valentine, K W G, 1974 Ecological changes induced by prehistoric man at Pitstone, Buckinghamshire, *J Archaeol Sci*, **1**, 343–51

Evison, V I, 1955 Early Anglo-Saxon inlaid metalwork, *Antiq J*, **35**, 20–45

—, 1958 Further Anglo-Saxon inlay, *Antiq J*, **38**, 240–4

—, 1963 Sugar-loaf shield bosses, *Antiq J*, **43**, 38–96

—, 1965 *The 5th century invasions south of the Thames*

—, 1968 Quoit brooch style buckles, *Antiq J*, **48**, 231–46

Eyre, S R, 1968 *Vegetation and soils: a world picture*

Fagg, C C, 1923 The recession of the Chalk escarpment and the development of the Chalk valleys in the regional survey area, *Trans Croydon Natur Hist Sci Soc*, **9.3**, 1–20

Falkner, H, 1907 Discovery of ancient pottery near Farnham in 1906, *SyAC*, **20**, 228–32

Farley, M, 1973 *Guide to local antiquities*, Bourne Soc

Farrant, N, 1973 Two weapons from the Thames, *Trans London Middlesex Archaeol Soc*, **24**, 157–8

Fasham, P, & Hanworth, R, 1978 Ploughmarks, Roman roads and motorways, in Bowen & Fowler 1978, 175–7

—, & Ross, J M, 1978 A Bronze Age flint industry from a barrow site in Micheldever Wood, Hampshire, *Proc Prehist Soc*, **44**, 47–67

Faulkner, P A, 1958 Domestic planning from the 12th to 14th centuries, *Archaeol J*, **115** (1960), 150–84

Field, D, 1983a Ham: the Edwards Collection, *SyAC*, **74**, 169–84

—, 1983b Two flint daggers from Kingston, *SyAC*, **74**, 207–8

—, 1985 Felday enclosure, Holmbury St Mary (TQ 108 447), *SyAS Bull*, **199**

—, & Needham, S P, 1984 A bronze palstave from north-west Surrey, *SyAC*, **76**, 115–17

—, & —, 1986 Evidence for Bronze Age settlement on Coombe Warren, Kingston Hill, *SyAC*, **77**, 127–51

—, & Woolley, A R, 1983 A jadeite axe from Staines Moor, *SyAC*, **74**, 141–5

—, & —, 1984 Neolithic and Bronze Age ground stone implements from Surrey, *SyAC*, **75**, 85–109

Finny, W E St L, 1927 The Saxon church at Kingston, *SyAC*, **37.2**, 211–19

Fisher, P F, 1982 *A study of the Plateau Gravels of the western part of the London Basin*, unpublished PhD thesis, Kingston Polytechnic

—, Dixon, A J, & Gibbard, P L, 1983 The Plateau Gravels of north Surrey, south Berkshire and north Hampshire, England, in Correspondence to the Editor, *Proc Geol Assoc*, **94.3**, 279–86

—, & Macphail, R I, 1985 The study of archaeological soils and deposits by micromorphological techniques, in *Palaeoenvironmental investigations: research design, methods and interpretations* (eds N R J Fieller, D D Gilbertson & N G A Ralph), Proc Assoc Envir Archaeol, Brit Archaeol Rep, **258**, 93–125

Flannery, K V, 1969 Origins and ecological effects of early domestication in Iran and the Near East, in Ucko & Dimbleby 1969, 73–100

Flower, J W, 1874a Notices of an Anglo-Saxon cemetery at Farthing Down, Coulsdon, Surrey, *SyAC*, **6**, 109–17

—, 1874b Notices of an Anglo-Saxon cemetery at Beddington, Surrey, *SyAC*, **6**, 122–4

—, 1874c Notices of a hoard of bronze implements found at Beddington, Surrey, *SyAC*, **6**, 125–6

Fowler, D, 1976 Wotton: excavations at St John's church, *SyAS Bull*, **127**

Fowler, P J, 1976 Agriculture and rural settlement, in Wilson 1976, 23–48

—, & Evans, J G, 1967 Plough marks, lynchets and early fields, *Antiquity*, **41**, 289–301

Fox, G E, 1905 Notes on some probable traces of Roman fulling in Britain, *Archaeologia*, **59**, 207–32

Fox, N Piercy, 1970 Caesar's Camp, Keston, *Archaeol Cantiana*, **84**, 185–99

Frere, S S, 1941 A medieval pottery at Ashtead, *SyAC*, **47**, 58–66

—, 1942 An Iron Age site near Epsom, *Antiq J*, **22**, 123–38

—, 1942–3 A Roman ditch at Ewell Council School, *SyAC*, **48** (1943), 45–60

—, 1944–5 Animal burial at Epsom, *SyAC*, **49** (1946), 93–4

—, 1946–7 The excavation of a late Roman bath-house at Chatley Farm, Cobham, *SyAC*, **50** (1949), 73–98

— (ed), 1961 *Problems of the Iron Age in southern Britain*, Inst Archaeol Occas Paper, **11**

—, 1974 *Britannia*, 2 edn

—, 1975 The origins of small towns, in Rodwell & Rowley 1975, 4–7

—, Hassell, M W C, & Tomlin, R S O, 1977 Roman Britain in 1976, *Britannia*, **8**, 356–449

—, —, & —, 1983 Roman Britain in 1982, *Britannia*, **14**, 280–356

—, —, & —, 1985 Roman Britain in 1984, *Britannia*, **16**, 252–332

—, & Hogg, A H A, 1944–5 An Iron Age and Roman site on Mickleham Downs, *SyAC*, **49** (1946), 104–6

—, & Hope-Taylor, B, 1950–1 [Saxon hut at Ham, near Kingston], in Report of the Council, *SyAC*, **52**, 101–2

Froom, F R, 1972a Some Mesolithic sites in south-west Berkshire, *Berkshire Archaeol J*, **66**, 11–22

—, 1972b A Mesolithic site at Wawcott, Kintbury, *Berkshire Archaeol J*, **66**, 23–44

—, 1976 *Wawcott III: a stratified Mesolithic succession*, Brit Archaeol Rep, **27**

Fuentes, N, 1983 Boudicca revisited, *London Archaeol*, **4.12**, 311–17

Gabel, G, 1976 St Catherine's Hill: a Mesolithic site near Guildford, *SyAS Res Vol*, **3**, 77–101

Gallant, L, 1966 Three Early Iron Age sherds from Beddington, Surrey, *SyAC*, **63**, 169–71

Gallois, R W, 1965 *British regional geology: the Wealden district*, 4 edn

Gardiner, J P, 1984 Lithic distributions and Neolithic settlement patterns in central southern England, in *Neolithic Studies: a review of some current research* (eds R Bradley & J P Gardiner), Brit Archaeol Rep, **133**, 15–40

Gardner, E, 1911 The British stronghold of St George's Hill, Weybridge, *SyAC*, **24**, 40–55

—, 1912 Some prehistoric and Saxon antiquities found in the neighbourhood of Weybridge, *SyAC*, **25**, 129–35

—, 1921 Effingham: plan of a Surrey earthwork, now destroyed, *SyAC*, **34**, 101

—, 1924 Bronze Age urns of Surrey, *SyAC*, **35**, 1–29

—, 1925 Prehistoric pottery from Weybridge, *Antiq J*, **5**, 74–6

Geikie, J, 1880 Discovery of an ancient canoe in the old alluvium of the Tay at Perth, *Scot Natur*, **5**, 1–7

Gelling, M, 1976a The evidence of place-names, in Sawyer 1976a, 200–11

—, 1976b *The place-names of Berkshire*, 3, English Place-Name Soc, **51**

—, 1977 Further thoughts on pagan place-names, in *Place-name evidence for the Anglo-Saxon and Scandinavian settlements* (ed K Cameron), 99–114

—, 1978a Place-name evidence in Berkshire, in Limbrey & Evans 1978, 123–5

—, 1978b *Signposts to the past. Place-names and the history of England*

—, 1979 *The early charters of the Thames valley*

Gerloff, S, 1975 *The Early Bronze Age daggers in Great Britain, and a reconsideration of the Wessex culture*, Prähistorische Bronzefunde, **6.2** (Munich)

Gibbard, P L, 1979 Middle Pleistocene drainage in the Thames valley, *Geol Mag*, **116.1**, 35–44

—, 1982 Terrace stratigraphy and drainage history of the Plateau Gravels of north Surrey, south Berkshire and north Hampshire, England, *Proc Geol Assoc*, **93.4**, 369–84

—, 1985 *The Pleistocene history of the middle Thames valley*

—, Coope, R G, Hall, A R, Preece, R C, & Robinson, J E, 1982 Middle Devensian deposits beneath the upper floodplain terrace of the River Thames at Kempton Park, Sunbury, England, *Proc Geol Assoc*, **93.3**, 275–89

—, & Hall, A R, 1982 Late Devensian river deposits in the lower Colne valley, west London, England, *Proc Geol Assoc*, **93.3**, 291–9

Gibson, J H, 1926 The Six Bells gravel pit at Farnham, *SyAC*, **37**, 88–9

Gillespie, R, 1984 *Radiocarbon user's handbook*, Oxford Univ Comm Archaeol Monograph, **3**

—, Gowlett, J A J, Hall, E T, Hedges, R E M, & Perry, C, 1985 Radiocarbon dates from the Oxford AMS system: archaeometry datelist 2, *Archaeometry*, **27**, 237–46

Gimmingham, C H, 1972 *Ecology of heathlands*

Girling, M, 1981 The environmental evidence, in *The Austin Friars, Leicester* (eds J E Mellor & T Pearce), Counc Brit Archaeol Res Rep, **35**, 169–71

—, & Greig, J R A, 1977 Palaeoecological investigations of a site at Hampstead Heath, London, *Nature*, **268**, 45–7

Godwin, H, 1940 Pollen analysis and the forest history of England and Wales, *New Phytol*, **39**, 370–400

—, 1962 Vegetational history of the Kentish Chalk Down as seen at Wingham and Frogholt, *Veröffentlichungen Geobotanischen Institutes, Stiftung Rubel, Zurich*, **37**, 83–99

Goodchild, R G, 1937 The Roman brickworks at Wykehurst Farm in the parish of Cranleigh. With a note on a Roman tile-kiln at Horton, Epsom, *SyAC*, **45**, 74–96

—, 1938a A priest's sceptre from the Romano-Celtic temple at Farley Heath, Surrey, *Antiq J*, **18**, 391–6

—, 1938b Martin Tupper and Farley Heath, *SyAC*, **46**, 10–25

—, 1946–7 The Celtic gods of Farley Heath, *SyAC*, **50** (1949), 150–1

Goodier, A, 1984 The formation of boundaries in Anglo-Saxon England: a statistical study, *Medieval Archaeol*, **28**, 1–21

Gover, J E B, Mawer, A, & Stenton, F M, 1934 *The place-names of Surrey*, English Place-Name Soc, **11**

Gower, M, 1983 The late Saxon *burh* at Eashing, *SyAC*, **74**, 225–6

Graham, A, 1978 Swan Street/Great Dover Street, in Bird *et al* 1978b, 473–97

Graham, D, 1986 A note on the recent finds of Bronze Age, Iron Age and Roman material and a site at Frensham Manor noted in an air photograph, *SyAC*, **77**, 232–5

—, & Millett, M, 1980 *Roman Neatham*

Graham, J, 1936 A Romano-Celtic temple at Titsey and the Roman road, *SyAC*, **44**, 84–101

Gravett, K W E, 1977 8 & 9 Littleton, *SyAC*, **71**, 305–9

Gray, P, 1978 *Charlwood houses*, privately circulated.

—, 1982 Cogman's Farm, Burstow: a Surrey base cruck, *SyAC*, **73**, 157–60

—, & Percy, K, 1985 Limpsfield's Domesday pits, *SyAS Bull*, **200**

Green, H S, 1980 *The flint arrowheads of the British Isles*, Brit Archaeol Rep, **75**

Green, L, 1977 Merton Priory: 12th century extension, *SyAC*, **71**, 95–100

Green, M J, 1976 *The religions of civilian Roman Britain*, Brit Archaeol Rep, **24**

Green, T, 1979 Techniques for studying comb signature distributions, in McWhirr 1979, 363–73

Greenwell, W, 1890 Recent researches in barrows in Yorkshire, Wiltshire, Berkshire etc, *Archaeologia*, **52**, 1–72

Grimes, W F, 1929–31 The Early Bronze Age flint dagger in England and Wales, *Proc Prehist Soc East Anglia*, **6** (1932), 340–55

—, 1960 *Excavations on defence sites 1939–45, part I: mainly Neolithic–Bronze Age*, Ministry Works Archaeol Rep, **3**

—, 1961 Some smaller settlements: a symposium, in Frere 1961, 17–28

—, 1968 *Excavation of Roman and medieval London*

Grinsell, L V, 1932 Some Surrey bellbarrows, *SyAC*, **40**, 56–64

—, 1934 An analysis and list of Surrey barrows, *SyAC*, **42**, 26–60

—, 1963 Puttenham – barrow on the Hog's Back, *SyAC*, **60**, 84

—, 1974 Disc barrows, *Proc Prehist Soc*, **40**, 79–112

Guildford Corporation 1957 *The Borough of Guildford 1257–1957: catalogue of an exhibition*

Hall, J, 1980 Hedgerow dating – fact or fantasy?, *Rescue News*, **23**, 3

Hall, M, 1981 Medieval Kingston, in *Archaeology of Kingston upon Thames* (ed B Woodriff), 31–52

Hammerson, M, 1978 Excavations under Southwark Cathedral, *London Archaeol*, **3.8**, 206–12

Hampton, J N, 1977 Roman Ashtead, in *Ashtead, a village transformed* (ed A A Jackson), 26–34

—, & Hawkins, N, 1983 Aerial survey and excavation of a cropmark site at Monument Hill, Woking, *SyAC*, **74**, 147–55

Hanworth, R, 1968 The Roman villa at Rapsley, Ewhurst, *SyAC*, **65**, 1–70

—, 1975 [Letters] A decline in the London settlement, *London Archaeol*, **2.13**, 345

—, 1976 Seale, Crooksbury: two dubious hillforts, *SyAS Bull*, **123**

—, 1978 Surrey: the evidence at present, in Bowen & Fowler 1978, 61–5

—, & Tomalin, D J, 1977 *Brooklands, Weybridge: the excavation of an Iron Age and medieval site*, SyAS Res Vol, **4**

Harbison, P, 1969 *The axes of the Early Bronze Age in Ireland*, Prähistorische Bronzefunde, **9.1** (Munich)

Harding, J, 1964 Interim report on the excavation of a Late Bronze Age homestead in Weston Wood, Albury, Surrey, *SyAC*, **61**, 10–17

—, 1967 Albury: Weston Wood excavations 1966/7, *SyAS Bull*, **36**

—, 1976 *Four centuries of Charlwood houses*

Harris, D R, 1969 Agricultural systems, ecosystems and the origins of agriculture, in Ucko & Dimbleby 1969, 3–16

Harrison, E E, 1961 A pre-Roman and Romano-British site at Charterhouse, Godalming, *SyAC*, **58**, 21–34

Hart, E, & Braun, H, 1941 West Humble chapel, *SyAC*, **47**, 1–11

Harvey, J, 1947 *Gothic England: 1300–1550*

Haslam, J, 1984a The towns of Devon, in Haslam 1984b, 249–83

—, 1984b *Anglo-Saxon towns in southern England*

Haslegrove, C, 1978 *Supplementary gazetteer of find-spots of Celtic coins in Britain, 1977*, Inst Archaeol Occas Paper, **11a**

Hastings, F A, 1965 Excavation of an Iron Age farmstead at Hawk's Hill, Leatherhead, *SyAC*, **62**, 1–43

Hawkes, C F C, 1971 Fence, wall, dump, from Troy to Hod, in Hill & Jesson 1971, 5–18

Hawkes, S C, 1982 Anglo-Saxon Kent *c* 425–725, in Leach 1982, 64–78

—, & Dunning, G C, 1961 Soldiers and settlers in Britain, fourth to fifth century, *Medieval Archaeol*, **5**, 1–70

Hazleden, J, & Jarvis, M G, 1979 Age and significance of alluvium in the Windrush valley, Oxfordshire, *Nature*, **282**, 291–2

Heales, A, 1883a Early history of the church of Kingston upon Thames with notes on its chapelries, *SyAC*, **8**, 13–156

—, 1883b History of the free chapel of St Mary Magdalene, Kingston upon Thames, *SyAC*, **8**, 255–356

—, 1898 *The records of Merton Priory*

Healey, E, 1973 The finds, in Philp 1973, 38–53

—, & Robertson-Mackay, R, 1984 The lithic industries from Staines causewayed enclosure and their relationship to other Earlier Neolithic industries in Britain, *Lithics*, **4**, 1–27

Heath, O M, 1932 Roman burials near Farley Heath, *SyAC*, **40**, 118

Hedges, J D, 1980 The Neolithic in Essex, in Buckley 1980, 26–39

—, & Buckley, D, 1978 Excavations at a Neolithic causewayed enclosure, Orsett, Essex, 1975, *Proc Prehist Soc*, **44**, 219–308

Henderson, J, 1984 The human remains, in Poulton & Woods 1984, 58–67

Henshall, A S, 1950 Textile and weaving appliances in prehistoric Britain, *Proc Prehist Soc*, **16**, 130–62

Hill, D, 1969 The Burghal Hidage: the establishment of a text, *Medieval Archaeol*, **13**, 84–92

—, 1978 The origins of the Saxon towns, in Brandon 1978a, 174–89

—, & Jesson, M (eds), 1971 *The Iron Age and its hillforts*

Hill, G F, 1906 Roman coins from Croydon (Constantius II, Constans, Magnentius, and Gallus), *SyAC*, **19**, 1–26

Hills, C, 1978 The archaeology of Anglo-Saxon England in the pagan period: a review, *Anglo-Saxon England*, **8**, 297–330

—, 1980 Anglo-saxon cremation cemeteries with particular reference to Spong Hill, Norfolk, in Rahtz *et al* 1980, 197–208

Hinnebusch, W A, 1951 *The early English friar preachers*

Hinton, D, 1977 Kingston: excavation in 1976: 4 Thames Street, *SyAS Bull*, **134**

Hinton, D A, 1981 Hampshire's Anglo-Saxon origins, in Shennan & Schadla-Hall 1981, 56–65

—, (ed), 1983 *25 years of medieval archaeology*

Hinton, M, 1981 *Medieval Kingston: archaeology and topography*, privately circulated

Hinton, P, 1982 Carbonised seeds, in P Drewett, Later Bronze Age downland economy and excavations at Black Patch, East Sussex, *Proc Prehist Soc*, **48**, 321–400

Hodder, I, & Hedges, J W, 1977 'Weaving combs', their typology and distribution with some introductory remarks on date and function, in *The Iron Age in Britain, a review* (ed J Collis), 17–28

Hogg, A H A, O'Neil, B H St J, & Stevens, C E, 1941 Earthworks on Hayes and West Wickham Commons, *Archaeol Cantiana*, **54**, 28–34

Hogg, A J, 1905–6 On human and other bones found at Whyteleafe, Surrey, *Trans Croydon Natur Hist Sci Soc*, **6**, 124–31

Holden, E, 1963 Excavations at the deserted medieval village of Hangleton, part 1, *Sussex Archaeol Collect*, **101**, 54–181

Holling, F W, 1964 Medieval pottery from the International Stores, Guildford High Street, *SyAC*, **61**, 103–6

—, 1967 The early foundations of St Mary's church, Guildford, *SyAC*, **64**, 165–8

—, 1968 Medieval pottery from Ash, *SyAC*, **65**, 139–42

—, 1971 A preliminary note on the pottery industry of the Hampshire–Surrey borders, *SyAC*, **68**, 57–88

Holmes, J M, 1949 Romano-British cemeteries at Haslemere and Charterhouse, *SyAC*, **51**, 1–28

Hooper, W, 1933 The pigmy flint industries of Surrey, *SyAC*, **41**, 50–78

—, 1937a A palaeolith from Surrey, *Antiq J*, **17**, 318

—, 1937b Palaeolithic flint from Reigate, *SyAC*, **45**, 140–1

—, 1945 *Reigate: its story through the ages*, SyAS special vol

Hope-Taylor, B, 1946–7 Celtic agriculture in Surrey, *SyAC*, **50** (1949), 47–72

—, 1950a Excavation on Farthing Down, Coulsdon, Surrey, *Archaeol Newsletter*, **2.10**, 170

—, 1950b The excavation of a motte at Abinger in Surrey, *Archaeol J*, **107** (1952), 15–43

Huband, H R, 1925 Farnham: discoveries during 1924, *SyAC*, **36**, 123–4

Hurst, J G, & Hurst, D G, 1964 Excavations at Hangleton, part 2, *Sussex Archaeol Collect*, **102**, 94–142

Jacobi, R M, 1973 Aspects of the Mesolithic age in Great Britain, in *The Mesolithic in Europe* (ed S K Koslowski), 237–65

—, 1976 Britain inside and outside Mesolithic Europe, *Proc Prehist Soc*, **42**, 67–84

—, 1978a Population and landscape in Mesolithic lowland Britain, in Limbrey & Evans 1978, 75–85

—, 1978b The Mesolithic of Sussex, in Drewett 1978b, 15–22

—, 1980a The Upper Palaeolithic of Britain with special reference to Wales, in *Culture and environment in prehistoric Wales* (ed J A Taylor), Brit Archaeol Rep, **76**, 15–99

—, 1980b The Mesolithic of Essex, in Buckley 1980, 14–25

—, 1981 The last hunters in Hampshire, in Shennan & Schadla-Hall 1981, 10–25

—, 1982 Later hunters in Kent: Tasmania and the earliest Neolithic, in Leach 1982, 12–24

—, & Tebbutt, C F, 1981 A Late Mesolithic rock shelter site at High Hurstwood, Sussex, *Sussex Archaeol Collect*, **119**, 1–36

Jackson, K, 1979 Queen Boudicca?, *Britannia*, **10**, 255

Janaway, J, 1974 Wonersh: Hallams Court, Blackheath, *SyAS Bull*, **106**

Jarvis, M G, Allen, R H, Fordham, S J, Hazleden, J, Moffat, A J, & Sturdy, R G, 1983 *Soils of England and Wales sheet 6: south-east England, 1:250,000*, Ordnance Survey

John, D T, 1974 *A study of soils and superficial deposits on the North Downs of Surrey*, unpublished PhD thesis, Univ London

—, 1980 The soils and superficial deposits of the North Downs of Surrey, in *The shaping of southern England* (ed D K C Jones), Inst Brit Geog Special Pub, **11**, 101–30

—, & Fisher, P F, 1984 The stratigraphical and geomorphological significance of the Red Crag fossils at Netley Heath, Surrey, *Proc Geol Assoc*, **95.3**, 235–48

Johnson, A, 1983 *Roman forts*

Johnson, B, 1975 *Archaeology and the M25, 1971–5*, SyAS

Johnson, D J, 1969 *Southwark and the City*

Johnson, S, 1980 *Later Roman Britain*

Johnson, W & Wright, W, 1903 *Neolithic man in north-east Surrey*

Johnston, D E, 1978 Villas of Hampshire and the Isle of Wight, in Todd 1978, 71–7

—, & Williams, D, 1979 Relief-patterned tiles: a reappraisal, in McWhirr 1979, 375–93

Johnston, P M, 1932 Notes on a medieval stone vaulted crypt at Wallington, *SyAC*, **40**, 123–5

Jones, G R J, 1976 Multiple estates and early settlement, in Sawyer 1976a, 11–40

Jones, M, & Dimbleby, G (eds), 1981 *The environment of man: the Iron Age to the Anglo-Saxon period*, Brit Archaeol Rep, **87**

Jones, M U, & Bond, D, 1980 Later Bronze Age settlement at Mucking, Essex, in Barrett & Bradley 1980a, 471–82

—, & Jones, W T, 1975 Crop-mark sites at Mucking, Essex, England, in *Recent archaeological excavations in Europe* (ed R Bruce-Mitford), 133–87

Jones, P, 1982 Saxon and early medieval Staines, *Trans London Middlesex Archaeol Soc*, **33**, 186–213

Jongerius, A, 1970 Some morphological aspects of regrouping phenomena in Dutch soils, *Geoderma*, **4**, 311–31

Jope, E M, 1961 Daggers of the Early Iron Age in Britain, *Proc Prehist Soc*, **27**, 307–43

—, 1964 The Saxon building stone industry in southern and midland England, *Medieval Archaeol*, **8**, 91–118

Keef, P A M, Wymer, J J, & Dimbleby, G W, 1965 A Mesolithic site on Iping Common, Sussex, England, *Proc Prehist Soc*, **31**, 85–92

Keeley, H C M (ed), forthcoming *Environmental archaeology: a regional review vol 2*, HBMC Occas Paper, **1**

—, & Macphail, R I, 1981 A soil handbook for archaeologists, *Inst Archaeol Bull*, **18**, 225–44

Keiller, A, & Piggott, S, 1939 Badshot long barrow, in Oakley *et al* 1939, 133–49

Kent, J P C, 1978a The origins and development of Celtic gold coinage in Britain, *Actes du congrès international d'archéologie, Rouen, 3–5 Juillet, 1975*, 313–24

—, 1978b The London area in the Late Iron Age: an interpretation of the earliest coins, in Bird *et al* 1978a, 53–8

—, 1981 The origins of coinage in Britain, in Cunliffe 1981b, 40–2

Kenyon, G H, 1967 *The glass industry of the Weald*

Kerney, M P, 1963 Late glacial deposits on the Chalk of south-east England, *Phil Trans Roy Soc London*, ser B, **246**, 203–54

—, Brown, E H, & Chandler, T H, 1964 The late glacial and post glacial history of the chalk escarpment near Brook, Kent, *Phil Trans Roy Soc London*, ser B, **248**, 135–204

Kerr, F G, 1971 East Clandon: a possible Roman dwelling site (TQ 058 524), *SyAS Bull*, **83**

Ketteringham, L L, 1976 *Alsted: excavation of a 13th–14th century sub-manor house*, SyAS Res Vol, **2**

—, 1977 Excavation of the church of St John the Evangelist, Coulsdon, *SyAC*, **71**, 101–10

—, 1980 Medieval building in Henley Wood, Chelsham, *SyAC*, **72**, 83–90

—, 1984 Excavations at Lagham Manor, South Godstone, *SyAC*, **75**, 235–49

King, D J C, & Renn, D F, 1971 Lidelea Castle – a suggested identification, *Antiq J*, **51**, 301–3

Knowles, D, & Hadcock, R N, 1971 *Medieval religious houses: England and Wales*

Knox, C, 1963 The meeting place of the hundred of Blackheath, *SyAC*, **60**, 86–7

Kukla, G J, 1977 Pleistocene land, sea correlations 1: Europe, *Earth Sci Rev*, **13**, 307–74

Kwaad, F J P M, & Mücher, H J, 1977 The evolution of soils and slope deposits in the Luxembourg Ardennes near Wiltz, *Geoderma*, **17**, 1–37

—, & —, 1979 The formation and evolution of colluvium on arable land in northern Luxembourg, *Geoderma*, **22**, 173–92

Lacaille, A D, 1963 Mesolithic industries beside Colne waters in Iver and Denham, Buckinghamshire, *Rec Buckinghamshire*, **17.3**, 143–81

—, 1966 Mesolithic facies in the transpontine fringes, *SyAC*, **63**, 1–43

Lambert, U, 1921 *Blechingley: a parish history*

—, 1929 *Godstone*

Lambrick, G, & Woods, H, 1976 Excavation on the second site of the Dominican friary, Oxford, *Oxoniensia*, **41**, 168–231

Lane Fox, Col, 1877 On some Saxon and British tumuli near Guildford, *Rep Brit Assoc Advance Sci*, 116–7

Lasham, F, 1893a Palaeolithic man in west Surrey, *SyAC*, **11**, 25–9

—, 1893b Neolithic and Bronze Age man in west Surrey, *SyAC*, **11**, 244–51

—, 1896 An 'urn field' at Merrow, Guildford, *SyAC*, **13**, 26–7

Lawrence, G F, 1890 The prehistoric antiquities of Wandsworth, *J Brit Archaeol Assoc*, **46**, 77–8

—, 1929 Antiquities from the middle Thames, *Archaeol J*, **86**, 69–98

Laws, A, 1976 Excavations at Northumberland Wharf, Brentford, *Trans London Middlesex Archaeol Soc*, **27**, 179–205

—, 1978 An Early Bronze Age axe from Harlington, in Bird *et al* 1978a, 39–43

Lawson, A, 1979 A late Middle Bronze Age hoard from Hunstanton, Norfolk, in Burgess & Coombs 1979, 42–92

Leach, P E (ed), 1982 *Archaeology in Kent to AD 1500*, Counc Brit Archaeol Res Rep, **48**

Leakey, L S B, 1951 *Preliminary excavations of a Mesolithic site at Abinger Common, Surrey*, Res Paper SyAS, **3**

Leakey, R E, 1981 *The making of mankind*

Lekai, L J, 1953 *The white monks*

Le Patourel, J, & Roberts, B K, 1978 The significance of moated sites, in Aberg 1978, 46–55

Leveson-Gower, G, 1869 On a Roman villa discovered at Titsey, *SyAC*, **4**, 214–37

Lewis, M J T, 1966 *Temples in Roman Britain*

Limbrey, S, 1975 *Soil, science and archaeology*

—, & Evans, J G (eds), 1978 *The effect of man on the landscape: the lowland zone*, Counc Brit Archaeol Res Rep, **21**

Little, R I, 1961 The excavation of a Romano-British settlement in King's Wood, Sanderstead, *SyAC*, **58**, 35–46

—, 1964 The Atwood Iron Age and Romano-British site, Sanderstead, 1960, *SyAC*, **61**, 29–38

Liversidge, J, 1968 *Britain in the Roman empire*

Lloyd, C W, 1962 Surrey, in Darby & Campbell 1962, 364–406

London Museum 1930 *London in Roman times*, London Mus catalogue, **3**

Longley, D, 1976 The archaeological implications of gravel extraction in north-west Surrey, *SyAS Res Vol*, **3**, 1–35

—, 1980 *Runnymede Bridge: excavations on the site of a Late Bronze Age settlement*, SyAS Res Vol, **6**

—, & Needham, S, 1979 Egham: a Late Bronze Age settlement and waterfront, *Current Archaeol*, **68/6.9**, 262–7

—, & Poulton, R, 1982 The Saxon cemetery at Upper West Field, Shepperton, *Trans London Middlesex Archaeol Soc*, **33**, 177–85

Longworth, I H, 1983 *Collared urns of the Bronze Age in Great Britain and Ireland*

Lousley, J E, 1976 *Flora of Surrey*

Lowther, A W G, 1927 Excavations at Ashtead, Surrey, *SyAC*, **37.2**, 144–63

—, 1929 Excavations at Ashtead, Surrey. Second report (1927 and 1928), *SyAC*, **38.1**, 1–17

—, 1930 Excavations at Ashtead, Surrey. Third report (1929), *SyAC*, **38.2**, 132–48

—, 1931 The Saxon cemetery at Guildown, Guildford, Surrey, *SyAC*, **39**, 1–50

—, 1933 Bronze–Iron Age and Roman finds at Ashtead, *SyAC*, **41**, 93–8

—, 1934 The Roman site near the parish church of St Giles at Ashtead, *SyAC*, **42**, 77–84

—, 1935a Excavations at Ewell in 1934. The Saxon cemetery and Stane Street, *SyAC*, **43**, 16–35

—, 1935b An Early Iron Age oven at St Martha's Hill, near Guildford, *SyAC*, **43**, 113–15

—, 1939 Bronze Age and Iron Age, in Oakley *et al* 1939, 153–217

—, 1944–5 Report on excavations at the site of the Early Iron Age camp in the grounds of Queen Mary's Hospital, Carshalton, Surrey, *SyAC*, **49** (1946), 56–74

—, 1945a Caesar's Camp, Wimbledon, Surrey, the excavation of 1937, *Archaeol J*, **102**, 15–20

—, 1945b Iron Age pottery from Wisley, Surrey, *Proc Prehist Soc*, **11**, 32–8

—, 1946–7a Excavations at Purberry Shot, Ewell, Surrey, *SyAC*, **50** (1949), 9–46

—, 1946–7b Pattern-stamped flue tiles from the Chatley Farm bath-building, in Frere 1946–7, 94–8

—, 1946–7c Iron Age pottery from sites at Ewell and Ashtead, *SyAC*, **50** (1949), 139–41

—, 1948 *A study of the patterns on Roman flue-tiles and their distribution*, SyAS Res Paper, **1** [undated]

—, 1949a Roman villa at Sandilands Road, Walton on the Hill. Excavations of 1948–9, *SyAC*, **51** (1950), 65–81

—, 1949b Cast bronze ornament of Late Bronze Age date, from St Catherine's Hill, Guildford, *SyAC*, **51** (1950), 143–4

—, 1949c Iron Age pottery from St George's Hill camp, Weybridge, *SyAC*, **51** (1950), 144–7

—, 1950 Report of group 'D': archaeology, *Proc Leatherhead District Local Hist Soc*, **1.4**, 4–5

—, 1953–4 Report on the excavation, 1946–7, of a Roman site at Farnham, Surrey, *SyAC*, **54** (1955), 47–57

—, 1957 A Late Bronze Age sword from Charlwood, *SyAC*, **55** (1958), 122–3

—, 1959a Cartographical survey of the area: the Saxon period, *Proc Leatherhead District Local Hist Soc*, **2.3**, 69–72

—, 1959b The date of the Roman buildings and brickworks on Ashtead Common, *Proc Leatherhead District Local Hist Soc*, **2.3**, 73–5

—, 1963a An enamelled bronze roundel of the Romano-British period, *Proc Leatherhead District Local Hist Soc*, **2.7**, 202–3

—, 1963b A Saxon burial found at Ewell, Surrey, *Antiq J*, **43**, 294–6

—, 1976 Romano-British chimney pots and finials, *Antiq J*, **56**, 35–48

—, & Goodchild, R G, 1942–3 Excavations at Farley Heath, Albury, during 1939, *SyAC*, **48** (1943), 31–40

Lukis, F G, 1843 *A brief account of the barrows near Bircham Magna, in the country of Norfolk* (Guernsey)

Lyne, M A B, & Jefferies, R S, 1979 *The Alice Holt/Farnham Roman pottery industry*, Counc Brit Archaeol Res Rep, **30**

Macdonald, J, 1976 Neolithic, in Collins *et al* 1976, 19–32

—, 1978 An Iron Age dagger in the Royal Ontario Museum, in Bird *et al* 1978a, 44–52

MacGregor, M, 1976 *Early Celtic art in north Britain*

Machin, E L, 1976 Report on the Mesolithic industry of Weston Wood, Albury, *SyAS Res Vol*, **3**, 103–11

Mack, R P, 1964 *The coinage of ancient Britain*, 2 edn

Mackney, D, 1961 A podzol development sequence in oak woods and heath in central England, *J Soil Sci*, **12.1**, 23–40

Macphail, R I, 1979 *Soil variation on selected Surrey heaths*, unpublished PhD thesis, Kingston Polytechnic

—, 1981a *Soil report on West Heath cemetery (1980), West Sussex, parts I and II*, Ancient Monuments Lab Rep, **3586**

—, 1981b Soil and botanical studies of the 'dark earth', in Jones & Dimbleby 1981, 309–31

—, 1982 *Soil report on Ockham Common (M25), Surrey*, Ancient Monuments Lab Rep, **3738**

—, 1983 Surrey heathlands and their soils, in Burnham 1983, 57–67

—, forthcoming A review of soil science in archaeology in England, in Keeley forthcoming

—, & Courty, M A, 1985 Interpretation and significance of urban deposits, in *Proc 3 Nordic Conf Applic Scientific Methods Archaeol* (eds T Edgren & H Jongner). ISKOS, **5** 71–84 (Finn Antiq Soc, Helsinki)

Major, A F, 1925 The archaeological survey of Surrey: Wallington, *SyAC*, **36**, 113–14

Malden, H E, 1900a *A history of Surrey*

—, 1900b Blechingley Castle, *SyAC*, **15**, 17–26

— (ed), 1902; 1905; 1911; 1912 *The Victoria history of the county of Surrey*, 4 vols

Manning, O, & Bray, W, 1804; 1809; 1814 *The history and antiquities of Surrey*, 3 vols

Margary, I D, 1956 *Roman ways in the Weald*, 3 edn

—, 1964 Dry Hill Camp, Lingfield, Surrey, *SyAC*, **61**, 100

—, 1973 *Roman roads in Britain*, 3 edn

Marsh, G, & Tyers, P, 1978 The Roman pottery from Southwark, in Bird *et al* 1978b, 533–82

Marshall, C J, 1924 A medieval pottery kiln discovered at Cheam, *SyAC*, **35**, 79–97

Martin, A B, & Treacher, L, 1910 Excursion to Limpsfield and Westerham, *Proc Geol Assoc*, **21**, 59–64

Martin, A R, 1933–4 *Franciscan architecture in England*, Brit Soc Franciscan Stud, **18** (1937)

Mason, R T, 1966 Old Court Cottage, Limpsfield, *SyAC*, **63**, 130–7

McCracken, J S, 1977a Merton Priory excavations, *SyAS Bull*, **135**

—, 1977b Wandsworth: Althorpe Grove, Battersea, *SyAS Bull*, **139**

—, 1980 Barnes: St Mary's parish church, *SyAS Bull*, **167**

—, 1981 St Mary, Barnes, *Bull Counc Brit Archaeol Churches Comm*, **14**, 9

—, 1983 Barnes: St Mary's parish church, *SyAS Bull*, **184**

—, 1984a King's royal observatory, Old Deer Park, Kew, *SyAS Bull*, **191**

—, 1984b Excavations at Merton Priory 1983: the infirmary, *SyAS Bull*, **196**

McGrail, S, 1978 *Logboats of England and Wales*, Brit Archaeol Rep, **51**

—, 1979 Prehistoric boats, timber and woodworking technology, *Proc Prehist Soc*, **45**, 159–63

McLees, C, 1982 *Medieval moated sites in western and central Surrey*, unpublished dissertation, Queen's Univ Belfast

McWhirr, A (ed), 1979 *Roman brick and tile. Studies in manufacture, distribution and use in the western empire*, Brit Archaeol Rep Internat Ser, **68**

—, & Viner, D, 1978 The production and distribution of tiles in Roman Britain with particular reference to the Cirencester region, *Britannia*, **9**, 359–77

Meaney, A, 1964 *A gazetteer of early Anglo-Saxon burial sites*

Meates, G W, 1979 *The Lullingstone Roman villa. Vol 1 – the site*

Megaw, B R S, & Hardy, E M, 1938 British decorated axes and their diffusion during the earlier part of the Bronze Age, *Proc Prehist Soc*, **4**, 272–307

Megaw, J V S, 1976 Gwithian, Cornwall: some notes on the evidence for Neolithic and Bronze Age settlement, in Burgess & Miket 1976, 51–66

—, & Simpson, D D A (eds), 1979 *Introduction to British prehistory*

Mellars, P A, 1974 The Palaeolithic and Mesolithic, in Renfrew 1974, 41–99

—, 1976 Fire, ecology, animal populations and man: a study of some ecological relationships in prehistory, *Proc Prehist Soc*, **42**, 15–46

—, & Reinhardt, S C, 1978 Patterns of Mesolithic land use in southern England: a geological perspective, in

The early postglacial settlement of northern Europe (ed P A Mellars), 243–93

Mercer, E, 1975 *English vernacular houses*

Merrifield, R, 1975 *The archaeology of London*

—, 1983 *London, city of the Romans*

Millett, M, 1974 A group of first century pottery from Tilford, *SyAC*, **70**, 19–24

—, 1979 The dating of Farnham (Alice Holt) pottery, *Britannia*, **10**, 121–37

—, & James, S, 1983 Excavations at Cowdery's Down, Basingstoke, Hampshire, 1978–81, *Archaeol J*, **140**, 151–279

Mills, P S, 1980 Excavations at Cromwell Green in the Palace of Westminster, *Trans London Middlesex Archaeol Soc*, **31**, 18–28

Milne, J G, 1948 *Finds of Greek coins in the British Isles*

Mitchell, G F, 1956 Post-Boreal pollen diagrams from Irish raised bogs, *Proc Roy Irish Acad*, ser B, **57**, 185–251

Moir, J R, 1929 Some hitherto unpublished implements, *Antiq J*, **9**, 10–12

Money, J H, 1960 Excavations at High Rocks, Tunbridge Wells, 1954–6, *Sussex Archaeol Collect*, **98**, 173–221

Moore, P D, & Webb, J A, 1978 *An illustrated guide to pollen analysis*

—, & Willmot, A, 1976 Prehistoric forest clearance and the development of peatlands in the uplands and lowlands of Britain, *6 Internat Peat Congress, Podzan, Poland 1976*, 1–15

Morris, J, 1959 Anglo-Saxon Surrey, *SyAC*, **56**, 132–58

—, 1966 Dark Age dates, in *Britain and Rome. Essays presented to Eric Birley on his sixtieth birthday* (eds M G Jarrett & B Dobson), 145–85

—, 1973 *The age of Arthur*

—, 1974 [Review of J N L Myres & B Green, *The Anglo-Saxon cemeteries of Caistor-by-Norwich and Markshall, Norfolk*, 1973], *Medieval Archaeol*, **18**, 225–32

— (ed), 1975 *Domesday Book 3, Surrey*, trans S Wood

—, 1982 *Londinium, London in the Roman empire*

Morris, R, 1983 *The church in British archaeology*, Counc Brit Archaeol Res Rep, **47**

Morton, A R, 1926 On the topography of the Cluniac abbey of St Saviour, Bermondsey, *J Brit Archaeol Assoc*, 2 ser, **32** (1927), 192–228

Moss, G P, 1972 An ancient trackway in the Weald, *SyAS Bull*, **88**

Mourant, A E, 1962 *Blood groups and the study of mankind*

Mücher, H J, 1974 Micromorphology of slope deposits: the necessity of a classification, in *Soil microscopy. Proc 4 Internat Working-meeting Micromorphology* (ed S K Rutherford), 553–6 (Ontario)

Muhlberger, S, 1983 The Gallic Chronicle of 452 and its authority for British events, *Britannia*, **14**, 23–33

Muller-Karpe, H, 1961 *Die Vollgriffschwerter der Urnenfelderzeit aus Bayern* (Munich)

Munby, J, 1975 A 15th century Wealden house in Oxford, *Oxoniensia*, **39**, 73–6

Musson, C R, 1954 An illustrated catalogue of Sussex Beaker and Bronze Age pottery, *Sussex Archaeol Collect*, **92**, 106–24

Musty, J, 1984 Science diary, *Current Archaeol*, **94/8.11**, 344

Myres, J N L, 1975 The Anglo-Saxon vase from Mitcham grave 205, *Antiq J*, **55**, 93–5

—, 1977 *A corpus of Anglo-Saxon pottery of the pagan period*

Nail, D, 1965 The meeting place of Copthorne Hundred, *SyAC*, **62**, 44–53

Nairn, I & Pevsner, N, 1971 *The buildings of England: Surrey*, 2 edn (rev B Cherry)

Nash, D, 1980 The Celtic coins, in R Downey, A King & G Soffe, The Hayling Island temple and religious connections across the channel, in *Temples, churches and religions in Roman Britain* (ed W Rodwell), Brit Archaeol Rep, **77**, 301

Neal, D S, 1981 *Roman mosaics in Britain: an introduction to their schemes and a catalogue of paintings*, Britannia Monograph, **1**

—, 1982 Romano-British villas – one or two storied?, in *Structural reconstruction* (ed P J Drury), Brit Archaeol Rep, **110**, 153–71

Neale, K, 1973 Stane Street (Chichester – London): the third mansio, *SyAC*, **69**, 207–10

Needham, S P, 1979a A pair of Early Bronze Age spearheads from Lightwater, Surrey, in Burgess & Coombs 1979, 1–40

—, 1979b Two recent British shield finds and their continental parallels, *Proc Prehist Soc*, **45**, 111–34

—, 1980a A bronze from Winterfold Heath, Wonersh, and its place in the British narrow-bladed palstave sequence, *SyAC*, **72**, 37–47

—, 1980b An assemblage of Late Bronze Age metalworking debris from Dainton, Devon, *Proc Prehist Soc*, **46**, 177–216

—, 1980c The bronzes, in Longley 1980, 13–27

—, 1981 *The Bulford – Helsbury manufacturing tradition: the production of Stogursey socketed axes during the Later Bronze Age in southern Britain*, Brit Mus Occas Paper, **13**

—, 1982 *The Ambleside hoard: a discovery in the Royal Collections*, Brit Mus Occas Paper, **39**

—, 1983 *The Early Bronze Age axeheads of central and southern England*, unpublished PhD thesis, Univ College, Cardiff

—, 1985 Neolithic and Bronze Age settlement on the buried floodplains of Runnymede, *Oxford J Archaeol*, **4**, 125–37

—, 1986 The metalwork, in O'Connell 1986, 22–60

—, & Burgess, C B, 1980 The Later Bronze Age in the lower Thames valley: the metalwork evidence, in Barrett & Bradley 1980a, 437–69

—, & Longley, D, 1980 Runnymede Bridge, Egham. A Late Bronze Age riverside settlement, in Barrett & Bradley 1980a, 397–436

Nevill, R, 1880 Esher Place, *SyAC*, **7**, 214–21

—, 1891 *Old cottage and domestic architecture in Surrey*

Nicolaysen, P, 1983 Three hand-axes from Surrey, *SyAC*, **74**, 201–2

—, forthcoming [Report on the bones from Badshot Lea]

Nortcliff, S, 1984 *Down to earth*, Leicester Mus Pub, **32**

North, O H, 1931 The Gosden Farm gravel pit near Bramley, *SyAC*, **39**, 144–5

Oakley, K P, 1939 Geology and Palaeolithic studies, in Oakley *et al* 1939, 3–58

—, Rankine, W F, & Lowther, A W G, 1939 *A survey of the prehistory of the Farnham district*, SyAS special vol

O'Connell, M, 1977 *Historic towns in Surrey*, SyAS Res Vol, **5**

—, 1980 The Wheatsheaf, Dorking: excavations in 1976, *SyAC*, **72**, 49–62

—, 1982 Burpham: excavation in 1978, *SyAC*, **73**, 97–100

—, 1983 The undercroft 72/74 High Street, Guildford, *SyAC*, **74**, 10–12

—, 1984 Green Lane, Wanborough 1979 (SU 920 495), *SyAC*, **75**, 185–93

—, 1986 *Excavations at Petters Sports Field, Egham*, SyAS Res Vol, **10**

—, forthcoming [Report on excavations at Stanwell]

—, & Needham, S P, 1977 A Late Bronze Age hoard from a settlement at Petters Sports Field, Egham, Surrey, *London Archaeol*, **3.5**, 123–30

—, & Poulton, R, 1983 *BPA pipeline Surrey*, privately circulated

—, & —, 1984 The towns of Surrey, in Haslam 1984b, 37–51

O'Connor, B, 1980 *Cross-channel relations in the Later Bronze Age*, Brit Archaeol Rep Internat Ser, **91**

O'Malley, M, 1978 Broom Hill, Braishfield: Mesolithic dwelling, *Current Archaeol*, **63/6.4**, 117–20

—, & Jacobi, R M, 1978 The excavation of a Mesolithic occupation site at Broom Hill, Braishfield, Hampshire, *Rescue Archaeol Hampshire*, **4**, 16–38

ÓRíordáin, S P, 1936 The halberd in Bronze Age Europe: a study of prehistoric origins, evolution, distribution and chronology, *Archaeologia*, **86**, 195–321

Orton, C, 1980 Excavations at 32, Burleigh Avenue, Wallington, 1921 and 1976, *SyAC*, **72**, 77–82

—, 1982 The excavation of a late medieval/transitional pottery kiln at Cheam, *SyAC*, **73**, 49–92

Osborne, P J, 1971 On the insect fauna of the organic deposits within the Wandle gravels, in D S Peake, The age of the Wandle gravels in the vicinity of Croydon, *Proc Trans Croydon Natur Hist Sci Soc*, **14.7**, 147–75

—, 1972 Insect faunas of Late Devensian and Flandrian age from Church Stretton, Shropshire, *Phil Trans Roy Soc London*, ser B, **263**, 327–67

—, 1974 An insect assemblage of Early Flandrian age from Lea Marston, Warwickshire, and its bearing on the contemporary climate and ecology, *Quaternary Res*, **4**, 471–86

Page, W, & Keate, E M, 1912 Romano-British Surrey, in Malden 1912, 343–78

Palmer, C P R, 1887 The Friar Preachers or Black Friars of Guildford, *The Reliquary*, new ser, **1**, 7–20

Palmer, S, 1970 The Stone Age industries of the Isle of Portland, Dorset, and the utilisation of Portland chert as artifact material in southern England, *Proc Prehist Soc*, **36**, 82–115

Parkinson, A J, 1968 Sanderstead: Iron Age and Romano-British occupation, *SyAC*, **65**, 126

Parnum, A, & Cotton, J, 1983 Recent work in Brentford: excavations and observations 1974–82, *London Archaeol*, **4.12**, 318–32

Parsons, E J S, 1970 *The map of Great Britain c 1360, known as the Gough Map*

Peacock, D P S (ed), 1977 *Pottery and early commerce. Characterization and trade in Roman and later ceramics*

—, 1979 Petrology of the querns from Holmbury and Hascombe, in Thompson 1979, 315

—, 1982 *Pottery in the Roman world: an ethno-archaeological approach*

Peake, D S, 1982 The ground upon which Croydon was built. A reappraisal of the Pleistocene history of the River Wandle and its basin, *Proc Croydon Natur Hist Sci Soc*, **17.4**, 89–116

Pearce, E M H, 1932 An account of the buildings of

Newark Priory with a note on its founders' family, *SyAC*, **40**, 1–24

Pelteret, D A E, 1984 The roads of Anglo-Saxon England, *Wiltshire Archaeol Natur Hist Mag*, **79**, 155–63

Pemberton, F F, 1971 Lower Kingswood: excavation at Rookery Farm (TQ 234 537 – TQ 244 541), *SyAC*, **68**, 190

—, 1973a A Romano-British settlement on Stane Street, Ewell, Surrey, *SyAC*, **69**, 1–26

—, 1973b Prehistoric and Romano-British settlement in Ewell, *London Archaeol*, **2.4**, 84–6

Penn, J, Field, D, & Serjeantson, D, 1984 Evidence of Neolithic occupation in Kingston: excavations at Eden Walk, 1965, *SyAC*, **75**, 207–24

Pennington, W, 1975 A chronostratigraphic comparison of Late Weichselian and Late Devensian sub-divisions, illustrated by two radiocarbon dated profiles from western Britain, *Boreas*, **4**, 157–71

Percival, J, 1976 *The Roman villa, an historical introduction*

Phillips, W, 1967 Bronze Age metal objects in Surrey, *SyAC*, **64**, 1–34

—, 1968 Flanged axe from Blackheath, *SyAC*, **65**, 130

Phillpot, J F, 1921 Flints found at Streatham, *SyAC*, **34**, 114–15

Philp, B, 1973 *Excavations in west Kent, 1960–1970*

—, 1981 The Medway megaliths, *Kent Archaeol Rev*, **64**, 77–92

Piggott, S, 1950 Swords and scabbards of the British Early Iron Age, *Proc Prehist Soc*, **16**, 1–28

—, 1954 *Neolithic cultures of the British Isles*

—, 1981 Early prehistory, in *The agrarian history of England and Wales* (ed S Piggott), 3–59

Pitt-Rivers, A, 1888 *Excavations in Cranbourne Chase, vol 2*

Pitts, M W, 1978 Towards an understanding of flint industries in post-glacial England, *Bull Inst Archaeol*, **15**, 179–97

—, & Jacobi, R M, 1979 Some aspects of change in flaked stone industries of the Mesolithic and Neolithic in southern Britain, *J Archaeol Sci*, **6**, 163–77

Platt, C, 1976 *The English medieval town*

—, 1978 *Medieval England*

—, 1981 *The parish churches of medieval England*

—, 1983 *Medieval castles in England and Wales*

Pocock, W W, 1858 Chertsey Abbey, *SyAC*, **1**, 97–121

—, 1864 Roman pavement, etc upon Walton Heath, *SyAC*, **2**, 1–13

Poole, C, 1984 Rectangular post-built structures, in Cunliffe 1984, 87–95

Potter, J H, 1977 Geological observations on the use of iron and clay at the site, in Hanworth & Tomalin 1977, 22–3

Poulton, R, 1978 Crop-marks at Stanwell, near Heathrow Airport, *London Archaeol*, **3.9**, 239–42

—, 1980 Cherchefelle and the origins of Reigate, *London Archaeol*, **3.16**, 433–8

—, 1986 Excavations on the site of the Old Vicarage, Church Street, Reigate 1977–82, Part 1, Saxo-Norman and earlier discoveries, *SyAC*, **77**, 17–94

—, forthcoming [Report on the 1954 excavations on the site of Chertsey Abbey], SyAS Res Vol

—, & O'Connell, M, 1981 Observations of the Esso pipeline construction in Surrey, *SyAS Bull*, **175**

—, & —, 1984a Recent discoveries south of Tyrrell's Wood golf course, near Leatherhead, *SyAC*, **75**, 289–92

—, & —, 1984b St George's Hill fort: excavations in 1981, *SyAC*, **75**, 275–80

—, & Woods, H, 1984 *Excavations on the site of the Dominican Friary at Guildford in 1974 and 1978*, SyAS Res Vol, **9**

Powell, T G E, 1958 *The Celts*

Preece, R C, Burleigh, R, Kerney, M P, & Jarzembowski, E A, 1983 Radiocarbon age determinations of fossil *Margaritifera auricularia* (Spengler) from the River Thames in west London, *J Archaeol Sci*, **10**, 249–57

Prendergast, M D, 1973 *The coarseware potteries of medieval Limpsfield*, privately circulated

—, 1974 Limpsfield medieval coarseware: a descriptive analysis, *SyAC*, **70** (1975), 57–78

Prest, J M, & Parrish, E J, 1949 Investigations on Walton Heath and Banstead Common, *SyAC*, **51** (1950), 57–64

Prestwich, J, 1891 On the age, formation and successive drift-stages of the valley of the Darent; with remarks on the Palaeolithic implements of the district, and on the origin of its Chalk escarpment, *Quart J Geol Soc*, **47**, 126–63

Pryer, K A, 1975 London Borough of Sutton: Romano-British cinerary urn and other vessels in modern cemetery, Bandon Hill, Wallington (TQ 299 647), *SyAS Bull*, **116**

—, 1977 Wallington: Bandon Hill modern cemetery (TQ 299 647). Romano-British finds, *SyAS Bull*, **134**

Pryor, F, 1980 *Excavation at Fengate, Peterborough, England: the third report*, Northamptonshire Archaeol Soc Monograph, **1**

—, 1982 Problems of survival: later prehistoric settlements in the southern East Anglian Fenlands, *Analecta Praehistorica Leidensia*, **15**, 125–43

Rackham, O, 1976 *Trees and woodland in the British landscape*

Radford, C A R, 1961 The church of St Mary, Stoke D'Abernon, Surrey, *Archaeol J*, **118** (1963), 165–74

Rahtz, P A, 1976 Buildings and rural settlement, in Wilson 1976, 49–98

—, 1982 The Dark Ages to 700, in *The archaeology of Somerset* (eds M Aston & I Burrow), 99–107

—, Dickinson, T, & Watts, L (eds), 1980 *Anglo-Saxon cemeteries 1979*, Brit Archaeol Rep, **82**

Rankine, W F, 1935 Discoveries in the gravels of the fifty-foot terrace at Farnham, Surrey, *Proc Prehist Soc*, **1**, 148–9

—, 1936 A Mesolithic site at Farnham, *SyAC*, **44**, 25–46

—, 1939 Mesolithic and Neolithic studies, in Oakley *et al* 1939, 61–132

—, 1944–5 Some remarkable flints from west Surrey Mesolithic sites, *SyAC*, **49** (1946), 6–19

—, 1946–7a Late Levallois point from C terrace, Farnham, *SyAC*, **50** (1949), 133

—, 1946–7b Mesolithic chipping floors in the wind blown deposits of west Surrey, *SyAC*, **50** (1949), 1–8

—, 1949a *A Mesolithic survey of the west Surrey Greensand*, SyAS Res Paper, **2**

—, 1949b Stone macaeheads with Mesolithic associations from south-eastern England, *Proc Prehist Soc*, **15**, 70–6

—, 1950–1 Mesolithic research in Surrey: with a tribute to Wilfrid Hooper LLD; FSA, *SyAC*, **52** (1952), 1–10

—, 1951a Quartzite pebble macaeheads with hourglass perforation and their distribution in England, *Archaeol Newsletter*, **4.4**, 53–5

—, 1951b Artifacts of Portland chert in southern England, *Proc Prehist Soc*, **17**, 93–4

—, 1952 A Mesolithic chipping floor at the Warren, Oakhanger, Selborne, Hants, *Proc Prehist Soc*, **18**, 21–35

—, 1953–4 Some palaeoliths from the Farnham terrace gravels, *SyAC*, **54** (1955), 1–9

—, 1956 *The Mesolithic of southern England*, SyAS Res Paper, **4**

—, 1960 The Warren Mesolithic sites, Oakhanger, Hants: discovery of Site V/VII, *Archaeol Newsletter*, **6.11**, 260–2

—, 1961a *A Mesolithic flaking floor at Oakhanger, Selborne, Hants; epitomised supplement to the abstract of the report published in Proceedings of the Prehistoric Society, 1960 Vol 26 pp 246–62*, privately circulated

—, 1961b *Further excavations at Oakhanger, Selborne, Hants: Site VIII*, Wealden Mesolithic Res Bull, privately circulated

—, Rankine, W M, & Dimbleby, G W, 1960 Further excavations at a Mesolithic site at Oakhanger, Selborne, Hants, *Proc Prehist Soc*, **27**, 246–62

RCHM 1925 *An inventory of the historical monuments in London, vol 2: west London*, Roy Comm Hist Monuments (England)

Reece, R, 1980 Town and country: the end of Roman Britain, *World Archaeol*, **12.1**, 77–92

Reid, A B L, & Frere, S S, 1954 The excavation of a fourth cave at Waddon, *Proc Croydon Natur Hist Sci Soc*, **12**, 144–51

Reid, E M, 1949 The late glacial flora of the Lea valley, *New Phytol*, **48**, 245–52

Renfrew, A C (ed), 1974 *British prehistory: a new outline*

Renn, D F, 1958 The decoration of Guildford Castle keep, *SyAC*, **55**, 4–6

—, 1960 The Anglo-Norman keep, 1066–1138, *J Brit Archaeol Assoc*, 3 ser, **23**, 1–24

—, 1967 The early church at Great Bookham, *Proc Leatherhead District Local Hist Soc*, **3.1**, 19–24

—, 1975 The River Wey bridges between Farnham and Guildford, *SyAS Res Vol*, **1**, 75–84

— (ed), 1983 Pachenesham, Leatherhead: the excavation of the medieval moated site known as 'The Mounts', *SyAC*, **74**, 1–46

—, forthcoming [Paper on Guildford and Betchworth castles]

Reynolds, P J, 1979 *Iron Age farm, the Butser experiment*

Riall, N, 1983 Excavations at Caesar's Camp, Aldershot, Hampshire, *Proc Hampshire Fld Club Archaeol Soc*, **39**, 47–55

Richardson, B, 1980 Excavation round-up 1979, *London Archaeol*, **3.14**, 384–9

—, 1981 Excavation round-up 1980, *London Archaeol*, **4.2**, 44–51

—, 1982 Excavation round-up 1981, *London Archaeol*, **4.6**, 159–66

Richardson, C J, 1923 Prehistoric site at Waddon, Croydon, *Antiq J*, **3**, 147–8

Richmond, I A, 1960 The Roman villa at Chedworth 1958–59, *Trans Bristol Gloucestershire Archaeol Soc*, **78**, 5–23

Rivet, A L F, 1964 *Town and country in Roman Britain*, rev edn

— (ed), 1969 *The Roman villa in Britain*

—, 1971 Hillforts in action, in Hill & Jesson 1971, 189–202

—, & Smith, C, 1979 *The place-names of Roman Britain*

Rixson, D, 1978 Summary of animal bones from all sites, in Bird *et al* 1978b, 603–5

Roberts, B K, 1982 The anatomy of the village: observation and extrapolation, *Landscape Hist*, **4,** 11–20

—, 1985 Village patterns and forms: some models for discussion, in *Medieval villages* (ed D Hooke), Oxford Univ Comm Archaeol Monograph, **5,** 7–26

Robertson-Mackay, R, 1962 The excavation of the causewayed camp at Staines, Middlesex, *Archaeol Newsletter*, **7,** 131–4

—, 1965 The primary Neolithic settlement in southern England: some new aspects, in *Atti VI Congresso Internazionale Scienze Preistoriche Protoistoriche, Roma 1962*, 319–32

—, Blackmore, L, Hurst, J G, Jones, P, Moorhouse, S, & Webster, L, 1981 A group of Saxon and medieval finds from the site of the Neolithic causewayed enclosure at Staines, Surrey, with a note on the topography of the area, *Trans London Middlesex Archaeol Soc*, **32,** 107–31

Robinson, H R, 1976 Fragment of a helmet cheek-piece, Barclays Bank site, 1969, in K Crouch, The archaeology of Staines and the excavation at Elmsleigh House, *Trans London Middlesex Archaeol Soc*, **27,** 77–80

Robinson, M, 1981 The Iron Age to early Saxon environment of the upper Thames terrace, in Jones & Dimbleby 1981, 251–86

Robo, E, 1935 *Medieval Farnham*

Rodwell, K, & Rodwell, W, 1975 Kelvedon, *Current Archaeol*, **48/5.1,** 25–30

Rodwell, W, 1975 Milestones, civic territories and the Antonine Itinerary, *Britannia*, **6,** 76–101

—, 1978a Rivenhall and the emergence of first century villas in northern Essex, in Todd 1978, 11–32

—, 1978b Buildings and settlements in south-east Britain in the Late Iron Age, in Cunliffe & Rowley 1978, 25–41

—, & Rodwell, K A, 1977 *Historic churches*, Counc Brit Archaeol Res Rep, **19**

—, & Rowley, R T (eds), 1975 *Small towns of Roman Britain*, Brit Archaeol Rep, **15**

Roe, D A, 1968a A gazetteer of British Lower and Middle Palaeolithic sites, *Counc Brit Archaeol Res Rep*, **8**

—, 1968b British Lower and Middle Palaeolithic hand-axe groups, *Proc Prehist Soc*, **34,** 1–82

—, 1981 *The Lower and Middle Palaeolithic periods in Britain*

Roe, F E S, 1966 The battle axe series in Britain, *Proc Prehist Soc*, **32,** 199–245

—, 1968 Stone mace-heads and the latest Neolithic cultures of the British Isles, in Coles & Simpson 1968, 145–72

Rose, F, 1953 A survey of the ecology of the British lowland bogs, *Proc Linnaean Soc London*, **164,** 186–211

Ross, A, 1968 Shafts, pits, wells – sanctuaries of the Belgic Britons?, in Coles & Simpson 1968, 255–85

—, 1970 *Everyday life of the pagan Celts*

Row, P, 1926 A burial of the Iron Age and a series of Early Iron Age occupation sites at Waddon, Croydon, Surrey, *SyAC*, **37.1,** 59–63

Rowlands, M J, 1976 *The production and distribution of metalwork in the Middle Bronze Age in southern Britain*, Brit Archaeol Rep, **3**

Rowley-Conwy, P, 1983 Sedentary hunters: the Ertebølle example, in *Hunter–gatherer economy in prehistory. A European perspective* (ed G Bailley), 111–26

Ruby, A T, 1950 Fourth interim report on excavations at The Mounts, *Proc Leatherhead District Local Hist Soc*, **1.4,** 5–8

—, 1951 Further interim report on excavations at The Mounts, *Proc Leatherhead District Local Hist Soc*, **1.5,** 4–6

Rumble, A R, 1976 Place-names and their context with special regard to the Croydon survey region, *Proc Croydon Natur Hist Sci Soc*, **15.8,** 161–84

Russell, M, 1982 Chaldon: Beaker pottery (TQ 324 549), *SyAS Bull*, **179**

Saaler, M, 1967 The search for the 'lost' village of Watendon, *Bourne Soc Local Hist Rec*, **6,** 3–6

—, 1970a Coulsdon: Acheulian hand-axe (TQ 298 587), in Extracts from the Bulletins of 1969, *SyAC*, **67,** 117

—, 1970b Coulsdon Woods Roman cemetery, *Bourne Soc Local Hist Rec*, **9,** 3–6

St Joseph, J K, 1953 Air reconnaissance of southern Britain, *J Roman Stud*, **43,** 81–97

Salmon, J E (ed), 1975 *The Surrey countryside: the interplay of land and people*, Brit Assoc

Sanford, R, 1970 Neolithic Twickenham, *London Archaeol*, **1.9,** 199–201

Sankey, J, 1975 The flora and fauna of Surrey, in Salmon 1975, 111–32

Saunders, P R, 1980 Saxon barrows excavated by General Pitt-Rivers on Merrow Downs, Guildford, *SyAC*, **72,** 69–75

Sawyer, P H (ed), 1976a *Medieval settlement*

—, 1976b Early medieval English settlement, in Sawyer 1976a, 1–7

Scaife, R G, 1980 *Late Devensian and Flandrian palaeoecological studies in the Isle of Wight*, unpublished PhD thesis, Univ London (King's College)

—, 1982 Late Devensian and Early Flandrian vegetation changes in southern England, in Bell & Limbrey 1982, 57–74

—, 1983 *Palynological analyses of West Heath barrows V, VII and IX, Sussex*, Ancient Monuments Lab Rep, **3942**

—, 1985 Palynological analyses of West Heath barrows V, VIII and IX, in P Drewett, The excavation of barrows V–IX at West Heath, Harting, 1980, *Sussex Archaeol Collect*, **123,** 51–9

—, forthcoming A review of later Quaternary plant microfossil and macrofossil research in southern England; with special reference to environmental archaeological evidence, in Keeley forthcoming

—, & Burrin, P J, 1983 Floodplain development in, and the vegetational history of, the Sussex High Weald and some archaeological implications, *Sussex Archaeol Collect*, **121,** 1–10

—, & Macphail, R I, 1983 The post Devensian development of heathland soils and vegetation, in Burnham 1983, 70–99

Schmidt, P K, & Burgess, C B, 1981 *The axes of Scotland and northern England*, Prähistorische Bronzefunde, **9.7** (Munich)

Schwab, I, 1978 106–114 Borough High Street, in Bird *et al* 1978b, 177–90

Scott, R, 1982 Chelsham: assemblage of worked flints from Slines Oak and Worms Heath, *SyAS Bull*, **176**

Seaby 1987 *Standard catalogue, coins of England and the United Kingdom*, edn for 1987

Seagrief, S C, 1956 *A pollen analytic investigation of the Quaternary period in Britain*, unpublished PhD thesis, Univ Cambridge

—, & Godwin, H, 1960 Pollen diagrams from southern England: Elstead, Surrey, *New Phytol*, **59**, 84–91

Sellwood, L, 1984 Combs of bone and antler, in Cunliffe 1984, 371–8

Sernander, R, 1908 On the evidence of post glacial changes of climate furnished by the peat mosses of northern Europe, *Geologiska Föreningens Stockholm Forhandlingar*, **30**, 465–78

Shaw, M E, 1970 A re-assessment of the material from the pagan Saxon cemeteries in Croydon, *Proc Croydon Natur Hist Sci Soc*, **14.5** (1966–73), 95–113

—, 1979 Croydon: hoard of Iron Age potin coins, *SyAS Bull*, **159**

Sheldon, H, 1975 A decline in the London settlement AD 150–250?, *London Archaeol*, **2.11**, 278–84

—, 1978 The 1972–4 excavations: their contribution to Southwark's history, in Bird *et al* 1978b, 11–49

—, 1981 London and south-east Britain, in *The Roman west in the third century* (eds A King & M Henig), Brit Archaeol Rep Internat Ser, **109**, 363–82

—, & Schaaf, L, 1978 A survey of Roman sites in Greater London, in Bird *et al* 1978a, 59–88

Shennan, S J, & Schadla-Hall, R T, 1981 *The archaeology of Hampshire from the Palaeolithic to the Industrial Revolution*

Shore, T W, 1897 [An ancient mound at Tooting], Notes of the month, *The Antiquary*, **33**, 353–4

Shurlock, M, 1868 [No title], *Proc Soc Antiq London*, 2 ser, **4** (1867–70), 118–20

Sibthorpe, A, 1831 Roman pavement at Worplesdon, in Surrey, *Archaeologia*, **23**, 398–403

Sieveking, G de G, Bush, P, Ferguson, J, Craddock, P T, Hughes, M H, & Cowell, M R, 1972 Prehistoric flint mines and their identification as sources of raw material, *Archaeometry*, **14.2**, 151–76

Simmons, I G, 1969 Evidence for vegetation changes associated with Mesolithic man in Britain, in Ucko & Dimbleby 1969, 110–19

—, & Tooley, M J (eds), 1981 *The environment in British prehistory*

Simpson, D D A, 1971a Beaker houses and settlements in Britain, in Simpson 1971b, 131–52

— (ed), 1971b *Economy and settlement in Neolithic and Early Bronze Age Britain and Europe*

Sims-Williams, P, 1983 Gildas and the Anglo-Saxons, *Cambridge Medieval Celtic Stud*, **6**, 1–30

Skelton, A C, forthcoming Nore Hill, Chelsham: a newly discovered prehistoric enclosure, *SyAC*, **78**

Skempton, A W, & Weeks, A G, 1976 The Quaternary history of the Lower Greensand escarpment and Weald Clay vale near Sevenoaks, Kent, *Phil Trans Roy Soc London*, ser A, **283**, 493–526

SLAEC 1984 Southwark & Lambeth Archaeological Excavation Committee, *Rescuing the past in Southwark*

Slager, S, & van der Wetering, H T J, 1977 Soil formation in archaeological pits and adjacent loess soils in southern Germany, *J Archaeol Sci*, **4**, 259–67

Smith, A G, 1970 The influence of Mesolithic and Neolithic man on British vegetation: a discussion, in *Studies in the vegetational history of the British Isles* (eds D Walker and R G West), 81–96

—, Grigson, C, Hillman, G, & Tooley, M J, 1981 The Neolithic, in Simmons & Tooley 1981, 125–209

—, & Pilcher, J R, 1973 Radiocarbon dates and the vegetational history of the British Isles, *New Phytol*, **72**, 903–14

Smith, C, 1977 A Romano-British site at Binscombe, Godalming, *SyAC*, **71**, 13–42

Smith, D J, 1969 The mosaic pavements, in Rivet 1969, 71–125

—, 1978 Regional aspects of the winged corridor villa in Britain, in Todd 1978, 117–47

Smith, I F, 1968 The pottery, in R Sanford, *Excavation at Church Street, Twickenham*, Borough Twickenham Local Hist Soc Paper, **12**

—, 1974 The Neolithic, in Renfrew 1974, 100–36

—, 1979a *Long barrows in Hampshire and the Isle of Wight*, Roy Comm Hist Monuments

—, 1979b The chronology of British stone implements, in Clough & Cummins 1979, 13–22

Smith, J T, 1978a Villas as a key to social structure, in Todd 1978, 149–85

—, 1978b Halls or yards? A problem of villa interpretation, *Britannia*, **9**, 351–8

—, 1980 The Roman villa at Rapsley: an interpretation, *SyAC*, **72**, 63–8

Smith, K, 1977 The excavation at Winklebury camp, Basingstoke, Hampshire, *Proc Prehist Soc*, **43**, 31–130

Smith, M A, 1958 Late bronze hoards in the British Museum, *Inventaria Archaeologica*, GB 35–41

—, 1959 Some Somerset hoards and their place in the Bronze Age of southern Britain, *Proc Prehist Soc*, **25**, 144–87

Smith, R A, 1902 Anglo-Saxon remains, in Malden 1902, 255–73

—, 1907 Recent and former discoveries at Hawkshill, *SyAC*, **20**, 119–28

—, 1908a The Weybridge bucket and prehistoric trade with Italy, *SyAC*, **21**, 165–9

—, 1908b Romano-British remains at Cobham, *SyAC*, **21**, 192–203

—, 1909 Romano-British remains at Cobham, *SyAC*, **22**, 137–54

—, 1917 Plateau deposits and implements, *Proc Prehist Soc East Anglia*, **2.3**, 392–408

—, 1924 Pottery finds at Wisley, *Antiq J*, **4**, 40–5

—, 1926 *A guide to the antiquities of the Stone Age*, Brit Mus, 3 edn

—, 1931 *The Sturge Collection 1: Britain*, Brit Mus

Sowan, P W, 1971 Walter Hellyer Bennett, *Proc Croydon Natur Hist Sci Soc*, **14.9**, 221–3

Spratling, M G, 1979 The debris of metal working, in Wainwright 1979, 125–49

Spurrell, F, 1885 Early sites and embankments on the margins of the Thames estuary, *Archaeol J*, **42**, 269–302

Stead, I M, 1984 Some notes on imported metalwork in Iron Age Britain, in *Cross-channel trade between Gaul and Britain in the pre-Roman Iron Age* (eds S Macready & F H Thompson), Soc Antiq London Occas Paper, new ser, **4**, 43–66

Steane, J M, 1985 *The archaeology of medieval England and Wales*

Steel, R, 1979 Abinger Roman villa (TQ 106 474), *SyAS Bull*, **160**

Steiner, P, 1923 Die römische villa von Bollendorf, *Trierer Jahresbericht*, **12**, 1–59

Stephenson, M, 1915 A Roman building found at Compton, *SyAC*, **28**, 41–50

—, 1916 Coins found at Abinger and presented to the museum by Lord Farrer, *SyAC*, **29**, 154–5

Stjernquist, B, 1967 *Ciste a cordoni (Rippenzisten): produktion – funktion – diffusion*, Acta Archaeol Lundensia, 4to ser, **6**

Stonebanks, J, 1972 *Coway Stakes at Walton-on-Thames*, Walton Weybridge Local Hist Soc Paper **9**

Straker, E, 1931 *Wealden iron*

Stratton, H J M, & Pardoe, B F J, 1982 The history of Chertsey bridge, *SyAC*, **73**, 115–26

Swanton, E W, & Woods, P, 1914 *Bygone Haslemere*

Switsur, V R, & Jacobi, R M, 1975 Radiocarbon dates for the Pennine Mesolithic, *Nature*, **256**, 32–4

Taylor, C, forthcoming [Paper on the worked flints from Waddon Caves]

Taylor, C C, 1974 *Fieldwork in medieval archaeology*

—, 1977 Polyfocal settlement and the English village, *Medieval Archaeol*, **21**, 189–93

—, 1978 Moated sites: their definition, form and classification, in Aberg 1978, 5–13

—, 1983 *Village and farmstead: a history of rural settlement in England*

Taylor, H M, 1978 *Anglo-Saxon architecture*, vol 3

—, & Taylor, J, 1965 *Anglo-Saxon architecture*, vols 1 & 2

Taylor, M V, 1960 Roman Britain in 1959, *J Roman Stud*, **50**, 210–42

Tebbutt, C F, 1970 Dry Hill Camp, Lingfield, *SyAC*, **67**, 119–20

—, 1974 The prehistoric occupation of the Ashdown Forest area of the Weald, *Sussex Archaeol Collect*, **112**, 34–43

Thomas, C, 1981 *Christianity in Roman Britain to AD 500*

Thomas, K D, 1982 Neolithic enclosures and woodland habitats on the South Downs in Sussex, England, in Bell & Limbrey 1982, 147–70

Thompson, E A, 1983 Fifth century facts?, *Britannia*, **14**, 272–4

Thompson, F H, 1979 Three Surrey hillforts: excavations at Anstiebury, Holmbury and Hascombe, 1972–77, *Antiq J*, **59**, 245–318

—, 1983 Excavations at Bigberry, near Canterbury, 1979–80, *Antiq J*, **63**, 237–78

Thompson, M W, 1960a The date of 'Fox's Tower', *SyAC*, **57**, 85–92

—, 1960b Recent excavations in the keep of Farnham Castle, *Medieval Archaeol*, **4** (1961), 81–94

—, 1961 *Farnham Castle*, official guide

—, 1967 Excavations in Farnham Castle keep, 1958–60, *Château Gaillard Stud*, **2**, 100–5

Thorley, A, 1971a Vegetational history of the Vale of Brooks, in *Guide to Sussex excursions*, Inst Brit Geog, 47–50

—, 1971b *An investigation into the history of native tree species in south-east England using the pollen analysis technique*, unpublished PhD thesis, Univ London (Kings College)

—, 1981 Pollen analytical evidence relating to the vegetation history of the Chalk, *J Biogeog*, **8**, 93–106

Thornhill, L, 1971 Croydon – two flint implements, *SyAS Bull*, **74**

Titford, C E, 1969 Stane Street: location of the posting stations, *London Archaeol*, **1.4**, 90–2

Todd, K R U, 1949 A Neolithic flint mine at East Horsley, *SyAC*, **51** (1950), 142–3

Todd, M, 1970 The small towns of Roman Britain, *Britannia*, **1**, 114–30

—, 1973 *The Coritani*

— (ed), 1978 *Studies in the Romano-British villa*

—, 1984 Excavations at Hembury (Devon), 1980–83: a summary report, *Antiq J*, **64**, 251–68

Tomalin, D, 1977 The quernstones, in Hanworth & Tomalin 1977, 81–5

—, forthcoming [Report on excavations at Gallibury Down, Isle of Wight]

—, & Scaife, R G, 1979 A Neolithic flint assemblage and associated palynological sequence at Gatcombe, Isle of Wight, *Proc Hants Field Club Archaeol Soc*, **36**, 25–33

Torbrügge, W, 1970–1 Vor- und frühgeschichtliche Flüssfunde zur ordnung und bestimmung einer Denkmalergruppe, *Bericht Römisch-German Komm*, **51-2** (1972), 1–46

Tupper, M F, 1850 *Farley Heath: a record of its Roman remains and other antiquities*

Turnbaugh, W A, 1978 Floods and archaeology, *Amer Antiq*, **43**, 593

Turner, D J, 1965a Site of the 'Roman station' at Merton, *SyAC*, **62**, 122–4

—, 1965b Carshalton: Orchard Hill, *SyAS Bull*, **12**

—, 1975 Medieval pottery kiln at Bushfield Shaw, Earlswood, *SyAC*, **70**, 47–55

—, 1977a Moated site near Moat Farm, Hookwood, Charlwood, *SyAC*, **71**, 57–88

—, 1977b Moated sites in Surrey: a provisional list, *SyAC*, **71**, 89–94

—, 1980 The North Downs trackway, *SyAC*, **72**, 1–13

—, 1986a Bodiam Castle: true castle or old soldier's dream house?, in *England in the 14th century. Proceedings of the 1985 Harlaxton Symposium* (ed W M Ormrod), 267–77

—, 1986b Bletchingley Castle excavations, *SyAS Bull*, **214–16**

—, forthcoming a [Paper on Thunderfield, Harrowsley and Thunderfield Castle]

—, forthcoming b [Paper on Betchworth church]

Turner, F, 1909 Objects found in the Thames at Runnymede, *SyAC*, **22**, 197–8

—, 1926 *Egham, Surrey: A history of the parish under church and crown*

Turner, J, 1962 The *Tilia* decline: an anthropogenic interpretation, *New Phytol*, **61**, 328–41

Ucko, P J, & Dimbleby, G W, 1969 *The domestication and exploitation of plants and animals*

Valentine, K W G, & Dalrymple, J B, 1976 The identification of a buried palaeosol developed in place at Pitstone, Buckinghamshire, *J Soil Sci*, **27**, 541–53

Vince, A, 1984 The Aldwych: mid-Saxon London discovered?, *Current Archaeol*, **93/8.10**, 310–12

—, 1985 The Saxon and medieval pottery of London: a review, *Medieval Archaeol*, **29**, 25–93

Vita-Finzi, C, & Higgs, E S, 1970 Prehistoric economy in the Mount Carmel area of Palestine: site catchment analysis, *Proc Prehist Soc*, **36**, 1–37

Wade, A G, 1927 Palaeolith from Farnham, *Antiq J*, **7**, 313–14

—, & Smith, R A, 1934 A Palaeolithic succession at Farnham, Surrey, *Proc Prehist Soc East Anglia*, **7.3** (1935), 348–53

Wade-Martins, P, 1980 *Village sites in Launditch Hundred*, East Anglian Archaeol Rep, **10**

Wainwright, G J, 1972 The excavation of a Neolithic settlement on Broome Heath, Ditchingham, Norfolk, England, *Proc Prehist Soc*, **38**, 1–97

—, 1979 *Gussage All Saints: an Iron Age settlement in Dorset*, DoE Archaeol Rep, **10**

Wait, G A, 1985 *Ritual and religion in Iron Age Britain*, Brit Archaeol Rep, **149**

Waldron, T, 1985 DISH at Merton Priory: evidence for a 'new' occupational disease?, *Brit Medical J*, **291**, 1762–3

Walker, L, 1984 The deposition of the human remains, in Cunliffe 1984, 442–63

Walls, T K, & Cotton, J F, 1980 Palaeoliths from the North Downs at Lower Kingswood, *SyAC*, **72**, 15–36

Walthew, C V, 1975 The town house and the villa house in Roman Britain, *Britannia*, **6**, 189–205

Ward-Perkins, J B, 1939 Excavations on Oldbury Hill, Ightham, 1938, *Archaeol Cantiana*, **51**, 137–81

—, 1944 Excavations on the Iron Age hillfort of Oldbury, near Ightham, Kent, *Archaeologia*, **90**, 127–76

Warren, S, 1977 Excavation of a Neolithic site at Sefton Street, Putney, *Trans London Middlesex Archaeol Soc*, **28**, 1–13

Waton, P V, 1982 Man's impact on the chalklands: some new pollen evidence, in Bell & Limbrey 1982, 75–91

Webster, G, 1969 The future of villa studies, in Rivet 1969, 217–49

—, 1970 The military situations in Britain between AD 43 and 71, *Britannia*, **1**, 179–97

—, 1975 Small towns without defences, in Rodwell & Rowley 1975, 53–66

—, 1983 The possible effects on Britain of the fall of Magnentius, in *Rome and her northern provinces* (eds B Hartley & J Wacher), 240–54

Welch, M G, 1975 Mitcham grave 205 and the chronology of applied brooches with floriate cross decoration, *Antiq J*, **55**, 86–93

—, 1976 Liebenau inhumation grave II/196 and the dating of the Anglo-Saxon cemetery at Mitcham, *Medieval Archaeol*, **20**, 134–6

—, 1978 Early Anglo-Saxon Sussex: from *civitas* to shire, in Brandon 1978a, 13–35

—, 1980 The Saxon cemeteries of Sussex, in Rahtz *et al* 1980, 255–83

Wheeler, R E M, 1929 'Old England' Brentford, *Antiquity*, **3**, 20–32

Whimster, D C, 1931 *The archaeology of Surrey*

Whimster, R, 1981 *Burial practices in Iron Age Britain: a discussion and gazetteer of the evidence c 700 BC – AD 43*, Brit Archaeol Rep, **90**

Whipp, D, & Platts, E, 1976 Westminster Hall excavation, *London Archaeol*, **2.14**, 351–5

Whitaker, W, 1864 Geology of parts of Middlesex, Hertfordshire, Buckinghamshire, Berkshire and Surrey, *Mem Geol Survey Great Britain*

Whitelock, D (ed), 1979 *English historical documents, 1: c 500–1041*, 2 edn

Whittle, A W R, 1977 *The earlier Neolithic of southern England and its continental background*, Brit Archaeol Rep Supp Ser, **35**

—, 1978 Resources and population in the British Neolithic, *Antiquity*, **52**, 34–42

—, 1980 Two Neolithics, *Current Archaeol*, **70/6.11**, 329–34

Wightman, E M, 1985 *Gallia Belgica*

Wild, J P, 1974 Roman settlement in the lower Nene valley, *Archaeol J*, **131** (1975), 140–70

Wilkinson, T J, forthcoming [Report on excavations on the M25 at Mar Dyke, Aveley, Essex]

Williams, D H, 1970 *The Welsh Cistercians*

Williams, D W, 1980 Excavations at Brewery Yard, Reigate, *SyAC*, **72**, 175–90

—, 1983 16 Bell Street, Reigate: excavation of a medieval and post medieval site, 1974–6, *SyAC*, **74**, 47–89

—, 1984 Excavation at 43 High Street, Reigate, *SyAC*, **75**, 111–54

Williams, J H, 1971 Roman building materials in south-east England, *Britannia*, **2**, 166–95

Williamson, F, 1960 'Bury' collection of flint implements from Farnham, Surrey, *SyAC*, **57**, 100

Williamson, T M, 1984 The Roman countryside: settlement and agriculture in north-west Essex, *Britannia*, **15**, 225–30

Wilson, D M (ed), 1976 *The archaeology of Anglo-Saxon England*

Wilson, D R, Wright, R P, & Hassell, M W C, 1971 Roman Britain in 1970, *Britannia*, **2**, 243–304

—, —, & —, 1974 Roman Britain in 1973, *Britannia*, **5**, 397–470

Winbolt, S E, 1923 Alfoldean Roman station: first report, 1922, *Sussex Archaeol Collect*, **64**, 81–104

—, 1924 Alfoldean Roman station: second report (on 1923), *Sussex Archaeol Collect*, **65**, 112–57

—, 1927 Excavations at Hardham Camp, Pulborough, April, 1926, *Sussex Archaeol Collect*, **68**, 89–132

—, 1929 A late Pleistocene flint point, *Antiq J*, **9**, 152–3

—, 1930 Excavations at Saxonbury Camp, *Sussex Archaeol Collect*, **71**, 223–36

—, 1932 Excavations at Hascombe Camp, Godalming, *SyAC*, **40**, 78–96

—, & Margary, I D, 1933 Dry Hill Camp, Lingfield, *SyAC*, **41**, 79–82

Winterbottom, M, 1978 *Gildas: the ruin of Britain*

Wood, E S, 1950–1 Neolithic sites in west Surrey, *SyAC*, **52** (1952), 11–20

—, 1953–4 The earth circles on St Martha's Hill, near Guildford, *SyAC*, **54** (1955), 10–46

—, 1965 A medieval glasshouse at Blundens Wood, Hambledon, Surrey, *SyAC*, **62**, 54–79

—, 1982 A 16th century glasshouse at Knightons, Alfold, Surrey, *SyAC*, **73**, 1–48

—, & Thompson, F H, 1966 A food vessel from Abinger Hammer, Surrey, *SyAC*, **63**, 44–50

Wood, M E, 1965 *The medieval English house*

Wooldridge, S W, & Linton, D L, 1933 The loam terrains of south-east England and their relation to its early history, *Antiquity*, **7**, 297–310

Wymer, J J, 1962 Excavations at the Maglemosian sites at Thatcham, Berkshire, England, *Proc Prehist Soc*, **28**, 329–54

—, 1968 *Lower Palaeolithic archaeology in Britain; as represented by the Thames valley*

—, 1974 Clactonian and Acheulian industries in Britain; their chronology and significance, *Proc Geol Assoc*, **85.3**, 391–421

— (ed), 1977 *Gazetteer of Mesolithic sites in England and Wales*, Counc Brit Archaeol Res Rep, **22**

—, 1985 *The Palaeolithic sites of East Anglia*

Yates, E M, 1961 A study of settlement patterns, *Field Stud*, **1.3**, 65–84

Yule, B, 1982 A third century well group, and the later Roman settlement of Southwark, *London Archaeol*, **4.9**, 243–9

Index

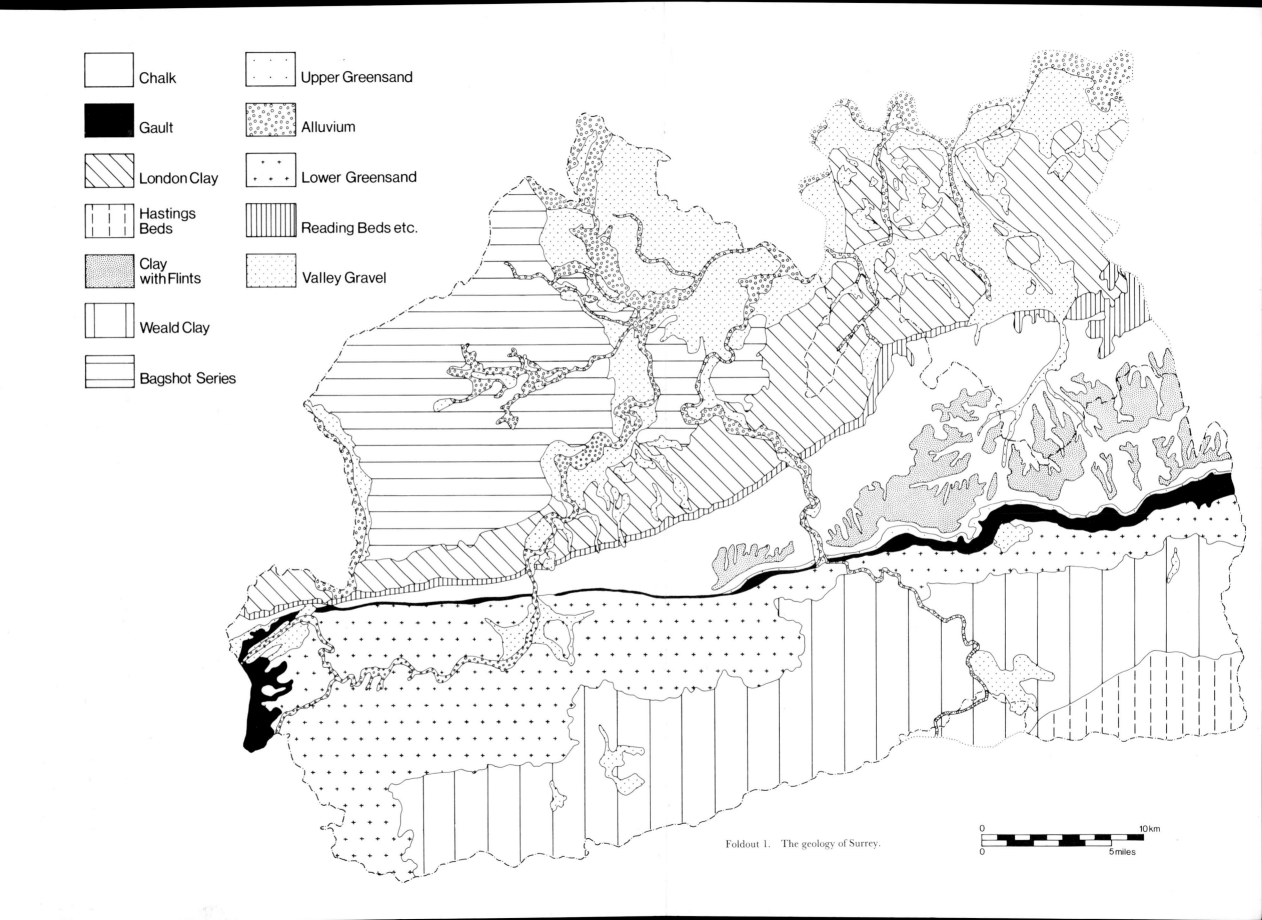

Legend

- Chalk
- Gault
- London Clay
- Hastings Beds
- Clay with Flints
- Weald Clay
- Bagshot Series
- Upper Greensand
- Alluvium
- Lower Greensand
- Reading Beds etc.
- Valley Gravel

Foldout 1. The geology of Surrey.

0   10 km

0   5 miles

Surrey Archaeological Society

The Society was established in 1854 'for the investigation of subjects connected with the history and antiquities of the County of Surrey'. Despite subsequent changes in administrative boundaries, the Society's objectives remain substantially the same, and the present area of interest includes the historic county up to the Thames.

The Society's headquarters are at Castle Arch, Guildford, where the Society's Library, which includes a large and diverse collection of research material, is also housed. Excavations and fieldwork are organised by the Society, the most recent major excavation being that of the Romano-British temple at Wanborough, near Guildford. The Society, through its various representatives around the county, is constantly vigilant on behalf of the conservation of old buildings and archaeological sites of known importance. There is a large and enthusiastic Surrey Industrial History Group and other active local and specialist groups of the Society.

Publication is an essential part of archaeological and local history investigations, and the Society publishes regularly and distributes free to members the *Surrey Archaeological Collections*, a journal of reports, articles and notes on a wide range of subjects. In addition, special volumes and research reports are published from time to time. A list of Society publications can be obtained from the address below.

Symposia, lecture courses and visits are organised and well-supported and the Society in a joint venture with Guildford Museum has recently set up a Young Archaeologists' Club for children from 8–16 years old. Society members keep in touch through the regular publication (ten issues a year) of the *Bulletin*.

Membership is open to individuals or groups interested in the work of the Society, and applications and enquiries should be addressed to the Honorary Secretary, Surrey Archaeological Society, Castle Arch, Guildford GU1 3SX.

Back cover: rescue excavations in 1986 inside the Tithe Barn at Betchworth (photograph by the excavator, D W Williams).